WORDS MADE FLESH

Writings in Pastoral and
Practical Theology

Elaine L. Graham

scm press

© Elaine Graham 2009

Published in 2009 by SCM Press
Editorial office
13–17 Long Lane,
London, EC1A 9PN, UK

SCM Press is an imprint of Hymns Ancient and Modern Ltd
(a registered charity)
St Mary's Works, St Mary's Plain,
Norwich, NR3 3BH, UK
www.scm-canterburypress.co.uk

British Library Cataloguing in Publication data

A catalogue record for this book is available
from the British Library

978 0 334 04194 8

Typeset by Regent Typesetting, London
Printed in the UK by
CPI William Clowes, Beccles, NR34 7TL

CONTENTS

Part Three Theology and Practice

Part Four Public Theology

Part Five New Technologies and Post/Human Futures

Epilogue

FOREWORD

Elaine Graham is the dean of British practical theologians. She has also been a colleague and friend for two decades. So it is a particular honour and pleasure to introduce the essays in this book, which provide a varied and fascinating picture of her professional interests and concerns.

Before saying more about the book, let me say something about its author. Elaine Graham has had an unorthodox and very distinguished career in practical theology. She habitually defies assumptions, breaks 'glass ceilings', and achieves 'firsts'. She did not have a traditional theological education, graduating initially in social science. Nor did she train for ministry. Instead, she worked for the Student Christian Movement and as a lay university chaplain. By means of this very practical induction into theology, she moved in the direction of practical theological research and education, undertaking postgraduate studies in social and practical theology at Manchester University that led to her appointment as lecturer in 1988. In only ten years she became the Samuel Ferguson Professor of Social and Pastoral Theology at Manchester in 1998 at the age of 39. She was, of course, the first woman and lay person ever to be appointed to this or any other chair in practical theology in Britain. Meanwhile she acquired a PhD by part-time study, became the founding chair of the British and Irish Association for Practical Theology, and published several books (including the influential *Transforming Practice*), while supporting her ailing predecessor and mentor, the late Tony Dyson.

Since 1998, Elaine Graham has been the first British president of the International Academy for Practical Theology, the administrative head of a very large department of theology and religious studies, a member of the churches Commission on Urban Life and Faith, and the author or editor of many papers and several books, including two landmark volumes on theological reflection. Her service to the Church of England was marked by the award of an honorary lay canonry at Manchester Cathedral in 2007.

Elaine is, then, an energetic and committed person – in practical theology (nationally and internationally), in theological education and innovation, in the university, diocese and city of Manchester, in the Church of England, and in exploring the intellectual and practical dimensions of Christian faith, especially as seen through the eyes of feminism. These commitments are reflected in *Words Made Flesh*.

The extent of her achievements might suggest an intimidating figure. This would be misleading. The self-effacing voice that emerges from these pages is certainly clear and unambiguous about its concerns and interests, but one of Elaine's great strengths as a writer and thinker is her sheer moderation and rationality. Formed in many ways by radical encounters with feminism, gender theory, political theology, and many kinds of social theory, her essays in practical theology are invariably well-informed, well-researched, judicious and gracious. She largely eschews polemic and her work entirely lacks stridency. Hers is a discourse of careful exploration and exposition, and well-supported, moderately expressed conclusions. It is the quiet persistence of her well-reasoned writings that adds to their power of challenging the reader to see and engage with the world differently.

There is no doubt that Elaine seeks to change the way in which humans encounter each other and their environment. There is clear focus on revaluing what might be considered unremarkable or commonplace, such as the experience of being embodied, the religious and domestic experience of women, and life in contemporary cities. She describes this as 'grounding theological reflection in the vernacular of human experience'. But she also transgresses into areas of life that many Christian believers and theologians ignore, are threatened by, or even find abominable: witness her explorations here into posthumanism and the futures of technology. Wisely, she does not write about anything and everything that occurs in the modern world. But she knows whereof she does write, and her insights, perceptions and arguments on the topics in which she is specialist are invariably worth attention. Her ruminations may begin with a school crib service, a visit to the cinema, an excursion into laboratory science, or a voyage into cyberspace, but they grow to encompass aspects of theological interest and concern illuminated by complex social theory. Whether exploring the nature and methods of practical theology, feminist pastoral care, religion, gender and culture, public theology in urban contexts, or the ethics of new technologies, Elaine always offers something of significance to discussion and debate, both theoretically and practically.

Over two decades, Elaine has explored in new ways what might be taken as a traditional Anglican emphasis on incarnational theology and the sacramental nature of common reality. She has adopted the pragmatic approach, common in Anglican as well as practical theologies, of looking at issues rather than systems and ungrounded theories. She does this in ways that might amaze or even offend many traditional Anglicans, unfamiliar with her emphasis on the embodied, gendered experience within technological and urban contexts.

Words Made Flesh is an approachable *entrée* to the thinking of one of the most significant feminist practical theologians presently writing. It is a pleasure to congratulate the author on the publication of significant material that represents two decades of work in the hope that there are at least two decades more of writing to come. I commend this work to students, practitioners and thinkers in many different disciplines and contexts, who will find material here that will make a difference to how they think and act.

Stephen Pattison
University of Birmingham
2009

INTRODUCTION

The painting that forms the cover of this book, Stanley Spencer's *The Resurrection with the Raising of Jairus' Daughter*, completed in 1947, is typical of so much of his other major work. It transplants biblical narratives into the landscapes of Spencer's own world. He frequently used the village of Cookham in Berkshire as a backdrop to his paintings: most famously in *The Resurrection, Cookham* (1926), which shows villagers, modelled on real-life subjects, rising from the tombs in Cookham graveyard on the Day of Resurrection.

Similarly, *The Resurrection with the Raising of Jairus' Daughter* uses the landscape of the everyday to explore themes of healing, death and resurrection. On the two outer panels, we see how the Day of Resurrection takes place in a very *ordinary* fashion, as the crowds raised from the dead emerge through the paving slabs and among the allotments, stopping to greet family and friends and to gossip with neighbours. Yet their *extraordinary* joy is evident from the way Spencer's figures embrace one another in reunion and celebration. For Spencer, the sacred and secular are indivisible, and the transcendent dimensions of human life emerge from, and blend seamlessly into, the everyday. This is exemplified beautifully by the tiny hand we glimpse in the top corner of one panel, seen waving the Union Flag; a reference, I think, to the bunting that would have hung in the streets for VE or VJ Day only a few years before. After all, if the Day of Resurrection was a red-letter day, then how best to celebrate it but through the same round of street parties and flag-waving as might accompany any major event?

Meanwhile, in the centre panel, Jesus is depicted in a simple terraced house, surrounded by disciples, where he rouses Jairus' daughter from her fatal sleep. The bedroom – Spencer liked bedrooms, but that is really another story – in which the gathering takes place is homely and unpretentious, but the figure of Jesus commands attention as he invokes words of resurrection to the young girl. Her poor father, however, is too absorbed in his grief to notice. Imagine his joy as someone prises his huge hands – Spencer liked hands, too: his subjects always have massive, touchy-feely, artisans' hands – from the bedpost and encourages him to look with new eyes at the scene behind him.

It should be clear by now why Spencer's work might appeal to a practical theologian. It touches on the deepest and profoundest issues of human experience – for Spencer, not just healing, death and resurrection, but sex, desire, loss and consummation – and roots these events in the 'vernacular' of ordinary life. The prosaic, the familiar and the ordinary become vehicles of the divine and the transcendent. Truly, the 'Word becomes flesh' for Spencer: but he was never coy about his subjects' embodiment, seeing beauty in the desires and flaws of human bodies, including (and especially) the emotional and sexual complications that often accompanied them. In that refusal to idealize or simplify the complexities of human living, Spencer's work affirms the reluctance of practical theology to over-systematize, or to privilege deductive over inductive principles. It is an insistence that every big event and every comprehensive narrative begins and ends in the particular of people's lives.

So the title I have chosen for this collection of essays says it all, in many respects. It is about work that has tried to explore the implications of an incarnational theology, of human embodied experience that is gendered and contingent, increasingly surrounded and shaped by technologies, and a way of thinking about and responding to God out of such experience. These essays mark 20 years of academic publication. It has been a timely opportunity to take stock of a body of work produced over that time.

Although these essays are not arranged chronologically, they do reflect certain themes in my work that have unfolded over time. I have grouped them according to major currents that ebb and flow throughout these past two decades, and in this introduction I hope to indicate some of the continuities and changes over that period. In some respects, no work can fail to incorporate elements of autobiography; but I am mindful of an accusation that is often levelled at practical and contextual theologians (myself included) on the part of those who stress the importance of a more inductive approach. They worry that theologies that begin with human experience struggle to progress beyond that perspective, and that practical theology is nothing but autobiography, phenomenology or anthropology. We do need to be clear, therefore, about what is distinctively theological about such inductive and experiential approaches, and to ask how the words of human action and reflection connect with the Word of God, in ways that transform the mundane into something remarkable. I will return to this question at the end of this introduction.

Parts 1 and 2 set out some of my earliest published work, and reflect the context of the late 1980s and early 1990s in practical and pastoral theology, especially the campaign for the ordination of women to the priesthood in the Church of England. It also traces my own emerging interest in feminist theology. My master's thesis surveyed English pastoral theology literature of the mid-twentieth century for references to women, either as recipients or agents of pastoral care. I was met, largely, by silence, as women's pastoral needs, let alone their contribution to pastoral ministry, were hardly mentioned. Some of that research is reflected in the first two essays in this collection, 'The Pastoral Needs of Women' (1989) and 'Pastoral Theology, Feminism and the Future' (1990), which set me on a journey to uncover more of the reasons behind the almost total absence of literature on women and pastoral care. As I went on, I began to experience the uncertainty and exhilaration of academic research, as I stepped into territory never before charted. Rather than uncovering ready data, I found the process to be one of tracing and needing to make sense of absence and silence. I chose to interpret these in terms of the prevailing structures of *sexism* and *clericalism*: a tradition that conceived of ministry as something exclusively undertaken by ordained men.

Gradually, however, I learned to develop strategies for analysing the hidden evidence. Like many feminist social scientists, historians, literary critics and theologians, I was learning that it was not that women had been inactive, but that history had not chosen to think their achievements to be of note. Later, I think I would have called this a deconstructive reading, or what my late colleague Grace Jantzen (2001) called 'reading against the grain', but at the time I was influenced by Rosemary Radford Ruether's proposal that feminist theology needed to proceed along a trajectory of 'critique' and 'reconstruction' (Ruether, 1983; 1993). First, one had to expose the silences and the biases, to listen to the hidden voices, and then to restore them to extant tradition and to reconstitute the nature of the discipline as a result. This I applied to pastoral care literature, and the essays in Part 1 explore different dimensions of this. They argue that pastoral theology must go beyond a mere consideration of 'adding women' into the exercise of pastoral care, towards a more radical reconstruction that reconfigures the entire notion of what it means to give and receive pastoral care. Where are the spaces for women's transformative ministry? How do the spheres of church, society and academy both constrain and encourage women's theological voices? This work therefore derives from the dictum of the broader women's movement that 'the personal is political', in that the dynamics of interpersonal care are rooted in deeper underlying structures. A critique of pastoral care as individualistic and ameliorative begins to emerge, in anticipation of a more comprehensive and inclusive model of pastoral action that strives for social and structural justice.

'The Sexual Politics of Pastoral Care', also included in this section, is taken from a collaborative publication which still ranks among my proudest achievements: *Life-Cycles* (1993), commissioned by SPCK and co-edited by myself and Margaret Halsey. I like to think that this project achieved in practice what the dynamic of critique and reconstruction points to in theory: of translating silence into speech, of beginning the corrective process not just of adding women into established conventions, but using their emergent perspectives to renew and reconstruct. We worked hard to ensure a diversity of voices (although, sadly, too predominantly White and middle-class) and styles of writing – academic essays, poetry, personal narrative, qualitative research – plus, in the shape of Celia Hart's compelling cover illustration, a visual representation of many of the themes of the book. Once more, pictures are able to express what text cannot say; and so, words take flesh. The converse was also true, however, as women's lived experience that had formerly struggled to be heard finally found the words with which to speak.

Part 2 of this collection is closely related to the material in Part 1, both thematically and chronologically, but widens the debate from issues of women's visibility in pastoral care literature towards underlying questions of the gendered nature of human experience, and the difference it makes to the practice and theory of pastoral care. 'Gender, Personhood and Theology' is a summary of my doctoral research: note how it models a particular form of critical correlation in the way it surveys secular social-scientific thinking and begins to draw out their theological implications. My argument was that assertions made around the time of the ordination of women to the priesthood often rested on unexamined claims about the 'feminine' nature of their pastoral gifts, and that much of feminist theology was under-theorized. In particular it was failing to acknowledge the complexities of wider debates within feminist theory, such as the nature of gender equality versus gender difference. Essentially, I was pointing to what I would now term the 'reflexive' nature of gender: not only that we inhabit a gendered culture into which we are socialized, but also that we are engaged in its remaking and reinterpretation by the exercise of our agency. Gender is not ontologically given, but constructed and reconstructed through social and cultural practices. It is not to be conceived as an entirely voluntary activity, but as a constituent part of social relations which emerge from the interplay of human agency and institutional structures (Graham, 1995b).

My conclusion, that gender is a form of practice, coincided with the emergence of scholars such as Judith Butler on the 'performative' nature of gendered identity, a theme I took further in my reconstitution of pastoral and practical theology in *Transforming Practice* (1996). I suppose this is probably the aspect of my work that has contributed most to debates about the nature of pastoral and practical theology, and coincided with its renaissance as an academic discipline in many parts of the world. Many of the themes I trace in that work – which are reflected in the essays in Part 3 – have been comprehensively charted, resulting in a shift away from a discipline calling itself 'applied theology' concerned with the activities of the ordained minister to one of a 'theology of practice' in which contemporary experience is placed in a dialectical relationship with the sources and norms of tradition in order to generate the *practical wisdom* by which the life of the whole Church – and not just ordained ministry – can be directed. Theological truth lies, as Duncan Forrester has put it, in the 'quality of relationships rather than in abstract principle, or a divine edict' (Forrester, 1997: 209). Rather, the words of our 'God-talk' take shape in the practices of human fellowship. Christian teaching is a living parable, rather than a set of moral prescriptions or applied truths.

Many of these essays also reflect the recurrent conviction on my part of the need to ground theological reflection in the vernacular of human experience. In '"The Story" and "Our Stories": Narrative Theology, Vernacular Religion and the Birth of Jesus' (2000) and '"What We Make of the World": The Turn to Culture in Theology and the Study of Religion' (2007), as well as my work on the ethical, political and theological implications of new technologies in Part 5, I use the voices of narrative and popular culture as theological resources. This arises out of my sense that in ostensibly 'secular' – or at least, post-Christian – cultures, it is often other forms of cultural practice beyond credal or institutional religion that serve as frameworks for people's articulation of fundamental world-views and values. The 'stories we live by' are indicative of our personal and collective norms and aspirations, and serve as orientating narratives by which we set our 'moral compasses' of meaning and action. I see this as a continuation of practical theology's perennial concern to interrogate the relationship between beliefs and actions. It may also be a contemporary version of the discipline's earlier fascination with the modern psychologies and psychotherapies as resources for pastoral care to the extent they offer significant insights into the human condition, and serve as secular conversation-partners for contemporary theology. If this is true, however, then this generation of interpreters will need to ensure that such insights are not simply uncritically adopted or used as 'quick fix' panaceas to enhance ministerial competence or ecclesial credibility. Instead, they must be used to forge a genuine framework of mutually critical correlation from which valuable syntheses may be generated.

The essays in Part 5 explore in particular some of the religious and theological referents and undercurrents in informing visions of what has been termed the 'posthuman', or concerns about whether new technologies will radically enhance, or fatally compromise, our humanity. It seems to me that such debates, as reflected in the views of both the technophiles and technophobes, constitute secular equivalents of religious myths of creation and fall, as they speculate about the nature of human responsibility in the face of profound power over life and death. It is intriguing to see how often such representations portray the exercise of human creativity through science and technology by recourse to the language of myth and religion, a theme I explored most fully in *Representations of the Post/Human* (2002). Perhaps theology has a role as a form of cultural critique here, since arguably it has a greater degree of 'literacy' in relation to the way old myths and symbols continue to circulate in many contemporary debates about our technologized future. Theology may actually be better-placed than many other disciplines to point to the durability of the language of the sacred and the transcendent in this respect, even (especially?) in non-religious or secular societies.

In my writing from this period, from the publication of *Representations of the Post/Human* on, I see a greater degree of courage on my part in asserting just such a critical and reconstructive task for theology. In particular, I identify the potential of Christian theological anthropology for a renewed understanding of what it means to be human. The argument implicit throughout those essays, articulated most effectively in 'In Whose Image? Representations of Technology and the "Ends" of Humanity' (2006), is that we need a doctrine of humanity as both 'creative' and 'creaturely': to affirm the God-given potential of human potential as co-creator, but also to remind us that humans are part of a universe that is not, ultimately, of their own making. While *Homo sapiens* may be uniquely privileged to participate in the making and remaking of the world, it is subject to a transcendent horizon that acts as a necessary curb to the excesses of hyper-humanism, which tends to elevate our own self-interest into objects of ultimate worship.

The theme of the role of theology in public life is more extensively explored in Part 4. By public theology, I mean the area of study that seeks descriptive and prescriptive understandings of the relationship between theological traditions and practices and public life. It is concerned not just with party politics, but individual and collective action in the spheres of global and local civil society, the role of institutional religion in aspects of economics and social policy and all manner of faith-related activism and witness for change. It informs the everyday faithful practice of the laity in their occupational and voluntary roles in government, business, welfare and civic duty, as well as considering the larger institutional and constitutional issues of Church and State. It is a form of 'practical theology' insofar as it seeks to reflect on practical issues and to offer theological resources for better and more faithful *praxis*.

The essays in Part 4 also reflect my own long-term association with the city and University of Manchester: the first industrial city, one of the cradles of modernity and microcosm of so many of the religious, cultural and economic changes to have affected Western societies in the past two hundred years. Its passage from post-industrial depression to a new buoyancy in the wake of a decade of urban regeneration has provided much case-study material for reflection on the nature of contemporary Christian social thought and practice. Two essays, 'Theology in the City: Ten Years after *Faith in the City*' (1996) and '"What Makes a Good City?" Reflections on the Commission on Urban Life and Faith' (2008) span that period of time, and chart the 20 years between a major piece of Anglican social thought, *Faith in the City* (1985) and its successor report, *Faithful Cities* (CULF, 2006). '"What Makes a Good City?"' reflects the core question at the heart of the latter's Commission for Urban Life and Faith (2004–6) and analyses the process of attempting to integrate an inductive and contextual way of doing theology into an official church report. The difficulties of such a task are also explored in 'Power, Knowledge and Authority in Public Theology' (2007), written for the newly founded journal, the *International Journal of Public Theology*. I would have to say that while I retain a commitment to doing theology collaboratively, my attempts to do theology *in committee* have proved less rewarding. Overall, however, this group of essays consider the business of generating theology about and to public issues, not least in exploring questions of theological method, and how the sources and norms of Bible, tradition, experience and culture might be deployed in the task of shaping both faithful practice and public debate.

Out of the Commission for Urban Life and Faith has come another fruitful collaboration: with Stephen Lowe, a fellow commissioner who has been committed to urban ministry for the whole of his professional life. 'Words of Encouragement from One Pilgrim to Another' (2007) was written for Stephen's commissioning as the Church of England's Bishop for Urban Life and Faith at Manchester Cathedral in November 2007. It is a departure from my usual style of writing, and was an attempt to practise what *I* preach about theology being a 'performative' discipline, as providing the words that direct the actions which bear witness to and realize the transcendent and transformative dimensions of reality. So this is a piece of theology that is 'practised' quite deliberately, in a context beyond the walls of the academy: something that seeks to make 'talk of God' a thing to guide the vocation of practical living, and to provide a glimpse of the sacred amid the everyday.

If theology is talk about God in order to orientate us towards faithful action, however, it is important to remember that we are always using fragile and contingent methods to speak of that which is, by definition, ineffable and beyond human reason. Perhaps theology needs to advocate a certain modesty in this respect; and a warning to 'mind your language' may actually be one of its best gifts to public discourse. It serves as a reminder of the simultaneous potency and fragility of words, their ability both to build and to destroy, to inform and to mislead.

Yet to believe that talk about God is merely a matter of representation – *nothing but* 'talk' – is to under-value the creative potential of the human imagination as vehicle of more profound disclosure. As I have argued in my work on technology, human capacity to create forms of representation such as myth, language and religion speaks in its own way of our being made in *imago Dei.* As humans, we are capable of creating material cultures of great beauty and sophistication; yet alone among the animals, we also possess the drive to manufacture worlds of *meaning* about those same activities. Our ability as a species to be creators of metaphysical worlds as well as material ones, therefore, to exercise the work of imagination as well as fabrication, and to move between these realms with seeming facility, is testimony to the possibility of human self-transcendence, as Philip Hefner (2003) has argued. Our powers of reflection on new worlds yet to be created constitute important normative and exemplary visions to guide the actions that bring those very worlds into being; in this way, once again, words have the power to take flesh into new realities, and to articulate the cycle of action-reflection-action that is at the very heart of practical theology.

That is one reason why I do regard (practical) theology as more than a phenomenology of action, or autobiography, or anthropology, precisely because it dares to place any claims about human values, actions or culture against the ultimate horizon of that which we call God. As an attempt to capture in words what is beyond human comprehension, however, it is necessarily always a pursuit that falls short of its goal. But, ultimately, if words fail us, then perhaps that is why it is all the more important that they 'take flesh' in ways that can testify more adequately to their transformative potential. So we return to the title of this collection. For the 'word made flesh' is essentially about a sacramental perspective on the world, reminding us that the prosaic and everyday dimensions of experience are not diversions from God's presence among us, but its very genesis.

Over the past 20 years, I have had the privilege of working with many fine and inspiring friends and colleagues. It is always invidious to single out anyone by name, but I would like to acknowledge some of them here: John Atherton, Chris Baker, Zoe Bennett, Malcolm Brown, Tony Dyson, Margaret Halsey, Reinier Holst, Ros Hunt, Grace Jantzen, Rachel Jenkins, Stephen Lowe, David Lyall, Stephen Pattison, James Poling, Ronald Preston, Will Storrar, Heather Walton and Frances Ward. My thanks also to Natalie Watson and production staff at SCM-Canterbury Press, and to Andrew Wilshere for technical and editorial assistance.

A NOTE ON TERMINOLOGY

Over the course of these twenty years, it is clear how terminology and definition in relation to the terms 'practical' and 'pastoral' theology have changed, even within the scope of the essays anthologized here. This may be regarded by some as evidence of lack of rigour and clarity within the discipline, but it might simply reflect evolving understandings of the discipline itself, as well as the different cultural, ecclesial and theological contexts (such as between the USA, UK, Germany or the Netherlands, Oceania or South Africa), within which research into practical theology and pastoral care takes place (see Graham and Rowlands, 2005). My own terminology in this collection bears witness to this variation, although I hope my usage is clear and consistent within each discrete piece of work. Nowadays, I would tend to use 'practical' to denote the generic activities of Christian ministry and 'pastoral' for the more interpersonal levels of care.

The British tradition, historically, tended to use the terms interchangeably to denote any issue affecting the practice of pastoral care and counselling, human education and development, through to questions of mission, ministerial formation, ecclesiology and public theology. I am increasingly moved to favour 'practical theology' for the discipline as a whole given my emphasis on the discipline as the study of Christian *practice*, and to locate pastoral theology as one of a number of practical theologies, distinguished by its emphasis on the theory and practice of the human life-cycle. The recent turn to method, especially in the Anglo-American tradition, also locates practical theology much more firmly as a broader meta-discipline which reflects on the nature of theological understanding in the light of Christian *praxis* in the world. The best elucidation of this, and the reasons why, essentially, all theology is practical theology, is to be found in Graham, Walton and Ward (2005; 2007).

Part One

FEMINIST THEOLOGY AND PASTORAL CARE

I

THE PASTORAL NEEDS OF
WOMEN

My aim in this research was to gain a clearer picture of how the pastoral needs of women has been portrayed within pastoral theology, and how that has influenced recent and current pastoral practice. My interest was in trying to piece together the kinds of attitudes that would have been prevalent within the past two or so generations, and that would still form the mainstream pastoral 'tradition'. I was searching in particular for images of women – their natures, their characteristics and destinies in life – as commonly presented in the literature of pastoral theology; and also the kinds of understandings that have emerged concerning notions of the 'ideal' or 'fulfilled' Christian woman. I studied various types of pastoral literature relating to women within three English denominations: Church of England, Methodism and the Baptist Union, and concentrating upon literature from a period beginning at the end of World War One and extending to the late 1960s. In all, there were five categories in my source literature:

1 'Academic' pastoral theology, sometimes written with the theological student or ordinand in mind, but more generally directed at ministers in pastoral charge, and developing issues to do with practical ministry, especially preaching and church or parish administration.
2 Literature relating to the pastoral ministry as exercised by women themselves, which was rapidly developing during this period, especially via the various Deaconess Orders existing in all three traditions at this time.
3 Associated with this was the area of 'moral welfare' work, which was a significant source of professional training and job opportunities for women who wanted to exercise a pastoral ministry. It is the most clear example of the ministry of women to women.

4 The pastoral activities of the various lay and auxiliary women's organizations – the Mother's Union, the Methodist Women's Fellowship and the Baptist Women's League. These represent a particular strand of pastoral care of women as voluntary, lay and peer-based.

5 Popular pastoral and devotional literature aimed at women, of which there appears to have been a significant genre. Book titles include Mrs Marshall's *Homely Talks with Mothers*; Violet Hodgkin's *A Challenge to Girls*; *Women's Place in Life*; and an entire series of *Stray Thoughts* – for Girls, for Mothers and for Teachers!

Findings

At no point was the issue of the pastoral needs of women addressed directly. Any discussion of women's roles viewed the question of their needs as self-evident and unproblematic, being seen to revolve 'naturally' around motherhood, family and domestic concerns. In the popular literature, the pastoral advice and uplift portrays women back to themselves as superficial, over-emotional, jealous, illogical, prone to 'nerves' – altogether irrational and dependent creatures.

Moreover, if the status of those caring for women pastorally is anything to go by, the pastoral needs of women were afforded low status and those involved in caring for them professionally were undervalued. For example, the work of professional moral welfare workers was marginalized by a church that put its clergy at the centre of pastoral action, and preferring not to engage with issues around women's needs, sexuality or relationships.

Conclusions

Broadly, my historical survey led me to maintain that the pastoral theology of this period was informed by two syndromes, namely 'sexism' and 'clericalism'. Women's needs were largely defined and articulated by men, who were the ones to decide what the 'ideal' of 'fulfilled' women would be, and who judged what would and would not be appropriate patterns of ministry for women. Although women probably constituted the majority of church members and pastoral 'clients' during this period, they were never regarded as the proper subject-matter of pastoral theology. This revolved instead around the activities of the ordained minister, who despite women ministers in the Free Churches was still regarded as definitively male. Women, by nature of their lay status *and* their gender, were therefore marginalized.

Suggestions for Future Research

Pastoral theology must embody a renewed vision of what it means to be human, taking into consideration feminist critiques of sexism and clericalism. This will inevitably have an impact on the way we talk about God, by introducing inclusive insights about God's nature and God's purposes for humanity which arise from actual pastoral experience. We also need to rethink our pastoral priorities and practices to take greater account of women's needs and experiences. It would be good to see the Church addressing itself more sympathetically to pastoral questions of relevance to the everyday lives of women, and listening to the stories of women that arise from those issues.

We may find that as well as having traditionally been a reactive and responsive discipline, pastoral theology must develop as a prophetic and prescriptive enterprise, with a clear view of how the Church might develop new ways of caring and acting to support women pastorally. In other words, pastoral care involves some kind of 'ethical imperative' which implicitly challenges roles, images and understandings of women's nature and needs which hamper and limit, rather than enhance, women's full humanity.

Finally, such insights about the needs of women will have dramatic impact on our understanding of the nature of pastoral ministry itself. This would involve a movement away from a concern with the pastoral agent towards greater attention to the needs of the cared for. Our pastoral care might also recognize that some of the best qualities of caring often go unnoticed when performed as a matter of course by women, and that as a Church we might do well to affirm those qualities: of passivity; of listening; of waiting; and of serving.

2

PASTORAL THEOLOGY, FEMINISM AND THE FUTURE

Contemporary pastoral theology has undergone a significant transformation in the past 15 years. As a discipline, it has experienced a renewal of its theoretical basis, due in part to a growing dialogue between itself and the human and social sciences. Changes within theology itself, perhaps most strongly within understandings of methodology triggered by the liberation theologies, have also played a part in causing a fundamental reassessment of much of the pastoral tradition as constructed over the first three-quarters of this century.

Considering the impact it has had on many disciplines – including many branches of theology – it comes therefore as a surprise to consider that the influence of feminism has been negligible during this most recent stage of development. No definitive work has been done to incorporate feminist perspectives into the emerging 'renaissance' of pastoral theology despite indications that such a move would be timely and significant. While it would appear that feminist insights concerning human nature, pastoral authority and the nature of caring would substantially challenge many long-held assumptions and practices, no substantive literature as yet exists. Obviously, some work has already been done as a by-product of the debate on the ordination of women which does relate to questions about the nature of ministry and therefore of the pastoral office. Yet as far as the other side of the question is concerned, that of the interests of the woman as *client* within pastoral care, no discussions appear even to have been initiated, however provisionally.

The aim of this chapter, therefore, is to offer some preliminary insights into what the tradition of pastoral theology does actually say about women, and in particular about the pastoral needs of women. Much of the evidence cited originated in research detailed elsewhere,[1] which

---

1 An account of the research appears in my article, 'The Pastoral Needs of Women'

aimed to reveal attitudes towards women's pastoral needs not just from a theoretical perspective – as in various works of what may be described as 'academic' pastoral theology – but also in terms of the nature of the pastoral care of women as carried out in practice. The material accumulated in the course of this research was intended to reflect the sort of pastoral literature which would have been generally influential and definitive for all those involved in the churches' pastoral ministry to women since World War One. These people were of course mainly clergy, but included deaconesses, moral welfare workers and ordinary members of church women's voluntary societies. From a survey of this pastoral 'canon', a number of central questions can be asked:

- What dominant images and assumptions about their 'needs' inform the pastoral care of women?
- Is it possible to discover prescriptive material concerning women's true nature, the Christian ideal as it relates to women's destiny and fulfillment, and assumptions about women's psychology, sexuality and social role?
- What, within pastoral theology during most of this century constitutes the ideal or 'healthy' woman?

Conclusions from the Research

1 **Invisibility** A major problem in undertaking a literature search for the type of material required lay in the difficulty of actually obtaining it. At no point was the issue of the needs of women as a client group addressed directly; much of the evidence was only gathered via inference, and is therefore oblique in character. This of itself is significant; and the time period studied, after all, predates the era of feminist consciousness and interest in the study of women as a sociological category. However, the fact of such invisibility and hiddenness has become a central criterion of much feminist historical research;[2] why, in this case as in many other instances, were issues of women's status and role within church and family considered self-evident and unproblematic? Why are women's needs accorded so little importance? Was it that they were not understood to have pastoral needs? Or was it assumed that any needs were automatically met without considered or significant attention being required? Two further findings many help to answer these questions.

(1989). The material is drawn from a period between the end of World War One and the late 1960s.

2 A variety of works have appeared on the theme of women's 'invisibility': for a good introduction, see Sheila Rowbotham's *Hidden from History* (Rowbotham, 1973).

2 **Biological Determinism and Reductionism** Women's needs were never addressed directly within pastoral theology because the nature of their needs are deemed to be self-evident and therefore beyond dispute. Put simply, it is taken for granted that women's roles and needs revolve around motherhood, family and domestic concerns. These tend to be justified on biological and naturalistic grounds, and it is interesting how psychology, which formed a major secular source for pastoral theology during the last generation – mainly through the influence of writers like Leslie D. Weatherhead – is used to bolster their perspective. For example, the work of Freud, Jung and Bowlby (to name the three most regularly cited) are quoted with approval, yet employed in a highly selective and uncritical fashion in order to present women's needs as those associated with fulfilment in motherhood.

3 **Low Status of Women** Women's needs, even when they are identified or explored, were not accorded much importance. Evidence for this fact can be drawn from the relatively low status of those involved in caring for them professionally. The opportunities for women to exercise pastoral ministry among other women seem to have been strictly circumscribed and, if anything, actually diminishing, especially after World War Two. External pressures on the churches, probably accelerated by wider social factors of secularization, encouraged a trend towards the enhancement of the professional status of the clergy, a process which served to marginalize women lay workers in parishes and elsewhere. As the role of the clergy became increasingly professionalized, women were refused the opportunity to follow suit and to enhance their status, both as individuals and as a group (Hall and Howes, 1965; Prelinger, 1986). An example of this can be found in the sphere of moral welfare work; as Church provision was superseded by many of the functions of the State, the mainly female staff saw their role as church professionals undermined, and the clergy failed to regard such work as having anything to do with the 'real' (parish-based) concerns of the Church. Similarly, the ill-defined status of deaconesses and women workers, especially in the Church of England, allowed clergy to set the terms of women's pastoral role.

Sexism and Clericalism

All three of these features can be placed within the framework of two major syndromes which served effectively to exclude and devalue the needs of women: 'sexism' and 'clericalism'. It is clear that throughout all the pastoral literature surveyed there is the assumption that men possess qualities that are unequivocally 'masculine', and women those which are equally clearly 'feminine'. However, inherent in this understanding is a belief that these qualities are biologically fixed and determined; and that the masculine attributes are intrinsically superior to the feminine. This can partly be traced to the legacy within the Christian tradition of 'dualism', a false partition of reality into body/mind, matter/spirit, emotion/reason. James Nelson (1983) identifies the way in which this division has resulted in the systematic and structured devaluation of women. He argues that men have traditionally feared the power of women in their capacity to reproduce and in their relative proximity to nature. The male psyche has sought to distance itself from these elements by projecting them on to women, who become associated with all that is alien and 'other'. The Divine image, on the other hand, is associated with what is spiritual, and therefore with all the qualities of masculinity; and so God becomes purged of all feminine attributes. Women therefore find it difficult to affirm themselves as being truly made 'in God's image'.

Just as dualism regards human nature as fixed and essentially polarized, so sexism assumes that gender attributes are all-determining in human behaviour. The interaction of these two within Christian anthropology means that women are regarded as essentially inferior, and destined by the simple fact of their biological sex to be 'misbegotten men'. Such arguments have been used to exclude women from the ordained ministry, on the lines that they cannot represent the higher and spiritual aspects of human experience, and that their gender is determinant of other vocations, hence the prevalence of motherhood – in an actual or surrogate sense – within the literature surveyed.

In addition, over the past few generations pastoral theology has reflected the dominance of 'clericalism', which assumes that the normative form of Christian ministry is the priesthood, and any alternative vocation is inferior. While the status of the clergy became more that of the 'professional' – as already noted – their pastoral training remained firmly rooted within tradition. The predominant model was that of 'apprenticeship', a curate or junior minister serving his title alongside a senior colleague, through whom the skills of the pastoral ministry would be communicated. As a model of training this was highly paternalistic, authoritarian and inherently conservative. It also tended to exclude women by virtue of their not being party to this clerical 'elite'. In addition, it meant that a clear institutional (and epistemological) separation occurred between academic theology and pastoral practice. The nature of pastoral theology during the period studied is therefore of a 'practical' and 'applied' discipline, largely written for newly qualified clergy already in post, with little theoretical or critical content.

Another feature of the pastoral material is its emphasis on the role of the minister, and not on the needs of the client. Pastoral theology was centred on the practical work of the clergy, because its function was seen to be one of providing 'applied' theology and practical suggestions of an administrative nature. Thus questions about the nature of the ministry itself, the relationship of the clergy to the whole Church, and of the Church to God and the world, were largely left unasked within literature primarily concerned with pragmatic 'hints and tips'.

The overwhelming concentration on the activities of the clergy once more served to marginalize women and render their pastoral needs invisible, despite their constituting the majority of the laity. Women were also invisible as the chief agents or initiators of pastoral care, because that was regarded as the province of the clergy – an office from which women were either excluded entirely, or else marginalized as unusual deviations from the masculine 'norm' of ordained ministry. What is considered healthy and ideal in the Christian life is distorted by the mechanisms of sexism and clericalism; and women's invisibility within the pastoral tradition bears witness to their exclusion from the source of power and self-determination. Women are denied the right to decide their own needs: sexism denies any opportunities other than those which conform to stereotypical notions of a 'woman's place'; dualism tells them that by their very nature they are inferior; and clericalism informs women – and all lay people – that any vocation other than that of a minister is inevitably second-class.

Towards an Inclusive Pastoral Theology

What are the implications of these arguments for the Church's pastoral care and for pastoral theology? It is no exaggeration to claim that the insights currently being offered by feminism present a considerable challenge to the role pastoral theology might exert, not simply as a discipline to enable Christian caring, but also as a critique of what the aims and ends of that pastoral task might be. It has already been demonstrated that, in the light of feminist critical perspectives, much of the inherited tradition of pastoral care falls short of offering women much more than limited and stereotyped images of themselves. It has also been suggested that the emphasis of pastoral theology on the activities of the pastoral agent – invariably the clergy – effectively blocks any systematic exploration of how practical pastoral care might develop perspectives and strategies based around the needs of clients, in this case the needs of women. Such critiques, directed as they are at the syndromes of sexism and clericalism, will therefore inevitably present a significant and fundamental challenge to traditional notions of the nature of pastoral ministry and to the Church's self-understanding as a whole. However, the function of such feminist criticism is not simply to highlight the inadequacy of the given tradition; it must also contribute to a renewed vision, towards something I shall later characterize as an 'inclusive' pastoral theology. The remainder of this chapter will therefore outline three major implications for pastoral theology of a feminist perspective: relating to the nature of pastoral care itself; upon notions of what it means to be human; and how we speak about God.

1 The Nature of the Pastoral Task

Part of the 'renaissance' of pastoral theology as a discipline has been the rediscovery of the corporate aspect of human life, and the need to ground pastoral care within a sense of social justice, as well as of individual well-being (Selby, 1983). Thus, a fundamental principle of pastoral theology must be that pastoral care should entail social analysis and critique in order to discern where the Church's pastoral priorities might lie. Feminist analysis has given a clear lead in this process, by affirming the notion that 'the personal is political'.

It is arguable, therefore, that the oppression of women represents a major pastoral and social priority for the Church. A renewed and inclusive pastoral theology must take insights from secular human sciences, and material from its own ethical tradition, in order to understand the pastoral mission of the Church. However, both processes of reconstructing the pastoral tradition – in the light of the Christian heritage and in the light of the contemporary situation – must be grounded within what Margaret Farley calls 'a moral imperative'.[3] An inclusive pastoral theology must of necessity be prescriptive; and as well as having been primarily practised as a reactive and responsive enterprise, pastoral care must now evolve as a prophetic and proactive discipline, with a clear view of how new ways of caring might develop in order to bring about greater justice and liberation for women – and for men.

This renewal of the aims of pastoral care can also be extended to a revaluation of its theoretical foundations and roots. As my survey of pastoral literature reveals, pastoral theology has in the past been guilty of taking secular traditions and disciplines and using them uncritically. This has been especially true of the influence of psychology upon much of the literature. Commentators like T. C. Oden have pointed to the way in which pastoral theology has in recent years become almost submerged beneath an over-enthusiastic adoption of secular psychotherapies, and that any explicit Christian content has been eclipsed (Oden, 1980). This criticism is certainly valid where the material I surveyed is concerned; little concerted effort was made by the pastoral authors to consult the Christian tradition in any depth. A rediscovery of the identity of pastoral theology cannot be undertaken without the same kind of critical awareness towards the Christian tradition as informs the social analysis. For example, questions

---

3 Farley (1975) argues that the changing roles of men and women constitute a challenge to traditional theology, but that Christian ethics can play a 'reconstructive' and prescriptive role.

relating to the status and use of biblical material raise key issues about the relationship between revelation, tradition and contemporary experience – issues central to the nature of theological construction itself.

Therefore, pastoral theology must engage in a critique of its own tradition, in order to understand how it has reflected – and to a great extent created – the cultural manifestations of the oppression of women. Any reconstruction of pastoral theology would therefore have to integrate alternative views, and especially those which reflect the experiences of those groups previously excluded from the dominant tradition. Thus the moral imperative of pastoral care must be self-critical in order to be authentic.

As such insights about the *needs* of women begin to influence understandings of pastoral ministry and the nature of the pastoral task itself, the overriding concern within pastoral theology with the pastoral agent will be replaced by a greater focus on the cared-for. In effect, pastoral theology and pastoral care will be provided with the resources to become much more client-centred.

Returning more specifically to the question of women's pastoral needs, it is clear that these must become more prominent within the pastoral priorities of the Church. It is to be hoped that it could address itself more sympathetically to pastoral questions of relevance to the everyday lives of women, and could listen to the stories of women which arise from these pastoral encounters. Examples of such priorities might be in areas such as health care issues of special concern to women; family-related matters in which women find themselves trapped and pigeon-holed into 'caring' roles; the problem of violence against women; and low pay and employment issues as they affect women.[4]

2 *Human Nature and Human Flourishing*

Pastoral theology must embody a renewed vision of what it means to be human, taking into consideration the experience and insights of feminism. For example, I have already argued that the kinds of values, attitudes and behaviour that are seen as commendable in women have been constructed within the distorting discourses of sexism and clericalism. As such they do not take account of women's objective experience. Two writers, Justes and McConnell (Justes, 1985; McConnell, 1981), writing from North American traditions of pastoral counselling, both make this point in emphasizing that counsellors must come to terms with the fact that their images of what is good and desirable within human nature have been informed by male-dominated understandings. For women to follow such traditional Christian models and ideals of self-sacrifice, self-

---

4 Contemporary issues of women's pastoral needs in relationship to work and employment are beginning to receive attention. (See Dawson, 1986; Borrowdale, 1989.)

abnegation and 'servanthood' is therefore to run the risk of falling into destructive sex roles, which are themselves – rather than the individual – the source of sin. Women may therefore have to rethink traditionally held notions of sin and virtue because they embody sexist assumptions.

It is for this reason that pastoral theology must allow itself to hear the feminist critique; but such an enquiry also serves to raise fundamental questions of what it means to be male *and* female, masculine *and* feminine, men *and* women; in other words, it is essential to see questions of anthropology – understandings of human nature – at the heart of this debate. A priority for pastoral theology must therefore be to explore the neglected areas of gender identity and formation. What assumptions do we have about the factors that make each of us uniquely male and female? How do we speak theologically and act pastorally as a result? How can we learn from other biological and social sciences – as well as rediscovering our own religious traditions? These kinds of question are imperative: a feminist reading of inherited pastoral tradition reveals the taken-for-granted opinions about women's needs and identities; yet that can only be corrected by a thoroughgoing examination of the roots of human gender differentiation and development the better to approach pastorally issues of sexuality, social roles, personality formation and patterns of family life, relationships and child-rearing. All these issues are related in some way to women's needs; yet they are also linked to the wider issue of how women and men can coexist in mutuality and justice.

3 Speaking about God

Finally it is hoped that such a renewed pastoral theology will also begin to make a difference to the way we talk about, and experience, the actions and presence of God. If we can accept the notion of theology and revelation as a process, and that humanity's changing and developing understanding of the world is an appropriate arena within which God can be experienced and encountered, then pastoral responses to human need can become a rich resource of theological reflection. Once we incorporate women's perspectives, the opportunity is created to augment the existing (male-dominated) tradition with new images and insights. For example, many authors have pointed to the way in which 'feminine' aspects of God challenge patriarchal and hierarchical notions of an estranged and authoritarian 'Father', and re-open alternative avenues of understanding the Divine nature as one of vulnerability and servanthood.[5] Given the central tradition within

---

5 One attempt to affirm the 'feminine' aspects of Divine imagery is Strachan and Strachan's *Freeing the Feminine* (1985) Dunbar: Labarum. Trible's *God and the Rhetoric of Sexuality* (1978) develops the study of the feminine in God and its implications for human sexuality and sexual identity.

pastoral theology of the *imago Dei* – humanity made in the image of God – such explorations raise fundamental questions about the meaning of personhood, and its relationship to Divine imagery.

It is hoped that such information might be used to advance the reconstruction of a body of pastoral theology that takes its responsibilities seriously in engaging in the world. Such a pastoral witness would be mindful of contemporary movements and also be self-critical of its own tradition. The changing experience of women has become a major issue to which Christian theology must respond in a variety of ways: not least pastoral theology, arising as it does from human need and human contexts. In this chapter, I have argued that the agenda for pastoral theology arises from such experience. However, in another sense, such responses are indicative of the way in which all pastoral theology that arises out of human need is always responding to the enduring questions and challenges of human existence. The central issues of the Church's pastoral agenda must always be questions relating to the nature of human destiny, ideals for Christian living, and the character and purposes of God. Thus, the reconstruction of pastoral theology, and in particular the inclusion of perspectives designed to encompass women's perspectives and experiences, is simply a restatement of the true purposes of the pastoral task.

3

THE SEXUAL POLITICS OF
PASTORAL CARE

How can women and men present a vision of human wholeness – a vision rooted in both Christian tradition and contemporary experience – which will help in the ecumenical task of renewing the Church? The Community study was – and is – at the heart of the ecumenical agenda. It reflects the realization that the world will come to believe not because of the clarity of our doctrinal formulations (important as this is), but because of the quality of our life as a loving, reconciling inclusive community in Christ. (Crawford and Kinnamon, 1983)

The Social Context of Pastoral Care

Attention to the novelty of women as agents and recipients of pastoral care is a matter which goes far beyond the mere process of 'adding in' a new constituency of pastoral ministers and clients to conventional models. Instead, it requires the Church to consider the nature of the core values at the heart of pastoral practice, and the implicit truth-claims of the Christian community as enacted and embodied in diverse patterns of pastoral ministry.

The maxim that 'the personal is political' is a familiar watchword in feminist circles. In recent years, such a claim has also come to prominence in much of the pastoral care literature, with respect to a growing awareness that relations between individuals cannot be immune from the dynamics of a wider network of social relations. Pastoral care literature is beginning to recognize that many of the problems and pressures faced by those who seek help are more than the sum of individual failings, bad decisions, or personal moral culpability.

Rather, pastoral carers must be sensitive to the social causes of health and illness; the influence of cultural norms and the dynamics of family life in the formation of individual personality; and the structural aspects of public policy and socioeconomic change which act to influence personal circumstances. Such a sensibility is reflected in speculations that pastoral strategy may involve attention to social change and political intervention, and not just to individual amelioration and adjustment. Such an understanding of the politics of pastoral care is beginning to be widely recognized, and is increasingly informing work that attends to the development of a pastoral care of women.

However, there is a second dimension to the politics of pastoral care, distinct from the factors that condition pastoral need, and which concerns the actual dynamics of the pastoral care relationship itself. At the heart of every pastoral encounter are unspoken values about the conduct of that and the aims and objectives to which pastoral practice is directed. In a fundamental sense, pastoral care is informed by ideals. It can never be the neutral carrier of uncontested or value-free objectives which are simply transacted between agent and client. Embodied in the apparently straightforward and uncontroversially benign tasks of pastoral care – classically defined as acts of healing, guiding, reconciling and sustaining – are assumptions concerning the nature of Christian faith and human destiny, patterns of authority in the Church, and the very character of God at work in the world.

Attention to the *politics* of pastoral care, therefore, begins with the realization that pastoral relationships cannot be isolated from their broader social and cultural setting, whether this be the political and structural causes of human need, or the extent to which culture shapes the values by which women and men live. This may not be immediately apparent to us, but a consideration of how such principles vary between historical epochs and cultures illustrates the impact of societal norms upon the Christian community's articulation of its own core values.

Symbols and Metaphors of Pastoral Care

One of the most enduring images in the history of Christian pastoral care is that of the pastor as shepherd: courageous, charismatic and solicitous. Yet increasingly, contemporary voices have spoken of their reservations at such a heroic model, which to present-day tastes appears authoritarian and paternalistic. The emphasis in many quarters of the Church today on the egalitarian nature of the Christian community and the priesthood of all believers is regarded as a reappropriation of such themes of mutuality and inclusiveness in surviving accounts of the early Church. Yet this does not sit well with the implicitly individualistic and undemocratic portrayal of pastoral ministry and Christian vocation embodied in the shepherd. If the pastor is the shepherd, it is argued, then it is unavoidable to think of the congregation or parish as sheep; hardly flattering or empowering!

As with many of the symbols and metaphors of the Christian tradition – forged in a social and cultural context and deploying concepts now foreign – the debate rages as to the possibilities of retrieving such imagery. Here, pastoral theologians are divided, some arguing that the shepherd is such a central icon of Christian pastoral ministry as to impel the contemporary Church to reclaim the model. Such discussions choose to emphasize the courage, unconventionality, and tenacity of the pastor. However, as with the debate on more obvious forms of exclusive language in theology – as, for example, the predominant image of God as Father – it is also argued that such metaphors are not merely sets of words, but reflect and perpetuate particular world-views and ideologies. In other words, the preferred images and expressions of theology – be they models of pastoral agency (shepherd, pastor, priest), metaphors for the ideal Christian life (soldier, servant), or concepts articulating the nature of God (Lord, Father, King) – speak to us most powerfully of the implicit values and power-relationships to which the Christian community subscribes. This may not be problematic for those who believe that Christian values are unchanging; but the truth is that they are historically and culturally conditioned, and that the language of the Church's pastoral ministry offers a graphic account of its prevailing models of human nature and destiny, the action of God in the world and the role of the Church in the work of salvation.

The use of shepherding imagery to encapsulate the Church's understanding of pastoral leadership and agency is therefore a clear example of metaphors from another age enduring into the modern era. Other aspects of pastoral care through the ages have been recognized as representative of more clearly historically conditioned and culturally specific norms. For most of the Christian era, a primary motif of pastoral care was that of pastoral discipline. The guidance and formation of the individual was seen in terms of demarcating the boundaries of the believing community, which was held to be absolute in its authority, both in dispensing the means of grace and salvation, and defining the terms of their mediation to the faithful. The authority of the ordained clergyman stemmed partly from his sociological status as an educated person in the community and, often, as a representative of an influential and wealthy patron. However, it was also derived from his theological and ecclesiological standing as the representative of God's law on earth through the Church mediated by Word and Sacrament.

Admittedly, Christian pastoral care has also been influenced by the nonconformist impulses of individual conscience, the liberating word of Scripture and the communitarian witness of the New Testament; but the dictates of institutional religion in the name of the claim that there can be 'no salvation outside the Church' have tended to be pre-eminent. This has served to emphasize the collective over the individual in the name of a model of Christian faith, which regards the corporate life of the believing community as paramount. Hence, pastoral discipline places its emphasis on practices which communicate and enforce the standards of the institutional *ecclesia* via practices of confession and absolution, moral examination and strictly administered access to the sacraments. However, this has to be placed in a historical and cultural context which predates modern democratic and egalitarian political ideals, and which places the rights of the individual as subordinate to concepts of the community as ordered according to the tacit authority of tradition and oligarchy.

Judged by the standards of later modernism, which implicitly shapes all our personal and corporate assumptions and values, this emphasis on pastoral discipline strikes us as punitive, morally regressive, and autocratic. Modern culture is founded upon such principles as the universality of human reason and personal freedom, especially in matters of religious belief and individual conscience. Thus the ideals informing notions of human destiny and fulfilment, and those exercises of pastoral agency deemed necessary to carry out the will of God do change with time, and the underlying values informing Christian ministry, in theory and practice, ought to be subjected to critical scrutiny. Any pattern of pastoral care, therefore, has to be understood as a creature of its time and place, reflecting and often enforcing particular cultural norms and values.

A Comparative Perspective on Culture and History

The implicit values of our time may therefore be more clearly mapped by bringing them into dialogue with the taken-for-granted norms of past epochs. The dissonance and incongruity between past and present sharpens our attention to the 'horizons' of our own day, as well as enabling us to identify the temporal continuities.

Such cross-cultural comparisons may also be ethnic or geographical. For example, the pastoral theologies now emerging from Africa and Asia originate in traditions and practices established by white Christian missionaries. For some, this influence represents nothing short of colonization by Western Christianity, which destroyed indigenous spiritualities and forms of religious expression, and attempted to impose alien norms and images of Christian vocation and virtue. Commentators maintain that although some Western values helped to differentiate the Church from traditional practices (and in many cases, offering more freedom to women in terms of greater educational, familial and economic opportunity), it also prevented the Church from developing an indigenous theology and spirituality which would articulate the gospel in a more culturally appropriate fashion.

Since the early years of the twentieth century, Christian pastoral care in Britain and North America has been conditioned by the fundamental revolutions in our intellectual and social order, symbolized by the figures of Marx, Darwin and Freud. Their thinking imbues our attitudes both towards the Christian historical tradition as well as current pastoral practice. If we see the audacity and genius of the earliest Christians in glimpsing and instigating an inclusive and egalitarian human community, it is not simply through the self-evidence of their vision, but also because our sensibilities have been sharpened by the critical perspectives and imperatives of modern socialism and, more recently, those of feminism and pluralism. Similarly, if nowadays we regard the exemplary pastoral carer as non-judgemental, supportive and empathetic, that is largely due to the influence of the post-Enlightenment psychologies and psychotherapies which affirm individual autonomy and self-determination as the primary virtues of human fulfilment. Therapeutic models of care in the quest for individual wholeness have replaced what is now seen as a repressive and negative emphasis on sin and conformity to churchly discipline; furthermore, this is regarded as proof of our generation's moral and theological progress – an idea which is itself a product of the Enlightenment. The extent to which the Christian community should live according to the norms and standards of its time, or adopt countercultural prophetic values, is of course a matter for pastoral and theological debate; but the fact is that pastoral care is neither immune from nor innocent of its social and cultural setting.

Power and Pastoral Practice

Pastoral relationships tend therefore to reflect and absorb the prevailing ideals by which norms of human virtue and moral value are judged. Power relations within a wider society – between women and men, black and white, lay and professional – cannot be prevented from invading the sanctuary of the helping relationship. Secular therapies have recognized for some years that the helping relationship can be far from neutral and benign, and that significant scope exists for abuses of power on the part of the counsellor, therapist, or expert. This is true not just in terms of the dynamics of the one-to-one relationship, but to the extent in which both parties are bearers of expectations and prescriptions about what is considered healthy, normal and good. Pastoral theology needs to be able to reflect critically on the implications of this for Christian pastoral practice.

Norms and ideals inform pastoral strategy by influencing certain choices regarding three main areas of care: questions of agency, priority, and aims and ends. When it comes to examining the norms that inform patterns of who cares for whom and by what means, decisions concerning the needs that merit pastoral attention and judgements on the appropriate virtues to be fostered and wrongs to be righted, it is important to recognize that such choices are not neutral, but have been influenced by already existing value systems.

The changing role of women within the churches highlights the significance of the *sexual* politics of pastoral care. Gender relations are reinforced in and forged by particular models of pastoral ministry. Pastoral care enacts a set of messages about authority and power in the Church, prescriptions for vocation and fulfilment in the Christian life, and understandings of the ways in which knowledge and service of God are attained. All have a critical impact on the treatment of women by the Christian Church: whether the prevailing, however unconscious, objective of pastoral practice is to liberate women, or to restrict them to norms of behaviour and patterns of self-development that serve to maintain male power within the Church.

One of the earliest formative theses of feminist theology illustrates the extent to which the values informing Christian pastoral practice are subject to patriarchal distortion. Valerie (Goldstein) Saiving (1979) argues that the standards of virtue by which the exemplary Christian life was judged ignored women's experiences. To elevate the ideals of service, self-abnegation and sacrifice may be an appropriate corrective to the patriarchal values of power and domination; but such ideals merely confirm women's subordination and serve to veil the unequal and exploitative nature of gender relations. Anne Borrowdale (1989) has developed this analysis, and illustrated how the Christian vocation to servanthood has become a licence for women's servility and submission.

Power Relations in Pastoral Agency and Pastoral Need

The use of images like that of the shepherd to delineate the scope and nature of pastoral care perpetuates models of care which emphasize individualism, professionalism and directivity. Historically, literature – popular and academic – reflecting on pastoral care has tended to concentrate upon the qualities that characterize the good pastor. Moreover, since its emergence as a specific discipline in the middle of the eighteenth century, pastoral theology has been synonymous with writings on the activity and characteristics of the pastoral agent. For most of Christian history, this also means that pastoral theology so understood implicitly restricts itself to the study of the pastoral agent – traditionally male, ordained and professionally accredited.

In the process, attention to the needs of the client, or to the dynamics and relationships within the Christian community as a whole, are obscured. Furthermore, the possibilities of other models of pastoral agency – for example pastoral care exercised by lay women – are also occluded, because what is assumed to constitute the normative pattern of Christian pastoral practice reflects the powerful and privileged status of the clergy. The considerable contribution and gifts of women as pastoral agents have been extensively undervalued and unacknowledged. Domestic responsibilities, mothering and all forms of service have been deemed natural and spontaneous when exercised by women, and therefore regarded as unexceptional models of Christian vocation. There have been many instances of women who have been regarded as harbouring inappropriate, and unfeminine, ambitions by pursuing ministries other than those to the traditional spheres of women's organizations, young people, children and education.

Women are thereby denied autonomy and recognition as pastoral carers; but it is also true that women's pastoral needs are also neglected and misrepresented. Traditionally, pastoral care has been informed by teachings and practices that rest upon the conviction that women's destiny is predetermined by virtue of their supposed connection with natural and maternal qualities. This is understood automatically to preclude them from positions of leadership or autonomous roles in church or society. The destiny and fulfilment of 'good' women rests in the vocation of wife and mother, roles which reflect the 'natural' order ordained by God. Pastoral need is determined in reference to such stereotypes; and pastoral care designed to ensure the inviolability of home and family.

Vital areas of pastoral need for women – questions of abortion, contraception, child care, sexuality, violence and sexual abuse – only began to feature as legitimate pastoral concerns once women achieved greater visibility and entered positions of leadership in the churches. Women's unequal position in society has also gone unchallenged by the churches because pastoral theology has never been sufficiently client-centred to allow such critical perspectives to be articulated.

Thus, both in terms of women's contribution as pastoral carers and in establishing the parameters of pastoral need, pastoral care has served to police and limit the horizons of women, by offering carefully circumscribed role models and visions of selfhood and self-fulfilment. Exclusive concentration on the person and role of the (ordained, male) pastor results in a pastoral theology that neglects the needs of (female) lay people and reflects the value-assumptions of a male hierarchy in ruling on questions of legitimate pastoral need and how to address it; in short, a pastoral theology that is both sexist and clericalist.

Two Models of Pastoral Theology

The values underpinning pastoral practice therefore embody particular conceptions of pastoral need and pastoral agency. However, they also act as vehicles of pastoral theology as well, in that they serve to articulate notions of the Divine through the exercise of care. What the Christian Church considers normative and desirable, and therefore seeks to foster in its life and work – via diverse forms of pastoral practice – is understood as a reflection of the nature of God. However, such values may actually be rationalizations of ideologies of sexism and clericalism in the name of the Divine will. A strategy by which such an implicit theology might be subjected to scrutiny – and restored to a more authentic state – is therefore essential for critical reflection on pastoral practice.

James Griffis (1985) writes about the implicit values which underpin pastoral practice, and argues that there are two distinct and oppositional models available within the Christian tradition. He identifies the tendency within mainstream churches towards what he calls the 'Constantinian' model of care, which embodies principles like control, order and the authority of law. In contrast, he delineates the characteristics of an alternative 'Liberation' model, emphasizing change, *metanoia* and innovation. Effectively, the choice is between a model of stability and maintenance, against one of liberation and transformation.

The sexist and clericalist model serves in many ways as an example of the Constantinian model: it restricts pastoral agency to male-ordained agents out of an implicit understanding that the grace of God works selectively, through the accredited channels of ordination and privilege. God is regarded as a similarly controlling and authoritative figure; Lord, King and Master of creation, to whom obedience and submission is due. Christian virtue is constituted as conformity to Divine authority.

By contrast, a liberative pastoral care takes as its inspiration the prophetic and apocalyptic ministry of Jesus, and a call for conversion rooted in an apprehension of God's transformation of the present via the creative and disturbing activity of the Spirit. Humanity is called into radical obedience to the Divine promise for the future, rather than required to preserve the existing order of structure and stasis. Pastoral agency, understood as the prerogative of all God's people, is directed towards the establishment of God's reign of justice and freedom from oppression.

Griffis insists that both models have their virtues: and certainly, the Constantinian model reminds us of the positive aspects of a theology of creation and natural virtue. It also emphasizes the importance of a pastoral ministry that is able to support and sustain those for whom stability and order is a token of the reassuring and consistent love of God at times of acute distress. However, it is also true that to restrict the boundaries of pastoral care to such pacifying and ameliorative functions narrows our ambitions concerning human response to suffering and need, effectively de-politicizing the gospel and refusing to regard pastoral care as reflecting the challenges of a God who is not only loving but just.

Feminist Theology and Pastoral Care

Is it possible to see in the paradigm of pastoral practice as liberation an effective model for the empowerment and pastoral care of women? A commitment to feminist praxis would mean modelling pastoral practice on theological values and insights that promised the empowerment of women and addressed their pastoral needs; but also to see those pastoral relationships as reflections of the Divine nature. Christian pastoral practice has the potential to reveal a God who is startlingly present in human encounter. In their relationships and actions of care, Christians believe they can effect some of the creative and redemptive work of God; but that such care will also express something of the Divine reality. Thus human pastoral relationships, however expressed, will also be to Christians in some sense a disclosure of God.

The Constantinian model assumes certain avenues for the disclosure and revelation of God, namely the established offices and structures of the Church and officially sanctioned avenues of pastoral practice. The Liberation model, by contrast, understands God to be at work in the faithful action of the poor and outcast in their struggles towards love and justice. A God who inspires such a mission would also inform pastoral practice that engaged in prophecy as well as service; in challenging social structures as well as servicing them; in exercising critical solidarity rather than unquestioning approval. The implications for the pastoral care of women would therefore promote a more proactive ministry, engaging with the structural and political dimensions of women's lives.

Attention to the needs of women in pastoral care alerts us to the reciprocal nature of the pastoral encounter. According to the traditional model, the pastor is the powerful and privileged agent through whom God works, by virtue of a special calling and superior qualities. God is understood to work from a position of strength and power; but this is rather contradicted by liberationist and feminist perspectives, which emphasize the vulnerability of God through the suffering of Christ, and identify the exclusion and pain of the poor and marginalized as experiences through which justice and redemption will be established. The compassion of Christ is thus not a striking of a sympathetic attitude from afar, but literally com-passion, or a suffering solidarity which willingly shares in the limitations of the human condition. Yet the resurrection is an assurance that the love of God is capable of embracing and transcending finitude and death.

The notion of the suffering God suggests that pastorally God is disclosed as much in the person and situation of the cared for as the carer. What does it mean therefore to talk of a God who is so vulnerable as to be in need of our care, who knows the pain of imperfection and death? It implies a God who enters completely into human affairs, refusing to be abstracted or distanced from the pain of the world. It certainly implies an end to models of care that are based on dualistic relationships of healthy/ sick, able expert/powerless client, shepherd/sheep, or ordained/lay; and invites us to consider models of mutuality and incarnate love as paradigmatic for pastoral theology. These are certainly recognizably feminist models, given that movement's promotion of values which emphasizes interconnectedness, mutuality and relationality.

Finally, such a liberationist model serves to break open our understanding of Christian caring, both in terms of personal agency and the corporate and symbolic nature of pastoral practice. A plurality of models of care are being reappropriated – often deliberately – by women in pastoral situations. Given the social and cultural expectations on women to exercise care – even if, as we have seen, that care goes unrecognized and unrewarded – they come to a closer recognition of the special gifts that caring requires and brings. Here are models and perhaps images that can take their place alongside the established ones of shepherd and pastor to inform Christian caring, and in the process open new avenues and metaphors to apprehend the nature of the Divine.

Important developments in deconstruction and literary criticism, as well as critical theory, have informed various perspectives in liberation theology and feminist criticism to suggest that any claim to absolute, final truth involves an occlusion of unvoiced and marginalized perspectives. As we have seen, pastoral care that reflects values of order, authority and hierarchy functions to bolster the position of the powerful. In the process, it sets limits on our apprehension of God's activity in the world.

By contrast, the gospel imperative of the bias to the poor involves practising pastoral strategies that empower such silenced groups, and ending those that perpetuate their marginalization. This involves pastoral ministries that not only embody the values of the powerless, but witness to models of truth that refuse the foreclosure of certainty: denying the false divisions and stereotyping (of gender, race, dis/ability and sexuality) that is born of the 'will to power'. Instead, pastoral values must affirm the mystery and complexity of human nature and the disturbing charism of the Spirit, an ethic of risk and *metanoia*, and thereby temper the more traditional emphases on order, structure and stability. Thus a feminist pastoral theology necessarily celebrates diversity, heterogeneity and provisionality, both in terms of human identity and of the possibility of absolute and ultimate truth-claims.

Such an appeal to the provisionality of experience and truth is not to collapse into relativism, or to deny the possibility of truth-claims; but it is to insist that such values can never exist in abstract and are necessarily linked to *praxis*. If pastoral practice is the embodied expression of Christian truth-claims, this means that the gospel and the Church's mission can never exist independently of the community which enacts and articulates these values. Pastoral care is not therefore the exercise of absolute eternal values, but more the enactment of provisional truth-claims that have to be tested out, in and through Christian practice. As the quotation at the beginning of this chapter testifies, the ultimate benchmark of authentic Christian *kerygma* is the quality of the faith community and discipleship into which the Church calls women and men. Pastoral practice that is directed towards forging authentic and gospel-related gender relations therefore serves as a crucial instrument of mission available to the Christian community.

This vision of theology is clearly incarnational and sacramental, and this seems consistent with the claims about knowledge, selfhood and community which feminists have seen fit to make in pursuit of women's emancipation. Tasks associated with the most fundamental, material and embodied human functions form the fabric of the everyday caring roles women have traditionally been required to undertake. As a result, the claims to experience arising from such gendered forms of labour tend to emphasize interrelationality and concretion as the fundamentals of selfhood and community – values often at odds with the dominant Western cultural ethos of autonomous, independent, atomistic individuals. Part of the oppositional project of feminism has therefore been to stand up for notions of the integrated and interrelated nature of human selfhood, which refuse the dualism and individualism of Enlightenment rationality. Similarly, feminist theory refuses the abstractions of empiricism and objectivism, which claim that truth and knowledge are in some way independent of the practices and subjects which generated them.

Such an appeal to the inseparability of knower and known, fact and value, theory and practice, reminds us that all knowledge, including theology, is contextual and situated, unable to abstract and divorce itself from the needs and interests of its generating community. Just as scientists are increasingly regarding scientific knowledge as the product of the social and human practice of doing science, so, too, all theology may be seen as pastoral, originating in the practice of the faith community. Such knowledge originates and returns to 'the present, the particular and the concrete', generated and tested in the crucible of Christian praxis, informed by values and norms themselves already forged as a result of situated and purposeful human pastoral encounters.

The challenge of women to pastoral care does not, therefore, simply require their inclusion in a tradition that remains otherwise unchanged. Instead, it is a programme for reconstituting the nature of pastoral values and the theological understandings that underpin Christian practice. Feminist evocations of difference and diversity eschew models of care that represent control and coercion; but open new avenues of discovering Divine truth as provisional and situated. Such values must be grounded in the reality of human community, in order to ensure their integrity and authenticity, and this may be done by rerouting such values back into pastoral practice as the human and embodied enactment of ultimate truth claims. Just as feminist theory challenges the traditional dualisms of theory and practice, body and spirit, emotion and reason, general and specific, truth and contingency, so such a model of theological truth defies the old conventions which claim that principles and eternal truths can be abstracted from the life of the communities which proclaim and enact them. Instead, there is the possibility of a theological sensibility that roots Christian values in the immediacy and concretion of interpersonal encounter, while witnessing to the paradox that at the very heart of such a dynamic of need and response is felt the transcendence which carries us beyond the knowable and certain into the realms of Divine disclosure.

4

FROM SPACE TO
WOMAN-SPACE[1]

One of the most evocative scenes I can remember from the cinema is
the closing sequence from Ridley Scott's *Thelma and Louise*. You may
remember how the two women have escaped from dead-end jobs and
relationships into a wild spree of crime, cars and the open road. But
eventually, this small bubble of freedom they have created must be
burst. Throughout the film the dominant mood has been one of wide
open spaces: of tall canyons and long dusty roads – and of the women's
sense of exhilaration as they break the normal conventions that prevent
women from moving and expressing themselves so freely. Certainly, to
carve out that space requires excessive, bizarre and often violent measures; but we are constantly reminded of the constraints and strictures
surrounding them, as women, trying to cut loose. There are many occasions in their adventures when Thelma and Louise are reminded that they
should not be encroaching on the male world of truck stops, highway
patrols and the open road; and the final denouement brings the harshest
lesson of all. Pursued by battalions of local police, their car reaches the
edge of a steep precipice. They have come, literally and metaphorically,
to the end of the road. They are still surrounded by wide open space; indeed, this final scene captures some especially breathtaking scenery. But
now, their panorama no longer points or leads them to freedom, but only
promises oblivion. Faced with the plunge off the cliff or a surrender to
the inevitable consequences of their transgression, they choose the point
of no return, and urge their car on, over the side and down to extinction.
For me, it is a powerful – and very visually alluring – portrayal of the rare
nature of women's freedom to participate in the particular genre of 'road

---

1 Adapted from a keynote address to the 1994 Summer School of the British and
Irish School of Feminist Theology.

movies', but also a tough reminder of how temporary and costly are these wide open spaces for women. Thelma and Louise win for themselves a period of sanctuary from their meaningless and drudge-like lives which far exceeds the normal parameters of women's horizons and territory. But ultimately they pay the price for going too far beyond the accepted standards of 'a woman's place' – and so oblivion and total disappearance must inevitably follow.

As I have hinted, the quasi-feminist message of this film seems totally tied up with the use of geographical and social or moral space that it evokes, deliberately, through its camera work and style of presentation. And its central notion of 'space' in relation to the women's search for freedom and self-respect remains with me as a powerful and evocative metaphor. So it interested me to observe that the subtitle of this summer school offered as the aim of this conference, 'To provide space for people to do theology together'. It seemed an ideal opportunity to explore further this theme of space, as it has been used within feminist theories, and how it might enable feminist theologians to go about their work. Certainly, the notion of space in feminist theory has proved to be a powerful vehicle by which to explore the dynamics of women's oppression and the source of alternative sensibilities.

Space: Society, Self and Knowledge

In a recent book, the feminist philosopher Seyla Benhabib discusses the prospects for a coherent and ethically responsible political philosophy in the wake of the collapse of universal 'grand narratives', and the 'end of history' (Benhabib, 1992). Despite widespread scepticism towards what Benhabib calls 'the legacies of modernity', she argues that any social theory and any practical politics must still engage with those precepts that stood at the heart of the Enlightenment project. While such commitments are not completely redundant, they are still in need of reconstruction, especially given feminism's exposure of their androcentric nature. So whatever the philosophical and political prospects are in our pluralistic, postmodern, fragmented times, she argues, we still find at the centre of our intellectual and practical concerns three core questions which must be resolved. These are: what is the nature of human community, and on what terms do we articulate our vision of the ideal society, and claims to justice, participation and solidarity? What is the essence of human nature and what do we believe are the sources of the self, the person? What is knowable, how do we know what we know and what can we value as truthful and reliable?

So it is those areas of 'society', 'self' and 'knowledge' that emerge as vitally contested 'spaces' for feminist theory and politics. I shall therefore explore feminist critiques of the division of human culture into 'public' and 'private' spheres as a fundamental aspect of the construction of gender difference; the evocation of subversive, distinctive feminine psychic space from which a new feminist identity and sensibility may be created; and the search for reliable and responsible spaces within the academy and feminist communities from which to generate new ways of knowing and acting.

In referring to 'feminist theory' I want in particular to draw upon the work taking place in the social sciences, philosophy, natural science, anthropology, psychoanalysis and cultural studies. It is my contention that feminist theology risks isolation from many of these insights if it does not take positive steps to engage in dialogue. By 'feminism' I mean that body of theory and politics – and the two are intimately related – which seeks to analyse and correct the exclusion and subordination of women in all its forms. But we must necessarily take account of the diversity of feminist work today; not just in its division into the various schools of liberal, radical, ecological, post-structuralist, womanist, socialist and so on; but in its global diversity and proliferation. As Rosemarie Tong says:

> That feminism is many and not one is to be expected because women are many and not one. The more feminist thoughts we have, the better. By refusing to center, congeal, and cement their separate thoughts into a unified truth too inflexible to change, feminists resist patriarchal dogma. (Tong, 1989: 7)

Despite these differences, the feminist sources I shall be using all share an understanding that inequalities of power lie at the heart of the relations between women and men. Feminist theorizing about how space is defined and policed to exclude and constrain women identifies the dynamics of gender inequality as resting in the institutions, conventions and practices of the system we call 'patriarchy'. Thus, although individual women and men may be autonomous agents, it is important to see that our individual and mutual destinies are also shaped and constrained by a patriarchal culture. We are therefore both the creators and creations of a gendered culture which establishes the conventions and hierarchies by which women and men are divided and differentiated. The relationships between women and men may be characterized to some degree by negotiation, consent and the willingness to collaborate and change; but there are significant ways also in which women are coerced, exploited and circumscribed by a system, administered and supported by men and women, which operates at a level beyond individual ill- or good-will.

Social Space

Many feminists argue that the demarcation of public and private space is integral to the construction of gender difference and the subordination of women. It is an area in which feminist theorists have done much creative and incisive work, in political theory, anthropology, history and economics. All focus on the central issues of how patriarchy creates a distinction between so-called 'male' space and 'female' space, and the symbolic and material means by which that division is effected, serving to place women, and that which is designated as 'feminine', into a separate and inferior sphere.

The dichotomy of public and private in many aspects of culture, and its connection with gender divisions, forms a major strand within anthropological studies. Twenty years ago, Sherry Ortner argued influentially and controversially that biological differences between women and men are inflated culturally into an entire symbolic and material system in which women are considered lesser, secondary and subordinate to men (Ortner, 1974). Ortner argues that this is so because the creation of human culture depends on the transcendence and socialization of nature. Women are identified with nature by virtue of their reproductive role, and men, as the creators of culture, seek to control and contain women as representatives of the natural order.

I think it is important to frame this argument in terms of the power struggle inherent in the creation of culture, and the way certain roles are rationalized and reified as inevitable. Commentators on Ortner's thesis have accused her of actually saying that women are ontologically closer to nature; but it is more properly regarded as an exposure of the conceptual and political machinery by which gender difference, and differential social roles, are constructed. The symbolic association of woman: nature/man: culture should therefore be regarded as the product of social relations; and such symbolism becomes an organizing and prescriptive framework for the way gender roles should be: that men belong 'naturally' in cultural, public and political spaces, whereas women must inevitably be confined to domestic, private, familial activities. So the equation of women with nature becomes a way of restricting and controlling their access to the world of men; and the bifurcation of nature and culture is extended to other evaluative distinctions, such as emotion/reason, body/mind, connectedness/detachment, subjective/objective, familial/social. All of them carve out a distinctively male sphere by circumscribing women's proper realm, appropriate role and specific characteristics; all organized around, and encapsulated in, the distinction of separate, inherently gendered, spaces.

Further studies explore how specific practices serve to protect the boundary between these gendered worlds. Gillian Rose has recently published a book in which she examines the work of feminist geographers who argue that unequal social relations and patriarchy are expressed and constituted primarily through spatial differentiation (Rose, 1993).

The segregation of the workplace is also a crucial dimension both of capitalist relations and gendered society. An outstanding feature of the 'world of work' is the degree to which women work only with other women, and men with other men, and the fact that occupations are quite distinctly differentiated on gendered terms, with women predominantly in catering, servicing, retailing and welfare sectors, whose strongly feminine ethos and low status serves to accentuate their ambivalent role as extensions of the 'domestic' sphere which only intrude into the public world of the paid economy on sufferance (Bradley, 1989). In studies of male-dominated workplaces, for example, everything from restrictive practices to sexual harassment serve to act upon women by implicitly reminding them that they do not belong, that they are invaders, aliens, guests, in male space (Bradley, 1989; Witz, 1993; Richardson, 1993).

Other feminists see a continuity between forms of violence by men against women such as rape, domestic violence and physical abuse, and other, supposedly less 'serious' behaviour such as sexual harassment at work or on the streets, obscene telephone calls, and so on (Hanmer and Maynard, 1987; Maynard, 1987). All are ways – highly sexualized ways, but many feminists see a clear link between patriarchal power and the construction of coercive heterosexual masculinity – in which men seek to control and police women. They may actually succeed in changing women's behaviour, as evidenced by studies of women's fear of crime which show that women do restrict their movements on the streets, do feel vulnerable at home alone and while travelling (Hanmer and Maynard, 1987: 105–9). Such considerations act as constant reminders to women that they have intruded upon men's space, that this is a man's world, and if they insist upon entering it they must take the consequences. We can only be there as outsiders or interlopers, or as objects for men's diversion and gratification. Whatever the case, in the patriarchal public space women must 'know their place' – and often this is to be 'seen but not heard'.

Other characterizations of violence against women see it as an assault on women's bodily integrity; in spatial terms, an invasion of our personal space. This suggests that the abuse and objectification of women's bodily space is crucial to the conduct of gender relations (Stanko, 1985; Kelly, 1988).

Women as 'pollutants' may be another way in which the boundaries between masculine and feminine space are drawn. Mary Douglas' work on taboo and boundaries emphasizes how rituals of cleanliness and purity are symbolic means by which we mark the threshold between inclusion and exclusion (Douglas, 1966). By transgressing the boundaries of public and private, women are 'out of place' and are regarded as contamination. To identify women as unclean, as Other, is a means by which the boundaries are implicitly acknowledged and reinforced; and become strategies of exclusion and foreclosure, founded on an insistence on clear distinctions between the spaces and ways of policing the entry- and exit-points of the separate realms.

Some of the most institutionalized and formal prohibitions against women's entering the male public realm have, of course, been removed over the past two hundred years. This has often come about as a result of economic and technological change, such as the huge shifts in economic organization over the past 40 years which have expanded women's job opportunities; but other, more overtly feminist contributions have been instrumental in legislating and campaigning for equal rights for women.

This has traditionally formed the central ambition of so-called 'liberal' feminism, which has sought to break down the dualism of nature and culture, public and private by extending the privileges of politics, education, paid employment and equality before the law to women on a par with men. This is an important project, rooted in an affirmation of the shared humanity of women and men; of a refusal to accept as innate, God-given or ontologically permanent the designation of separate spheres, nature as female, and culture as male. It urges upon us the realization that such a demarcation is the result of human agency, that women and men share a common culture, that women's exclusion from the public is 'cultural', and not 'natural'.

But on the other hand, as the women's movement in the West over the past 30 years has discovered, it is still in so many ways a man's world. For women striving for recognition – or even for a decent living wage – in the public world, the constraints of their private obligations bear down hard upon them. The phenomenon of the two-career woman has created a 'double bind' in which the pressure of competing with men on their own terms is compounded by continuing expectations concerning domestic and familial responsibilities. Such images of ourselves as good mothers, loving wives and competent homemakers are more than a matter of external cultural stereotyping, but are often deeply internalized. In other words, we have formal (even if not substantive) equality in one sphere; but the dichotomy remains, and arguably women are still constrained by the dual spheres and the persistence of 'the ties that bind' within what is still regarded as an exclusively female, domestic sphere of responsibility (Glendenning and Millar, 1992).

Thus, a dilemma for feminism begins to emerge. If equal participation in male space on patriarchal terms proves unsatisfactory, is the solution to return to the female province in a search for truly woman-centred politics? Or does this merely capitulate to the nature/culture division and perpetuate a patriarchal system which is only too happy to sanction women's repudiation of a shared public culture?[2]

One possibility might be to seek strategies that enable us to inhabit a space 'which is neither the masculine public nor the feminized private' (Rose, 1993: 130) or as Adrienne Rich puts it, to create a world where

---

2 See Grosz (1990: 332–44) for an elaboration of the 'equality/difference' debate.

'work [might] be as meaningful as love and friendship in our lives' (Rich, 1980a). In a sense, this is a reiteration of the old feminist nostrum that 'the personal is political': a refusal to tolerate as individual and private that which actually owes its shape to structural and political factors.

The essays in *Life-Cycles*, a collection about women and pastoral care, show this essential connection between the traditional feminine world of 'pastoral care' and the wider dynamics of social policy and church politics (Graham and Halsey, 1993). Women's 'caring' role has been for too long sequestered in the private space of home, affection, family ties and feminine duty; but by speaking about those experiences, the gendered division of labour on which women as carers rests, the assumptions about the essentially female nature of care, we begin to glimpse a wider story. Such a process brings out into the open space of public scrutiny the everyday experiences of women, the taken-for-granted fabric of their lives as carers, and begins to ask deeper questions about the inevitability of such activities. It also stresses that women's interventions into 'male' arenas can display appropriate competence but also sow the seeds of new patterns of achievement and relationship.

Subjectivity and Selfhood

Within contemporary feminism, a generation of French-speaking writers have taken themes from classical psychoanalysis and married them with linguistics and literary criticism. Psychoanalysis is a troubled and ambivalent discipline for feminists, but it does offer a perspective that encapsulates an inspired fusion of body and mind, of psyche and soma, in its insistence that human mental and psychological states have their origins in the earliest desires and physical demands of infancy. Through the work of writers such as Luce Irigaray, Julia Kristeva, Hélène Cixous and Michelle le Doueff, a new style of feminist theorizing has emerged. Opinion remains divided, but what I want to concentrate on here is the emphasis on the retrieval and creation of autonomous and subversive 'space' that such writers commend within the conventions of language, psychoanalysis and literature.

For these writers, the discipline of classical psychoanalysis relates the story of the infant's entry into culture – and patriarchal culture at that. Following the French structuralists and the psychoanalyst Jacques Lacan, they place great weight on the significance of language, both for the ordering of society and the development of individual 'subjectivity' (our personality and consciousness). Language has an importance in reflecting and symbolizing an entire 'symbolic economy' of gender relations within which the representation of personhood and subjectivity is androcentric – normatively male. But in tandem with this there is the idea that language is also the primary medium by which we are formed as individuals;

33

language, and the infant's acquisition of speech, are central to the formation of adult gender identity. (See Tong, 1989 for an introduction to psychoanalytic feminism.)

In a patriarchal society, women are silenced by their lack of representation within the androcentric linguistic order, represented by the metaphor of the phallus. Women are 'Other' (de Beauvoir, 1979 [1949]: 16ff.), they lack any linguistic privilege, and therefore possess no definitive identity, but exist as non-beings, invisible, nameless and marginalized.

However, the premises of Lacanian and Francophone feminist psychoanalysis are that the patriarchal, so-called 'symbolic' order, while structured around the dominance of the phallus, is also founded upon the rejection and repression of the world of the 'imaginary', which is analogous to the realm of pre-Oedipal polymorphous pleasure. Yet these forces of desire – embodied in the id, the sphere of polymorphous pleasure – persist, emerging at critical points in our development.

Conventionally, of course, the pre-cultural imaginary is the world of the maternal, the domestic and the feminine. So all those qualities (of desire and undifferentiated sensuality, of unity with maternal love) are associated both with the imaginary (the pre-cultural, pre-linguistic) and with the feminine: and all are represented by the unconscious, which, according to Freud, is where all these aspects are lodged after the formation of the ego. So they do not disappear, but remain within the unconscious; and despite the superficial stability of the ego, the conscious, rational self, the forces of desire and sensuality threaten to fracture and invade the public, ordered world. Similarly, therefore, the powers of the imaginary, feminine realm serve as a constant reminder of the failure of the socialization process, of the possibility of subversion by the forces of the unconscious, with its chaotic, fluid and destabilizing presence. Kristeva terms this the 'chora' or semiotic, the unspeakable, pre-discursive space which exists prior to language, associated with the maternal, a site of resistance and disruption of the symbolic (Irigaray, 1985; Kristeva, 1981; 1984).

So for these Francophone feminists, such 'spaces' are evoked in order to celebrate, and locate, a new identity for women which defies the patriarchal metaphysics founded on women's 'non-being', silence and invisibility. They transform this non-being into a subversive 'otherness' which is not contained or circumscribed by patriarchal discourse. A new symbolic system is required; a distinctively woman-centred identity that is grounded in women's differential experience of the body, of their different and problematic relationship to language, of their psycho-sexual and maternal positions, of coming to terms realistically with the negative symbolism and representation of women. Starting from here, Kristeva and Irigaray hope to construct a new symbolic economy which values women's distinctiveness and provides them with a source of positive identification. In a sense, therefore, Irigaray and Kristeva use language – and the significance of language in reflecting and structuring our innermost identity as gendered persons, and its importance in representing access to power and privilege and other cultural values – as a powerful tool to construct a proper space within which women can discover themselves free of patriarchal distortion and prescription.

Here, therefore, is to be found the source of an alternative feminine identity, which is subversive, uncontrollable, indefinable according to the linear monolithic standards of the patriarchal phallus (the dominating system of language). It is the place of women's identity and self-affirmation into which the patriarchal system cannot, quite literally, penetrate.

Hence, also, the importance of what is known as 'writing the body': women's embodied selfhood, as the absolute source of differential knowledge and identity, resting beyond the confines of language, becomes the vantage point for women's creative and transformative energy (Jones, 1986). For Irigaray, writing is 'a space of subjective creation' (Braidotti, 1991); much of her work is about strategies for carving out a woman-centred space within which an alternative metaphysics may be practised and a truly feminist politics, uncompromised by androcentricism, might be realized. 'The women's movement is for Irigaray the privileged space of elaboration of new discursive practices, which enables the political evolution of feminism' (ibid.: 64).

Kristeva identifies metaphors and historical examples in which femininity and resistance or subversion have been linked, and attempts to explore their significance for the women's movement today. She is becoming interested in the prophetic and critical potential of spirituality and religion, seeing this as 'revolutionary poesis' (Kristeva, 1984), a form of expression in which altered states of consciousness, non-rational and symbolic forms of meaning, narrative and ritual, may overturn rationalistic and literalistic systems.

This seems to me to have tremendous potential for feminist theology, and touches on some practical examples of how such a trend in feminist theory might be developed. Why are these feminist writers deliberately evoking the language of transcendence, religious ecstasy and mysticism? Kristeva talks about the 'radical trinity of subversion', derived from the feminine unconscious, of 'madness, holiness and poetry': all challenge the linear rationality of the patriarchal symbolic, all provide means through which alternative states of consciousness and expression might flower (Grosz, 1989). And of course, historically, women have been prominent as prophets, mystics, charismatic visionaries and millenarian leaders. Is this one sign of the 'protest' of the normally silenced and marginalized finding a different voice, drawn from the space of otherness and non-being?

Certainly, such thoughts have led me to revaluate the power of women's liturgies, poems and rituals, as potential sources of a new creativity drawn from the imagination, the unconscious and the embodied. This idea identifies language, and women's representation or invisibility within religious language, as a primary site of struggle and renewal for feminist theology. So, the various 'women-church' and 'women-space' groups that focus on exploring and fostering new forms of spirituality and ritual may be about reclaiming women's existence within a symbolic economy that conventionally renders them invisible, unspeakable (Ruether, 1985; St Hilda Community, 1991; Walton and Durber, 1994).

I am convinced that these areas are tremendously fertile spaces for theological discourse; both as places where we can create and foster new vehicles of human expression, but also as spaces within which we can go beyond the boundaries of logic and established language, into the mysterious and unspoken, there perhaps to encounter the transcendent.

Knowledge

One way in which women experience patriarchal knowledge at its most powerful and excluding is via its manifestations in science and technology. Wajcman examines how even a new and supposedly gender-neutral discipline such as information technology is rapidly becoming a male preserve, especially in schools; interestingly, she expresses in spatial terms the barriers that exist against women and girls: 'Most women never approach the foreign territory of these masculine areas' (Wajcman, 1991: 217).

The new reproductive technologies are another area of scientific innovation where, despite much of the rhetoric, discoveries are driven less by women's needs and more by medical and scientific values. Of course, medicine is not monolithic, nor is it thoroughly malevolent; but there is evidence to suggest that many of the policy-makers and practitioners are operating out of implicit understandings of women's role and destiny as centred upon motherhood, and motherhood, at any cost, and that the dynamics of new reproductive technologies ignore many of women's demands in pursuit of high-prestige, high-risk procedures (Stanworth, 1987). This area seems a very contested and paradoxical space, bounded by the expanding limits of medical knowledge and technology, where science may be seen to offer many advantages to childless women, even though the options may be largely determined by strict views of the 'maternal instinct'. Here again is a space where economic factors, social policies, cultural expectations, medical and scientific knowledge and professional power and expertise all intersect, and create a space which women may experience as extremely contradictory:

Thus, medical and scientific advances in the sphere of reproduction – so often hailed as the liberators of twentieth-century women – have, in fact, been a double-edged sword. On the one hand, they have offered women a greater technical possibility to decide if, when and under what conditions to have children; on the other, the domination of so much reproductive technology by the medical profession and by the state has enabled others to have an even greater capacity to exert control over women's lives. Moreover, the 'technical possibility' of choosing an oral contraceptive or in vitro fertilization is only a small aspect of reproductive freedom. For some women, motherhood remains their only chance of creativity, while economic and social circumstances compel others to relinquish motherhood altogether. (Ibid.: 231)

Science, both as a body of knowledge and a form of practice, therefore, has often appeared to be the implacable foe of the women's movement and a highly influential and significant factor in the construction and maintenance of patriarchal ideologies and policies. Proper scientific knowledge is portrayed as pure, objective and value-free, reflecting a notion of rationality as encapsulating pristine logic, untainted by the interests or perspectives of the knower. Such a view of rationality is typically associated with the world and activities of men; objectivity, domination, creativity, intellect are qualities associated with the building of culture. Inevitably, they become opposed to the characteristics equated with women: subjectivity, irrationality, affectivity: the qualities of home and family. Science is therefore culturally associated with masculinity, and with the public realm of the masculine; any woman entering the field is thought to be surrendering her 'true' nature. The sphere of instrumental technical reason has traditionally been defined as a male activity – as an intellectual space into which women may not stray – and is predicated on an exclusion of all that is irrational, emotional, subjective and 'feminine'. Here again we encounter the dynamics of exclusion and foreclosure; in order to circumscribe the (exclusively) androcentric sphere of reason, all ambiguity and alternatives are rendered 'Other' and alien.

The feminist responses to these dilemmas reflect the diversity of feminist theory and practice. Some perspectives seek to invert the oppositional nature of male science and female invisibility, and develop an analysis that sees a feminist alternative as originating in the repressed and marginalized values currently represented by women. These varieties of radical feminism or ecofeminism tend to equate objectivity and domination with male control and consciousness, and argue for a renewed woman-centred epistemology, which affirms the 'feminine' qualities of empathy, closeness to nature, co-operation and nurture (Jaggar, 1983: ch. 5; Plumwood, 1993: ch. 1).

However, objections have been raised to such a woman-centred science, primarily that it simply perpetuates patriarchal evocations of women's characteristics as deriving from their maternal, naturalistic and relational qualities: an inversion of the old nature/culture distinction. It still locates women, and women's ways of knowing in a separate, essentially 'feminine' sphere, even though it serves as a source of protest against the ecophobic tendencies of patriarchal technological rationality. It seems to me that such a perspective assumes that different ways of knowing are rooted in biology, and not in social experience or in the circumstances of the scientific process itself. This is related to the issue of where we locate ourselves as feminists in relation to knowledge, intellectual enquiry and scientific practice. Knowledge is not just about abstract 'ideas' that live in our heads; indeed, that may be one 'idea' that serves to deflect critical attention from the links between knowledge and power. Rather, knowledge, just like anything else, is organized, and manifests itself, spatially. Knowledge consists as much of practices and institutions – the processes and places responsible for its generation, transmission and perpetuation – as it does of words, concepts and theories. In this respect, therefore, it is important to view from a critical standpoint how 'knowledge space' has served to privilege certain groups, and in particular to serve patriarchal interests, and how feminists might seek to begin to change some of the organizational and epistemological aspects of exclusive knowledge.

It may therefore be important to distinguish between feminist science and feminine science when attempting to construct feminist epistemologies which do not cede the realm of rationality back to men, and which fully acknowledge women's participation in the creation of culture and social relations. But the problem of how to cede space to women, of how women enter the androcentric world of objectivity and scientific instrumental rationality, is parallel with that of entering the public world of politics. Can the 'space' of science cede a place to women without requiring women to adapt to patriarchal standards and criteria? If there is a separate and alternative way of knowing, what are its origins and how do we articulate it?

In her insistence upon knowledge and cognition as human practice, the feminist scientist Mary Hawkesworth proposes a renewed attention to knowledge as a located, spatial phenomenon (Hawkesworth, 1989). Knowledge as practice becomes something clearly bound by language, rules of procedure, validation and theorization, all of which have their origins, not outside or beyond that which is known in some Platonic realm of ideal reason, but within the very realm of human agency:

In this view, 'knowledge' presupposes involvement in a social process replete with rules of compliance, norms of assessment, and standards of excellence that are humanly created. Although humans aspire to unmediated knowledge of the world, the nature of perception precludes such direct access. The only possible access is through theory-laden conventions that organize and structure observations by according meanings to observed events, bestowing relevance and significance on phenomena, indicating strategies for problem solving, and identifying methods by which to test the validity of solutions. Knowledge, then, is a convention rooted in the practical judgements of a community of fallible inquirers who struggle to resolve theory-dependent problems under specific historical conditions. (Ibid.: 548–9)

As the primatologist Donna Haraway observes, a notion of scientific knowledge as objective, universal and value-neutral represents an impossible form of human knowing because it denies its own embodied and 'situated' character (Haraway, 1991: 183–201). Whereas Hawkesworth uses the theme of practice, Haraway evokes the metaphor of vision – as embodied and situated. The idea of infinite vision, of seeing all in a universal and final perspective, is plainly ridiculous, and to make such a claim is, effectively, to 'play God'. Thus an epistemology modelled on such assumptions should be rejected. Instead, Haraway argues that an insistence on the 'particularity and embodiment of all vision' comprises 'a usable, but not an innocent doctrine of objectivity' (ibid.: 189).

Gillian Rose echoes this by arguing that detachment, universality and objectivity are implicit denials of the spaces from which we all must speak: 'Masculinist rationality is a form of knowledge which assumes a knower who believes he can separate himself from his body, emotions, values, past and so on, so that he and his thought are autonomous, context-free and objective' (Rose, 1993: 7).[3] Thus, this attempt to evade the spatial, located and politically committed origins of knowledge is the major flaw of universalist patriarchal epistemologies. So, in terms of constructing alternative feminist ways of knowing, we look to found them not on 'innate' differences in knowing, but upon the context and applications of knowledge and the conditions of its generation: on the processes and spaces of knowing, rather than the qualities of detached and disembodied knowers.

But if the social location of knowing is at issue, our commitment to the locatedness of intellectual enquiry, then the nature of the 'spaces' within which we assemble and practise as knowers becomes more critical than ever. And in particular the question arises of whether the academy is a responsible and appropriate space for feminist and inclusive knowledge; and what the relationship between feminist theology and academic theology should be.

---

3 In deference to this commitment to 'situated' knowledge, I would ask the editors of *Feminist Theology* to identify the contexts from which their contributors write. Patriarchal knowledge likes to cloak its own origins, but given that we all speak from some vantage point, it is important to be able to trace the opinions and perspectives of feminist debate to their specific locations.

Academic institutions are ambivalent places at best for feminists. The feminist philosopher Kate Campbell talks about the academy as a 'harbour' for feminism: 'building it up and replenishing it in some ways ... but at the same time given to running it dry, keeping it within walls, seeing to its overall containment' (Campbell, 1992: 2) – and, one may add, very vulnerable to turns of the tide. Some argue that by their very nature, universities and academic institutions cannot embrace feminist ways of knowing. This is because the academy is built on epistemological criteria (in other words, values about what it means to know, and what it means to be a knower), which implicitly exclude women. Although many of the material obstacles against women achieving creative and intellectual excellence have been removed, places of higher education are still not 'woman-friendly'. Whether the modern university is organized as a medieval monastic community or as a free-market corporate business, neither model has proved particularly conducive to more inclusive and open values of continuing education and adult access, collaboration, and socially responsible knowledge regardless of commercial outcome.

Does this mean therefore that feminists should abandon such institutions? Here I return to Donna Haraway's representation of situated knowledge as 'usable but not innocent': emanating from spaces that necessarily embody compromise and paradox, but capable of careful transformation into forms of responsible knowing. If we are to construct alternative ways of knowing, and reconstitute ourselves as authentic knowers, I do not believe this will come via a denial of reason as an abstract, de-contextualized ideal; instead, it will be a renegotiation of the spaces in which knowledge is contested, a refusal of existing boundaries; but including a recognition that, like it or not, this space, this language, this metaphysics is, for the time being, all we have. Our oppressions and our resistances, our constraints and innovations will come from this very space, which is contradictory. 'Women no less than men, though undoubtedly in a different fashion, are products of culture and cannot coherently claim for themselves an a priori purity or absence of contamination by its values, its language or its myths' (Gatens, 1991: 95).

To abandon the quest for knowledge feels too much like reverting to the patriarchal stereotypes that decree that women are unfit to be knowers, to accept uncritically the dichotomy that 'men theorize, and women experience'. The reality is that responsible and reliable knowledge, as presented by feminist philosophers, does offer us a way of prizing rigorous and systematic enquiry within a socially responsible context. Alison Peacock speaks on behalf of many women – myself included – who have spent too long fighting to be accepted as intelligent and female to surrender a claim to an intellect, an independence of judgement and the chance of educational excellence:

For some women, leaving the system is an act of protest, intended to challenge traditional academic priorities and goals. It may proclaim that caring for other people does matter, and that the price of academic success is too high. It may affirm a deep conviction that the quality of a person's mind ought not to be the sole determinant of worth, and that systems which promote such a partial view of human life are deeply flawed. Yet, however valid the criticisms implied in the action, the effectiveness of opting out as a strategy for women needs to be questioned. It cannot be seen as a radical challenge to the education system if, at the same time, opting out confirms prejudices about women's abilities and commitment to their work. It may even contribute towards the creation of a parallel set of feminist prejudices, in which a decision to remain within the system is seen as a selfish betrayal of sisterhood rather than womanhood! Most important of all, leaving moves women into the margins, so that mainstream education remains unchallenged and unchanged. Given that disadvantage still restricts girls in compulsory schooling, a mass exodus of able and principled women is scarcely beneficial. (Peacock, 1993: 75–6)

I wonder whether we, at this summer school, can use the ambiguities of our position to good effect. As a community of scholars, however temporary, we actually transcend the divisions of 'inside' versus 'outside' academia; in the words of bell hooks, we are both at the centre and the margins; and thus challenge the relative positions of both. We have the opportunity to use the insights from 'academic' feminism but to integrate them, and test them, in the crucible of feminist praxis. I have argued that the boundary between academic and lay, between reason and emotion, is constructed in order to keep women securely within one category; but can we find ways of refusing to recognize those boundaries, and transgress them creatively instead?

I suspect that feminist theology may be singularly blessed in this respect. This was brought home to me recently in giving a presentation to the newly formed 'Women's Studies Network' at my university, which is effectively a body convened of all the women who teach gender or feminist courses and do research in these areas. I approached my task of introducing some of the main themes in feminist theology with trepidation; some feminists are very hostile to religion, and I feared that to talk as I wished about the importance of spirituality, liturgy and politics as sites and locations of feminist theologizing would appear quaint and unrigorous. Yet it was my conviction that feminist theology, perhaps uniquely of all the feminist academic disciplines, has access to a wider constituency beyond the academy by virtue of its accountability to women in the Church, in base communities, women-church and other movements. Feminist theology therefore already crosses the boundaries of many different locations; and in order to give an authentic overview of the phenomenon called 'feminist theology' to the Network, I was insisting on a multiplicity of origins and locations and a diversity of contexts, vocabularies and concerns. These included the global and liberationist contexts of feminist, *mujerista* and womanist theologies; the collaboration between academic and ecclesiastical theologians; and the proliferation of Christian, post-Christian and goddess theologies and thealogies. I also felt it was important to give due homage to the influences of the theologies of liberation from the two-thirds world, which understand the people as agents of theological discourse.[4] For them the collaborative and practical nature of even the most esoteric scholarship is second nature.

So to speak and create theology from many different places challenges what it means to know and how we become knowers; we must make sure we are represented at the core, but also work hard to extend the boundaries. Higher education is becoming more exclusive, particularly because of the contraction in student grants and the increasing emphasis on cost-effectiveness. So I think we have to find ways of collaborating so that there is a flow between the different contexts – not an anti-intellectualism, but an academic rigour that includes as one of its criteria for valuable knowing the realm of useful and transformative knowing.

Conclusion: From Space to Woman-Space

I have been suggesting that women frequently experience space as paradoxical: as with the ambiguity of the new reproductive technologies, for example, or the strategic dilemma between reclaiming patriarchal space and creating an alternative, separate feminist territory. But perhaps this is not unhealthy; it reminds us that we are never entirely free of the contested nature of the space in which we find ourselves. Nowhere is pristine or entirely free of patriarchal encroachment; even the blissful realm of separatist imaginings requires a political and strategic will to be brought to birth. Yet I believe that this warns us against collapsing into utopianism, an implicit denial of our spatial location, by pretending that we can retreat to an Archimedean standpoint, situated beyond our immediate historical context or material experience. This space – however compromised, however contradictory – is all we have; and we can only construct our alternative ways of knowing and acting from the place in which we find ourselves (Rose, 1993: 159–60).

I drew earlier on the work of Donna Haraway, and her insistence on a form of 'situated knowledge' as affirming the given-ness of our immediate context. She suggests that to be a responsible political and intellectual

4 In reality it is an alliance of grass-roots and specialists in basic ecclesial communities. (See Boff and Boff, 1986; Hebblethwaite, 1993.)

agent is to acknowledge that we are finite, embodied and fragile creatures, not disembodied superhumans who can abstract ourselves from
our own material perceptions and contexts.

> So, not so perversely, objectivity turns out to be about particular and
> specific embodiment, and definitely not about the false vision promising
> transcendence of all limits and responsibility ... Feminist objectivity is
> about limited location and situated knowledge, not about transcend-
> ence and splitting of subject and object. (Haraway, 1991: 190)

The very embodied, contextual and located nature of 'space' thus implies ways of knowing and acting that require us as feminist theologians
also to concentrate on the concrete, the immediate and the practical.
The situated nature of knowledge is a means of grounding the vantage
point of feminist vision and feminist theologizing in the specific, spatial
and located, grounding its claims to authenticity and validity in the very
affirmation of its 'situated' and value-directed nature. This form of theology regards the practical transformation of the material world as the
primary goal of theological understanding; in that respect, it is very close
to the notion of 'praxis' or 'practical wisdom' within the theologies of
liberation. Thus, it is important to look for spaces within which theology as a form of 'practical wisdom' might take place; and I have tried
to highlight already existing forms of feminist theological praxis as ways
of using, and renegotiating, new forms of 'woman-space' in the areas of
ministry and pastoral care, spirituality, liturgy and academic theology.
But ultimately, it requires us to create theologies that proceed from a
particular space and material experience; that engage critically with their
contexts, and exist as bodies of knowledge only in order to transform
and redeem the world.

So finally, as we inhabit the space of this summer school and act within
it to create new feminist theologies, I offer you some ways of characterizing that space, drawn from feminist theories. Perhaps it will be helpful,
overall, as we continue throughout this week, to think of that space as
political, subversive and provisional.

This space is political, because all of us, in various ways, depend on
the labour of others to make it possible for us to be here. Whether that is
the labour of the domestic and bursary staff in this college; or the labour
of partners, relatives and friends in organizing childcare; or in terms of
the sacrifice of money and time to afford the fees or protect this space in
our busy schedules. This sense that our space is not easily won, and that
we are all privileged occupants of this space, must, I believe, require us
to adopt a responsibility for the way we use this space. I have identified
how patriarchy uses space to exclude and divide; can we be more generous in our creation of space, in our refusal of boundaries that keep us

43

in and others out? A reminder of those who are not here, of our global relationships to those beyond this immediate space, will be important aspects of our coming together.

This is also a special, set-apart space in which, for the duration of the summer school, we are set free to dream dreams. It is a space for experimentation, where the novel and extraordinary can flourish. This may generate entirely new forms of vision, unencumbered by established routines; and in this respect, it is a sanctuary, a retreat. However, as with any retreat, the question of the long-term discipline we learn on returning whence we came is also important. Can we take advantage of the exceptional nature of this space – this very sense of dis-location that it offers – to foster a genuinely lasting renewal and change; to use it as a place of prophetic and subversive vision, as well as enjoyment and recreation?

We have, in a sense, been brought together temporarily for this week in this space; and this suggests to me that we are pilgrims in this space, coming together from our various contexts, testing our different perspectives, learning from diversity. Pilgrims of course tell stories to one another, and the narrative tone continues well this notion of the situated, concrete and material nature of our acting and knowing. Just as this space is a luxury for many, so we must celebrate its creation but regard its provisional and temporary nature as an encouragement and place of succour on the longer journey that we all must take.

So, this week, as feminist theologians gathered in this place, we claim the right to speak and act within the public realm, create new visions and dream daring dreams and tell stories of our shared journey; and in the process, I believe we will find new ways of creating theology together.

5

A VIEW FROM A ROOM

Feminist Practical Theology[1] from Academy, Kitchen or Sanctuary?

Introduction: Beyond Sexism and Clericalism

In this chapter, I want to reflect on certain general social and religious dimensions which shape Christian ministry and practical theology in Britain today: issues of secularization, pluralism and the changing role of women. I shall do so from the vantage-point of my own context as a woman academic in an urban university in northern England. I will continue by discussing how a feminist practical theology is actually emerging out of Christian feminist praxis. The story of one particular 'woman-church' community – the St Hilda community – which serves both the pastoral and liturgical needs of its members, will illustrate my argument. I conclude by arguing that feminist practical theology emerges from the encounter between faith and practice in the form of the values embodied and enacted in the diversity of pastoral responses to women's changing needs and perspectives. In the development of a feminist practical theology in Britain, it has been crucial to counter the invisibility of women. The stimulus for my own initial researches in practical theology was the churches' pastoral neglect of much of the fabric of women's lives.

---

1 In a British context the terms 'pastoral theology' and 'practical theology' are often used interchangeably. I shall use the term 'practical theology' for purposes of consistency with other contributors. My own understanding would regard practical theology as the critical study of the theological values which underpin and inform a diversity of Christian practices, extending beyond the activities of pastoral care and counselling to encompass preaching, Christian formation, spiritual direction, liturgy and congregational studies.

Women's experiences of motherhood, work, ageing, caring and inequality, not to mention their attempts to realize a vocation to the Christian ministry, were notably absent from the pastoral care tradition.

My subsequent examination of the pastoral care literature of the modern period in Europe and North America revealed that the exclusion of women was deeply entrenched in the tradition (Graham, 1989). Until the first quarter of the twentieth-century, women were excluded from the ordained ministry in most Christian denominations in Britain. By virtue of their lay standing, women were deemed unqualified to undertake any kind of ministry or pastoral care; yet, in reality, many women did exercise significant pastoral tasks while maintaining successful professional careers. Such contributions were afforded little status: Christian pastoral care was equated with clerical definitions of ministry, thereby devaluing anything not carried out by the clergy.

Some of the pastoral care literature of this period did feature women as the recipients of pastoral care, but the overwhelming focus on the activities of the pastoral agent meant that the experiences and perspectives of the pastoral client were afforded little authority. In the few discussions of the pastoral needs of women, they tended to be characterized in stereotypical form, as neurotic, dependent and unstable.

The effect of these 'clericalist' and 'sexist' paradigms was to establish a tradition of practical theology which operated from the perspective of the male, ordained pastor; one in which any kind of 'client-centred' commitment was unknown. The genesis of a feminist practical theology begins with the exposure and critique of such an androcentric tradition (Graham, 1990). However, it cannot stop there. 'Critique' must necessarily be followed by the task of 'reconstruction'. Accounts of pastoral care that take women's experiences seriously and value them as givers and receivers of care, challenge exclusive and prescriptive definitions and set out a more authentic picture of the diversity of methods and contexts of Christian ministry.

Speaking from a Context

Looking out from my office at the University I see a cherry tree in full blossom. At the time of writing, in late spring, the tree is at its most magnificent, although the rain showers quickly dampen its splendour and scatter the pink petals like confetti.

I am lucky to have such a spectacular tree outside my room; most of the rest of the campus is stone, concrete and red brick, and it straddles one of the busiest main roads into Manchester city centre. Apart from my garden enclave, therefore, this is a very urban context. It is also one of the largest higher education complexes in the Western world: a network of institutions dedicated to the pursuit of intellectual excellence. The mock Gothic buildings reflecting the University's Victorian origins are now surrounded by computing, science and engineering labs, their plate glass exteriors adding to their inscrutability. In one older building is the room where the first computer was built (in the 1940s these prototypes filled a room the size of a lecture theatre). A few blocks away is the laboratory where Rutherford first split the atom.

From the second floor of my building I can look out over the University campus to the areas known as Moss Side and Hulme, two of the most economically disadvantaged areas in Britain, and graphic testimonies to urban decline and social polarization. The landscape of these areas has been dramatically altered in the past few years. The once-lauded social housing experiments of the 1960s are steadily being demolished, replaced by new 'model' housing developments, the result of partnership between the City Council and local business. This is 1990s social policy, in which any talk of social engineering to end inequality has been replaced by the more cautious rhetoric of 'urban regeneration' (HMSO, 1995: 93–102).

Today the headline in the newspaper reads, 'The End of the Welfare State' (Guardian, 8 May 1996: 1). For anyone involved in health and welfare provision or for those concerned as consumers of education, medical care, housing, local social services or income support, such a verdict confirms what we all already feared: the State, funded by public taxation and expenditure, can no longer be relied upon to bear the primary burden of support for those in need, or to intervene as a vehicle of social change.

Such a withdrawal from interventionist or social democratic policies is a legacy of 18 years of Conservative government, in which the values of individualism, free enterprise and competitiveness were prized, and the functions and responsibilities of government were reduced to a minimum. The people of Hulme and Moss Side bear the real burden of such policies, as social polarization grows and social commentators speak of a decay of communities and the growth of an increasingly alienated 'underclass'.[2]

Many of my students live and work in areas like Moss Side and Hulme: in East Manchester, Stockport, Liverpool, Leeds and right across the North-West of England. The stories of such areas, prone to

---

2 See the report of The Commission on Social Justice, Social Justice: Strategies for National Renewal (1994) and Manchester Health for All Working Party, Health Inequalities and Manchester in the 1990s (Manchester City Council, 1993). Indicators of differentials in income and of poverty suggest that social inequality in Britain has increased in the past 15 years. For example, in 1979, one child in ten lived in poverty; in 1993, the proportion was one in three (Commission on Social Justice, 1994: 31). Other social research suggests that women are especially vulnerable to the factors that contribute to poverty: low pay, job insecurity, family dependants, old age (Glendenning and Millar, 1992).

disproportionate incidence of poverty, unemployment, ill-health and crime, form the subtext for our scholarly discussions. But they are stories in which hope leavens the despair. In many areas, the Church remains the only major organized body of the statutory or voluntary sectors to maintain its buildings and services. It therefore acts as a focus of community organization and endeavour, and the Christian community is valued for its willingness to 'keep faith' with the inner cities.[3]

Frequently, the stories of inner-city communities feature leading roles for women. Church involvement in Greater Manchester has focused on the support of credit unions, voluntary (and locally-run) associations in which money is collectively saved and lent independently of big business or local loan sharks. Women are prominent in such groups, as organizers and clients, and thereby take a prominent role in actively creating and generating the hope and mutual reliance which are so vital for survival.[4]

Such stories, and many more like them, offer our academic discussions a necessary focus. The central issue is essentially about the relationship between faith and values on the one hand, and collective and individual action on the other. Whether this be the theological convictions that impel the churches to denounce government policies on housing, immigration or unemployment, or the religious roots of politicians' 'conviction politics',[5] such debates remind us that economic and social policies which shape the life of the nation often derive from ethical and religious beliefs and world-views.

Our practical theology programme at Manchester therefore traces the origins of notions of citizenship, participation and community which underly the changing horizon and fabric of inner-city Manchester. We examine the religious values and beliefs that have shaped the churches' intervention in social and political debates, and which inform the everyday relationships and interactions between church and community. We explore how the theological tradition of humanity created in the image of God might inspire the values of Christian ministry. And we ask how

---

3 The British churches have maintained a constant flow of reports and programmes related to the plight of the inner cities. The best known of these is The Archbishop's Commission on Urban Priority Areas, *Faith in the City* (1985), which brought the Church into open conflict with the Thatcher government, and which put paid to the description of the Church of England as 'the Conservative party at prayer'. For a fuller (and critical) account of this, see Clark (1992).

4 Jenkins (1989) gives an account of various women's initiatives in Salford, Greater Manchester.

5 Margaret Thatcher was the epitome of such a concept. It is said that her values of self-reliance and individualism derived from a strict evangelical Protestant upbringing. Interestingly, the current (1997) Labour Prime Minister, Tony Blair, also attributes his political formation to Christian values: in his case, the Scottish communitarian philosopher John Macmurray. Despite the secular nature of British society, therefore, religion still represents a significant factor in public moral and political discourse. See Allison (1990), Bryant (1993).

patterns of individual pastoral care and social action serve as the 'incarnation' of the truth-claims of Christian theology.

Religion, Culture and Gender in Contemporary Britain

However, other aspects of life in Britain decisively shape the context within which practical theology is conducted. It may come as a surprise to some readers if I say that Britain is a very secular society. This statement has to be qualified, of course: religious behaviour and affiliation is by no means uniform in Britain today. But practical theologians must take their context seriously; and one feature that strikes any observer of the British scene is the steady decline in long-established religious institutions. While the origins and causes of such decline are still hotly debated, it is broadly the case that the mainstream Christian denominations are losing active members at an unprecedented rate (Davie, 1994). The same is true of Anglo-Jewry, whose numerical decline is causing significant anxiety and comment (Englander, 1993).

Yet the precise religious contours of British society are sometimes hard to trace. Despite such low levels of formal participation in the Christian churches, the vast majority of Britons still retain a degree of informal, non-denominational, religious sentiment. Studies consistently reveal that two-thirds of interviewed samples express a belief in God, with significant proportions admitting to regular times of prayer (Greeley, 1993). The so-called 'Celtic fringes' of the North of Ireland, Wales and Scotland also display a stronger persistence of formal church-going than urban England, for example (Davie, 1994: 94–105). This is the context in which practical theology is conducted, and it is important to remember that formal religious affiliation is a minority interest amid a non-participating, but nevertheless religiously sympathetic, population.

If Britain is no longer a Christian country – even if not quite a *post*-Christian one – due to the decline in formal participation, then the presence of ethnic minorities is also an important feature of our current context. The British Empire may well have been dismantled finally in the years immediately after 1945; but a colonial past has endured in the political, economic and cultural ties between Britain and Africa, the Caribbean and South Asia. The result has been the growing prominence of British Islam – there are now well over a million Muslims in Britain – and the troubled relationship between African-Caribbean Christians and the 'white-majority' churches, a matter to which I shall return later (Lewis, 1994; Wilkinson, 1993). While British cultural, ethnic and religious pluralism is potentially very significant for society and the churches, most branches of contemporary theology, including British feminist Christian theology, have largely failed to reflect this context in which the primacy of Christianity can no longer be taken for granted.

49

Christian Feminism and the Church

The changing role of women in the British churches cannot be fully appreciated outside the historical development of Western feminism. The women's movement in Britain owes most of its impetus to the broader campaigns of socialism and trade unionism, and to self-consciously woman-identified programmes such as women's refuges, abortion reform and cultural feminism. The religious underpinning of early feminist activism has, however, been underplayed. Until recently, the academic study of feminism reflected an overwhelming hostility to religion. Christian feminism in Britain struggles against isolation within the women's movement as well as lack of acceptance within the churches.[6]

Today, women's calls for change resound throughout society. These calls are now being augmented by voices from the Christian community in the shape of Christian feminists of all denominations and backgrounds. Some choose to work for change within the institutional churches, while others locate themselves beyond the religious structures in order to pursue a new kind of spiritual quest for women.[7] Women have achieved some degree of recognition in the Free Church (Protestant) traditions; but the prospects in the Roman Catholic Church look as bleak as ever. There are a number of pressure groups for women's ministry in the Roman Catholic Church but I suspect that many women and progressive lay men have chosen to channel their energies into world development and peace and justice campaigns out of sheer frustration at ever shifting the institution on its conservative stance towards women's wider participation (McEwan, 1991).

Any discussion of women and the Church, and especially questions of ministry and practical theology, is inevitably dominated by the question of women's ordination to the priesthood in the Church of England, a campaign which ran from the mid-1970s until the early 1990s. It was an epic struggle and defined so much of the preoccupations and priorities of Christian feminism during the 1970s and 1980s (Dowell and Williams, 1994; Field-Bibb, 1991). Many Christian feminists would admit to some ambivalence at the pre-eminence of this one issue during this period. For example, media coverage focused on the novelty of women priests in the Anglican context at the expense of acknowledging the existence of women ministers in other denominations, let alone examining their

---

6 The gulf between academic feminist scholarship and feminist theology in Britain is a seriously neglected issue. I have attempted to address this question in 'Feminist Theology: Myth, Mystery or Monster?' (1997).

7 Daphne Hampson is the best-known British feminist theologian/philosopher to argue that feminism and Christianity are incompatible. Her journey through the campaign for women's ordination in the Anglican tradition towards a more 'post-Christian' spirituality is recorded in *Theology and Feminism* (1990). For an extended debate between British feminist theologians of varying perspectives, see Hampson (1996).

achievements and problems. Similarly, sections of the women's movement in the churches remained robustly laicized, and resented the suggestion (as they saw it) that Christian feminism might simply be equated with equal opportunities for women in the priesthood, thereby avoiding wider questions about the nature of ministry and leadership in the churches. Nevertheless, the campaign for the ordination of women in the Established Church served as an important focus for mobilizing many women and men; and although many did not move beyond the single issue of priesthood (and actively eschewed any association with feminist theology) many others were radicalized by the experience into further exploration of more overtly feminist issues (Dowell and Williams, 1994: 49–58).[8]

The struggle of women in church and society is therefore a major factor informing my activities as a professional practical theologian. Local factors, once again, shape my story. The University of Manchester was the first institution in Britain to offer undergraduate or graduate programmes in feminist theology. Like any good religion, feminist theology at Manchester has its own myth of origin. The legend goes that a prestigious (male) guest lecturer spoke of feminist theology as 'taking the whingeing [whining, complaining] out of the kitchen and into the seminar room'. The resulting outcry culminated in the first version of the course (launched in 1986 and entitled 'Women, Men and Christian Theology') which I continue to teach to this day.

At one level, of course, this description was a typically patriarchal insult, suggesting that women in the academy could never properly shed their domestic preoccupations. Ironically, though, I am also aware of a great deal of 'kitchen table theology' taking place within British Christian feminism, insofar as theology is discussed and practised in contexts which extend well beyond the confines of the academy. In Manchester we have attempted to straddle the boundary between academic and popular theology by running regular 'Saturday Schools' in feminist theology, which are organized and run by graduate students and open to the public as part of the University's continuing education provision.

Such an approach recognizes that a university course or qualification is but one among many routes into, and expressions of, feminist theological commitment, and that academic endeavour must be accountable to a wider community. The context and conviviality of the (metaphorical) kitchen table, as well as the rarefied air of the academy, are thus acknowledged and affirmed as legitimate starting-points for our theologizing.[9] This amounts to an alternative feminist epistemology, crucial to

---

8 For a discussion of the experiences of women deacons in the Church of England prior to the 1992 vote, see Treasure (1991).

9 For examples of feminist theology which seeks to integrate the experiential and the conventionally academic, see Russell (1985) and The Mud Flower Collective (1985).

the development of a feminist practical theology: starting with experience, it also seeks to integrate the values of affectivity, justice and care with those of rationality and agency.[10] We need, however, also to be wary of over-romanticizing the kitchen context, in case it communicates another kind of domestic captivity for women. Feminists speak of privileging and articulating women's experience, but there is a danger of re-stereotyping the perspectives from which women speak. We may wish to claim the right to have our kitchen table recognized as a site of legitimate theological work, to see the world of nurture and family as important vantage-points from which to locate theological insights: for it is, after all, where many women do the bulk of their pastoral care. Economic reality also dictates that many women write at their kitchen tables because they cannot gain research grants or high-status university positions. A celebration of the experiential and informal roots of Christian feminism must not, however, be used as a device to imprison women in a domestic space or deny them access to academic excellence and wider opportunities. Women also have to insist on their right to take their legitimate places in the seminar room, the lecture theatre and the laboratory.

The many local Christian feminist groups meeting in kitchens, sitting rooms and church halls are therefore a vital part of the contemporary feminist theological scene. It would be mistaken, however, to regard these informal groups as merely the consumers of feminist theologies which are actually generated elsewhere. Such groups are also the producers and originators of important and vital work. They are in fact the sources for an alternative epistemology for feminist practical theology: they are spaces in which diverse experiences and ways of knowing may be articulated.

Feminist Theology and Feminist Praxis

Christian feminists are often accused by religious opponents of falling prey to 'secular' ideologies concerning women's liberation. Such a view assumes that those gullible enough to embrace the divisive and confrontational world-view of feminism are automatically abandoning their Christian principles in favour of a purely secular creed (Oddie, 1984; Leonard, 1989).[11] Yet this perspective ignores the decisive links between nineteenth-century first-wave feminism and Christianity in Britain and the United States.[12] It also implicitly precludes Christians from acknow-

---

10 One example of attempts to construct a feminist way of knowing derived from everyday relationships and activities of work, care and experience may be found in Rose (1994).

11 For an extended discussion of the views of such opponents of Christian feminism, see Furlong (1991: ch. 4).

12 Figures such as Josephine Butler, Elizabeth Cady Stanton and Sojourner Truth

ledging the presence of God at work within social or philosophical movements other than Christianity.

By contrast, I would argue that feminist theological critiques of androcentricism and hierarchy in the Christian tradition, and the reconstruction of more inclusive visions, are not merely motivated by secular feminism. The practical endeavours of feminist theologians to create more authentic and inclusive communities and ministries are informed by a vision of transcendence, justice and hope which is actually profoundly theological.

A recent volume of essays on women and pastoral care, entitled *Life-Cycles*, was the first attempt to articulate an agenda for practical theology informed by feminist consciousness and action (Graham and Halsey, 1993). First, it enabled the voices of women's experiences of pastoral care, and the diversity of their needs and contexts, to be heard. Second, it suggested that 'pastoral care' embraces more than personal counselling or support and that the process of giving and receiving care is about building relationships of mutuality and empowerment, of presence at the cutting edge of social change, of solidarity with the marginalized and of the provision of symbolic, ritual and theological resources by which people can make sense of their lives. By this token, critical and reconstructive practical theology starts with experience, attempts to place an individual story in a social or collective context, locates the personal story in relation to the stories of faith (both historical and contemporary) and finally encourages new models of practice to blossom which embody and enact renewed visions of faith. Such renewed practice may be, as contributors to the volume suggested, liturgical, or it may be embodied in new patterns of ministry, or expressed in 'breaking open' the fixed truths of Scripture and tradition. Fundamentally, such a transformation of praxis envisages a renewed feminist pastoral care to be 'word made flesh' (ibid.: 234):

> Christian pastoral practice has the potential to reveal a God who is startlingly present in human encounter. In their relationships and actions of care, Christians believe they can effect some of the creative and redemptive work of God, but that such care will also express something of the Divine reality. Thus human pastoral relationships, however expressed, will also be to Christians in some sense a disclosure of God. (Graham, 1993: 220)

I now turn to an illustration of one particular inclusive liturgical and reflection group, the St Hilda Community, which represents some of the most profound and innovative theology in Britain today. It is significant,

---

are all examples of those whose commitment to the rights of women was inseparable from a devout faith.

however, that this group is actually undertaking the theological task of critique and reconstruction from the vantage-point of practical and pastoral concern. It is therefore out of specific pastoral responses to the complexities of women's experiences, that is, out of feminist praxis,[13] that some of the most exciting feminist theology is emerging.

From Exile to Sanctuary: Liturgy, Community and Theology

The origins of the St Hilda Community lie in the exclusion and marginalization of women within the Church and the agonizing progress towards the ordination of women in the Church of England. It took nearly two decades, from the Church's General Synod declaring in 1975 there was 'no fundamental theological objection' to women priests, to the vote finally being passed in favour of women's ordination in November 1992. The first women were ordained priest in March 1994 (Dowell and Williams, 1994: 113–15).

These were wilderness years for many women and men in the Church of England. Their frustration and alienation was also shared to greater or lesser extent by other denominations. Traditions which did admit women to ordained ministry often afforded them less than equal standing and respect (McEwan, 1991). This general dissatisfaction coupled with the feeling (already noted) that the scope of feminist change was not exhausted by the single issue of ordination, encouraged activists to explore new avenues. One outcome was the establishment of informal worshipping communities concerned to promote women's ministry. They were not necessarily eucharistic, although on many occasions Nonconformist women ministers or Anglican priests from overseas presided. The groups' intention was more to create liturgical and spiritual 'spaces' in which non-sexist and inclusive practice could be fostered. The St Hilda Community was one such, and serves as a good case-study because of the amount of attention it has received. Its story is recorded in a collection of liturgies and prayers, *Women Included*. Accompanying essays tell the story of the St Hilda Community from its early beginnings in a college chapel in the East End of London (St Hilda Community, 1991: part I).[14]

Many aspects of the St Hilda experience mirror familiar contours of the

---

13 I use the term 'praxis' to mean value-informed and value-directed action, or 'truth as practicable', to paraphrase Jürgen Moltmann. The primacy of praxis as an arbiter of authentic theological understanding owes much to liberation theology. For a discussion of its relevance for feminist theology, see Hogan (1995).

14 The Community started meeting in 1987, was evicted from St Benet's by the Diocese of London in 1989, moved to Methodist premises nearby and continued to meet right up to the first ordinations in 1994. Meetings are now held more informally in members' homes.

'Women-church' movement.[15] As well as this global referent, however, the St Hilda Community, in common with many similar groups throughout Britain, also introduced elements of indigenous Christian tradition. The inspiration for the St Hilda Community is the historical figure of Hilda of Whitby (AD 614–80), abbess, teacher and theologian. As an influential supporter of Christian missions and scholarship, she occupies a prominent place in the history of the English Church. As an example of a powerful woman in Christian antiquity, she has also been adopted as a proto-feminist icon by many women and men in the Church. She therefore served as a highly suitable and inspirational 'patron saint' for a liturgical community concerned to retrieve and renew women's ministry in the Church (Furlong, 1991: 7–8).

The St Hilda Community is also interesting in that it combined both pastoral and theological dimensions in its liturgical practice. It quite deliberately set out to be a place where the wounds of exclusion and sexism could be healed. Monica Furlong, a founder member, and Suzanne Fageol, a priest ordained in the United States and occasional president, both comment on the powerful hurts and emotions which were frequently disclosed in the context of public worship (ibid.; Fageol, 1991: 16–26).[16]

Thus, the St Hilda Community was always more than an experimental liturgical workshop: it was also genuinely an alternative community which provided a nurturing, supportive antidote to a patriarchal Church. A deliberate policy was made whereby anyone attending a liturgy was considered to be part of the Community while they were visiting; and mutual care took precedence over set liturgies or formal proceedings: 'Nurturing and care-giving always take precedence over worship. If we cannot care for one another, how can we possibly hope to incarnate effectively the One in whose name we gather to worship?' (Fageol, 1991: 21). There was therefore an essential unity between hearing the stories of human hope and suffering, and enacting an alternative community which sought to transform current practice by prefiguring new ways of living.

From Women-church to God-talk

While the St Hilda Community is one of the better-known alternative liturgical groups, there are many such networks in varying degrees of organizational shape. Yet they represent an important focus for the devotional and spiritual lives of many who find the institutional churches restrictive

---

15 See Ruether (1986). The 'women-church' movement, established in the United States and subsequently spreading throughout the world, is a network of alternative worship, liturgy and social action groups. Ruether's model is one of 'spirit-filled community' existing in critical parallel to the institutional Church.

16 St Hilda liturgies used dance, silence, symbolism as well as new forms of words; an emphasis on the creative use of space is also noteworthy (Fageol, 1991: 22).

or stifling. Circulating among these groups is an extensive array of liturgies, rites and prayers, some of which draws from established ecumenical sources such as the Community of Reconciliation at Taizé, the Iona Community, or the published work of contemporary writers such as Janet Morley, Brian Wren and Jim Cotter (Morley, 1988; Wren, 1989; Cotter, 1988; Ward *et al.*, 1995; Ward and Wild, 1995). Yet, in the best spirit of 'kitchen-table theology', such work probably represents the tip of an iceberg of ad hoc, unpublished creative writing distributed among and between such groups and communities. Much of this material which first came to birth in alternative worship groups has now filtered into mainstream congregations. It is therefore clear that one of the most significant legacies of such groups has been to force the question of inclusive language in worship on to the pastoral and liturgical agenda of the institutional churches.

Feminist theology is often accused by conservative commentators of being obsessed with so-called 'inclusive language'. It is argued that such a preoccupation with forms of words has nothing to do with theology (as a discourse of eternal truths) and reflects, once more, the extent to which feminist theologians are merely parroting the concerns of the 'politically correct' secular world. The complex matter of the relationship between human consciousness, cultural context and symbolic imagery[17] is thus reduced to the simplistic notion that feminist liturgists and theologians seek merely to swap all references to God as Father with those of God as Mother. Often these arguments are further bolstered by the accusation that Christian feminists are 'goddess worshippers'; another method of decrying the legitimacy of feminist claims, of course, by placing them 'beyond the pale' of orthodox belief (Oddie, 1984; Leonard, 1989).[18]

The reality is far more nuanced, and more profound. It is not a question of mere forms of words but relates to theological questions about who God is for us. Language about God is crucial to our experiences of God, and to our spirituality, because language does not simply reflect, but also actively shapes, human consciousness (McFague, 1983). Inclusive language is one means of enabling worshippers to envision new models of Divine agency. Inclusive imagery for the worshipping community also helps women to feel visible as full participants in the Body of Christ.[19]

---

17 The work of Sallie McFague provides a well-argued and provocative exposition of the philosophical underpinnings of religious language. She argues for a clear link between images of the sacred and Divine and patterns of social relations. Language is necessarily shaped by cultural and political context, but must always be seen as provisional and contingent: a 'Model' not an 'Idol' (McFague, 1983; 1987).

18 For a reasoned defence of inclusive language, see Carmody (1994).

19 See Liturgical Commission (1989): note that this report welcomes cautiously the idea of inclusive language for congregations but refuses to be drawn into debates about language for God. For further discussion on the inclusive language debate, see Morley (1984: 56–70).

As Christian women we need to celebrate our creativity, on all levels. We are called to open the church, and men, as well as ourselves, to the idea that we are originally blessed in the image of God and as connected to the rest of creation ... St. Hilda's members have constructed whole liturgies around the celebration of God as our Mother, as the one who gives birth to and nurtures us into creative adulthood. The Hebrew bible is a rich source for such wisdom and celebration. There we find images of God as Holy Wisdom who teaches us spiritual discernment and God as 'ruach', the feminine wind-energy who brings creation out of chaos. (Fageol, 1991: 24)

Clearly, what I have already said about a Christian community 'incarnating' and embodying its truth-claims in its collective practice is fundamental to the self-understanding of the St Hilda Community. This is apparent in the way the community resolved the dilemma of appropriate leadership and presidency. Faced with the non-availability of women's priestly ministry (legally at least), and a preference not to have male presidents at its liturgies, the St Hilda Community had to search for new models. It was decided to undertake a collective adoption of actions normally restricted to the priest: absolution, Eucharist and blessing. In the corporate actions which developed as a result, mere expediency was transformed into a powerful symbolic expression of shared ministry and community:

Mutual absolution takes the form of a shared general confession, drawn from various sources, feminist and other ... This sacramental act, normally preserved as the priest's, is powerful when done personally and as a shared ministry of the whole body of Christ. The depth of forgiveness, given and received, brings us all closer to God and to each other as images of God incarnate. (Ibid.: 20)

Insofar as the St Hilda liturgies occupy a perilous space between critique and reconstruction, there will always be a tension between the old and the new. Finding a comfortable resting-place in an androcentric tradition is not easy, and feminist theology is beset with choices about the extent to which the historical tradition can be retrieved as 'usable' and 'woman-friendly', or else abandoned completely as corrupt and irredeemable.[20] One strategy of reconstruction is to recover formerly hidden voices and testimonies from the past and consciously to celebrate them. The lives and examples of Hilda of Whitby and Julian of Norwich have been valorized by Christian feminists in Britain and beyond in just such a fashion.

---

20 Such choices inform much of the debate in Hampson (1996) and formed the central issue in the dialogue between Hampson and Ruether. See Hampson and Ruether (1987).

But is this alternative 'herstory' ever quite so rich and unproblematic as the malestream history? It is, after all, a heritage of scraps and fragments: and while feminist theologians may pride themselves on their enterprise of 'searching for lost coins' (Loades, 1987) this arguably still only amounts to the gathering of the small change of Christian history. Feminist practical theologians are compelled to assert that 'tradition' is never a final and absolute authority for contemporary praxis. It is clear from the examples discussed earlier that the voices and contexts of the present, reflecting the changes, complexities and contradictions of 'women's experience', have the right to challenge the fixity and authority of the past. In the meeting of horizons between past and present, heritage and experience, the practical, concrete and immediate demands of gender justice calls forth new theological insights; an admission that the tradition as it stands is not adequate.

This is clearly illustrated with reference to the St Hilda Community, where many of the liturgies and prayers have deliberately rewritten traditional forms in a conscious reappropriation. Some of the most well-known, and widely-used, feminist prayers are Janet Morley's 'Collects' (designated prayers for the day in the Anglican tradition). They rehearse the themes and cadences of traditional forms but deploy startling new imagery:

> God our mother,
> you hold our life within you;
> nourish us at your breast,
> and teach us to walk alone.
> Help us so to receive your tenderness
> and respond to your challenge
> that others may draw life from us,
> in your name. Amen. (St Hilda Community, 1991: 45)

The St Hilda Community is one example of how women's naming of their experiences, their purposeful enactment of caring practice and their conscious attempts to reclaim the sacred are actively contributing to a recreation of Christian tradition in theory and practice. Although the Community was always open to women and men, it also had a special vocation by which it 'existed to give space to women' (Fageol, 1991: 18). This metaphor of space is one to which I find myself returning (see Graham, 1995a). It is a powerful idea by which to explore many creative avenues in feminist theology: to what extent is all pastoral practice, be it counselling, preaching, listening, telling stories, times of meditation or worship, essentially about creating the space in which human and Divine encounters can flourish?

Underpinning and articulating feminist models of care, community and worship are renewed visions of the Divine, and it is here that we can see how new theological responses are being forged. I detect clear parameters of a novel and exciting feminist practical theology in which there is no separation between Christian practice and 'God-talk' because each feeds and stimulates the other. Incongruously perhaps, practical theologians are wont to quote the Church of England Alternative Service Book to illustrate this point: 'Christians are formed by the way in which they pray, and the way they choose to pray expresses what they are' (Alternative Service Book, 1980: 10; Furlong, 1991: 5); but for me, this is an excellent example of feminist pastoral praxis in which reflection and action, word and deed, are fused into a life-giving theology. Feminist liturgical communities like the St Hilda Community are therefore essentially doxological, shaped by their purposeful encounters with the Divine in worship, and defined by an attempt to embody and enact their theology in their collective practice, as forms of 'words made flesh'.

Conclusion: New Horizons

In the midst of emergent voices within practical theology a feminist perspective is galvanizing the discipline and pointing to new challenges for the future. I wish finally to identify three crucial priorities for feminist practical theology in Britain: dialogue with the discipline as a whole, dialogue across ethnic and racial boundaries and dialogue with 'secular' feminists.

Issues of social inequality continue to occupy practical theologians, reinforcing work which has already argued for a clearer commitment to 'the politics of pastoral care' (Selby, 1983). Significantly, Stephen Pattison in a recent work on the relationship between liberation theology and pastoral care has identified gender issues, and more specifically women's lack of status and power in relation to mental health, as a major priority for pastors, health care chaplains and policy-makers (Pattison, 1997).

While feminist theology and gender issues may be making some impact on academic practical theology, however, Christian feminist theology still faces challenges of its own. There is much to be done to address issues of religious pluralism and racial injustice although, gradually, the voices of Black Christian women are breaking through. The experience of exclusion from many white-majority denominations in the years following mass immigration from the West Indies after 1945, has been decisive in forging Black British Christians' self-understanding and is similar to the collective memory of slavery for African-Americans. Women in Black-majority churches are beginning to tell their stories: naming experience, resisting exclusion and remaking the tradition in their own ways (Pitts, 1990).

A final question concerns how a Christian feminist practical theology might respond to the spiritual needs of women who have left the churches or choose to channel their energies into other forms of spirituality. Can

suitable spaces – studies, kitchens, sanctuaries, churches, pulpits – be created in which fruitful dialogue can take place? How will Christian feminists break down the barriers of suspicion and indifference on the part of
'secular' feminists? These are all critical tests of the ultimate reality and
relevance of a feminist practical theology, in its ability to offer anything
of worth to a society beyond the Christian walls.

Feminist theory may offer some important clues as to the future direction of feminist practical theology. I have identified a number of locations
and contexts for such theological action and reflection: academy, kitchen
and sanctuary. All are an essential part of the vitality of contemporary
feminist practical theology, witnessing to the fact that we cannot separate
theory from practice, the esoteric from the everyday, intellectual discovery from social responsibility. These various contexts speak well of our
experiences as women in modern Britain; but does such diversity militate
against coherence? Significantly, contemporary feminist theory argues
that pluralism and difference are a necessary part of our thinking and
acting. To assume one dominant story or framework is to risk marginal-
izing and silencing those whose experiences do not correspond with the
'master narrative'. Yet the alternative is not to collapse into relativism
or the babel of competing voices. As Donna Haraway argues, we can
recognize that the voices of difference represent 'situated knowledges', all
of which reflect legitimate vantage-points (Haraway, 1991: 187–96). To
be clear about the space from which we speak and act is, for Haraway, a
guarantee of an ethically responsible perspective on truth:

> Feminists don't need a doctrine of objectivity that promises transcend-
> ence, a story that loses track of its mediations just where someone
> might be held responsible for something, and unlimited instrumental
> power. We don't want a theory of innocent powers to represent the
> world, where language and bodies fall into the bliss of organic symbi-
> osis. We also don't want to theorize the world, much less act within
> it, in terms of Global Systems, but we do need an earthwide network
> of connections, including the ability partially to translate knowledges
> among very different – and power-differentiated – communities. We
> need the power of modern critical theories of how meanings and bodies
> get made, not in order to deny meanings and bodies, but in order to
> build meanings and bodies that have a chance for life. (Ibid.: 187)

I take heart, therefore, from the understanding that feminist practical
theologies, born of pastoral practice, directed towards specific aims and
ends of care, nurture and celebration, can claim to be 'situated knowledges' about justice, love and the Divine.

It is hard to negotiate some of the differences, and the competing loyalties that often arise, let alone gain recognition from institutions that

frequently attempt to constrain or categorize us within their domains. Feminist practical theologians, whether they work in the academy, the Church, at home, or in the political world, need to be mutually accountable and supportively critical. In Manchester, we try to embody these different contexts and perspectives, and to engage with one another in collaborative praxis in teaching and learning together; and I hope that, like the cherry tree, our work is the sign of a blossoming forth of vital and vibrant new life.

Part Two

RELIGION, CULTURE AND GENDER

6

GENDER, PERSONHOOD AND THEOLOGY

One of the most significant phenomena within the Western Church over the past 25 years has been the emergence of feminist theology. Fuelled by the second wave of the modern women's movement, drawing upon the theoretical and critical stances of academic feminism, and inspired by Latin American liberation theology, feminist theologians have achieved a remarkable body of work in a relatively short time. They have sought to establish the opportunities and validate the methods by which women, long silenced as theological subjects, may articulate their perspectives and contribute towards the reconstruction of a more 'inclusive' theological discipline.[1]

Such theological developments both reflect, and promote, pastoral and policy concerns associated with the proper roles and relationships of women and men within the Christian Church. These are concerned with the appropriate ordering of the Church's ministry and practice; the validity of women's priestly ministry; the use of 'inclusive' language in liturgy; and the deployment of 'masculine' and 'feminine' attributes and characteristics in the metaphorical naming of God and God's actions in the world.

However, many of these debates conceal unexamined assumptions. One of the fundamental tenets of feminist theology has been its appeal to 'women's experience' as a corrective to androcentric tradition, and as a foundational source of knowledge upon which to base a theological reconstruction (Ruether, 1993: ch. 1). Yet, with the possible exception of Pamela Dickey Young's attempt to qualify and categorize women's experience (1990: ch. 3), there has been little attention to the substance

---

1 See Ruether (1993) and Loades (1990) for general introductions to feminist theology.

of such claims to a unique knowledge and experience founded on a distinction of gender.

Similarly, as relations between women and men move from hierarchy to community, the nature of their respective roles and functions is thrown into relief. Some versions of the relative positions of women and men may regard their relationships as determined by the laws of nature; others will argue that a culture which objectifies and subordinates women is the primary site of gender division. In either case, protagonists will fashion their notions of the ideal and authentic community on the basis of their assumptions about the significance and origins of gender difference for human destiny.

For example, support for the greater participation of women in church life, especially in the ordained ministry, rests on a conviction that no ontological barrier exists to the equal exercise of women's pastoral and sacramental ministry (Edwards, 1989: ch. 10). Yet many of those same advocates would assert that women do also bring a different dimension to ordained ministry and priesthood, based on 'feminine' characteristics and disposition. Such practical strategies and theological visions are founded on two distinct understandings of human nature: one of a commonality of women and men with a shared nature, and one of a radical distinctiveness of women from men, whether such difference is considered innate or socially constructed.

These are issues which concern the nature of human experience; but this is also a question of theological language. The 'maleness' of God as portrayed in traditional Christian religious language has been criticized as denying the full humanity of women, because male experience is implicitly privileged and rendered normative and superior by its exclusive use in representing the Divine. Conversely, female humanity is relegated to a derivative, 'misbegotten' and subordinate status (Ruether, 1993; Joseph, 1990). This is an important debate, not least because it confronts the way in which theological language which draws upon gendered metaphors for God is shaped by human values concerning the nature of gender identity and relationships.

Such debates therefore expose the extent to which such practical and contemporary issues are subtended by much deeper assumptions about gender as a category of human experience and human nature. However, the confusion of such questions in theological circles reveals the lack of sustained attention so far given to an analysis of the phenomenon of gender as it affects church policy, theological discourse and religious practice. This chapter represents an attempt to begin such an enquiry. It is a deliberately interdisciplinary engagement with contemporary critical studies of gender, with a view to presenting such insights in dialogue with theological studies. This discussion will focus on three major subject disciplines – anthropology, biological science and psychoanalysis – in which feminist and postmodern enquiries have converged to challenge many of the notions of the fixity and dichotomy of gender identity and difference. They offer profound implications for our understanding of the very foundations of human culture and identity, and I shall consider the implications of some of these for theological studies in my concluding observations.

What is Gender?

Within the human and social sciences, three clear dimensions of the critical study of gender may be discerned:

1 **Gender identity:** the origins, formation and acquisition of the individual characteristics and personality traits that denote male and female, men and women, 'masculine' and 'feminine'. This area is often associated with psychological tests for 'sex differences', which seek to identify empirically the respective qualities of masculinity and femininity and their contribution to an individual's sense of self

2 **Gender relations:** patterns and prescriptions concerning gender norms and roles; customs and cultural expectations concerning marriage, sexuality and familial arrangements; the relative position of women and men before the law, education and the State; work and the sexual division of labour; the distribution of wealth and material opportunities and rewards.

3 **Gender representations:** this aspect refers to the deepest structures of culture, and how gendered metaphors are used to order and shape our perceptions in ways that far exceed simple ideas about women and men. Many other binary distinctions, such as culture/nature, reason/emotion, mind/body, and so on, are imbued with gendered connotations which associate each pairing with the primary dichotomy of 'masculinity'/'femininity'. However, most cultures also order such binary pairings hierarchically, reinforcing the subordination of all things associated with the feminine. Gender difference then becomes part of a perceived reality in which human experience and the natural order are axiomatically divided into two mutually exclusive and ontologically separate halves.

Critical Theories of Gender

It seems appropriate to begin a survey of critical theories of gender with an influential piece of analysis: the distinction between 'sex' and 'gender', as advanced by Robert Stoller in 1968:

> With a few exceptions there are two sexes, male and female. To determine sex one must assay the following conditions – chromosomes,

external genitalia, internal genitalia, gonads, hormonal states, and secondary sex characteristics. One's sex, then, is determined by an algebraic sum of all these qualities, and as is obvious, most people fall under one of the two separate bell curves, the one of which is called 'male', the other 'female'.

Gender is a term that has psychological and cultural rather than biological connotations: if the proper terms for sex are 'male' and 'female', the corresponding terms for gender are 'masculine' and 'feminine', these latter being quite independent of (biological) sex. Gender is the amount of masculinity and femininity found in a person, and obviously, while there are mixtures of both in many humans, the normal male has a preponderance of masculinity and the normal female a preponderance of femininity. (As quoted in Oakley, 1972: 158–9)

Stoller's definition, and the distinction between 'sex' as natural, biological and physiological, and 'gender' as psychological and cultural, was theoretical orthodoxy for 20 years. It was of immense heuristic and political value to the emergent feminist movement, because it enabled scholars to argue that women's subordinate and secondary position was due to socially constructed, and not naturally occurring, patterns of gender division. This offered a means of refuting those 'naturalistic' arguments which rooted differences between women and men in the immutable logic of biological imperative; instead, it could attribute the foundations of gender identity to social and cultural factors.

Sex, Gender and Science

In a commonplace sense, the tendency to refer to 'the opposite sex' reflects a taken-for-granted assumption that gender characteristics are not only tangible and quantifiable, but oppositional and dichotomous. However, critical studies of the tests for 'sex differences' in psychology and biology do suggest that a false bipolarity has often been imposed on a sample, emphasizing statistical bipolarity between males and females and ignoring significant similarities and overlaps (Archer and Lloyd, 1982; Doyle and Paludi, 1992: chs. 3–4). Gender difference is thus associated with the possession of certain mutually exclusive cognitive and affective traits, rather than representing two extremes of a statistical continuum: women and men as discrete categories of being, rather than persons of diverse, yet shared, qualities.

The history of medicine, the philosophy of science and the sociology of knowledge have all challenged positivist claims to objectivity of scientific research and the value-freedom of empirical data (Harding, 1986). Feminist critics of research into 'sex differences' have made use of such perspectives to maintain that what counts as the 'facts' about gender, and the social inevitability of biological laws, must be regarded as social products, generated by human processes of enquiry. That these researches take place in social contexts which already assign women and men to separate and hierarchically ordered spheres is held to be of paramount importance for conditioning their findings. The view that nature will determine and override any other factor in shaping social and cultural organization may more properly be reversed. Scientific enquiry and theorization has frequently drawn upon social and political metaphors for its characterisation of nature; and in viewing much of the evidence through a framework of gender dichotomy, researchers have reified and exaggerated gender difference (Birke, 1982).

Anthropology, Nature and Culture

Over the past generation, the question of gender has achieved prominence in anthropological studies thanks largely to the efforts of feminist scholars; but theirs is not the sole interest in promoting gender debates, because critical studies of gender relations are seen as indispensable to wider questions of a culture's social, symbolic and economic structures and practices. Marilyn Strathern characterizes this feature thus: 'what happens to women cannot be comprehended unless we look at what happens to men and women, and ... what happens in that realm cannot be comprehended without attention to the overall social system' (Strathern, 1987: 287). The priority of attention afforded gender in anthropology thus makes it uniquely privileged in serving to elucidate wider issues: the nature of human agency, especially in terms of the relationship between nature and culture; the universality (or otherwise) of gender differentiation and symbolism; and the relationship between gender systems and other institutions and social structures.

One significant aspect of the study of gender relations across the disciplines is the almost universal extent to which gender is expressed in dualistic or binary terms, despite – as I have detailed – considerable scepticism towards the psychological and biological evidence for absolute polarities. Anthropologists have detailed the ubiquity of gender dichotomy, and how it imbues other categories: nature/culture, raw/cooked, domestic/public, gathering/hunting, profane/sacred. Men are seen as controlling public and social arenas, possessing clear status, occupying dominant roles, whereas women are confined to the margins, defined only in terms of their relationships to men (Yanagisako and Collier, 1990).

Anthropologists have sought to explain such a strong cultural connection between binary characterizations and gender inequality. Sherry Ortner argued controversially in 1974 that women's universal association with the world of nature, by virtue of their child-bearing and child-rearing practices, was the reason for their subordination (Ortner, 1974).

Thus gender relations are inextricably linked to the pre-existent opposition of nature and culture. However, Ortner's hypothesis regards the social and cultural distinctions between women and men as reducible to biological function, thus inevitably consigning women to a separate realm of nature and embodiment. Such analysis fails to recognize that the demarcation of the boundary between nature and culture, and the consignment of child-rearing inevitably to the domestic and 'feminine' world is itself a social construction: the product of human agency and interpretation. Cross-cultural evidence would indicate, for example, a greater diversity in the cultural representation of the binary categories themselves, suggesting that gender divisions, as founded upon the axiomatic separation of nature and culture, are not solely derived from the imperatives of biological and reproductive difference (Yanagisako and Collier, 1990).

Thus, anthropologists reject notions of gender divisions as resting upon universal, a priori distinctions between nature and culture, and of women and men as occupying ontologically separate spheres by virtue of an all-determining biological sex difference. Instead, they have turned to alternative explanations of gender hierarchy, which emphasizes the cohabitation of culture and social practices by women and men. Such perspectives affirm the importance of human agency, or practice, in the process of generating gender differences:

> Women and men are products of social relations, if we change the social relations we change the categories 'woman' and 'man'. On both political and intellectual grounds we would argue that to put it at its bluntest, social relations determine sex differences rather than biological sex producing social divisions between the sexes. (Brown and Jordanova, 1982: 393)

The historical analyses of writers such as Peggy Reeves Sanday (1981) and Gerda Lerner (1986) have helped to trace the actual processes by which specific patterns of economic production, familial relations and symbolic exchange have served to structure relations between women and men. Cultural representations and categorizations of gender are not the reflection of a pre-existent world of nature, but specific strategies and interpretations which serve to exaggerate and polarize gender difference. Rather than the expression of absolute difference, therefore, gender is more properly to be understood as the suppression of similarities:

> In other words I would see ideological intention ... in the desire to produce a dichotomy (nature vs. culture) out of a set of combinations (all the meanings that nature and culture have in our culture, rich in semantic ambiguity). *It is the same logic which creates 'opposition' out of 'difference'.* (Strathern, 1980: 179, my emphasis)

Attention has therefore shifted to the various transformative practices in which human beings engage, via structures of kinship and marriage, economic activity and the division of labour, in order to understand the processes that determine cultural categories of gender.

Psychoanalysis: Gender, Subjectivity and Knowledge

Classical, or Freudian, psychoanalysis occupies an especially influential, if ambivalent, place in theories of gender. Its analysis of the development of raw infant into socialized adult affords the acquisition of gendered traits and characteristics a crucial significance in the formation of personal identity. As a discipline, it debates the core questions of human 'subjectivity' (identity, motivation and consciousness), and the relative significance of individual psyche, early experience and social norms in the creation of an adult, gendered personality. However, the contribution of psychoanalysis to theories of gender has attracted fierce debate.

Feminist opposition to Freudian psychoanalysis has focused on his representation of the feminine personality as problematic, and his assumption that the attainment of adult heterosexual masculinity is normative. The depiction of femininity as 'lack' of a penis, the clitoris as an 'immature' equivalent, and a concentration on vaginal sexuality as normative for adult females, are regarded as veiled rationalizations for penetrative heterosexual activity and women's reproductive destiny (Freud, 1971).[2] In contrast to the active, inherently 'masculine' auto-eroticism of the pre-Oedipal infant, femininity is a denial or reversal of earliest sexual desire.

Such a reading of psychoanalysis presents 'penis envy' as something inevitable, decisively redirecting psychosexual development at an immature stage. The girl must sublimate her deprivation in a properly feminine expression of adult sexuality – namely, motherhood. If not, she is deemed not to have properly resolved the Oedipus experience, and risks an unfulfilled and psychologically unstable future brought about by her rejection of the true feminine vocation. Psychoanalysis thus implies that the feminine condition is necessarily one of passivity, limited intellectual capability, lack of autonomy, tendency to neurosis, and an innate predisposition to a maternal and domestic role.

However, accusations of psychic determinism misjudge the more complex model of human development within Freud's thought, which admittedly tends to conceptualize the biological drive as an irrevocable, instinctive force, but which also regards the individual's psychological reaction and adjustment to the discovery of anatomical difference as the central well-spring of mature subjectivity.

---

2 For a feminist critique (and reappraisal) of classical psychoanalysis, see Flax (1990).

One could argue that Freud's 'anatomy is destiny' is not only part of his rejection of irrational responses to notions concerning women ... but also his attempts to ground future discussions of masculine and feminine characteristics in the body's presentation of itself in the social world. Taking the female body as given, Freud wanted to explain the diversity of sexual development in terms of the real and apparent differences as they are perceived by the individual. His concern with the unconscious was to add another layer of truth to the question of one's being, to see how one's social personality is a consequence of one's biology. Freud's views ... have to be understood within this framework of grounding an understanding of character and personality in the interplay of biological and psychic factors. (Farganis, 1986: 14–15)

Freud's work may therefore be read as an insistence upon gendered subjectivity as contingent upon the entry into culture, and a model of selfhood which, while biologically and morphologically rooted, is not deterministic. This in itself is implicitly anti-biologistic, as it portrays gender identity as emerging from a psychosexual struggle in early childhood, and therefore as something that is attained, rather than innate. As much of Freud's own clinical practice revealed, the maintenance of an untroubled and consistent adult Ego was constantly disrupted by the repressed memories, desires and demands of the Unconscious Id, suggesting to many commentators that gender identity is not fixed and unitary, but fragmented and constructed.

To many critics, therefore, psychoanalysis offers an account of human identity in its 'natural' state as having greater potential for diversity, plasticity and uninhibited expression than actually allowed for by 'cultural' mores. Critical theorists of gender have therefore turned to psychoanalytic perspectives as offering more satisfactory alternatives both to biologically derived accounts of gender and to sociological theories of 'sex roles' and socialization, because they are able to take account of the strongly internalized nature of gender identity while offering a critical pattern of causation. Effectively, the discovery of sexual difference is only rendered meaningful upon the child's entry into adult or familial culture, when anatomical difference assumes a social significance for the adoption of particular gender roles.

Difference and Embodiment

Such an insistence upon the social context of embodied and psychosexual experience is of enormous significance for theories of gender. The role of embodied experience in the formation of gender identity has long been problematic; a persistent criticism of Stoller's early definition was its exclusion of biological and morphological experience in the formation of gender. Many biological scientists proposed a greater interaction between 'biology' and 'environment' for this reason, allowing the interpretation of biochemical, hormonal and physical changes to impinge upon the formation of identity (see Hubbard, 1990).

Women's embodiment as a distinctive and subversive source of feminist politics has long been a key characteristic of 'radical' feminism (see Tong, 1989: chs 3–5). In the writing of a Francophone neo-psychoanalytic group – especially Julia Kristeva, Luce Irigaray and Hélène Cixous – the marginality and invisibility of the feminine in patriarchal representation is elevated as a radical subversion of the 'phallogocentric' order (ibid.: ch. 8; Grosz, 1989; Whitford, 1991). Following the psychoanalyst Jacques Lacan, gender identity is defined in relation to the possession or otherwise of the rights to speech, as a sign of the privileges of patriarchal society. Gender identity is located at the point of entry into adult culture, represented by the acquisition of language by the speaking subject. The child's relationship to language is symbolic of its position in the 'Phallic' order of the Father. The primacy of masculine discourse under patriarchy thus relegates femininity to non being, lack and silence. Women's symbolic absence from patriarchal culture thus equates their gendered identity with the undifferentiated pre-Oedipal, pre-linguistic realm. The French feminists refer to the source of this unique sensibility as one of jouissance – satiation, sensuality, orgasm – to denote an almost metaphysical quality, derived from the polymorphous desire of the 'Imaginary', pre-cultural world. Jouissance encapsulates, and expresses, a uniquely feminine sexual and sensual desire, unformed and unmarked by the Law of the Father. Hence, the importance of what is known as 'writing the body': women's morphology, as the absolute source of differential knowledge and identity, resting beyond the confines of language, becomes the vantage-point for women's creative and transformative energy (Jones, 1986).

The presence of such autonomous expressions of women's sensuality and bodily self-possession in a society that privileges Cartesian dualism and disembodied rationality is refreshing and challenging. The strategy of 'writing the body' reminds us that gender cannot be an intellectual construct alone: it involves us as psychosomatic beings, inhabiting bodies as well as minds. This alternative perspective roots our gendered identities in the embodied and material practices of work, intimacy, reproduction, ageing and everyday social relations. However, such a strategy of itself cannot rest unexamined; as critics have argued, no woman's experience of herself and her body is as transparent and unambiguous as many feminists would claim. Such a metaphysical evocation of subjectivity effectively collapses women's identity and the processes of gender differentiation back into biological difference. If women's difference from men rest not in social relations and human practice but in some pre-discursive, pre-Oedipal sphere, the source and nature of gender is effectively placed beyond critical scrutiny. Gender is once more theorized as a precondition to social relations, rather than their product.

The challenge for critical studies of gender is therefore to reappraise the ontological and epistemological significance of the body, and the way in which morphological and biological characteristics can assist accounts of gendered experience without 'enclosing us in our differences' (de Beauvoir, 1987) by recourse to forms of determinism. The celebration of difference represented by radical feminists is significant, but only insofar as it directs critical attention to the generation of material, not metaphysical, differences within human agency, language and society.[3]

Implications for Theology

Notions of gender difference as deriving from fixed and innate characteristics, and of women and men as occupying ontologically separate spheres, have been contested by alternatives which see gender as a relational rather than abstract or reified term, and which regard gender divisions as one fundamental dimension of a wider order of social relations. Culture is thus the creator, rather than the precursor of gender; the 'natural' dichotomies of which gender has appeared to be an inevitable product are themselves the results of a gendered system of scientific practice and categorization.

The idea of gender as a form of social relations thus regards women and men, not as ontologically separate, but as cohabitants of culture and nature, generating the material and symbolic relations out of which gender in all its dimensions originates. Such a model of causation challenges unicausal and deterministic understandings, and requires attention to the interplay of human agency and institutional structures in the generation and regeneration of social systems and gender 'regimes'.[4]

An enquiry into the nature of gender roles, development of gender identity and the scope of gender relations therefore goes far beyond simple questions about the differences between women and men. Gender is a complex, dynamic and self-reflexive phenomenon; and a 'theology of gender' will not be a straightforward application of selected categorical statements about empirical differences.

Instead, theology itself must engage with the pluralism and complexity of interdisciplinary theories of gender at a number of levels. First, such perspectives portray a human nature that is not essential, but existential; many critical studies of gender display a scepticism concerning a universal or supra-cultural 'human nature' that endures

---

3 Segal (1987) provides a critique of 'essentialist' and 'radical' feminism on these grounds.

4 Connell (1987) adopts the most comprehensive analysis of this kind.

throughout history and outwith social conditioning. Although certain biological imperatives may persist – reproduction, nourishment, survival – these are always already intertwined with cultural elaborations; we cannot extricate ourselves from our present context and formulate a metaphysical model of human nature. So whatever human nature may be, even if there are universal common elements, they remain inaccessible to our understanding beyond the medium of our own culture and interpretation.

Such a rejection of an essential human nature outwith the relations and interactions of human culture bears significant implications for theological anthropology, and for the Christian doctrine of the *imago Dei*. It challenges notions of an eternal, pre-existent human nature, and suggests that theological teachings concerning a God-given order of creation or natural law which pre-ordains separate functions for women and men may be untenable. The challenge is to contemplate human nature as contingent and contextual, but also to consider the ethical and political implications of such a 'non-realist' understanding. Does such a dissolution of the subject, and a disavowal of any notion of personhood that is independent of human discourse, inevitably lead to an anti-humanism? Or can ethical and political value-commitments be founded on some enduring notion of the person that does not collapse into metaphysics or essentialism?

However, while gender is a complex and constructed phenomenon, it is not merely an incidental aspect of our experience. The decisive impact of gender as a form of social relations is suggestive of a model of human nature as profoundly relational, requiring the agency of culture to bring our personhood fully into being. This resounds with other perspectives that emphasize such an identity as thoroughly compatible with a Trinitarian model of God. In a recent version of this, the multivalent and interactive nature of the Divine is reflected in human relationships of mutual and non-coercive affirmation. Authentic human being is thus only fully realized – recognized and made concrete – within human communities that respect the dynamism and provisionality of personhood (see McFadyen, 1990).

In their use of gendered metaphors for God, therefore, theologians are reminded that gender is an artefact of human culture, and not a metaphysical category. However, faith-communities can only use human terms and images by which to apprehend the Divine. The substitution of 'feminine' terms to replace patriarchal images of Father, King and Lord in inclusive liturgies and prayers are no more 'value-free' than patriarchal language, although arguably they represent important aspirations on the part of worshipping communities to count women's experiences as equally holy, and worthy of imaging the holy, as those of men. However, they do nothing to dispel the fundamental limitations of using human experience to apprehend the Divine, but rather remind us of the provisional and meta-phorical nature of all 'God-talk'.[5]

An understanding of social relations as the generator of gender differences, and of practice as the creator of any social order is not to be mistaken for voluntarism. Rather, the experience of living in any human society is one of being an active, creative agent, while simultaneously recognising the constraints and sanctions – be they moral, material or ideological – which proscribe a wider set of choices or lifestyles. Any gender system is generated by the practices and conventions of science, technology, work, reproduction and cathexis, familial relations and religion; but these are all self-reflexive activities, involving acts of will and free agency as well as being constrained by the dictates and material sanctions of institutions and structures. If the 'causes' of gender are constituted in, and enacted through, material, embodied and symbolic practices, then the role of religious practices and ideologies in the creation and maintenance of gendered systems becomes a crucial area of study. How do religious practices, institutions and symbolic practices serve to reflect, reinforce and create particular dynamics of gender identity, gender roles and representations?

Critical studies of gender also refute the implicit idealism and dualism of the rational intellectual self unencumbered by embodied subjectivity. Authentic analysis of gender must be informed by accounts of human bodiliness. However, it has been the rule that embodiment is regarded as an exclusively female quality, and that the female gender is marked with the signs of carnality, non-rationality and biological determinism. The challenge is to find ways of speaking which cast bodies as the primary source and medium of our relationship to the world, as a kind of 'vantage-point' for experience, while lending diversity and provisionality to such accounts. It may well be that there is a definitive difference between inhabiting a male body and a female one; but we must recognize the extent to which our understanding of our bodies, and of ourselves as bodies, is always culturally constructed and mediated.[6]

Thus, while bodies are creative agents through which we effect change, experience sensory perception, manipulate technology and interact with others, they are also constrained by relations of objectification and patterns of finitude. Theological traditions that have disregarded bodily experience in the articulation of spiritual and ethical verities may well need to be reformulated as a result. This is especially true in areas of sexual and reproductive ethics; but may also be relevant in areas of pastoral care

---

5 Sallie McFague's work (1983; 1987) has become well known in this area.

6 Martin (1987) is a sophisticated analysis of women's own experiences of embodiment and reproductive processes. Such accounts speak of alienation and empowerment. See also Nelson (1992a) for a recent attempt to 'write the body' from a critical perspective on masculinity.

associated with women and medicine, ageing, sexuality, celibacy, body image and violence against women.[7]

The challenges within critical theories of gender to an essential human nature, the transparency of Self and language, and to Platonic categories of masculinity and femininity are mirrored within a wider body of social theory, where feminist and post-structuralist 'deconstructions' of metaphysics has produced similarly contingent and reflexive models of value, meaning, identity and truth. Critical studies of gender are therefore no less vulnerable to the challenge of generating new sources of principle and value in the wake of the dissolution of metaphysics, natural law or objective truth as 'foundational' epistemological criteria. Yet the debate is gradually moving towards the simultaneous rejection of essentialism and categoricalism with the hope for clear and binding ethical and political principles derived from sources other than such varieties of foundationalism (Baynes *et al.*, 1987; Barker *et al.*, 1992; Benhabib, 1992).

I have already related how models of gender identity and relations are perceived as grounded in processes of human practice. It is significant that many commentators are turning to notions of human culture and meaning, and thus accounts of 'truth' and 'value' as grounded in the purposeful and value-directed practices and activities of human communities. The impasse of postmodernism is resolved not by turning away from its critique of metaphysics and dominant rationality, but by insisting that purposeful, coherent and binding values can be articulated from within the core of human activity and value-directed practice.[8]

Such a perspective translated into theology would speak of the contingency and situatedness of human existence and knowledge, and the provisionality of our apprehension of the Divine. 'Truth' would be understood as realized within and through human practices and material transformation. This is very close to notions of *praxis* – value-informed and value-directed action – as the foundation of theological discourse. It would however add a feminist critique of such claims to truth and value by attending to latent aspects of domination and exclusion in the formulation of such values. A 'theology of gender' must therefore address itself critically to the contribution of Christian practices, values and theological metaphors to the creation and maintenance of specific

---

7 See various essays on violence against women, sexual abuse, childbirth, depression, sexuality and pastoral care in Glaz and Moessner (1991) and Graham and Halsey (1993).

8 For example, Habermas (1987); Bernstein (1985). Two recent contributions in theological studies to the debate about values after postmodernism are Browning and Fiorenza (1992) and Berry and Wernick (1992). However, there is much more to be done in articulating theological praxis as the basis for public – and gender-inclusive – values.

gender ideologies and relations. In formulating alternatives, it must look to the practices of the Christian community as the source of both received wisdom and future reappropriations. Practical strategies in the form of pastoral care, worship, adult formation and direction, social action and preaching, might serve to foster the values, relationships and truth-claims of a more 'gender-inclusive' community.

7

WORDS MADE FLESH

Women, Embodiment and Practical Theology[1]

Introduction

In this chapter, I want to contribute to the development of what the North American theologian James Nelson has termed 'Body Theology' (Nelson, 1992b). Feminist theology has famously characterized the dualism of classical Christianity – and in particular, its valuing of the spiritual over the material – as one of the fundamental aspects of the denigration and subordination of women (Ruether, 1983). One of the corollaries of this is the ambivalence, to say the least, exhibited by the Christian tradition towards the facts of human embodiment. However, in what follows, I wish to argue two things: first, that critical attention to the experience of embodiment is a necessary, if problematic, aspect of women's passage from subordination to selfhood; and second, that an exploration of the pastoral, ethical and theological dimensions of embodiment might point us towards a new model of 'Body Theology' from a practical theological perspective. I will propose that embodiment is more than an 'issue' exciting our compassion; rather, it points us to the performative, incarnational nature of all theology. I want to argue that bodily *practice* is the agent and the vehicle of Divine disclosure; and the faithful practices of the Body of Christ are 'sacraments' of suffering and redemption. Feminist theology is finding new impetus, I believe, from its encounter with practical or pastoral theology, because it is being enabled to root itself in the stories of women's pains and joys: to articulate words about God out of the human passage through the life-cycle. Out of the concrete, embodied and dynamic stories of life – and in particular, out of women's pursuit of

---

1 Originally published as 'Woorden tot vlees gemaakt: belichaming en praktische theologie' in de Haardt *et al.* (1998).

79

words and deeds that empower and bring to speech those formerly rendered silent and invisible – new theological voices are making themselves heard.

In recent years, feminist writers have broken new ground in the discipline of pastoral or practical theology.[2] New insights are bringing distinctively feminist perspectives to bear on the area of women giving and receiving pastoral care (Ackermann and Bons-Storm, 1998). Feminist practical theologians are seeking to address issues of gender and power in the churches; and to correct the androcentric nature of pastoral care. The central concern has been to expose systems of patriarchal theory and practice that create and justify a world in which women are ignored or misunderstood, and to call attention to 'a gap between the promise of redemption and liberation on the one hand, and on the other the reality of subtle or brutal marginalization and exploitation of women going on inside and outside the churches' (Bons-Storm, 1996: 15). Through their writing, feminist practical theologians have been advocates for those trapped in the 'terrible silence' (ibid.: 31) of patriarchal church and society, arguing that women have been unable to reveal their true feelings for being stifled by prescriptive ideals of the perfect wife, mother, daughter, colleague, and so on. But alongside the critical task, there is a reconstructive project too: a more adequate theological language and appropriate models of pastoral care through which women can articulate a more credible and liberative account of their lives, relationships and spiritual aspirations.

Feminist practical theology is not simply committed to challenging the status quo, but also to finding forms of healing and empowerment for women: a practice to match the theory. It is this insistence that care cannot be conducted without critical and rigorous analysis, that practice and theology are inseparable, that distinguishes such work. These pioneers of a feminist practical theology, a discipline both critical and reconstructive, offer hope for the renewal of the Christian community, a renewal characterized by new patterns of relationship as well as new apprehensions of the Divine.

In asking what it might mean to do practical theology from a feminist perspective, many writers have focused on the importance of the representation of women: correcting distorted and ideological portrayals – which often lead women themselves to believe the misrepresentations – but also finding new articulations of women's experiences. Thus, for example, the telling of one's story is crucial to the construction of a more authentic self (ibid.: 58–61).

This quest for authoritative spaces from which women can speak for themselves is reflected in many works in feminist practical theology: of releasing women from the bonds of false expectation and allowing them

---

2 For the purposes of this discussion, I shall be using these terms interchangeably.

to tell forth their own reality (Graham and Halsey, 1993; Moessner, 1996; Miller-MacLemore, 1994). Yet while I concur with the importance of such a project, I cannot simply assume that once women start telling their stories they will instantly shed the false illusions of patriarchal accounts and emerge, free of oppression, as the tellers of completely authentic, totally self-actualized narratives. The transition from silence to speech is never easy.

One example of the problems feminist-inspired theory and practice has encountered in attempting to articulate a more 'genuine' account of women's lives may be seen in relation to the issue of embodiment. In the drive for women's self-definition the nature of embodied subjectivity has proved difficult and controversial. Patriarchal representations, in religion,[3] medicine, biological and psychological sciences, the arts and philosophy portray women as misbegotten and abnormal males, inhabiting a lesser sphere of nature and emotion, in contrast to men who occupy the superior world of culture, reason and transcendence (Graham, 1995b; Lloyd, 1984). With such a dualistic characterization, however, goes a further association of women equated with the body and men with the mind. Women are thus denigrated and excluded from the cultural domain by virtue of their links with the non-rational, capricious and profane body.

Feminist theory and politics has therefore inherited an ambivalence towards the body. 'Liberal' feminists prefer to reclaim women's rationality and intellectual equality with men, regarding embodiment as a barrier to emancipation. Simone de Beauvoir is a famous example of such a perspective, arguing that femininity is so associated with body, sex and finitude that if women are to aspire to autonomy they must transcend their bodiliness (de Beauvoir, 1979).

Other feminists seeking to ground a claim for women's distinctive or oppositional experience within bodily difference have been derided as 'essentialists' uncritically valorizing a fixed biological foundation for gender difference, merely reversing but not abolishing the determinism of patriarchal gender dualism. Many feminists have shown themselves nervous about women's embodiment because it is associated with all manner of patriarchal theories of female inferiority, whether that be hormones, maternal instinct, penis envy or brain deficiency. If 'biology is destiny', then it is best avoided, or transcended, altogether:

This improper body is quarantined for fear that its ineluctable immediacy will leave us no space for change, no chance to be otherwise, no

---

3 In a recent book exposing the sex industry in South-East Asia, Rita Nagashima Brock and Susan Thistlethwaite argue that the ambivalence of Christianity and Buddhism towards the material and bodily world, and especially a belief that embodiment is a barrier to spiritual enlightenment and communion with the Divine, still acts as a powerful cultural factor in the denigration of women (Brock and Thistlethwaite, 1996).

place from which to engender a different future. According to this view, the politics of representation remain inseperable from what are commonly understood as the biological facts of the body's existence. (Kirby, 1991: 91)

But there are signs of new approaches to embodiment. Francophone traditions of 'writing the body', which were initially interpreted as essentialist by Anglo-American feminists, have now been reappraised as constituting not a collapse into the discourse of biological determinism, but a new way of configuring the relationship between bodily representation and identity (Braidotti, 1989: 89–105). Creative appropriations of women's embodiment can defy 'phallogocentric' constructions and celebrate the body in new ways. Thus, 'anatomy is always/already just another moment in culture's refiguring of itself' (Kirby, 1991: 96). Accounts of women's embodiment that serve to constrain, misrepresent and foreclose can be rejected as social constructions rather than scientifically or divinely derived 'truth': women reclaim the right to exercise their own 'imaginations' in speaking, acting and writing the body; and the authoritative nature of this process lies in its ability to envision and make possible a more wholesome human community:

> The epistemic authority of such experiences lies not in their ontological foundations in some absolute truth, but in their possible moral status: namely, to what extent do such experiences sustain, advance, enhance, or extend a socionatural environment conducive to perpetuating further human creativity itself? In short, the ultimate epistemological issue is justice itself. (Cooey, 1994: 116)

I have argued so far that although it may be problematic, the quest for reconstructed selfhood through the telling of stories must always involve the experiences of embodiment. And a feminist practical theology needs to seek ways of bringing bodies into speech, both in the ways it reconstructs practical caring and reconfigures our images of the Divine. Practical theology will need to start by listening to people's experiences of embodiment, especially those places where appearance and reality seem out of step. The stories of giving and receiving care – which are always *embodied* stories – are the ideal vantage-point from which to begin. Those who give and receive pastoral care are confronting all the time dilemmas of illness, sexuality, poverty, disability and ageing. And the pastoral encounter itself is always necessarily and variously embodied: the touch, be it informal or as a ritual of anointing or healing; or the reassurance of eye contact, the one-to-one conversation.

So practical theology begins with embodied experience in its practice of care; but its theology is never disembodied, either. It seems to me that practical theology is well-placed to affirm the centrality to Christian life of Word and sacrament as a concrete, tangible expression of the divine–human encounter. After all, at the heart of the Christian faith is the mystery of the incarnation: of God sharing human life in the form of the person of Jesus. Christians acknowledge the reality of God's self-revelation in the form of a human life; but a practical theology that tells stories of embodiment can really examine what it might mean for God to be revealed in a human *body*, broken and suffering, whose resurrection proclaims that love is stronger than death.

All these concerns root us in the reality and complexity of human experience; but they propel us into deeper questions of suffering and salvation out of which theological reflection might be generated. And so a good motto for a practical theology rooted in embodied experience but concerned also to embody Divine grace may be in the words of James Nelson in his influential study, *Embodiment*: 'What does it mean that we as body-selves are invited to participate in the reality of God?' (Nelson, 1989: 9).

Where's the Body?

We may wish to regard our bodies as the most intimate and transparent repository of information about ourselves, but the ambivalence within feminism shows that bodies are never innocent of social construction or unmarked by the dynamics of power and difference. Bodies are therefore both the agents and objects of culture, 'both location and artifact of human imagination' (Cooey, 1994: 7), creative imagining subjects and socially constructed products:

> Bodies are not generic but bear the markers of culturally-constructed difference ... Conditions of embodiment are organized by systemic patterns of domination and subordination, making it impossible to grasp individual body practices, body regimes and discourses about the body without taking power into account. (K. Davis, 1997: 14)

Formerly subordinate groups, defined and constrained by patriarchal constructions, have sought to find new, more empowering ways of talking about themselves as bodily agents as well as objects. Black, gay and lesbian, subaltern or post-colonial, feminist or disabled political movements and critical theories have provided such space: but those who speak from the vantage-point of such subject-positions often still find themselves defined in opposition to a hegemonic and unexamined norm of white, able-bodied, first-world straight masculinity which is never itself required to own up to its own embodied nature. What would it mean for men to 'write their bodies'? There is an urgent need for dominant, privileged groups to become critical about their own racial, sexual and gender identity, and begin to make it possible for everyone to think from the body; or else bodily experience is restricted to a property of those speaking from a position of 'difference', which in practice means the abnormal, problematic, victimized body. It is therefore essential that embodiment is affirmed as a common human trait, even though our experiences may be diverse and characterized by inequality of representation, access to resources and self-determination.

I would therefore wish to emphasize an alternative model of embodiment which should guide our thinking and theologizing about the body. We need to understand bodies as occupying the intersection of nature and culture, construction and agency. They are not merely passive, fleshly husks in which the 'real' self is trapped, nor simply the repositories or objects of cultural forces. Bodies are active agents in the construction and mediation of our world; the creators, as well as the creations, of human social relations. This model rejects the view that 'society' (as an abstract force) inscribes 'values' or 'meanings' (as disembodied principles or values) on to human bodies. It means that every aspect of social reality is always already an embodied reality. The effects and dynamics of power, truth, reason, good and evil never exist as transcendent ideals; they remain to be embodied, enacted and performed in human communities as forms of bodily practice. So the deepest dynamics of the social, political and economic order are always incarnated into persons/bodies-in-relation.

From 'The Body' to 'Our Bodies'

In seeking more nuanced and constructive ways of bearing witness to human embodiment, therefore, I look for clues in the mass of material within social theory and cultural studies which makes a shift from the formal analysis of 'The Body' to the more narrational and phenomenological emphasis on 'our bodies' (Graham, 1995b: 128–9).

A constant theme in this literature is the sense in which, far from being mute and agnostic, bodies offer us epiphanies of meaning which, while locating us firmly in space and time, also take us beyond mere flesh and blood to confront and reveal deeper threads. Consistently such accounts focus on the disclosive nature of pain and suffering; the power of illness to take us beyond the limits of taken-for-grantedness, out to the margins of existence.

Some writers attribute this to the disruptive nature of pain or illness. Leder argues that phenomenologically the 'normally' functioning body is self-effacing: most bodily activities, such as digestion and muscle functioning, take place at such an automatic and unconscious level that we are hardly aware of their taking place (Leder, 1990: ch. 2). The usual task of bodily movement is actually to take us beyond our material existence, into a world of communication and creation: a kind of self-transcendence which Leder terms the 'ecstatic' (ibid.: ch. 1). But pain renders our customary disregard for bodily functioning problematic:

> The disruption and constriction of one's habitual world thus correlates with a new relation to one's body. In pain, the body or a certain part of the body emerges as an *alien presence*. The sensory insistence of pain draws the corporeal out of self-concealment, rendering it thematic. No event more radically and inescapably reminds us of our bodily presence. Yet at the same time pain effects a certain alienation. The painful body is often experienced as something foreign to the self. (Ibid.: 76)

So this rupture of pain brings uncertainty and disorientation, halting us in our tracks, silencing our usual bodily fluency. Yet the very strangeness of such bodily dissonance compels us to explore its contours more thoroughly; because however strange and unsettling, however unrecognizable and distorted the world of pain may be, it invites us beyond the margins of taken-for-granted existence into new, uncharted territory.

Other sources develop this revelatory theme of dissonant bodies, arguing for the inherently moral nature of such bodily testimonies. The locatedness and specificity of the body in pain, and its journey to the edges of existence, constitutes an ethical imperative to counter the relativism of postmodern theory in the form of the cry of suffering:

> Ultimately there would be no ethics of the body, but rather all ethics would take the body as its fundamental point of departure ... The reason is simple: only bodies suffer. Only by a studied concentration on the body can we bear adequate witness to this suffering. Only an ethics or a social science which witnesses suffering is worthy of our energies or attention. (Frank, 1991: 95–6)

However, I wonder whether the narrative disclosure of suffering bodies might not also be echoed by other kinds of bodies-in-extremis. I say this, mindful of my earlier point about a practical theological hermeneutics of the body needing to eschew accounts of bodily experience that assume that only 'abnormal' bodies are real. But this establishes an absolute dichotomy of sickness/health, a distinction belied by many of the studies of disability and chronic pain which call into question the 'normality' of a perfectly functioning healthy body by using the language of 'temporarily able bodies' (Shildrik and Price, 1996: 106). This reminds us that we are all prone to cyclical fluctuations of bodily well-being and that any kind of demarcation – most especially an ontological distinction – between able/disabled actually polarizes and distorts lived experience.

Thus, it is the capacity of bodily dissonance or ambivalence of many kinds to confront us with the fault-lines of pathology and normality, sickness and health that structure the taken-for-granted substance of embodiment. Stories of bodily experience that transgress boundaries and unsettle taken-for-granted categories literally bring us to our senses, bringing us face-to-face with the artifice of even the most intimate aspects of our world. We realize how the abstract forces of economic, religious, cultural and political power may also be written on our bodies; how the texture of embodiment renders tangible the texts of social construction (Schenck, 1986: 43–54). As well as stories of suffering bodies, therefore, I would wish to privilege other narratives that challenge ideas of bodily naturalism, fixity or uniform ability.[4] Such bodily ambivalence and dislocation affords opportunities to review the way in which the underlying values of our culture are enacted and embodied, through the eyes and voices of those whose bodily integrity or identity has been discounted or denied by the hegemonic mainstream.

So bodies offer a 'vantage-point' from which the complexity of human experience, as creator and creation of culture, can be experienced and analysed. Bodies are the bearers of important narratives, some of which unsettle superficial or entrenched understandings; and such unexpected stories excite compassion and serve as the foundation for new moral narratives of hope and obligation.

But in focusing on the disclosive potential of such narratives of exclusion and ambivalence, we are also invited to encounter the theological dimensions of such a commitment. To what extent can narratives of embodiment act as disclosures of Divine reality and activity; bodies as incarnating theological truth-claims?

One case-study may help to illustrate how a practical theology of embodiment enables us to appreciate the complexity of bodily experience as well as suggesting ways in which the creative potential of bodies might be brought to life. It helps us to pursue further the question of how the experiences of bodily dissonance might be given voice within practical theology, and interpreted into a meaningful narrative. Can practical theology

---

4 I have in mind a number of categories: 'hybrid' bodies, at the boundaries of nature, culture and technology, such as those portrayed in the work of Donna Haraway, who presents us with challenging visions of a future in which we are all 'cyborgs' or amalgams of flesh and technology (Haraway, 1991). Bodies of 'difference' are narratives in which the dynamics of race, gender and sexuality find concrete expression. Paula Cooey's *Religious Imagination and the Body* (Cooey, 1994) is a case-study of the depiction of women's embodiment which reveals how patriarchal culture finds corporeal expression. Brock and Thistlethwaite's recent study of prostitution articulates the bodily dimensions of global dynamics of colonialism, sexism, racism and poverty; these forces are literally inscribed on the bodies of women and children and enacted in their sexual and economic relations with male clients (Brock and Thistlethwaite, 1996). Stories of 'ageing' bodies would also be instructive; a process we all share but which implicitly introduces the possibility that our embodied experience is changing, fluid, evolving, capricious and not fixed or controllable.

and the practice of care affirm the integrity of 'different' bodies; and enable the transformation of the chaos of pain, loss and dislocation into life-giving words and deeds?

The significance of Nancy Eisland's book, *The Disabled God* (1994) is limited if we pigeonhole it into a special category of 'theology of disability'. In fact, Eisland avoids the objectification of disability as an 'issue' of interest only to those directly affected, or else merely requiring the compassion and concern of the able-bodied. Instead, Eisland transforms a 'theology of disability' into a practical theology of embodiment, in which all bodies – albeit diverse and heterogenous – become sources of experiential and theological disclosure.

Eisland chooses to highlight the changing definitions of disability, thus characterizing it as a cultural – and political – rather than biological or medical phenomenon (Eisland, 1994: ch. 1). She also focuses on narratives of pride and self-empowerment, singling out the lives of two women with disabilities as stories of achievement, affirmation and self-esteem as much (if at all) as about limitation and suffering – or even of 'pluckiness'. The point is, that all (bodily) lives encounter degrees of difficulty and contingency; but a range of definitions of 'embodiment', to encompass prosthetic limbs, use of wheelchairs, diverse physical sensations and accomplishments, brings all bodily experience into question, counters any attempt to ontologize disability, and destabilizes any fixed dichotomies of bodily ability (ibid.: 31–47).

Bodies as 'Sacraments' of the Divine

The theological significance of the broken body is firmly privileged in Eisland's practical theology. She illustrates how disabled lives might be a revelation of Christ-like ministry in today's Church and world. In the bodies of those living with chronic illness and disabilities, we glimpse the suffering but transfigured incarnation of the Almighty: the scandal of the Divine embodied in a finite, broken human body – 'God in a sip-puff wheelchair' (ibid.: 89). Eisland embraces a theology of the cross from the vantage-point of bodies rendered problematic by exclusive definitions of physical normality and integrity, and turns such judgements on their head. The disabled God is at work in the broken bodies of the faithful; not all-powerful, nor helpless, but a survivor, interdependent with others in mutual care (ibid.: 103).

This is, for me, impressive theological reflection. But I want to close my observations with one final, and vital, point. Eisland does not content herself with merely stating this theology as a matter of disembodied principle, or with a call for a change of attitudes. She takes her argument into the realm of Christian pastoral *practice*, and discusses in particular how the enacted and performative realms of liturgy and ritual might themselves be embodiments of her theology of disability. So the emphasis is on how faithful (and corporate) practice might enable people of faith to relate and enact stories of suffering and redemption. Eisland focuses upon the Eucharist as a sacramental act which rehearses and incarnates the drama of a body crucified and resurrected. The corporate communion of the eucharistic body of Christ is the visible sign of a practice of resistance to exclusive and foreclosive understandings of personhood, opening our horizons to a more generous apprehension of the nature of God. The Eucharist, for Eisland, incarnates (in liturgical practice) the 'disabled God' in whom the signs of suffering and impairment are shown not as weakness or failure but as strength and solidarity (ibid.: 114).

I have thus been arguing that the task of the practical theologian is to examine how (embodied) pastoral practices constitute a 'Christian' (or faithful) identity – an identity which, of course, is always already performative. We thus begin with bodily experience, in the narratives of our bodies;[5] but we end, too, with bodily practices and sacraments as the incarnations of the Divine in our midst. While I have concentrated on Eisland's depiction of the Eucharist, there is undoubted scope to develop further studies of other corporate acts as symbolic enactments of the Christian narrative.

A practical theology of the body/our bodies is therefore never merely the statement of principles; more the cultivation of the *habitus* of the body[6] whereby the words of suffering and redemption may become flesh. If theological values have any substance, they will exist in primary form as bodily practices – clinical, liturgical, kerygmatic, prophetic – and only derivatively as doctrines and concepts. Practical theology essentially gives voice to the 'body language' of the Christian faith:

> The body practices of the Church are a physical language – the routines, rules and practices of the body, conscious and unconscious. In the Church, the body practices are the physical discourse of inclusion and exclusion. The practices reveal the hidden 'membership roll', those whose bodies matter in the shaping of liturgies and services. (Eisland, 1994: 112)

Conclusion

Practical theologians, whatever their context, are seeking to make sense of the values that underpin faithful and purposeful practices of care. It

---

5 Might this involve a new understanding of the 'living human document' of Clinical Pastoral Education? (See Holifield, 1983: 244–7.)

6 Farley (1983) advances a *habitus* model of practical theology as the discipline which cultivates faithful *praxis*.

is in humanity's flawed and faltering attempts to realize the values of unconditional love, healing and liberation that the Divine is ultimately revealed. So it is precisely in the dynamics and practices of human care that Christians embody their truth-claims (see Graham, 1996b). Bodily practices are sacraments of the Divine at work in human relationships; and the vocation of the Body of Christ is thus, as Melanie May has put it, to 'become the flesh of our words' (May, 1995: 88).

8

FROM 'TERRIBLE SILENCE' TO 'TRANSFORMING HOPE'

The Impact of Feminist Theory on Practical Theology

Introduction: Feminist Theory and Practical Theology

A recent collection of essays, entitled *Liberating Faith Practices: Feminist Practical Theologies in Context*, brings together a selection of leading scholars in the field of feminist practical theology (Ackermann and Bons-Storm, 1998). As such, it represents a significant opportunity for the international practical theological community to assess this work so far. What, if anything, distinguishes practical theological scholarship from a feminist perspective; what impact has feminist theory made upon practical theology; and what are the implications of this for the wider academy?

Feminist practical theology has been slow to come to maturity. While feminist systematic, biblical and ethical scholars can trace a heritage of nearly 40 years,[1] feminist practical theologians have only begun to make a significant impact on their discipline since 1990. Systematic attention to feminism and gender in academic practical theology was a long time coming;[2] yet arguably, the field of practical theology is crucial as the

---

1 Valerie Saiving Goldstein's 'The Human Situation: A Feminine View' (1960) is widely acknowledged as the first work in second-wave feminist theology. Mary Daly's *The Church and the Second Sex* (1968) is often regarded as the first major text, although Margaret Brackenbury Crook's *Women and Religion* (1964), by a Unitarian minister and theologian, is an important, neglected, early work.

2 This chapter will not be debating the reasons for this tardiness, although it is likely that the twin syndromes of 'sexism' and 'clericalism' have a lot to answer for. Within a

forum within which the concrete, specific and immediate pastoral needs of women are articulated, and where the mismatch between women's insights and the paucity of their treatment within the Christian tradition is most acutely experienced. This is therefore a crucial, if neglected, area of feminist theological work: as Rebecca Chopp has argued, feminist theology is inevitably drawn into debates about 'what counts as tradition, how experience is conceived, and how theology itself interprets, guides, or governs Christian life' (Chopp 1996: 181). Thus, a major litmus test of theological authenticity must be its practical effectiveness, and not simply its philosophical coherence or historical fidelity.

As feminist practical theologians have come to the fore, however, it is noticeable that they have held many themes and approaches in common. Much of the writing in the field over the past decade has concentrated on the exposure of androcentric biases and silences in the received tradition, and the importance of giving voice to women. It has also pursued, but with perhaps less consistency, a reconstruction of the tradition in order to retrieve the liberating threads which, it is hoped, are contained within religious teachings and practice. The emergence of feminist practical theology has therefore operated within a dynamic of *critique and reconstruction*: countering women's invisibility within the pastoral care tradition, and developing new models of care founded on feminist values.

In this chapter, I wish to place the emergence of feminist practical theologies in the context of the debates within second-wave feminist theory. I will argue that while conventional accounts of secular feminist thought follow particular theoretical demarcations, this already abstracts us away from the practical realities of feminist struggle. It is more appropriate to speak of crucial 'moments', mediated by significant sayings or phrases, which encapsulate important practical and theoretical moments of postwar feminism in the West.[3] As it found a voice, feminist practical theology reflected many of these themes, as I shall hope to indicate.

However, I will then move to introduce a second set of feminist aphorisms, characteristic of mature feminist debate by the early 1990s. These speak of greater heterogeneity and ambivalence within theoretical work, and warn against reductionist accounts or universalized notions of what constitutes women's experience and emancipation. While feminist practical theology shares much of this later mood, asking important questions

---

discipline dominated by an androcentric (male-dominated) clerical paradigm, women were afforded little opportunity as non-male, non-ordained persons to be recognized as agents or as clients of pastoral ministry. (See Ackermann and Bons-Storm, 1998: 1–8; Graham, 1998: 130.)

3 Unfortunately, space prevents me from assessing the constructive contributions to practical theology informed by critical studies of men and masculinity. This must await a separate review; but two excellent recent examples in this area are Neuger and Poling's *The Care of Men* (1997) and Pryce's *Finding a Voice* (1996).

about the nature of its own theorizing and transformative practice, it has largely failed to reflect the complexities of women's passage from silence into speech. Nevertheless, it is my contention that feminist voices are lending an important vitality to practical theology's mission to occupy the places 'where human suffering evokes ... a religious response' (Miller-McLemore, 1998: 179).

Mapping Feminist Theory

[T]he story of feminist theory begins in political history. (Grant 1993: 28)

A textbook introduction to contemporary feminism normally follows a standard pattern, which may be simplified into something like this (Humm, 1992). From its genesis in religious and political radicalism in seventeenth-century Europe, the women's movement attained greater coherence during the Enlightenment by appealing for women's inclusion into the 'Rights of Man' founded on universal human rationality. 'First wave' feminism developed in the US and Britain within a context of wider abolitionist and suffrage campaigns. In the twentieth century, women's participation in war-time economies, involvement in civil rights movements and the advent of labour-saving innovations precipitated 'second-wave' feminism in the US and Europe after 1945, consolidating into a full-blown phenomenon by the late 1960s. By the end of the century, however, much of the vitality of feminism had dissipated, fragmenting under the pressure of 'difference' within the women's movement (race, sexuality, dis/ability, class, post-colonial issues), and economic and political retrenchment. Some proclaimed this new era as one of 'post-feminism', exposing the redundancy and irrelevance of the women's movement; others, as the opening of a new chapter in 'a new and improved post-Enlightenment humanism' (Grant, 1993: 184).

Such introductory works generally choose to organize second-wave feminist thought according to particular theoretical classifications. Thus, liberal, radical and socialist/Marxist schools of thought constitute the heart of theoretical feminism by the late 1970s (Jaggar, 1983), joined by subsequent theoretical developments, such as psychoanalytic, womanist and postmodern feminism by the early 1990s (Tong, 1989; Humm, 1992; Evans, 1995).

In this overview, however, I want explicitly to avoid a portrayal of second-wave feminism that simply reproduces such theoretical demarcations. Increasingly, I think such a presentation of feminism as primarily to do with theoretical distinctions is a commentators' construction, and should only be used heuristically and tentatively. Feminist theory is, as it were, the secondary source; but its categorizations are the products and not the precursors of what we might call the 'primary' voices of feminist thought and action. I have therefore chosen to emphasize the degree to which feminist thought was born of practical dilemmas and campaigns and have accordingly selected some well-known quotations as paradigmatic in their articulation of core principles.

1 'The problem with no name': countering women's invisibility

This phrase is taken from Betty Friedan's trenchant classic, *The Feminine Mystique* (1963). Friedan speaks of the mismatch between the youthful aspirations of a generation of women in the United States – symptomatic of changes occurring throughout the Western world after 1945 – and the realities of later life. Women who had tasted unprecedented independence and opportunity, especially in terms of education and employment, experienced a drastic contraction in their horizons once married and cloistered in suburbia. Why, if marriage, motherhood and domestic concerns were so natural and fulfilling to the feminine condition, did such women find themselves frustrated, guilty or, frequently, severely depressed?

Friedan spoke for a generation of women who found that no adequate language existed for a satisfactory diagnosis of women's dissatisfaction. Simone de Beauvoir's *The Second Sex* (1949) also articulated the enigma at the heart of women's identity. Man has named himself as normative, as 'Self', and women are designated as their eternal 'Other', and regarded as secondary, misbegotten and derivative (de Beauvoir, 1949 [1988]: 15–18). However, de Beauvoir insists: 'one is not born, but rather becomes, a woman' (ibid.: 295): a radical and deeply influential insight, prompting a generation of feminist theory which challenged the naturalism of gender difference, by arguing that women's nature – and gender inequality – was socially, rather than biologically, produced. Later work, particularly in medical, psychological and educational fields, confirmed the extent to which, empirically, the qualities and attributes designated as 'feminine' were afforded lower value (see Archer and Lloyd, 1982; Fausto-Sterling, 1985): 'The image of women that we in the twentieth-century Western world have been socialized to accept is the image of woman as less important than man' (Young 1990: 54).

In attempting to put words to the silences of their malaise, feminists often deployed existing theoretical frameworks to help them articulate the source of the problem. Liberal political theory provided a vocabulary of equality and the possibility of women claiming, on the basis of a shared humanity, a common rationality and agency with men. Marxism and socialism offered economic reasons for women's secondary status. But these perspectives only prompted those active in the women's movement to undertake further action and reflection, in order more adequately and systematically to grapple with the theoretical vacuum.

Part of the feminist project, therefore, was to correct the historical effacement of women's experiences, to move from silence to speech. It is notable that second-wave feminism featured many literary works in an attempt both to deny women's lack of excellence or cultural significance and also to counter the famine of patriarchy by retrieving positive role models and resources for women's autonomous voice. Reflecting on her quest to revive interest in the African-American novelist Zora Neale Hurston, the womanist writer Alice Walker describes going to search for Hurston's unmarked grave, and finding it obscured and overgrown by weeds (Walker, 1984: 93–116). This is a powerful metaphor for the indifference towards the cultural achievements of women, but a reminder that despite such neglect, women still have a proud heritage.

2 'Ain't I a Woman?': Affirming the value of 'women's experience'

> That man over there says women need to be helped into carriages, and lifted over ditches, and to have the best place everywhere. Nobody ever helps me into carriages, or over mud-puddles, or gives me any best place! And ain't I a woman? Look at me! Look at my arm! I have ploughed, and planted, and gathered into barns, and no man could head me! And ain't I a woman? I could work as much and eat as much as a man – when I could get it – and bear the lash as well! And ain't I a woman? I have bourne thirteen children, and seen them most all sold off to slavery, and when I cried out with my mother's grief, none but Jesus heard me! And ain't I a woman? (Collins, 1991: 14)

Strictly speaking, the famous declaration of the African-American preacher and campaigner, Sojourner Truth, predates the period on which I wish to concentrate by over a century. But it reminds us of the continuity between 'second wave' feminism – born of technological and economic advance, made possible by women's entry into the labour market under wartime conditions in the 1940s in Britain and the US and fostered by the civil rights and trade union movements of the 1960s – and its earlier precursors a century earlier, in particular the anti-slavery campaigns in the US of the mid-nineteenth century.

Sojourner Truth explodes the 'naturalism' of women's frailty and subordination by pointing to the bodily evidence of a different life of hardship. She challenges perspectives that decreed that women were, by nature 'ladylike' and genteel, and points to her experience of having to work and support her children. Yet her story is not one of victimhood or dependence, but one of resistance and self-respect. External prescriptions will not daunt Sojourner Truth from bearing witness to her own integrity and self-definition against a culture that may have refused to recognize white women as political subjects but denied Black women – as slaves and Africans – their very humanity. The centrality of 'Ain't I a Woman' to the feminist canon of self-affirmation serves to remind us that issues of gender and women's role cannot be separated from questions of race and class and affirms a different kind of women's integrity and power, to construct new, positive images of Black womanhood.[4]

3 'The Personal is Political': from private lives to social change

This slogan captured the conviction of the early women's movement that women's dilemmas transcended mere personal dissatisfaction. Like Friedan's 'problem with no name', women seeking to articulate their frustration with their personal roles and expectations were confronted with a lack of appropriate analysis. Progressive politics, such as the civil rights movement and trade unionism, advanced manifestos for the ending of economic, social and racial injustice; but within many such campaigns the position of women remained unproblematic. The most notorious example of this double standard is surely Stokely Carmichal's comment that in radical politics, the only place for women is on their backs (Coote and Campbell, 1982: 13); but is also reflected in the jokey aphorism of early 1970s socialist feminism in Britain: 'men make the policies, women make the tea'!

The notion of the *personal as political* therefore crystallizes two important principles of second-wave feminism. First, it is a repudiation of the idea that women's situation was merely attributable to individual choice or destiny. Rather, feminists insisted that structural factors were responsible, the beginnings of analysis which attended to the *institutionalization* of gender relations, to the roots of women's inequality in entrenched social structures, and not simply the product of 'bad faith' on the part of individual women or men. It also spoke of a refusal to 'blame the victim' for the systematic and structural oppression of women, who were understood instead as unwilling compliants in a system of male domination (or 'patriarchy') in which the exercise of power transcended individual choice.

The second dimension of the personal as political concerned feminists' growing concentration upon the actual mechanics of oppression: the beginnings of a link between women's public lack of opportunity and the dynamics of personal and domestic relations. Indeed, the most graphic

---

4 For further discussion, see hooks (1982), Haraway (1992) and Alliaume (1998).

– and, as it turned out, most intractable – dimensions of male domination were traced to women's everyday lives. The sexual division of labour in the home, and the patterns of emotional labour by which men received support from women who had been socialized into suppressing their own needs, were regarded as part of an interlocking system which, as Row-botham, Segal and Wainwright argued, 'radically extended the scope of politics':

> because of the form of oppression which it confronts, the women's movement has radically extended the scope of politics and, with this, has changed who is involved in politics and how. Much of the oppres-sion of women takes place 'in private', in areas of life considered 'per-sonal'. The causes of that oppression are social and economic, but these causes could only be revealed and confronted when women challenged the assumptions of their personal life, of who does the housework, of the way children are brought up, the quality of our friendships, even the way we make love and with whom. These were not normally the subject of politics. (Rowbotham, Segal and Wainwright, 1979: 12)

Thus, in contradiction of leftist and civil rights minimization of the women's movement as personal and trivial, early feminist practice in-sisted upon the political nature of women's experience and growing clarity of the nature of their oppression. The early feminist practice of 'consciousness-raising' was not, therefore, to be belittled as either gossip or therapy, or as unnecessary diversion from the real priorities of the class struggle. By using personal experience as a critical faculty, women could begin to understand the nature of the *anomie* and dislocation to which Friedan first so powerfully gave voice. Consciousness-raising – beginning with experience – was a political activity, and provided the forum by which individual 'problems with no name' would become collectivized:

> One of the first things we discover ... is that personal problems are political problems. There are no personal solutions at this time. There is only collective action for a collective solution. (Hanish, 1969: 76, quoted in Grant, 1993: 37–8)

However, parallel traditions also existed which saw fit to address as-pects not accommodated within an equal rights model: issues of women's reproductive rights, their physical safety and integrity at the hands of vio-lent or abusive partners and sexual freedom and self-determination. This strand, which is often associated with 'radical' feminism, emerged from practical campaigns to protect women against rape, domestic violence and sexual harassment. Sexuality, regarded by liberal society as private and unregulated, thus became a particular focus of feminist interrogation. In the words of Catherine MacKinnon, 'sexuality is to feminism what work is to marxism: that which is most one's own, yet most taken away' (MacKinnon, 1989: 3). Radical feminism therefore advanced an analysis which located women's oppression in men's control over women's sexual autonomy, either overtly through forms of sexual violence, or more subtly, such as institutions of marriage and 'compulsory heterosexuality' (Rich, 1980b: 631–90).

While not constituting the elaborately theorized and intense focus on 'The Body' characteristic of later gender theory in the 1990s, 'radical' feminism of the 1970s did begin to articulate attention to embodied difference and to sexuality as a site of contestation that was to become an abiding, albeit problematic and contested, theme of feminist theory.

I have taken a narrative rather than a theoretical approach in my overview not in order to adopt an anti-intellectual position nor to downplay the sophistication of the theoretical corpus generated by certain historically or contextually shared preoccupations. After all, by the early 1980s feminist writing was attaining a tentative, but tenacious, foothold in the academy. However, it is my point that the body of knowledge 'feminist theory' has always existed in a dialectical relationship with the more practical concerns of feminist political campaigning:

> Theory enables us to see immediate needs in terms of long-range goals and an overall perspective on the world. It thus gives us a framework for evaluating various strategies in both the long and the short run, and for seeing the types of changes that they are likely to produce. Theory is not just a body of facts or a set of personal opinions ... Feminist theory relies on the underlying assumption that it will aid the liberation of women. Feminist theory, therefore, is not an unengaged study of women ... While feminist theory begins with the immediate need to end women's oppression it is also a way of viewing the world. (Bunch, 1992: 172)

Given that early feminism was intent upon articulating the hidden voices of women rendered invisible by patriarchy, there was a tendency to believe that the 'hearing into speech' was itself a complete emancipatory act. The elucidation of *women's experience* – as affirmation of identity, as critical vantage-point, and as criterion for transformative action – was, therefore, a fundamental element of early feminism, being firmly rooted in women's passage from silence to speech. As we shall see, while the articulation of women's experiences was a fundamental criterion of feminist, and feminist theological, critique and reconstruction, it was later to become the object of much reappraisal. Women's experience as a foundational category of feminism became deeply problematic in its tendency to become reified and universalized.

Feminist Practical Theologies: From Misogyny to Counter-Narrative

Systematic attention to issues of the pastoral care of women and to the insights of feminist critique and reconstruction on the part of practical theologians have only made an impression in the last ten years. Yet a survey of work published in practical theology from a feminist perspective by the early 1990s reveals startling commonalities, broadly reflecting the ambitions of second-wave feminism as already outlined. Thus, the first generation of feminist practical theology can usefully be surveyed in terms of its *protest against the exclusion and objectification of women* within the Christian pastoral tradition; its emphasis on pastoral care as *finding a voice for women,* and the empowering nature of 'hearing into speech'; and of *transforming the life of the Church and society* in the light of such 'counternarratives' to the traditions of neglect and denigration.

1 Listening to the Silence

Carrie Doehring identifies an emergent body of feminist pastoral counselling with a distinctive 'perspective, assumptions, ethics, goals and tasks' (Doehring, 1992: 23). It seeks to *render visible* the 'underground' sufferings of women subjected to sexual and domestic violence, and to bring such experiences to the surface (ibid.: 24). Other work similarly begins with protest against women's 'terrible silence' in the Christian pastoral tradition (Bons-Storm, 1996: 31). Many emphasize, like Doehring, the Church's sanctioning of misogyny in various forms: the idealization of images of servanthood and sacrifice (Gill-Austern, 1996: 304–21); models of God as judgemental and punitive, silencing women's distress at abuse or injustice (Garma, 1991: 133; Clarke, 1986: 17; Addy, 1993: 80–90); or teachings imputing women's lesser ontological status to men (Crawford and Kinnamon, 1983: 70–5; Kanyoro, 1991).

As a second stage, Doehring goes on to *name* the 'harsh, punitive puritanical God, a false God of the patriarchal tradition' (1992: 25): images and patterns of care which sanction hierarchical relations of submission to the perpetrator of abuse and which implicitly commend self-abnegation. However, a third element, of *reconstruction*, is present in the call for feminist counselling to exorcise the false gods and replace them with what she terms 'life-giving Gods'. This transformative task will be effected with the aid of liberating therapeutic practice:

As feminist pastoral counsellors, we are called to name the sin of patriarchy and to rediscover the roots of our faith in the empowering theme of liberation that has been the deep structure of our faith for thousands of years. One of our tasks is to evaluate models of pastoral counseling from a feminist perspective and to create new models which reflect the potential for empowerment in our relationship with clients and our relationship with God. (Ibid.: 26)

For Emma Justes, both psychology and theology have reflected androcentric perspectives, thereby eclipsing consideration of women's true needs and characteristics:

> Both theology and psychology have defined female as different, as 'other', and have built traditions and theories that proceed to ignore that difference. To truly understand the difference we must begin to hear about humanity from a female perspective. (Justes, 1985: 281)

Here, therefore, we detect clear echoes of second-wave feminist concerns symbolized by de Beauvoir's characterization of woman as 'Other'. For Justes, theological teaching has sanctioned a view of women as secondary and invisible; but patriarchal prescriptions about the inevitability of male dominance assume the normality of women's subordination, requiring women to take responsibility for failed or abusive relationships. Thus, Justes also identifies the need to regard the *personal as political*, enabling counsellors and caregivers to challenge the tendency to 'blame the victim' by assuming that it is women's inevitable fate to be the objects of male aggression, objectification or abuse, or to require them to be forgiving, or that domestic mistreatment of women by men is tolerable or uncontroversial (ibid.: 285–91).

2 Finding a Voice

The focus on the critical and reconstructive force of 'women's experience' is paramount: there is a strong emphasis on narrative, especially in the European contributions. Women's lives as primary data, and the importance of naming the hidden dimensions of women's stories – those 'seldom heard' (Milhaven, 1991), let alone the subjects of prayers and preaching – form the overwhelming model for this time. It is believed that women's experiences – frequently matters normally rendered taboo in the Church – and the worlds revealed through 'the praxis of caring' (Tamez 1989: 4), will contribute valuable new insights.

In *The Incredible Woman* (1996) Riet Bons-Storm is concerned to construct a pastoral care that will enable women to speak their lives authentically and without fear in a world where frequently they are ignored, belittled or misunderstood. Once more, the ideological nature of patriarchal ideals are contrasted with the more authentic self-understandings of women. The pastoral task is to release women from the distorted versions of their true feelings and aspirations; what women want from pastoral care is not what they have traditionally received. Thus, Bons-Storm talks of moving from 'unstory' to self-narrative (Bons-Storm, 1996: 58–61) and the need to practise 'counternarratives' (ibid.: 111) founded in women's authentic experience.

Visibility and finding a voice are perennial themes: Bons-Storm emphasizes the liberating power of 'listening to women's silences' (ibid). *Life-Cycles: Women and Pastoral Care*, published in Britain in 1993, discerns in the growing ecclesial and public profile of women a glimpse of a renewed future. Women may occupy areas regarded as marginal by patriarchal Church structures, such as urban ministry, social work and part-time theological education; but it is in these realms that the innovative work, practical and theological, is emerging (Graham and Halsey, 1993: part IV).

Many of the stories told by women in these volumes tell of the ambivalence and complexity of their lives, and stress the struggle women have to find and sustain integrity and full personhood. Frequently, women tell of the precarious balance they maintain between caring and autonomy (Kennedy, 1993: 10–18; Lewin, 1993: 43–58; Miller-McLemore, 1991: 63–85). But throughout, the echoes of the refrain, 'and ain't I a woman?' can clearly be heard:

> Why can I not be a mother *and* a whole person? ... I will not cut down my truth to a remnant. It is not right to ask anyone to do so because it means mutilating what there is of God in each of us. My son and daughter are the best part of my love and life, but they are not all that I am. I would be committing a crime if I asked them to be everything to me. As a family we cannot live in the golden glow of a stage-set. Our lives are not a tableau. (Kirby, 1993: 139)

In an article on the care of older women harbouring secrets of long-ago abuse, Emma Justes considers how such care will require particular stages of attentive listening. Note, again, how they reflect patterns already discerned: a dynamic we might identify as *attending, naming and acting*:

> There are three stages that can be considered as involved in care related to older women's secrets. First, caregivers must communicate some willingness to hear about the secret ... Second, the secret must be heard ... Third, it is important to be willing and able to *continue* to hear about the secret ... to enable the man's new movement toward wholeness and spiritual fulfilment. (Justes, 1996: 246–7)

Justes sketches a process of care that is nicely mutual: for every experience told, possibly for the first time in years, there must be one who is prepared to listen. Similarly, the disclosure of a secret must be acknowledged for its gravity and preciousness; and a telling forth must be accompanied by patient acceptance. Such mutuality of care, an avoidance of hierarchy, a wish to embody new patterns of community and co-operation are crucial in feminist practical theology: from the collaborative nature of feminist liturgies, to the frequent dialogical or conversational model of feminist preaching, to attempts at non-hierarchical or non-directive patterns of feminist spiritual direction or counselling.[5]

Such attention to collegiality reflects an attentiveness to hearing one another into speech – readily apparent in the example quoted from Emma Justes – born of a commitment to the critical and transformative value of women's experience. The stories of exclusion and empowerment are therefore crucial primary sources for feminist practical theologians, and constitute their main resource for critique and reconstruction. A relational model of selfhood provides the pattern for the exercise of care and the practice of faith and is another expression of the feminist conviction that the personal is political, amounting to a rejection of individualistic and privatized diagnoses of either women's ills or new visions of renewed community. Thus, Bonnie Miller-McLemore envisages the focus of pastoral theology not as the 'living human document' after Anton Boisen and Charles Gerkin, but the 'living human web'; and Pamela Couture argues for practical theology as conducted within analyses privileging the 'social ecology' of women's pastoral needs (Miller-McLemore, 1996: 2–26; Couture, 1996: 96; Couture, 1991). Furthermore, as Christine Neuger argues, given the systemic and entrenched nature of patriarchy, collaborative and structural strategies are essential if women are to create new possibilities (Neuger, 1993: 195–209).

Thus, feminist practical theologians find themselves moving beyond perspectives which simply 'add women' towards challenging many of the assumptions about the practice of Christian care, and the conception of the discipline. *Life-Cycles* insists upon the connection of the individual story to the social and structural context: experiences of education, work, marriage and motherhood are profoundly political. In the face of women's pastoral needs revealed as structural injustices rather than personal failings, the pastor must become more proactive and sensitive to 'the sexual politics of pastoral care' (Graham, 1993: 210–24). Such a vision of ministry is more than ameliorative; it challenges the spiritualization and privatization of religious belief and pastoral care.

---

5 This attitude is also exemplified in the collaborative style of many of the publications: one hopes this is a genuine reflection of women's desire to work together (see Moessner, 1996: 3) and not an indication of academic resistance to feminist monographs.

3 Engaging with the Theological: From 'Terrible Silence' to 'Transforming Hope'

Carrie Doehring's article locates the significance of pastoral care and therapeutic practice as actually addressing theological issues: of the power of religion to hold captive and, as Doehring claims, to release. Feminist pastoral care requires more than good therapeutic technique: it necessitates a critical engagement with theological language, Church structures and ministerial practice as crucial arenas of feminist protest and reform. Doehring asserts the benevolence and liberatory import of the Christian tradition, but is less specific on the hermeneutical journey necessary to effect a retrieval of the 'authentic' tradition.

Like other works published at this time, the essays in an important collection from the US, *Women in Travail and Transition*, reiterate the importance of a new fund of knowledge, grounded not in patriarchal institutions or sexist imaginings of what women want, but in psychological perspectives that take women's lives seriously. The reconstructive task is dependent on the critical explosion of new ways of knowing: 'in order to develop a gender-free understanding of human experience, we first need to develop the woman-centred formulations that have escaped conscious articulation' (Glaz and Moessner, 1991: 195). The therapeutic conversation, informed by feminist psychology, provides the crucible of alternative knowledge to enable women to break the silence (ibid.: 115, 159, 205).

Glaz and Moessner also hint at the importance of exploring theological issues and of grounding renewed pastoral practice in feminist theology; 'The pastoral situation focuses theological reflection' (ibid.: 193). But it is not clear what theological tools might be deployed or how the Christian tradition (in the shape of images, narratives, doctrines or institutions) might itself exercise an ideological or liberating power. The task appears to be to reassure women that 'the tradition' is inclusive and life-giving, in contrast to the patriarchal nature of psychology (ibid.: 55). Thus, there is talk of the 'promise of transforming hope' (ibid.: 104) but less clarity on how it is practised or made manifest in the life of the Church; of how less wholesome models of God can be transformed to 'better' images (ibid.: 119–20, 136, 152).

Modelled on the pastoral cycle of liberation theology, the essays in *Life-Cycles* attempts to move from experience to social analysis to theological reconstruction. In its emphasis on the practices of women giving and receiving care, it opts for narrative accounts of how women are already reconstructing ways of doing theology: liturgical innovations, re-reading the Bible, reconceiving theological education and ministerial practice. The structure of *Life-Cycles* perhaps represents the most explicit attempt to evaluate the impact of feminism not simply as giving voice to women but in terms of the possibilities women's perspectives offer for renegotiating the theological tradition. Yet it is still hard to avoid the assumption that the articulation of women's stories will automatically elucidate the egalitarian nature of the gospel, although many of the voices explicitly address the hermeneutical complexities of changing Christian practice, asking whether faith is a source of nourishment or diminishment; a curse or a blessing:

> what if the stories from the store of faith are simply inadequate vehicles to convey a woman's experience of rape, infertility, or loving other women, for example? What if the world of our experiences cannot happily be clothed with an existing Christian narrative, or enclosed within a scriptural framework? What then? (Walton, 1993: 195)

Clearly, feminism has started to make an impact on practical theology, in its ambitions towards the restoration of the voices of women, an explicit advocacy of the full humanity and participation of women, and action directed towards dismantling systems of domination and hierarchy. Reflecting a sensitivity to the political as well as the personal, feminist practical theology has exhibited a shift of emphasis away from ameliorative care of the individual towards 'prophetic, transformative challenge to systems of power, authority, and domination that continue to violate, terrorize, and systematically destroy individuals and communities' (Miller-McLemore, 1996: 16). In this respect, feminism has been one of the forces that has galvanized practical theology to return to wider vision of pastoral ministry as encompassing social injustice as well as individual distress (Couture and Hunter, 1995; Pattison, 1997).

Yet for me this trajectory of feminist critique and reconstruction carries a number of problems, which will become the subject of the closing stages of the chapter. How does feminist care-giving actually empower women to move from the shadows and margins of silence into speech? Will women instinctively know and do the truth once they have been able to adopt the role of fully speaking subjects? Is it enough to 'find a voice', as much of the literature implies? The actual processes of retrieval, reconstruction and renewal imply complex epistemological and hermeneutical considerations: attention to priorities concerning the sources and norms of authentic theological discourse which are not given sufficiently detailed attention.

A transition from so-called 'modern' to 'postmodern' perspectives in recent feminist theory problematizes some of the fundamental concepts upon which feminist practical theologians have relied: an appeal to the self-evidence and universality of 'women's experience' and a commitment to women's ability to find therapeutic value within a reconstructed theological tradition.

Reconstituting Feminism: Difference, Subjectivity, Gender

Much of my argument so far has been to place the intellectual and theoretical claims of feminism within its own historical location: and feminism, too, is a product of modernity. Modernity introduced a discourse of human rights, of reason, empiricism and science; and it allowed women and their male allies to exploit that discourse of enlightenment and emancipation to advance the cause of women.

The threshold of modernity/postmodernity must be seen as necessitating a re-examination of the logic of Enlightenment feminism: first, in its claims to speak for all human conditions; second, that events can actually bear out the faith in progress and the self-evidence of human reason in all things; and third, its ability to provide an authentic and reliable account of 'reality'. Current feminist theory has problematized many of the categories on which second-wave feminism was founded: the transparency of women's experience, the self-authenticating nature of women's agency and empowerment, the comprehensive scope of feminist knowledge (Flax, 1990). I shall therefore now move to three further moments in late second-wave feminism which crystallize this critical transition, before debating their significance for feminist practical theology.

1 'Changing the Subject': Diversity and Unity in Women's Experience

The core ideals of second-wave feminism – autonomy, agency, self-determination, freedom from objectification or prescriptive stereotyping – have already been outlined. But what if some women's experiences do not conform to a feminist analysis: what if women's narratives of self-expression do not explicitly reject patriarchal images and values? Mary McClintock Fulkerson's concern in *Changing the Subject* (1994) – based on ethnographic studies of women in 'conservative' churches in the US – is that the orthodoxies of liberal feminist theology risk overriding the experiences of many women.

The women of her study use the language of servanthood, submission to the Lord and self-effacement: anathema to the motifs of affirmation, autonomy and empowerment within liberal feminism. Yet for these women, such language is a way of guaranteeing the authority of the Holy Spirit for their actions: they work within the conventions of their culture to gain a degree of freedom, albeit closely circumscribed, but real nevertheless. Language in this situation does not simply name reality; it works to engineer a degree of agency. The language of poor white women in Pentecostal congregations is, argues Fulkerson, unintelligible to a feminist analysis that assumes that language and subject-positions are transparent. Fulkerson insists that there must be allowance for greater contradictions and complexity; language and action is dependent upon context. The meanings and choices for the women of Fulkerson's study are not determined: they are generated in and through 'signifying practices' that are institutional, liturgical and embodied as well as linguistic. The women ministers deploy the resources available to them in the exercise of agency, self-determination and autonomy; but because they retain, to a certain extent, the vocabulary and conventions of their traditional surroundings, such strategies seem unfamiliar and discordant to the external commentator (Fulkerson, 1994: 285–98).

Thus, it is the attention to the specificity of their resistance to invisibility and marginalization and to their articulation of dignity and self-affirmation which marks, for Fulkerson, an appropriately feminist response. By 'changing the subject', alternative perspectives are brought to light, and it is apparent that there is no one definition of women's experience, nor one self-evident route to liberation. Women will have many different ways of exercising autonomy, agency and authority: 'a woman is not a "fixed text" or a natural subject, the same thing regardless of culture and historical period' (Fulkerson, 1996: 138).

I read Fulkerson's study as a timely recollection that the founding principles of feminism were not a prescriptive appeal to universalizing categories but a series of calls to action that sought to activate what Fulkerson affirms as 'the full humanity of women, which I take to include agency, self-assertion and creation – the entire range of the productive capacities of women' (ibid.: 132). A respect for diversity among women and the complexities by which subjectivity is generated calls for restraint in the universalizing use of 'women's experience'.

2 The 'Sensible Transcendental': Embodiment, Religion and Secularity

The work of the feminist psychoanalyst and philosopher Luce Irigaray defies much of the secularizing tendency of second-wave feminism, and discomforts many feminist philosophers and theorists who find they have to engage anew with concepts of religion and theology. It requires feminist practical theologians to think very radically about the nature of religion and how it functions for women, as well as disturbing many of the assumptions about feminist aspirations towards equality with men.

Irigaray argues that the Western 'symbolic' – the world of language, culture and society – is built on male superiority and privilege, an analysis derived from the work of the psychoanalyst Jacques Lacan, who taught that gendered identity comes about at the point of a child's entry into culture designated by the child's acquisition of language (Lacan, 1977). Lacan draws an analogy between anatomical difference – after Freud, derived from the possession or lack of a penis – and the structures of language, ordered around the privileged signifier of the 'Phallus'. The term 'phallogocentricism' communicates the co-incidence of a social order based on language – *Logos* – and the anatomical privilege of masculinity. As non-male, as 'Other' to the phallic economy, woman is relegated to non-being, confined to the pre-cultural, pre-linguistic realm of the 'imaginary', often associated with the female, especially the maternal, body (Irigaray, 1977).

Irigaray is therefore critical of those varieties of feminist politics which locate women's emancipation in terms of their equality with men. This simply condemns them to conformity to androcentric standards (Irigaray, 1993a: 9–14). Instead, if women's representation as 'Other' within the deep symbolic of patriarchy is fundamental, then it must be radically remade into a truly woman-centred subjectivity – and politics – founded on the sexual specificity of women. It is this that fuels feminist neo-psychoanalytic scholarship: to imagine a primal state of multiple, dissonant subjectivities that is not identical to the stable construct 'Woman' but which retains elements of self-possession and resistance such that the patriarchal symbolic can never master her. This process of remaking is necessarily a matter of giving voice to, and speaking from, the female body as the site of sexual difference (Irigaray, 1998: 198–224).

As an ethical norm, Irigaray proposes not equality, because women can never aspire to being more than the errant 'Other' to man. Rather, gender justice is predicated on radical difference that makes possible new forms of reciprocity and intimacy between women and men. Thus, we are returned to the body: avoided in much second-wave feminist thought as condemning women to an 'essentialist' or biologically determined, transcultural identity; but here offered in Irigaray's work as the necessary site of all feminist politics and ethics.

An alternative 'Symbolic' must be founded on the female sexuate body and the sensations repressed and unvoiced within the monolithic order of the Phallus. But because this representation of (embodied) feminine subjectivity is not available within the prevailing discourse, such an alternative is necessarily utopian. And here Irigaray begins a turn to theology, to ideas of 'becoming divine' as a necessary aspect of women's empowerment. Women have to reinvoke the Divine for themselves, because nothing else will fulfil a task so fundamental in nature: 'What we need, we who are sexed according to our genre, is a God to share, a verb to share and become ... It is indispensible for us to be God *for us* so that we can be divine for the other' (Irigaray, 1993b: 11).

This turn to theology and metaphysics is not a predictable association of women with idealized spirituality. Nor is it an attempt to retrieve female goddesses from prehistory. Irigaray's idea of God serves as an ideal – a 'horizon' towards which women can aspire. In order to achieve full humanity women need a female Divine who can open up the possibility of a transfigured female body. It is women's 'lack' – of Phallus, of speech – that is reconfigured, not as absence or void but as a sacred space: it is in the 'spaces' of the body, and between bodies, that the Divine becoming will be apparent.

Irigaray's Divine is not a distant, transcendent being divorced from the material, immanent world – this is the God created by men in their own image in order to rationalize and sacralize their own dis-embodied denial of the maternal. Hers is not a God 'out there', against whom we measure our finitude and imperfection, but: 'a *sensible transcendental* that comes into being through us' (Irigaray: 1993c: 129).

Irigaray is therefore deliciously subversive, on three counts. First, she uses the patriarchal association between women and emptiness, silence and lack and reappropriates it to convey a notion of women's bodies as the 'threshold of transcendence' (Braidotti, 1994a: 184): a place of liminality and incompleteness, but also a becoming – a *telos* – in which all human essences remain unfinished and unfixed.

Second, Irigaray subverts the patriarchal denial of women's spirituality: that women are denied spiritual, rational identity because they are in some way more bodily, carnal and earth-bound. Rather than our ideas of transcendence being based on separation, disembodiedness, universality, omnipresence, Irigaray argues that women only reach towards, attain and realize the Divine in and through our specific and particular embodiment. Irigaray argues that women need a God who shares their specificity, and invites them to perfection and wholeness from that very point:

> The most intimate perception of the flesh escapes every sacrificial substitution … This memory of the flesh as the place of approach is ethical fidelity to incarnation. To destroy it risks suppressing *alterity*, both God's and the Other's. (Irigaray, 1986: 256)

Contrast this with modernity's (and feminism's) call to social transformation, that appeals to the death of God and of religion as representing forces of superstition, tradition and ecclesial authority which obstructs the project of human empowerment. However, Irigaray argues for a re-enchantment of the world: the transformation of feminist practice and consciousness is impossible without the reconfiguration of our concepts of the Divine. And along with that goes a feminist imagination that locates itself in the *poesis* of embodied subjectivity, with explicit links to a Christian understanding of the Word made flesh.

Here is a third element of Irigaray's thinking that promises to be revolutionary for feminist practical theology: her reconception of themes of *embodiment* and identity. Irigaray's return to the materiality of embodied subjectivity may actually *reverse* the earlier feminist nostrum by arguing that 'the *political* is the *personal*': we cannot depend on abstract notions of rights or universal human nature to undergird our political programmes, but must rather begin from the fleshly reality of our bodies.

In her notion of the 'sensible transcendental', therefore, Irigaray names two taboos in secular feminism – religion and the body – as fundamental sites of subjectivity, agency and ethics. She is both reminding us of the concretion and specificity of feminists' appeals to critical and transformatory knowledge, and of its radical incompleteness and lack of closure. Like women's 'excess' to the patriarchal economy, there is something about our aspirations towards full humanity that can never be totally realized: only to be glimpsed as a horizon of human becoming. Irigaray stresses that identity is always elusive. We will have to resort to extreme measures – to the extent of invoking religion and the body – to imagine 'a realm of personal identity ... apart from social constraint' (Scott, 1992: 35).

3 'Gender-as-a-verb': Performativity and Identity

Just as various strands of feminist scholarship have served to problematize core concepts of women's experience and subjectivity, so too the very fundamental category of gender has also been subjected to renewed scrutiny.

The tendency has been to regard gender as a property, as a cluster of characteristics in some way biologically or physiologically derived, constituting 'real' characteristics, traits and tendencies. However, contemporary theorists argue that gender cannot be seen as a pre-existing category of absolute difference – either extrapolated from biological difference or socially 'constructed' – but rather as a set of interrelated variables of identity, relationship and representations which are constantly being generated through a variety of material and symbolic practices (Connell, 1987; Graham, 1995b). Masculine and feminine identities are not determined by a pre-given, unchangeable biological substratum. They are created by and reflect structures of power, language and social practices and our struggles with and against these structures.

Some of the most influential theorists at work today, such as Judith Butler, take the contingent and fluid nature of gender identity further, and perceive it as a 'performative' reality, a 'regulatory fiction' (Braidotti, 1994b: 61): a form of social relations that constructs subjects as male or female, heterosexual or homosexual, masculine or feminine. Gender is enacted or 'iterated' in particular ways according to a pre-existent heterosexual economy. Gender is thus a normative activity by which categories such as feminine, masculine, heterosexual, woman and man are constructed and regulated (Butler, 1990). The shift from gender as a property or given category – from 'gender-as-a-thing' to 'gender-as-a-verb' (Braidotti, 1994b: 67) – indicates the shift from ontology to performativity; what appears to be the mere living out of categorical qualities is actually a series of *accomplishments*.

Butler's critics have associated the idea of performativity with choice or voluntarism, a charge that Butler in more recent work has gone some way to defusing. While I remain critical of Butler's disregard for the sociological realities of gender identity, relations and representations, and the extent to which gender is always already institutionalized, it is clear that she wishes to trace how gender is 'naturalized' as a taken-for-granted category (so that 'gender-as-a-thing' is accepted unquestioningly), and how alternative approaches might shock us into realizing that we *make the difference* and *practise* gender in its individual, interpersonal and institutional forms.

In later work, however, Butler develops a discussion of the articulation of a more overtly political sensibility (Butler, 1997). Here, I think we see an attempt to counter accusations of nihilism and anti-humanism within post-structuralism, in order to cultivate a spirit of solidarity with the victims of *différance*, those groups and identities occluded by dominant discourses, and to work for ways of retrieving the integrity of the marginalized. Butler argues that formerly 'abject' categories (such as homosexuality) can be reconstituted by the exercise of agency that reinvests them, via processes of renaming, as worthy and valuable. The reclamation of terms such as 'queer' by the gay and lesbian community is reminiscent of African-American adoption of terms such as 'Black', not as words of abuse but of pride; a strategy that deliberately robs such words of power and ironically invests them with dignity.

This has interesting parallels with Sojourner Truth's statement which synthesizes traditional images of femininity with ideas of the dignity of labour, and transforms the term 'woman' into one of pride and self-possession. It also reminds us of the continuing importance of retrieving and naming the stories of those silenced by oppression. These mere words have a tangible political impact, not least in the way they restore a measure of self-determination to subjects who were formerly the objects of others' wounding speech.

From Women's Experience to Feminist Theory

Given the historical impact of feminist themes of visibility, affirmation, autonomy and agency, it is no wonder that the category of 'women's experience' emerged as the criterion against which such principles could be tested and around which feminist theory and politics could coalesce. However, its potency rests chiefly in its oppositional force, as an expression of that which has been subordinated, trivialized, naturalized and silenced. As Rosemary Ruether has said in a famously quoted phrase:

> The use of feminist theology lies not in its use of the criterion of experience but rather in its use of *women's* experience, which has been almost entirely shut out of theological reflection in the past. The use of women's experience in feminist theology, therefore, explodes as a critical force, exposing classical theology, including its codified traditions, as based on *male* experience rather than on universal human experience. (Ruether, 1993: 13)

However, the viability of 'women's experience' as a *constructive* category is open to question. As all three writers surveyed above suggest, notions of identity and the subject – the very category 'woman' – are variously problematized. One is certainly not born a woman, as de Beauvoir declared; but Butler, for one, would take this further and argue that the process of being and becoming woman (or man) is *never* complete, but forever performative. There is, as Butler says, no 'doer behind the deed': no prediscursive subject who remains constant outside or independent of a performative context.

As Fulkerson's use of post-structuralist theory indicates, one effect has been to see the female feminist subject recast 'not as yet another sovereign, hierarchical and exclusionary subject, but rather as a multiple, open-ended, inter-connected entity' (Braidotti, 1994b: 66). Arguably, 'woman' is not a monolithic, universal or self-evident category, and this renders ideas of 'women's experience' as a foundational category very fragile.

Neo-psychoanalytic feminists constitute woman not as substantive identity, but as lack or absence effected by patriarchal structures of representation and denial. It is Irigaray's genius to have identified this problem: how to articulate that which is, under patriarchy, unspeakable? The problem is precisely that feminism tries to build its emancipatory praxis on something that by its very nature is absence, enigma and invisibility.

Liberating Faith Practices

> Human agency and hope combine in the search for healing. We have to make our hopes happen. (Ackermann, 1998: 89)

By the mid-1990s, feminist practical theology was acquiring confidence and theoretical sophistication, with particular emphasis on the use of liberation theology and critical social theory. In particular, attention turned to the elucidation of the epistemological claims of theology as *praxis*, and the privileged position of a feminist vantage-point to declare the inseparability of theory and practice: 'Theological knowledge is gained from a commitment to the examination of women's experience of oppression and to envisioning a liberative alternative' (Hogan, 1995: 163).

Transforming Practice, published in 1996, begins with a recognition of the challenges to traditional models of practical theology. Feminism, along with liberationist and narrative theologies, stresses the critical, transformative and performative nature of identity and knowledge; these thus constitute my core sources and norms for a reconstructed 'theology of practice' (Graham, 1996b: 112). Critical attention is paid to the *habitus* of making and reshaping the world: how subjects get made, and how values are enacted within the purposeful practices of intentional communities. Ethical and theological judgements about the authenticity of communities' beliefs can only be granted from within phenomenological study of faith practices. These will always be situated, embodied, contingent, eschatological, open-ended. This is not a surrender to nihilism, but a recognition that Christian 'truth' is incarnated in the performative, embodied practices of intentional communities: 'Theology now becomes not an abstract series of philosophical propositions, but a performative discipline, where knowledge and truth are only realizable in the pursuit of practical strategies and social relations' (ibid.: 204). The title of *Liberating Faith Practices*, the volume introduced at the beginning of this chapter, plays with two meanings. It signals a consideration of faith practices that liberate, while also pointing towards possible ways in which practices of faith might themselves be freed to reflect new realities. What does this collection tell us about the future direction of feminist practical theology? Can we discern themes of contingency, contextuality and particularity emerging; of knowledge as provisional, and the importance of transforming knowledge at the heart of feminist *praxis*?

Themes identified in earlier works are still evident: for example, contributors still refer to the importance of telling forth the hidden realities of women's lives – 'the power to decide what is true and good rests with men' (Bons-Storm, 1998: 11) – and of naming, giving voice and breaking women's silence. This may be about women naming themselves and their concerns as holy, enabling them to reclaim sacred space (Graham, 1998: 129–52) or countering the invisibility of women with disabilities (Eisland, 1998: 103–28) or of liturgical 'lament' as the lifting of a veil of silence over suffering (Ackermann, 1998: 75–102).

But there is a greater attention to the complexity and diversity of women's situations, as in Nancy Eisland's reminder that differential bodily capabilities confound universalizing definitions of gender as the primary category of experience or analysis. Similarly, themes of women's agency and choice are emphasized, as in Barbara Nichols' discussion of women's role in new reproductive technologies (Nichols, 1998: 153–74).

Moreover, a greater concentration on the *theological* task is also apparent. Contributors stress the importance of providing hermeneutical models, and of rooting care in a hopeful imagination which is the anticipation of God's transforming actions. Practical theology is described as the 'critical theory of religiously transmitted *praxis* in society' (Bons-Storm, 1998: 13). It should be orientated towards excavating the implicit truth-claims of religious and cultural institutions, examining the extent to which such communities of faith are the embodiment of practical theological wisdom. The contributors draw largely upon liberationist traditions: of theology as *praxis*, and of regarding theology as knowledge for transformation; as an interpretative framework by which people make sense of the world, providing a benchmark by which they judge reality:

> Practical theology is context-specific. It does not try to subsume the particulars of people's lives into universal truths, but embraces the specifics of different lives as the grounding for the work on an ongoing reflection and action, based in the conviction that God-talk matters. (Nichols, 1998: 157)

The most novel – and the most persistent – theme is therefore the performative and contextual nature of faith, expressed in the commitment to a praxis model. 'Truth' is determined by that which defines the route from captivity to freedom, judged by a 'hermeneutic of healing' (Ackermann, 1998: 80; Bons-Storm, 1998: 9–26). The insights of the tradition are judged according to their capacity to embody the hopes for justice of the poorest of the poor:

> Authority is understood, not as the power of a particular teaching or text to speak of God, but the power of a particular teaching or text to inspire consent to faith and love in a community that struggles to find the message of God's love in solidarity with those who have been marginalized and denied the full empowerment of that love. (Russell, 1995: 107)

Truth is enacted and embodied, therefore, in the search for justice: in the healing not just of individuals but of the body politic (Ackermann), and in the eucharistic practice of a gender-inclusive liturgical community (Graham) which is a prefiguration of reconciliation between humanity and God.

However, the turn to *praxis* within recent feminist practical theology is not necessarily sufficient to make it distinctively, or adequately, *feminist*. In fact, there may be good reasons to require of feminist practical theologies a certain 'hermeneutics of suspicion' towards uncritically assimilating liberationist emancipatory models. While liberationist and feminist theologies share a political commitment to justice and an epistemological grounding in models of truth as transformatory knowledge, it is still important to ask whether the aspirations of feminism can simply be exhausted by generic campaigns. This criticism gains added force given evidence from revisionist studies of basic ecclesial communities which suggest that, despite a superficial discourse of egalitarianism, women still find the culture of liberation theology exclusive and inhibiting (Alvarez, 1990; Burdick, 1993).

While honouring the turn to *praxis* that characterizes much contemporary practical theology, therefore, feminists cannot simply harness themselves to a programme that seeks to totalize its subjects or predetermine its own ends. There will always be a tension between feminist ambitions towards women claiming and celebrating a shared humanity with men, and forging their own definitions of equality and agency, especially those rooted in embodied subjectivity. Feminist practical theologians must not merely become assimilated into gender-blind or universalized accounts. While heavily indebted to liberal and liberationist models of human flourishing, they would do well to listen to the more radical, albeit unsettling, emphases of Fulkerson, Butler and Irigaray. A properly complex and adequate feminist theory – not one which reproduces patterns of patriarchal determinism and exclusion by basing itself upon universalizing accounts of women's experience – needs a way of illuminating the subject as multiple, differentiated and provisional, and setting its own epistemological ambitions to embrace the Otherness and mystery at the heart of transforming hope.

Conclusion

I have been reluctant to portray the protagonists of what we call 'second wave feminism' as greatly preoccupied with establishing theoretical orthodoxies. My contention has been, rather, that they were concerned to advance the cause of women, to shift the balance of power in gender relations and to establish new social, cultural and familial models based on visions of equality and collegiality between women and men. It may not be an exaggeration to claim that feminist theory as conceived is better understood as a form of *praxis*: value-laden and value-directed action, emerging from specific historical projects and, once consolidated, serving as the accumulated body of wisdom by which further analysis and action is guided.

The 'problem with no name' had to find some kind of vehicle from silence to speech. Feminist theory has functioned as a means of accumulating wisdom, and as a way of articulating and analysing problems not accorded space or due attention within 'malestream' thinking. I have therefore stressed the symbiotic relationship of theory and practice, rather than the autonomy and inevitability of feminist theory; and in choosing a model of praxis I find important similarities between feminist theory and current self-understandings of practical theology that emphasize its critical, interpretative and transformative potential. The designation of feminist theory and feminist practical theology as bodies of practical wisdom is also designed to insist upon their contextual, multiple and provisional nature: their genesis is in concrete, specific and material interests, but something of their vision remains unexhausted by pragmatic demands. There must be space for a utopian, even eschatological sensibility:

> The full implications of feminism will evolve over time, as we organize, experiment, think, analyse, and revise our ideas and strategies in light of our experiences. No theory emerges in full detail overnight; the dominant theories of our day have expanded and changed over many decades. That it will take time should not discourage us. That we might fail to pursue our ideas – given the enormous need for them in society today – is unconscionable. (Bunch, 1992: 173)

9

'ONLY BODIES SUFFER'

Embodiment, Representation and the Practice of Ethics

In December 1991 three elderly South Korean women filed a lawsuit against the Japanese government claiming systematic enslavement and abuse as a result of their treatment at the hands of the Imperial Army during World War Two. As their case unfolded, and women's groups took up their cause, the full scale of their story emerged (L. K. Davis, 1994; Palley, 1994). It was revealed that as many as 200,000 young women from South-East Asia, especially Korea, were forcibly conscripted by the Japanese forces and drafted to work as prostitutes throughout South-East Asia and the Pacific during the 1930s to 1945. Corralled in small cubicles, the women were required to have sex with as many as 30 men a day (Chung, 1997; Howard, 1995). The plight of these so-called 'comfort women'[1] was subsequently suppressed for nearly 50 years, preventing the women from making public their experience. Many readers may judge such a conspiracy of silence as amounting to an extension of the original abuse, serving only to prolong the deleterious effects of the original trauma, and from which release has taken the best part of a lifetime.

Such a story confronts its hearers with suffering and injustice on a scale that is unimaginable. The fate of the comfort women is one among many expressions of the militarism, genocide and totalitarianism that have habitually scarred the twentieth century and undermined the 'grand narrative' of civilization and progress, revealing it to be more a product of the naive confidence of Western modernity than a moral universal. Yet even if one model for enlightenment and emancipation is shaken,

---

1 Often referred to as *Jungshindae*, which literally means 'conscripted worker'.

the question still remains: where are the resources for cultivating a moral sensibility appropriate to the horrifying scale of the evil and inhumanity of Auschwitz, Bosnia and Rwanda?

It is significant to note that one version of a reconstructed moral discourse – one cautious of universals and grand narratives, but determined nevertheless not to abandon the moral and political vision of human emancipation – draws upon the social theory of the body. To place the body at the centre of moral and social theorizing reflects a conviction on the part of many scholars that the human body serves as the surface upon which the most controversial and pressing dilemmas of the day are made flesh. Questions of war, peace, hunger and torture involve bodily containment, flourishing or coercion. It is bodies that bear most tangibly the marks and effects of cultural, political and economic trends, such as the use and abuse of medical advances or the growing encroachment of computer technologies on the human body to the extent of blurring the boundaries between organic and cybernetic life (K. Davis, 1997; Frank, 1990; Scott and Morgan, 1993; Shilling, 1993; Turner, 1984).

One figure, the sociologist Arthur Frank, has been especially influential in the turn to the body in recent social theory, particularly as an advocate of an 'ethics of embodiment' (Frank, 1991b).[2] Frank's position is well encapsulated in the following statement, found at the end of his 1991 essay surveying the future of the sociological study of the body. He argues that the body possesses a moral imperative of a compelling nature, capable of disclosing powerful truths about the human condition:

> Ultimately there would be no ethics of the body, but rather all ethics would take the body as its fundamental point of departure ... The reason is simple: *only bodies suffer.* Only by a studied concentration on the body can we bear adequate witness to this suffering. Only an ethics or a social science which witnesses suffering is worthy of our energies or attention. (Frank, 1991b: 95, my emphasis)

Frank's comments identify questions of bodily representation and theorization as ultimately questions of accountability and moral disclosure; and since the essay cited above, Frank has developed further the links between embodiment, suffering and ethics. He has advanced a compelling portrayal of the 'wounded storyteller' as moral exemplar, whose odyssey through pain represents what Frank terms a 'pedagogy of suffering' (Frank, 1995: 182). He argues that (suffering) bodies constitute narratives of pain and redemption sufficient to regenerate our moral vocabulary.

In this chapter, I propose to examine Frank's model of the representa-

---

2 For discussions of Frank's influence, see Davis (1997), Shilling (1993: 93–9). For further discussions of the ethics of embodiment, see Diprose (1991; 1994) and Schenck (1986).

tion of suffering bodies in narratives of 'the wounded storyteller' as a case study of the connections between representation, gender and experience. While his account is courageous, inspirational and evocative, it contains a number of elements with which I wish to take issue. In particular, Frank's work ignores the extent to which the passage into speech of the wounded storyteller is always already circumscribed by concealed dynamics of gender and race. Some stories get told; but others, Frank's 'chaos' narratives, remain on the margins of acceptable speech because the prevailing system of gendered and racialized privilege renders their bearers mute and invisible. In particular, women – their bodies and voices – are so fundamentally absent from patriarchy that they cannot possibly occupy the same narrative spaces as men. This is graphically illustrated when we reconsider the emerging stories of the comfort women of Korea and Japan, whose bodies (and minds) bear the marks of suffering and coercion, but whose passage to speech exposes Frank's (and others') neglect of the gendered nature of bodies and their stories of wounding and healing.

Such ingrained gender representations need restructuring, and Luce Irigaray's remaking of the symbolic of patriarchy is similarly focused on suffering bodies. However, her task is to remake the metaphysics of embodiment and ethics via an ambitious project of reconfiguring our very concepts of divinity and transcendence. So while Frank's wounded storyteller may serve as moral exemplar – and spark our efforts to relate similar narratives of hope and obligation – it seems that without Irigaray's concept of 'Divine becoming', and new representations of identity, community and responsibility, we will simply be stuck with telling the same old stories. 'Physical pain has no voice, but when it at last finds a voice, it begins to tell a story' (Scarry, 1985: 3).

Frank develops his ethics of embodiment in two works: *At the Will of the Body* (1991) is based on his own encounters with serious, life-threatening illness, first a heart attack at the age of 39, and then cancer treatment a year later. The theme of Frank's most recent book, *The Wounded Storyteller* (1995), develops in more detail the association between bodies in pain and the search for a postmodern ethics.

Frank speaks of illness as a 'dangerous opportunity': one's entire identity is undermined by the power of illness to confound habitual certainties and dislocate one from former preoccupations. It is a process of afflicted bodies 'dissolving' physical and social certainties, depriving the sufferer of his or her taken-for-granted abilities to function. The experience of pain is a central element of the debilitating potency of illness (Frank, 1991a: 34), a kind of surrendering of personal and professional competence and control.[3]

---

3 A theme later reiterated in Frank's discussion of Sacks (1984); see Frank (1995: chs 5–6).

But bodies dissolve and lose their self-possession in other ways: central to Frank's analysis is his distinction between 'illness' and 'disease' (Frank 1991a: 13–21), and the way in which both conditions are representative of contrasting sociological epochs. Disease is the condition of modernity, a medicalized version of one's condition, which is necessarily clinical and objectifying, and symbolized by the passive acquiescence of the patient in the high-tech medical facility. Illness, by contrast, is redolent of the opportunity postmodernity presents to take control of one's condition:

> Illness is the experience of living through the disease. If disease talk measures the body, illness talk tells of the fear and frustration of being inside a body that is breaking down. Illness begins where medicine leaves off, where I recognize that what is happening to my body is not some set of measures. What happens to my body happens to my life. (Ibid.: 13)

The healing story can only thus emerge from the reclamation of the body that chooses to defy medical objectification. The body 'is not a territory to be controlled by either the physician's treatment or the patient's will' (ibid.: 62), it has a mystery and a wisdom of its own. The integrity of the body, despite our attempts to maintain the control of assurance, progress and normality, is the best moral teacher (ibid.: 115–27). 'At the centre of narrative ethics is the wounded storyteller. What is ethical is found in the story, and the story depends on the wound' (Frank, 1995: 169).

This contrast, between the diseased body held captive in the logic of modernity which prizes technological progress and scientific panaceas, and the narratives of illness which facilitate the advent of the wounded storyteller, may be simplistic but is crucial to Frank's analysis. The paradigm of modernity is one of restitution: a notion that suffering and illness have closure, and the narrative of pain can be rendered coherent via medical intervention. The primacy of technical expertise dominates the experiences of illness; the patient surrenders him/herself to the care and power of the professional.

While the restitution narrative is firmly entrenched within modernity, Frank's model of the 'chaos' narrative represents the stories which lack any coherence or resolution within the paradigm of restitution. Chaotic tales are untellable, representing merely a 'hole' in the narrative that cannot be filled. 'The story traces the edges of a wound that can only be told around. Words suggest its rawness, but that wound is so much of the body, its insults, agonies, and losses, that words necessarily fail' (ibid.: 98). This is a strand of thinking about the body which may be traced back to the work of Elaine Scarry: the body is 'unmade' to a point of mute pain that removes self and body from language, culture and representation (Scarry, 1985). It is actually the representation of pain into coherent narrative that transforms the body from flesh to words; and, for Frank, constitutes (in the sense of comprising and constructing) its ethical imperative. The drive to speak, to portray, to communicate – to become the master of one's own narrative and the teller of one's own tale – is thus at the heart of his account.

The process of recovering one's voice is therefore a journey through suffering, but one redeemed by one's capacity to connect with others, thereby forging a moral sensibility grounded in communicative intersubjectivity. It is a movement from passivity to activity, isolation to community, and from objectification to self-actualization. This is the ethical heart of Frank's system:

> The idea of telling one's story as a responsibility to the commonsense world reflects what I understand as the core morality of the postmodern. Storytelling is for an other just as much as it is for oneself. In the reciprocity that is storytelling, the teller offers herself as guide to the other's self-formation. The other's receipt of that guidance not only recognizes but values the teller. The moral genius of storytelling is that each, teller and listener, enters the space of the story for the other. Telling stories in postmodern times, and perhaps in all times, attempts to change one's own life by affecting the lives of others. Thus all stories have an element of testimony. (Frank, 1995: 17–18)

The conditions under which Frank believes the wounded storyteller has been able to thrive is thus characterized by him as a shift from modern to postmodern times. While Frank's characterization of the contours of modernity and postmodernity is sketchy – he admits: 'I make no attempt to define postmodernism'[4] (ibid.: 4) – it seems to me that Frank's distinction between the two epochs is concerned with questions of personal freedom and autonomy. The 'postmodern' is a corrective to the 'modern' in that the proliferation of people's own stories releases them from the imposed and ideological fabrications of modernity: 'Much of postmodernity – haunted by the question of how to write after Auschwitz – is a struggle to work out what aspects of modernity can be preserved while scrapping the modernist telos' (ibid.: 112).

Thus, the 'postmodern' narrative of illness begins when the patient can reclaim their capacity for telling their stories for themselves. There is a sense that illness is a reality which, in bringing us to our senses, provides some kind of ethical constant: 'Even in postmodern times, even among the various selves that each of us is, a bedrock of the really real remains. Its name is often pain' (ibid.: 72).

---

4 Frank seems to use 'postmodernism' to delineate the historical and sociological condition, whereas I prefer to refer to this as 'postmodernity', and reserve 'postmodernism' as the term for the intellectual enquiry into the state of postmodernity.

This means, I think, that Frank's work is ultimately as much about stories as it is about bodies. He takes the turn to narrative in much postmodern theory as his cue for pursuing the idea of narrativity as underpinning social life. 'Events are contingent, but a story can be told that binds contingent events together into a life that has a moral necessity' (ibid.: 176). In the absence of metaphysical truths, people must construct their worlds via story; but they inherit and receive the world narrationally too (Loughlin, 1996). People may no longer rely on 'grand narratives' to sustain them in the illusion that there really is a truth out there; but they subsist upon the local stories in which they participate.

Instead of the dominance of 'restitution', therefore, the paradigm here is the patient in 'remission'. While the temporarily seriously ill may tolerate being taken over in the name of recovery – even cure – the long-term chronically sick and cancer patients in remission will not tolerate permanent colonization of this nature. Relieved of the pressure to 'get well soon', the remissioner takes responsibility for their stories of illness as a way of defining themselves on their own behalf. No longer content to be the object of another's colonizing gaze or construction (that of the medical expert, or the prescriptive logic of recovery, or the depersonalizing trajectory of invasive treatment), the postmodern wounded storyteller resists medical reductionism and their objectification and infantilization at the hands of the 'master narrative' of science or its practitioners.

Thus the 'remission society' exposes the flaws and presumptions in the restitution narrative. Modern medicine aims at an invulnerability and control which the frailty of the body belies. There can be no medical – or indeed ontological – distinction between 'healthy' and 'sick': one may not even be in the process of 'becoming' well. The remission patient forever remains transient, a citizen of two worlds. They recognize that as the teller of their story they emerge changed, transfigured even, from the journey of illness and treatment.

This is the beginning of what Frank terms the 'quest' story which feature the 'hero'[5] who journeys through tribulation to eventual resolution. The destination is not victory but interestingly – 'atonement' (Frank, 1995: 119). The hero journeys to the heart of suffering but returns – changed, not necessarily, if ever, 'cured' – to tell the 'inspirational' story to others. It appears not to be so much the content of the story – not a moral fable – as the embodiment of transfigured suffering and courage which reaches out as a source of grace to others. The storytellers bear the 'marks of pain' (ibid.: 127) on their flesh – flesh made words, in an inversion of traditional Christian typology of incarnation. The hero is not a victor but a 'suffering servant'.[6]

---

5 Frank cites Joseph Campbell's work at this point.
6 Frank evokes the figures of Bodhisattva and Christ as paradigms of this process.

Such figures cannot speak of ultimate closure or abstract ideals of progress and healing; they can only bear witness to their own wounded vulnerability and perseverance, an offering that invites empathy and calls forth community. Those who bear witness to the testimony are summoned to become a certain kind of person by virtue of the invitation to hear the story – and thus to realize and bring into flesh the words, and into words the flesh, of the wounded narrator: 'the listener must be present as a potentially suffering body to receive the testimony that is the suffering body of the teller' (ibid.: 144). The sharing of stories is one of the ways in which the communicative (other-related) body shares its pain and encounters the recognition of another. Stories heal by virtue of the shared bonds they create, and ill people's stories are therefore moral acts, eliciting care as the appropriate response of those hearing these narratives. 'The wounded storyteller is a moral witness, reenchanting a disenchanted world ... Postmodern times may be pandemonium, but they are not a void. Illness stories provide glimpses of the perfection' (ibid.: 185).

However, despite Frank's insistence that the assumption of illness is necessarily a vocation of vulnerability, vestiges of the modern narrative of self-actualization and control linger on. The ethical significance of the narrative process of illness seems, for Frank still, to be about personal responsibility: 'In postmodern times, becoming a narrator of one's own life implies an assumption of responsibility for more than the events of that life. Events are contingent, but a story can be told that binds contingent events together into a life that has a moral necessity' (ibid.: 176).

Frank's 'postmodernism' thus emerges supremely as an era of liberal individualism. See the emphasis here – mirrored throughout his book – upon choice and responsibility: 'People, especially ill people, may not choose their bodies, but as body-selves they remain responsible for their bodies, and they choose how to exercise this responsibility' (ibid.: 41).

This connects with a perennial theme in Frank's work, already identified: that of illness as disruption and interruption of personal success, competence and progress. It mirrors his earlier distinction between 'disease' – the medicalized, objectifying discourse about one's condition – and 'illness' which is the lived, phenomenological experience through which one achieves a greater degree of autonomy and self-definition.

However, I take issue with Frank's basic premises in this respect. He takes what he calls 'postmodernism' to be a state in which everyone is equally free to tell their story (free of authoritarian, totalizing regimes) and that no one is complicit in silencing anyone else. This is a 'free market' of storytelling, postmodern clearly in Frank's terms insofar as a multiplicity of voices proliferate, but essentially a state in which narrative has been deregulated: a democracy of wounded healers! We are all now authors of our own lives:

> In stories, the teller not only recovers her voice; she becomes a witness to the conditions that rob others of their voices ... Those who have been objects of others' reports are now telling their own stories. As they do so, they define the ethic of our times: an ethic of voice, affording each a right to speak her own truth, in her own words. (Ibid.: xii–xiii)

Here, we see again Frank's characterization of postmodernity as the culmination of personal responsibility to tell one's stories; but note also the language of 'robbery' and 'recovery'. Is there a primal state of innocence in which everyone is the author and agent of their story, only to have it subsequently distorted or misappropriated? If so, what robs us of that capacity to relate our lives? Whatever that may be, it is clear that the finding of one's own voice occurs not if, but *'when* the capacity for telling one's own story is reclaimed' (ibid.: 7, my emphasis).

By stressing the narrative as the epitome of self-actualized agency, Frank glosses over issues of power and difference in the construction of bodies, stories, suffering and recovery. What of those who have a story, manifest in bodily distress, and yet who cannot speak for lack of an audience, or who are constrained not merely for want of listeners but by virtue of altogether more intractable factors? Some bodies may be legitimate groundings of the kind of personal agency suggested by Frank's process; but others are denied any realization of personal autonomy, subjectivity or moral authority. It seems inadequate therefore simply to follow Frank's logic without also asking how some bodies become constituted as bearing the credibility to be classed as fully human, liable to be heard into speech; and other bodies still have to struggle to gain any kind of hearing.

Despite Frank's careful gender-inclusive language, and his use of Audre Lorde's *Cancer Journals* as one of his source texts, Frank's narratives are implicitly gendered and racialized. Gender and race are both systems of social relations, founded on power and difference, in which representations of the body are fundamental. Gender oppression and racism both become embodied in quasi-scientific discourses which reduce complex biological factors to deterministic processes and which feed representations of women, indigenous and Black peoples as inherently more 'animalistic' or 'closer to nature' than white males.[7] Such 'scientific' evidence must be subject to the hermeneutics of suspicion and exposed as perennial pieces

---

7 For a critique of the deterministic and reductionist tendencies in sociology, see Lewontin *et al.* (1984).

of rhetoric by which the powerful exclude subordinates from full humanity and participation. Physical coercion, dispossession of rights, enforced
segregation and other forms of bodily control are crucial tools of gendered and racialized regimes (Turner, 1984; Foucault, 1977). The power
to resist such representations (in their widest forms: as discourse, as portrayals and as control of physical and political space) and to construct
alternative models of identity and self-representation is a critical element
of Black and feminist political and theoretical empowerment (see Lorde,
1984). However, as such movements testify, it is not achieved without
significant struggle, often against considerable resistance.

Systems of hierarchy and exclusion also manifest themselves in the
differential occupation of bodily space, in physical violation, unwanted
touch or gaze. Iris Young argues that gender relations in particular are
enacted within bodily space; women's experience of themselves as embodied is often one of confinement and restriction, not of personal agency. It
is not simply illness that 'robs' women of ourselves; we may never fully
come into self-possession in the first place:

> Insofar as we learn to live out our existence in accordance with the
> definition that patriarchal culture assigns to us, we are physically in-
> hibited, confined, positioned, and objectified. As lived bodies we are
> not open and unambiguous transcendences that move out to master a
> world that belongs to us, a world constituted by our own intentions
> and projections. (Young, 1990: 153)

The experiences of the comfort women of Korea serve as a graphic example of the silencing of gendered and racialized bodies. The bodies (and
minds) of the comfort women continue to bear the scars of what Davis
characterizes as 'one of the most extreme expressions of territorial, ethnic, and gender domination resulting from the masculine abuse of power,
domination [sic], and aggression documented in the twentieth century'
(L. K. Davis, 1994: 236). Their experience gives graphic detail to the way
in which the structural forces of poverty, colonialism, racism and sexism
find material and specific expression in the bodily abuse of women and
children.[8]

But why has it taken so long for the stories of the comfort women to be
told; and why is it only now that their sufferings have been given voice?
The answers to these questions suggest that Frank's analysis fails to take
sufficient account of the circumstances under which bodily narratives
are acknowledged and legitimated, and the resistances which often circumscribe the wounded storyteller: of denial, collusion and self-interest.
Frank does not see that the dichotomy between 'disease' and 'illness' is

---

8 An analysis pursued in greater detail by Brock and Thistlethwaite (1996).

not the only locus of dispossession, and the silencing wrought by the patient's powerlessness at the hands of medical attention is paralleled by other forms of objectification and exclusion.

Why could these women not transform their story from one of 'chaos' to 'quest'? Until the campaign for reparations was launched, most former comfort women suffered unnoticed, often disowned by their families, living in poverty and suffering chronic illness as a result of their ordeal (Buckley, 1994: 171–2; Chung, 1997: 2–3). Strong structural factors were at work which created a culture of silence. Stories are always given voice within a political context; we might say that cultural factors predisposed the comfort women to a life of 'abjection' because their experiences, inscribed upon their suffering bodies, transgressed too many cultural taboos for their society to tolerate. Confucianism and Calvinist Christianity in Korea contribute towards patterns of social order and social interactions built upon elaborate observations of honour, shame and social status. Women are still regarded as the property of their fathers prior to marriage and of their husbands afterwards: so for a woman to be 'defiled' sexually casts her as damaged goods, with dire consequences for the honour of her family (Chung, 1997).

Religious beliefs, institutions and practices sacralize and perpetuate gender hierarchy by sanctioning dualistic metaphysics in which women are associated with nature, the body and matter, while men are depicted as closer to the world of the spirit and the intellect. In their examination of the religious and theological roots of the sex industry in South-East Asia, Rita Brock and Susan Thistlethwaite suggest that Confucianism, Christianity and Buddhism perpetuate powerful cultural and ideological motifs which foster the subordinate and exploited status of women in this region. These religious systems emphasize the symbolic association of women with the body, which is regarded negatively as an obstacle to spiritual enlightenment, thereby enclosing women in the realm of the profane, and sanctioning the objectification of women as lesser forms of humanity (Brock and Thistlethwaite, 1996: 90–1). This suggests that religious images play a powerful role in shaping gender and racial representations which, judging from the experiences of the comfort women, served as a powerful inhibiting factor to women's achieving equal status as wounded storytellers.

The true nature of the abuse of the comfort women was also obscured by a refusal to sanction the seriousness of the systematic rapes which they had to endure. Recent work on violence against women has emphasized that it is a phenomenon not committed only by exceptionally pathological individuals, but is something likely to be perpetrated by 'normal', often respectable and responsible, men (see Poling, 1991). Similarly, the campaign for an official recognition of the existence of the comfort women insisted that the rapes were not spontaneous acts of cruelty by sadistic men, or even the excesses of ill-disciplined troops; quite the contrary. It was a systematically sanctioned programme to ensure soldiers did not contract venereal disease and to prevent the occupying forces from consorting with the local population (Chung, 1997: 2–3).

Thus, the feminist-inspired campaigns had to overcome the reticence of the comfort women – many of whom sought to repress the trauma of their experiences – and the culture of shame which surrounded the women's 'going public'. The comfort women faced resistance to their efforts to name their experiences as violence to body and mind, and to acknowledge the physiological and psychological effects felt in the present as manifestations of a systematic and calculated programme in the past. The culture of denial prevented the comfort women from being able to claim their status as active participants in the hostilities. But the telling forth of their stories as casualties of war could not take place until they were properly named as legitimate combatants; only then could they begin to relate their narratives. For years, therefore, the comfort women were politically and institutionally invisible; but the healing narrative could not be told while their very existence was denied. The first step was therefore visibility.[9]

Here are stories of bodily confinement, abuse and suffering which have been silenced for a lifetime, only now to be told, and heard. The effects of totalitarian political rule and militarism may be seen, inscribed on the bodies of such women; but, in a sense, these bodies also still bear the scars of subsequent years of denial. Bringing to light such testimony required more than the presence of a sympathetic fellow-sufferer: major cultural shifts had to occur. Political movements had to argue for the legitimacy of these women's bodies as appropriate speakers and actors of their pain. Much of that was to do with reconfiguring women's status and giving them the right to speak for themselves, and challenging a patriarchal and racist culture which denied them justice.

Power and difference do not therefore disappear in postmodernity, although their effects and traces may become more diffuse. But we cannot simply rest the emergence of the wounded storyteller on personal responsibility, without looking at the ways in which some narratives are geared actually to the reinforcement of such relationships of inequality. We can be complicit in some power relations while victimized ourselves by others; and while Frank dissolves the boundary of health/sickness, he is less perceptive on the dichotomies of power/powerlessness. Nor is he

---

9 The Korean-American journalist Yunghi Kim has been instrumental in bringing the story of the comfort women to public attention via a series of photographs. The visual nature of her intervention underlines the importance of making the bodies of the comfort women tangible and real amid the political and familial denial. Kim says: 'The most important thing the pictures did was give these women a face, show them as real people' (Lacey and Kim, 25 May 1997).

alert to the possibility that the 'fellowship' of wounded storytellers may still be divided along the fault-lines of power and difference.

I suspect that Frank's inability to accommodate such dynamics, and his gender-blindness in particular, may be traced back to his characterization of the 'chaos' narrative. He unconsciously attributes entrapment in such chaos in a way that contains within it unexamined gender representations. If Frank's depiction of 'chaos' is examined through psychoanalytic, especially Lacanian, eyes, it is possible to identify the echoes of a long-standing tradition that depicts women as inherently chaotic, silenced and voiceless:

> Hearing is difficult not only because listeners have trouble facing what is being said as a possibility or reality in their own lives. Hearing is also difficult because the chaos narrative is probably the most embodied form of story. If chaos stories are told on the edges of a wound they are also told on the edges of speech. Ultimately, chaos is told in the silences that speech cannot penetrate or illuminate. The chaos narrative is always beyond speech, and thus it is what is always lacking in speech. Chaos is what can never be told; it is the hole in the telling. (Frank, 1995: 101–2)

The chaos story seems to adopt a Lacanian feminized subject position in Frank's analysis: associated with embodiment; unrealized in, and marginal to, speech (and therefore culture); the lack, or hole; it is enigma, mystery and 'Other' to its hearers (who occupy the normal world of privileged speakers); these chaotic bodies/stories cannot be 'penetrated' or rendered coherent by the Phallic order which only acknowledges those who can conform to its particular bodily/linguistic economy. We can only conclude that the chaos story resembles the Imaginary world beyond patriarchal speech, space and time: as Frank remarks, chaos narratives have no flow, no future, present or past to structure them (ibid.: 108). To the mainstream world, chaos narratives comprise 'vulnerability, futility, and impotence' (ibid.: 101): much as the patriarchal symbolic characterizes women's incoherence and invisibility due to their incidental relationship to the Phallus as universal signifier.

Within Lacanian psychoanalysis, sexed identity is contingent upon entry into culture designated as the structure of language ordered around the privileged signifier of the Phallus. Woman's sexed identity is predicated upon lack of such anatomical/linguistic privilege. She is relegated to non-being – by virtue of being non-male – a characterization that can be traced back to Freud's theories of the castration complex, in which the female child discovers the absent penis as a fateful affliction, a 'punishment personal to herself, a 'scar', a 'wound to her narcissism' (Freud, 1986 [1925]: 407).

Lacan's analysis of woman's absolute silence and invisibility under the Law of the Father should serve as a warning, as it does to his one-time disciple and critic Luce Irigaray. For Irigaray, feminist politics founded on appeals to the common humanity of women and men rest on presuppositions about human nature which frequently, on closer scrutiny, are implicitly those of male human nature. Woman can only glimpse the void of her absence, enclosed in phallogocentric constructions. Irigaray is therefore critical of those varieties of feminist politics which locate women's emancipation in terms of their equality with men; this simply condemns them to conformity to androcentric standards (Irigaray, 1998: 198–214). Instead, if women's representation as 'Other' within the deep symbolic of patriarchy is fundamental, then it must be radically remade into a truly woman-centred subjectivity – and ethics – founded on the sexual specificity of women.

Irigaray's representation of embodiment is not a literal or essentialist reading. Rather, she is practising a 'poesis' of the body: a creative rendition which is actually trying to recreate the very terms of representation themselves. One of her objectives is to subvert the terminology of 'wound', 'lack' and 'hole' as appropriate characterizations of women's subjectivity. However, this process of remaking goes beyond metaphor or literary device: her insistence on the real, sexuate body is an affirmation of the material bedrock of women's identity. Her poesis of the body is a subversion of phallogocentric representations of women's embodiment; whereas patriarchy portrays women as deficiency and blankness, Irigaray's celebration of the body is an assertion of women's Being – but on terms of her own making (see Irigaray, 1985; Stockton, 1994).

Rosi Braidotti has championed an interpretation of Irigaray as articulating a uniquely feminine symbolic. In referring to Irigaray's notion of the body as 'threshold of transcendence' (Braidotti, 1994a: 184), I take Braidotti to be hinting at the body as a liminal thing, an inhabitant of indeterminacy and margins, transitory and fluid; and it underlines Irigaray's insistence that a renewed feminist symbolic is both morphological and theological/metaphysical. It can neither be reduced to discourse nor to biology.[10] For without addressing the entrenched symbolic of sexual difference, it will be impossible to reconfigure questions of identity and sexuality. The subject must be linked to the sexed body, because this is the foundation of women's real, lived experience, representing the lack of reciprocity in the symbolic order of patriarchy; but it also serves as the site of an alternative symbolic founded on bodily pleasures, unspeakable

---

10 Just as Irigaray insists on the liminality of bodiliness, so too I detect similar strains in Donna Haraway's work. Her emphasis on the future of feminist strategy via the artful manipulation of new technologies tells us that it is less to the essence of bodies and rather to their boundaries that we must attend (Haraway, 1991 – bodily practice is dynamic and contextual, but of course always already material).

and irreducible to the monolithic order of the Phallus. But because this representation of (embodied) feminine subjectivity is not available within the prevailing discourse, such an alternative is necessarily utopian and teleological:

> Women are alienated not from some past body they have known but from a future body owed to them. These are bodies women have not yet been allowed to see, to fashion, or to listen for, even though these bodies already resist their dominant constructions, particularly where these bodies appear as holes in the dominant Symbolic. (Stockton, 1994: 28)

Such a vision exists in the repressed and unvoiced arena of the female body; but not as hole or void, but more appropriately, as sacred space. Women do not become divine by abandoning their bodies; rather, the sexual body is caught up into the Divine: 'spiritual becoming and corporeal becoming are inseparable' (Irigaray, 1998: 203). The material and the transcendent are undivided.

This turn to theology and metaphysics is not a predictable association of women with idealized spirituality but a means to convey the manner in which the Divine represents a horizon of incompleteness and becoming – a telos – in which all human essences remain unfinished and unfixed. Is Irigaray's evocation of 'the divine' thus an ultimate deferral of essentialism; not a projection of human finitude onto the Divine (cf. Feuerbach) but an acknowledgement that no representation of the mystery that is human identity is ever complete?

> Love of God has nothing moral in and of itself. It merely shows the way. It is the incentive for a more perfect becoming. It marks the horizon between the more past and the more future, the more passive and the more active – permanent and always in tension. God forces us to do nothing except become. The only task, the only obligation laid upon us is: to become divine men and women, to become perfectly, to refuse to allow parts of ourselves to shrivel and die that have the potential for growth and fulfilment. (Irigaray, 1993b: 68–9)

Thus Irigaray argues that women must necessarily reclaim their relationship to the Divine, and to regard the horizon of divinity as an essential element to their own becoming. Irigaray elaborates on the Lacanian notion that 'the feminine' is inconceivable in positive terms, but only as 'deficiency or atrophy' (Irigaray, 1985: 61). But not only does patriarchy construct femininity as the 'Other' in order to define and bolster normative masculinity, it also conceptualizes God as the 'guarantor' of masculine subjectivity. 'Man can exist because God helps him to define his gender (genre), helps him orientate his finiteness by reference to infinity' (Irigaray, 1993b: 61). God as self-sufficient, immutable, omniscient and non-material serves as the perfect idealized Other to masculine identity. This God as a projection of patriarchal desires must be distant and distinct from man in order to function as a perfect ideal. The existing sexual symbolic depends on a radical dualism between man/God and man/woman in order that the latter element of each pair can function as the 'Other' to masculine identity. When Irigaray reconceives the notion of Divine, she does not simply duplicate the schism between man and God. Her notion of transcendence is very different: the Divine is continuous, even intimate with, the human, rather than abstracted and distant. But Irigaray's notion of divinity proceeds from the encounter between man and woman: as sexually distinctive beings, certainly, but as co-equal subjects whose discovery of one another provokes wonder. This is necessarily a bodily, sexuate – but debateably still a (hetero)sexual – encounter, because Irigaray insists that it is in and through bodily practice, sexually differentiated, that the beginnings of such perfect community are founded. But this is grounded in the realization of both the integrity (wholeness) and potential of the other: they are precisely not alike. Thus, Braidotti's idea of the body as 'threshold' is so apposite: 'Where the borders of the body are wed in an embrace that transcends all limits ... each one discovers the self in that experience which is inexpressible yet forms the supple grounding of life and language. For this, "God" is necessary, or a love so attentive that it is Divine' (Irigaray, 1993c: 18–19).

So transcendence is not to be interpreted as other-wordly, or disembodied, but rather the recognition of the mystery at the heart of human encounter. Hence Irigaray's term, 'sensible transcendental': 'A birth into a transcendence, that of the other, still in the world of the senses ("sensible") still physical and carnal, and already spiritual' (ibid.: 129).

Susan Parsons, significantly, nominates Irigaray's work as in part a project to reconfigure the *imago Dei* in terms that value and accommodate women (Parsons, 1996: 234). Yet Irigaray's characterization is also profoundly Christocentric, and one which consciously uses the crucified Christ on the cross as the representation of Divine solidarity with the silenced and suffering women. The 'wounds' of women's lack (and perhaps their material oppression?) now become symbolic of Divine becoming in their equation with the lacerated, bleeding body of Christ on the cross (Irigaray, 1974: 200). Irigaray thus reappropriates the derogatory metaphor of hole, gash or wound into a motif of Divine disclosure.

It is intriguing to see that religious and theological language peppers the work of both Frank and Irigaray, and how the figure of God informs their respective ethical sensibilities. For example, Frank relates the story of Jacob wrestling with the angel (Genesis 32.22–32) to illustrate the value of the heroic 'quest' narrative. The wound to Jacob's hip is evidence of the fact that the story cannot be told independent of the (brokenness of the) body. Jacob pits his body against the angel and is wounded – lastingly. Without those marks of engagement and suffering he cannot enter into a new phase marked by the assumption of a new name – Israel. However, Jacob's travail also entails wrestling with God:

> Jacob's story is about the complexity of resistance to *what readers of the story can only call God*. God is the mystery of what Jacob wrestles with. This mystery is not named until the end of the story ... Jacob's impulse toward what is retrospectively known as God is curiously expressed as resistance: Jacob contests the divine. (Frank, 1995: 181, my emphasis)

By wrestling, resisting and being vulnerable to a wound, Jacob encounters God and finds himself to have been on holy ground; but it is the embodied immanence of the human wrestling that sanctifies the ground: 'resistance is never worked out once and for all; the self must continue to wrestle and continue to be wounded in order to rediscover the ground it now stands on as sacred. To be is to wrestle with God' (ibid.: 182).

Irigaray's account takes the religious and metaphysical references which exist in the margins of Frank's text and gives them voice. However, the 'wound' which for Frank signifies excess of embodiment unrationalized by speech, and therefore unrepresentable, is precisely the genesis of Irigaray's characterization of bodily experience which also becomes an avenue of Divine disclosure. The wounds of Frank's narrative of chaos attain new value in Irigaray's telling: they are analogous to women's 'holes', but are consecrated as sacred epiphanies. They now function more as stigmata which may designate unspeakable suffering within conventional logic, but within Irigaray's alternative symbolic, wounds are compared to the 'lips' (a reference to women's labia which displaces imagery of women's vulva as gash or hole) which become the source of an alternative poesis of desire and empowerment.

For Irigaray, the wound is the hole in patriarchal discourse, which both silences women (designated 'lacking') and becomes the sacrament of Divine becoming (the Passion of Christ identifies with the wounds of women). Whereas Frank uses the figure of the 'hero' as his mythic ideal (an image which, once more, privileges the male character in myth and legend), Irigaray's model for the wounded healer may best be that of 'abject Other': one who assumes the realm of liminality, silence and effacement in order to bear the stigmata of suffering on her body with pride and not shame.

We appear, therefore, to have two avenues for an ethics of the body, which we might call respectively Frank's 'narrative' and Irigaray's 'poesis'. While Frank concentrates on 'narratives' of the body, some of which record the discovery of wonder and mystery – 'to what readers of the story can only call God' (ibid.: 181) – Irigaray prefers 'poesis': a radical reshaping of the metaphysical and theological presuppositions upon which women ground their concepts of self, Other, relationality, community – and ethics.

Irigaray reshapes the symbolic of bodily representation to counter women's invisibility. She also argues that women must radically rework religious symbolic – starting with bodies – in order to articulate new forms of moral community. At the heart of this theological project is the identification of women's 'wounded' status – their lack of phallic privilege barring them from full participation in the narrative order of ethical storytelling, relegating them to the chaotic imaginary. But by reappropriating the 'chaotic' wound as the Passion of Christ, Irigaray conjures up the repressed sacred of modernity and places it not at the margins but at the centre of her revised ethics of sexual difference. Thus, suffering bodies – but bodies as the 'threshold of the Divine' – are the agents by which women retrieve their stories and transform the 'wounds' and 'holes' of patriarchal discourse into an empowering, and moral, narrative. 'Is not God the name and the place that holds the promise of a new chapter in history and that also denies this can happen? Still invisible? Still to be discovered? To be incarnated? Arch-ancient and forever future' (Irigaray, 1993b: 72).

Part Three

THEOLOGY AND PRACTICE

10

PASTORAL THEOLOGY: 'THERAPY', 'MISSION' OR 'LIBERATION'?[1]

In a book entitled *The Christian Pastor and the Working Church*, published in 1898, Washington Gladden, a leading figure in the Social Gospel movement, attempts a definition of the field of pastoral theology. Gladden's characterization of pastoral theology as the study of the work of the minister and the management of the Church is typical of many definitions, both historical and contemporary:

> This book is intended to cover the field of what is known as pastoral theology. The technical phrase is not well chosen: theology, by any proper sense of the word is not connoted by it. It deals with the work of the Christian pastor and the Christian church. Its subject is applied Christianity. (Gladden, 1898: v)

Pastoral theology ever since has been dismissed as the Cinderella of theological studies, occupying itself with the pragmatic and relatively untaxing practicalities of 'applied Christianity'. Its uncertain position in the academy may not be helped by the eclectic mixture of academic theologians, theological college tutors, pastoral counsellors, educationalists, health care chaplains and church advisors on social responsibility, urban ministry or international affairs that make up its constituency in the UK. Certainly such interdisciplinarity does impart a vigour and richness to discussion; but pastoral theology is, at least in academic circles, vulnerable to charges that it lacks a clear epistemological or theoretical focus.

---

1 This chapter has been slightly adapted from the article that originally appeared in *The Scottish Journal of Theology* (1995).

We can date the emergence of pastoral theology in the modern era with the various projects to categorize the study of theology that took place in German seminaries from the seventeenth century. The most significant of these is found in the work of Friedrich Schleiermacher (1768–1834). Schleiermacher's theological encyclopedia, *A Brief Outline on the Study of Theology*, first published in 1811 (Schleiermacher, 1966 [1811]), identifies three branches of theology: 'philosophical' (apologetics, polemics, or 'the idea of Christianity'); 'historical' (dogmatics, church history, exegetical theology: Christianity as it has been manifested historically); and 'practical' theology (homiletics, liturgy, church government, pastoral care and Christian education).

All the various sub-disciplines of theology find a scientific unity in their status as, in Schleiermacher's words,

> an assemblage of scientific elements which belong together not because they form a constituent part of the organization of the sciences, as though by some necessity arising out of the notion of science itself, but only insofar as they are requisite for carrying out a practical task. (Schleiermacher, 1966 [1811]: 19)

For Schleiermacher, all three branches of theology share a common focus, in providing the resources for the exercise of church leadership and the practice of the Church. The congregational reality serves as the validating norm for Christian theology. Theological discourse is thus related to practical ministry, validated ultimately not by reference to philosophical verities but to ecclesial reality and activity. Pastoral theology is therefore the theory of collective pastoral practice; its technical objectives to perfect and maintain the life of the church (Burkhart, 1983).

It is important to note in passing that there has been disagreement over the real implications of Schleiermacher's categorization: is he emphasizing the activities of ordained ministry in the service of the Church, or focusing on the entire gathered community? Is he actually conceiving of practical theology as an applied or primary discipline? In practice, his successors have tended to emphasize the former of each of those pairs. From the beginning of the modern era, practical theology was equated with the sphere of Christian ministry, and designated as the application of systematic and doctrinal teaching. The notion of practical theology in the service of congregational reality was effectively narrowed into what Edward Farley has famously termed 'the clerical paradigm' (Farley, 1983a: 85); and the wider ecclesial pursuits of liturgy, Christian formation, preaching, exegesis and evangelism have become specialist areas of expertise, estranged from the discipline of 'pastoral studies' as focused upon personal care, direction and guidance. So the unity of all these tasks for Schleiermacher within the general practice of church life – in its historical and contemporary contexts – was gradually eclipsed (Farley, 1983b; Burck and Hunter, 1990). Practical and pastoral theology was attenuated into a collection of specialist disciplines, with a consequent diminution of theological significance.

So from the beginning, there has been a tension within the self-understanding of pastoral theology: is it concerned with the specifically clerical or the generally ecclesial; should it focus on the one-to-one context of care and counselling or the wider activities of liturgy, social action and Christian formation; and what is the relative status of disciplinary resources – from biblical studies to the modern psychologies – in informing pastoral practice? But such debates carry deeper considerations. These concern the nature of the pastoral task, its aims and objectives; the guiding metaphors which convey the dynamics of giving and receiving care; the predominant notions of expertise and authority which shape our image of the pastoral agent; and the sources and norms – secular and theological – of pastoral activity, indeed of all Christian action.

Pastoral theology in the modern era is therefore characterized by a whole variety of implicit understandings of, and answers to, these questions. In this chapter, I want to identify three such versions that I believe have been especially influential and continue to shape contemporary practice and debate. All three tell a particular story about the nature of pastoral care, about the dynamics of giving and receiving care, about the authoritative resources used to inform Christian action, and about the ultimate aims and ends to which such activities are believed to be directed. I also want to say that they all serve as implicit witnesses to particular theological narratives. Far from being an applied and unreflective discipline, therefore, pastoral literature contains a wealth of theological understandings about the ways in which suffering humanity may be offered deliverance and healing from their distress; visions of human destiny and flourishing; and maybe even occasional glimpses of the nature and will of Divine activity in the midst of human experience. All three of my types – of pastoral theology as therapy, mission and liberation – are therefore implicitly value-laden, with the capacity both to disclose ultimate commitments and to embody them in practice. For reasons of limited time, all my models are necessarily idealized constructs, or ideal types; but I hope also to stress that they all involve real figures and emerge from actual historical contexts.[2]

I would like to suggest that all three contain important insights and help us understand the historical and contemporary nature of pastoral theology. However, I will conclude by asking whether we need, if not a fourth model, then an overarching framework. Pastoral theology

---

2 John Patton identifies three governing paradigms for pastoral care and counselling: classical, clinical and communal–contextual (Patton, 1993).

needs to point us to the theological values at the heart of purposeful and transformative action – to refuse a distinction between words and deeds, faith and action. It is amid the necessarily unsystematic character of human action and relationships, that we glimpse the essentially *theological* nature of human practical wisdom. The lesson we can learn from this study is that all theology is ultimately *practical* (and contextual) theology, rooted in human experience and informing faithful and transformative practice.

Therapy

We cannot consider any of our models independently of their social and historical context, and the *therapeutic* model is no exception. It is frequently equated with the dominance of pastoral counselling in Christian ministry; but it emerged from a complex network of relationships, personalities and cultural trends. It is firmly rooted in the growth of the modern psychologies in North America and Britain from the end of the nineteenth century. Historically, there were two strands to this: the European analytic tradition – one represented by Sigmund Freud, Carl Jung and Alfred Adler – and another by the North American empirical and pragmatic tradition, associated especially with William James and John Dewey (Lyall, 1995: ch. 1). There is no denying the enormous energy and innovation that the adoption of the modern psychologies effected among the caring and medical professions – not least within the practice of Christian ministry, despite Freud's celebrated antipathy towards religion (Fuller, 1986; Holifield, 1983).

One of the earliest alliances between Christian ministers and psychiatrists and medical practitioners was the 'Emmanuel Movement' in Boston, USA at the start of the twentieth century. The Revd Elwood Worcester, minister of Emmanuel Presbyterian Church, saw the modern psychologies as a tremendous resource for the enhancement of Christian ministry. He believed that the unconscious was a powerful regulating force in human personality and was a means by which moral growth could be effected. The work of the so-called 'religion and health' movement grew from there, bringing together psychiatrists, physicians, clergy, theologians and health care chaplains – sometimes in specialist units for care and counselling, sometimes in the training of clergy, other times in theological discussions and seminars.

An early and decisive factor in the establishment and consolidation of the therapeutic paradigm was its assimilation into theological colleges and seminaries. In 1925, Richard Cabot, patrician New Englander, Unitarian, medical physician, had come up with a proposal for a 'clinical year' for divinity students similar to that of medical training. Cabot teamed up with a Presbyterian minister, working as a hospital chaplain, called Anton Boisen to formulate a scheme of training known as Clinical Pastoral Education. The student would carefully record the details of a visit or pastoral conversation and reflect on it within a tutorial setting. Cabot and Boisen believed that so-called 'verbatim' accounts of pastoral encounters were akin to written texts in their potential for interpretation. By focusing on the 'living human document' of the pastoral interview, valuable insights could be gained into the dynamics of the therapeutic process and of pastoral ministry itself (Stokes, 1985).

However, Clinical Pastoral Education was from the start a divided movement; in fact the movement split in the 1930s, with Boisen going to Chicago and Cabot remaining in New England. It is clear that much of the schism resulted from the different personalities and approaches of its two founders. Cabot regarded CPE as a valuable technical tool, instrumental in furnishing trainee medical practitioners and clergy with competence and expertise. He was deeply suspicious of the emerging profession of psychiatry, believing that all mental illness was organic in origin. Cabot's scepticism towards psychoanalytic perspectives which located mental disorders in the patient's unconscious contrasted with Boisen's conviction that mental illness was not organic but psychodynamic – even symptomatic of spiritual malaise and dislocation (Snyder, 1968).

It is impossible to regard Boisen's opinions on this matter as unaffected by his own life-experience. For his own adult life was characterized by intermittent periods of severe mental breakdown, including a psychotic crisis that hospitalized him for nearly a year at the age of 44. Metaphor has long been a powerful vehicle within pastoral theology; and perhaps we can see Boisen as the archetype of Henri Nouwen's 'wounded healer'. Vulnerable and troubled though Boisen was, upon recovery from his bouts of depression he would resume his work as a hospital chaplain, but renewed – paradoxically – by the insights afforded through his own disability. Such unique and privileged insight convinced him that recording and reflecting upon the living human document of his own life was nothing less than an encounter with the deepest dynamics of human suffering and salvation (Hall, 1968; Nouwen, 1968).

Within a generation of its beginnings, the therapeutic model was in the ascendancy, and was to prove equally influential for another generation. In New York, a small group of psychoanalysts, physicians, psychiatrists, pastoral tutors, theologians and clergy met regularly between 1942 and 1945 to discuss a shared interest in the dialogue between religion and medicine, especially the modern psychologies and psychotherapies (Holifield, 1983: 231–49). Among the members was Paul Tillich, who regarded the modern psychologies as providential. He believed they were enabling contemporary culture to explore and articulate its deepest anxieties and existential problems to which theology could respond with renewed clarity and purpose. Other members of that group included those who were to become the leading figures in pastoral theology, counselling, psychology and theology over the next 30 years: Seward Hiltner, Hannah Tillich, Eric Erikson, Rollo May and Carl Rogers. As writers and practitioners, these people popularized forms of Christian care closely modelled on the dynamics of therapeutic practice, and advanced perspectives on human personality founded on varying degrees of psychology and theology in synthesis.

Carl Rogers is perhaps the best-known of this generation of popularizers of psychotherapy and counselling (Rogers, 1942; 1951; 1961). Yet as well as being a consistent advocate of humanistic psychotherapy, his career and work also illustrates the interconnectedness of religion and psychology within the therapeutic paradigm. Rogers is perhaps best known for his advocacy of 'non-directive' counselling, forged within a generally humanistic perspective that regards self-actualization as the most reliable pattern of human development. This seems to reflect a particularly Enlightenment commitment to the powers of human reason being the most authentic and progressive source of truth and emancipation; and in this respect we might see Rogers as a highly secular exponent of existentialist therapy. In this respect, Rogerian counselling, as exemplary of the values informing the ascendancy of the therapeutic in pastoral theology, has provoked fierce controversy. Opinion is divided as to whether such principles represent the secular equivalent of Christian love and forgiveness; or whether they have been responsible for eclipsing Christian traditions of pastoral discipline and moral guidance and evacuating pastoral activity of any ethical or normative content whatsoever.

Such criticism of the therapeutic model often therefore accuses it of submitting to the 'cheap grace' of the secular psychotherapies: of becoming so assimilated into the secular humanist world-view that it abandons any distinctive Christian perspective. This may have been true in some of the more popular forms; but such an accusation does not stand up to closer scrutiny.

Undoubtedly, the therapeutic paradigm owes a great deal to the pressures of secularization, of the loss of clear roles and status for the Church and the temptation to adopt new caring techniques that offered a safe rationale. But the question is whether this represents an abandonment of theological values or merely their transposition: of attempting to discern the signs of the times within the therapeutic movements, and use their best insights for the renewal of pastoral care. After all, Rogerian therapy was received by many Christian ministers as an attractive antidote to theological traditions that over-stressed human sinfulness, self-abnegation and Divine judgement. The power of 'unconditional positive regard', and the absolute freedom of the client to find paths of growth and forgiveness via the therapeutic relationship, all appeared to resonate with Christian values, while articulating them in terms accessible to modern culture. A leading figure in British client-centred therapy, Brian Thorne, has staunchly advanced this view, and argues that person-centred counselling is profoundly theological, characterizing it in a recent essay as a 'spiritual discipline' (Thorne, 2007).

Some commentators go further, to argue that there is a much greater continuity between Rogers' style of therapy and older Christian understandings of the person. For a start there is Rogers' own Presbyterian background, and the fact that many Christian ministers and counsellors saw Rogers' advocacy of 'unconditional positive regard' as at the very least a valuable corrective to the moralistic admonition that often passed for Christian pastoral guidance. Robert Fuller argues that Rogers owes much more than is recognized to an earlier religious tradition in which the healing process of pastoral counselling is not merely humanistic authentication but spiritual fulfilment (Fuller, 1986:159–72). The human unconscious is not self-sufficient but an avenue between the individual and a higher, possibly transcendent, realm. In this, Fuller places Rogers in a tradition of theological engagement with the human psyche that dates back to the Puritan Divines:

> Like Jonathan Edwards, Ralph Waldo Emerson, and William James, Rogers holds that authentic human action is a direct function of an inward identification with Being itself. According to the Rogerian notion of authenticity ... by opening ourselves to the raw impressions of nature we can take hold of the spiritual principle of things. Thus 'psychological congruence' is to Rogers what 'consent to Being in general' was to Edwards, 'Divine influx' to Emerson, and incursions from the 'subliminal self' to James. All point to the psychological process whereby individuals can apprehend, and become inwardly connected to, an immanent divinity. (Fuller, 1986: 170)

It may be possible to argue, against the critics, therefore, that there is less discontinuity between humanistic psychology and earlier theologians such as Edwards or even Schleiermacher, who regarded one's inner reality and disposition as a reflection of and pathway to the transcendent. Thus Rogers' popularity within Christian pastoral counselling and his status as axiomatic of the therapeutic model in pastoral theology is upheld as the modern fulfilment of earlier religious traditions rather than their antithesis.

However, some of the other emphases of pastoral care as therapy may need to be questioned. Some critics have attacked the popularity and proliferation of pastoral counselling as representing an implicit overcommitment to *crisis ministry*, to curative and pathological patterns at the expense of preventative or developmental interventions (Lambourne, 1983; Lyall, 1995: 36–7). This resistance to the therapeutic model as necessarily leading to a medicalization of pastoral care is therefore one of the most contentious issues in contemporary pastoral theology. In addition, criticisms are voiced about the implicit *power relations* within the counselling relationship, especially in some Rogerian models in which it seems to be assumed that inequalities of gender, class and race can somehow be bracketed out of the therapeutic process. But human self-actualization does not take place independently of a social context. While it would be wrong to brand all pastoral counsellors as obsessed with the psychodynamic, individualist and clinical at the expense of a wider social critique, the very focus on the integrity of the person may impede a full consideration of collective and structural dimensions, of issues of cultural difference, and of the necessity of struggles for social justice as well as individual wholeness.

Concern over the ethical consequences of pastoral care and counselling relates not only to its alleged abandonment of traditional patterns of moral guidance, and ideals of Christian perfection, but also to the sense in which the modern psychotherapies were themselves in crisis as to their own values and standards (Crews, 1993). As questions of the abuse of clients, professional ethics and the role of psychotherapy in wider issues of social justice have come more to the fore in the worlds of therapy, so the lingering dissatisfaction within pastoral theology has intensified. Most particularly, these have focused on the extent to which therapy can successfully contain within itself implicit questions of value; and the responsibility of pastors and counsellors in a Christian, or religious context, to establish a clear normative framework for their work:

> Except in some more conservative circles, the Church now primarily seeks to maintain warm relations, communicate acceptance and support, and help confused, depressed, or otherwise broken people regain some initiative and control without paying too much attention to the specific moral or spiritual direction of their lives. (Browning, 1982: 10)

This trend towards locating Christian care – and the discourse of pastoral theology – within a clearer normative framework therefore leads me into my second model: pastoral theology as *mission*, with a corresponding emphasis on the Christian community as the agent of pastoral action.

Mission

Within Protestant traditions, the past 20 years has seen an increasing attentiveness to what Don Browning has termed 'the moral context of pastoral care'. Browning argues for a rearticulation of a clearer moral context to pastoral care – not in any authoritarian sense, but in terms of regarding Christian pastoral care, especially counselling, as the articulation of the core normative principles of Christian life. '[L]ove or communitas are meaningless and formless concepts without a concept of moral norms, judgements and structures' (Browning, 1976: 77). Browning's subsequent work therefore concentrates on his understanding of the discipline as the excavation and interrogation of the activity of the Christian community as embedded in its layers of moral reasoning.

This connects with work by writers such as Stanley Hauerwas who similarly regards the Christian life as the telling and retelling of classic Christian narratives in which the core ethical and exemplary precepts of the gospel are embodied (Hauerwas, 1981). Such a concern may also be traced in the resurgence within North American practical theology of the genre of congregational studies: interdisciplinary, often collaborative, research projects in which the stories, social context, decisions, power structures and 'practical wisdom' of local church congregations are regarded as redolent of faith commitments and corporate truth-claims (Dudley, 1983; Hopewell, 1987).

Such a shift to the communal context of Christian pastoral care, and an emphasis on the life of congregations in Protestant traditions, is matched by a parallel movement within Roman Catholic pastoral theology. It is here in the emphasis on the study of the 'Church in the World' that we see most clearly how pastoral theology as *mission* is closely allied to Roman Catholic moral theology. Traditionally, pastoral and moral theology were engaged with the maintenance and monitoring of the boundaries of the Church. Moral theology was responsible for ruling on the fitness of the individual to receive the sacraments, according to their degree of devotion and penitence; pastoral theology made the link between such moral adjudication with the practice of ministry in terms of the administration of the sacraments of the Mass, confession and absolution (Duffy 1983; 1990; Kinast, 1990).

From the beginning of the twentieth century, therefore, there grew up a greater focus on the pastoral ministry as the 'Church's self-fulfilment in the ever changing situation'. The Second Vatican Council (1962–65) used the pastoral as the central organizing focus of many of its documents: on ecumenism, communication, the liturgy and the ministry (McCarthy, 1990; Brennan, 1967).

Vatican II also brought about a deeper and more inclusive sense of the identity of the Church, which was understood to be less about the inclusion into a strictly sacramental life, and more about the Church in terms of its mission to and calling in the world. The conciliar documents affirm the priesthood of all believers, of the Church as the people of God, of its life and work in dialogue with the contemporary world. The vocation of the laity was to serve as the Church in the world – be that in pastoral care activities, in secular employment, or in the commitment of many individuals and groups to the causes of social justice. The Council effectively understood that if God was at work in the world redeeming God's creation, then to be a Christian was to be actively involved in that task, understood as the building up of the world in truth, justice and love. The layperson 'redeems the world from within ... while the priestly ministry is "chiefly and professedly to the sacred ministry"' (Schuster, 1967: 365).

Pastoral practice – as embodied in the entire life and work of the whole Church – was therefore the living and temporal expression of a wider, universal Body of Christ, conceived as the fulfilment of God's purposes and activities in the world. The theologian Karl Rahner was perhaps the most articulate exponent of this shift in Roman Catholic pastoral theology, and was influential in shaping much of the tenor of the Second Vatican Council. In *Theology of Pastoral Action*, Rahner argues that the Church exists not for itself, but to proclaim and enact the gospel in human society; pastoral practice is the living expression of the Church's mission to the world:

> Pastoral theology deals with the action of the Church. It is pastoral because it engages concrete circumstances, it is theological because it reflects systematically on the nature of the Church and analyses the circumstances which confront the Church today ... The work of pastoral theology begins only when Christians here and now and at a local level incarnate the Church's nature. (Rahner, 1968: 25)

Starting with theologians such as Rahner, therefore, and affirmed by Vatican II, we can see how a theology of the Church in the world assumed centre stage within much Roman Catholic thinking in the second half of this century; and it is this emphasis on the people of God, reflecting on experience, living out the gospel in faith and action, that has shaped their understanding of pastoral theology. All theology is essentially pastoral, for it is driven by the concrete, the immediate and the practical.

The strengths of the missionary model lie in its rooting of pastoral action within the life of the Christian community and the collective ministry of the congregation. It resists the clinical and individualistic tendencies of pastoral counselling; it concentrates on activities of formation and vocation, not simply curing and healing. However, I wonder whether the missionary model restricts its sources and norms too closely to the received wisdom of the tradition. Can the Church prevent a diligent and concerted attention to building up the skills and contributions of the faithful from becoming an unhealthy obsession with the inner workings of the Church? Also, given that its pastoral discipline emerged essentially from the practices of maintaining and demarcating the boundaries of the Church, is there a danger that the interests of the institution and the powerful militate against an open, pluralist, inclusive community?

While the recovery of pastoral discipline may be seen as a vehicle of the cultivation of Christian qualities within the life of the community of faith, it may be used to exert a judgemental and moralistic exclusion of all those who in any way deviate from a particular stereotype of 'good Christian'. 'Community' is a notoriously vague concept; it may express collective solidarity and belonging, but it may also be a metaphor for foreclosure and the abuse of power. 'Mission' therefore raises crucial questions about the boundary between Church and world; and whether a model of pastoral theology can be simultaneously Church-related *and* public and inclusive. The imagery of the Church in the world as temporal expression of a universal Body of Christ may also suggest that the structures and values of the Church are still in some way independent of history, and that human action is merely the outworking of an a priori ordering of faith. Yet this may serve to reinforce the view that contemporary experience should conform to the historical teachings of the magisterium at the expense of being truly responsive to contemporary insights and challenges.

Any model of 'mission' as informing the values of pastoral action must therefore remember its eschatological and not just its ecclesiastical imperatives. The documents of the Second Vatican Council speak of the Church as called to be a prophetic sign of the promise of the Kingdom yet to come; and so the life of communities that proclaim and embody such values must be both gathered *and* outward-looking; faithful *and* prophetic.

Liberation

This leads appropriately into my third model, that of pastoral theology as 'liberation'. There are perhaps three clear strands informing the emergence of this model, deriving from sociological and theological sources.

First, we must consider traditions of Roman Catholic social and ecclesial thinking that were renewed by the emphasis on the pursuit of social justice as an integral part of the Church's proclamation of the gospel throughout the 1960s. The Papal encyclicals of John XXIII and Paul VI display the beginnings of a sharper and more radical social critique (McCarthy, 1990; Baum, 1987). *Gaudium et Spes* (1962) not only affirmed the secular vocation of the laity but placed that in the context of the calling of the 'People of God' in working for peace and justice. *Populorum Progressio* (1967) condemned the global imbalance of trade between what we would now call 'North' and 'South' and focused attention on the massive debt crises of many Third World economies. The process continued with *Laborem Exercens* (1981), teaching that society must recognize reality and legitimacy of struggles of oppressed social groups. Fidelity to the gospel entails solidarity with the marginalized; the 'signs of the times' are to be discerned in the advance of history towards freedom and emancipation (McGovern, 1989).

The second influence is the German political theology of figures such as Jürgen Moltmann, Dorothee Sölle and Johannes Baptist Metz – himself a student of Karl Rahner – in its protest against the 'privatization' of theology (Sölle, 1984; Metz, 1984; Moltmann, 1984; Browning, 1985). Since the Enlightenment, the practice of faith has become ideological: individualistic, existential and domestic. While not wishing to decry the call to individual repentence and faith within the gospels, political theology is unequivocal about the status of the Christian message as 'public proclamation' which must necessarily call the faithful to a life of what Metz characterizes as 'liberty, peace, justice, reconciliation' (Metz, 1969: 114) and which pursues a structural as well as interpersonal agenda of care:

> The Church must mobilize that critical potency that lies in her central tradition of Christian love. Indeed it is not permissible to restrict love to the impersonal sphere of the I-Thou. Nor is it enough to understand love as charitable work within a neighbourhood. We must interpret love, and make it effective, in its societal dimension. This means that love should be the unconditional determination to bring justice, liberty, and peace *to the others*. (Metz, 1969: 117)

Such an insistence upon 'the concrete relation between the Church and the world' (ibid.: 115), and Christians as critical, liberating people of faith, found a ready audience in Catholic social movements emerging from Latin America from the 1950s. The practice of such liberating communities predates liberation theology by a generation; but certainly Vatican II gave the theologians emerging from the base communities permission to articulate their own way of 'doing theology'. Latin American theologians therefore fused two principles. After Marx, they argued that all knowledge reflects and serves particular concrete social interests; and after their own readings of Scripture, they argued that faithful action necessitated a 'preferential option for the poor' (McGovern, 1989). Thus, they argued that theological truth was that body of practical knowledge which authenticated and fuelled such service and justice for the poor. The commission, then, was to restore full humanity, right relation and justice to the oppressed. At its heart was the notion of theology as *orthopraxis* in which the truth of the gospel is measured by its ability to bring life, right relation, justice and full humanity into the world:

> The truth of God-language and of all theological claims is measured not by their correspondence to something eternal but by the fulfilment of its claims in history, by the actual creation of communities of peace, justice and equality. The creation of liberation faith and liberation theo-

logy is practice, or, more specifically, the process of liberation in history. (Welch, 1985: 7)

A recent example of the assimilation of liberationist perspectives into Western pastoral theology is Stephen Pattison's *Pastoral Care and Liberation Theology* (Pattison, 1997). Pattison indicts the discipline, and most pastoral practitioners, as neglectful of any critique of structural and policy dimensions to human need. In an extended case study of mental illness and the practice of health care chaplains in psychiatric institutions, he argues that the overwhelming predominance of the therapeutic approach obscures the real dynamics of mental illness – its origins, diagnosis and treatment. He presents a formidable array of evidence to indicate massive – and ever-widening – inequalities of access and provision in health care, personal social services and welfare benefits. Thus, it is appropriate to think of 'the poor' as constituting a significantly dispossessed class in Britain today, and those who have experienced mental illness, of whatever type or severity, as further disadvantaged and marginalized by the standard of care they receive. Pattison integrates many feminist critiques of the high incidence of mental illness among women, and the role of the Church in reinforcing models of feminine passivity and self-abnegation.

Pattison therefore applies the critique of theology as individualistic and apolitical to pastoral care, seeing it as privatized and ameliorative, failing to identify or act against the underlying dynamics of injustice. A liberation model, argues Pattison, would emphasize the interrelationship between low socio-economic status and ill-health, the comparative power of the medical and psychiatric professions to determine patient treatment and the influence of gender, race and class discrimination in the provision of care and institutional treatment. A pastoral theology concerned to address the exclusion and invisibility of 'the poor' would therefore need to adopt a more interventionist and preventative stance, aiming for justice, addressing structures, critical of power dynamics in caring relationships.[3]

Properly understood, therefore, the liberationist approach to pastoral activity is one in which the people (the poor) are the agents of theological action and reflection. However, I wonder whether it fully succeeds in this task. Too often the adoption of liberation theology in the West is seen simply as a call to politicize the Church – or in Pattison's case, to see the structural and political dimensions of pastoral ministry. The result in Western cultures, where the poor have historically been absent from organized religion, is that the professionals or church pressure groups campaign *on behalf of* the poor through church-related pressure

---

3 For a feminist application of this model, see E. L. Graham, 'The sexual politics of pastoral care' (1993).

groups, rather than grappling with the implications of the challenge of empowerment.

Moreover, the revolutionary spirit of liberation theology rests in its identification of the experiences and interests of those on the 'underside' – be that of the economic order or the mental health system – as the most authentic perspectives against which *praxis*, or value-directed action, is to be judged. It takes seriously the prospect of the experience of the marginalized as theologically authentic, and of true orthodoxy as resting in liberative practice (*orthopraxis*).

Liberation theology tells the story of the power of the poor in history, but it is chastening to remember that we have by some accounts reached 'the end of history' where such utopian and progressive grand narratives have fractured (Forrester, 1994). The nature of the ultimate vision that can possibly inform pastoral praxis in such a fragmented context still remains to be seen. Perhaps what some people have suggested as liberat*ing* theology would more adequately convey the provisional and tentative sense of the future of human history. While faithful praxis may wish to operate within a framework of hopeful anticipation, therefore, we must also resist the doctrines of progress and emancipation that undervalue the tasks of helping one another to live well and truthfully within situations where, frequently, there are no cures and answers. This is the task of the pastor that the early Christians termed 'sustaining' – clearly distinguished from 'curing' (Clebsch and Jaekle, 1964). Once again, however, this reminds us of the eschatological nature of Christian hope. Humanity may be partners with God in God's redemptive activity, but ultimately, human healing and salvation are gifts of God, contingent upon Divine grace.

Each of the three models outlined above reveals implicit understandings of the pastoral task, but they also serve as potential bridges between the pastoral and the theological. Paul Halmos talked about the 'faith of the counsellors' to denote the implicit values of the practitioners and techniques of non-directive counselling (Halmos, 1965); but it is true that truth-claims and metaphors of Divine action imbue all forms of pastoral activity.

The *therapeutic* model, therefore, emphasizes as its key activity the practice of personal care, support and healing. The primary locus of such a model is upon the interpersonal encounter, the intimacies of listening, conversation and solicitous concern. The primary agent of care is characterized as counsellor, skilful guide, solicitous companion; the therapeutic pastoral practitioner owes obvious debt to time-honoured traditions of healer – but of souls instead of bodies. The theological dimensions to this model lie in its emphasis on the implicit values of healing and reconciliation. The interpersonal encounter characterized by unconditional positive regard is thus seen as analogous to the compassion and grace of the

Divine; and skilful listening and guidance is understood as the path to self-acceptance, forgiveness and healing.

The *missionary* model identifies the community of the Church at its centre – whether that is the 'Congregation' of Protestant studies, or the universal Church of the Second Vatican Council. The communal life of the Church is the primary pastoral agent; the activities of baptism, Eucharist and ministry the essential tasks, in that they are corporate liturgical acts in which the processes of initiation and incorporation are effected. Given the emphasis on building up Christian vocation and fellowship, it draws upon ecclesiology, adult education and catechesis to guide its strategy. Theologically, this model might be seen as reflecting values of *koinonia* and *kenosis*; the visible presence of the Church in the world as the present and tangible expression of God's grace; the Church as partner in God's self-giving and costly presence within the world; community as the essential mode of human living in reflection of the Trinitarian fellowship of the Divine.

For the *liberative* model, the objectives of pastoral activity are translated into those of social transformation, of action for justice. The agents of this pastoral activity are, classically, 'the poor'. In contrast to the therapy model, which liberationists characterize as privatised, elitist and individualistic, pastoral practice as liberation takes place in the public, political domain: in medical and other welfare institutions, or via social policy measures, political intervention or maybe community development. The theological language is 'Kingdom'; the imagery that of 'prophet': salvation embraces the entire inhabited universe, not merely disembodied souls. Nor is the gospel to be misused as a consolation in the next world for social injustices in this one.

To describe the concerns of pastoral theology as chiefly those of the pursuit of human wholeness, the actions of the Church in the world, or the realization of justice and equity, therefore, is to capture important dimensions of its disciplinary identity. Yet they find a primary unity in the domain of practice, a focus which is capable of uniting the original vision of Schleiermacher with a liberationist emphasis on *praxis* in which theology is cast as a 'performative' discipline. Such a model defies Washington Gladden's characterization of pastoral theology as devoid of theology, being merely 'applied Christianity'. There is no such division between theory and practice.

Schleiermacher's identification of the practical as the pinnacle or 'crown' of theology suggests that he did not just conceive the relationship as a hierarchy of dogmatic over 'applied' theology, but as something in which all theology is united within the general rubric of ecclesial life. Practice is both the source and application of theological understanding; but even though Schleiermacher was effectively characterizing theology as a form of 'practical wisdom', he and later interpreters were unable to consolidate this into his system. But the notion of 'praxis' enables an emphasis to develop which regards values and truth-claims as meaningful only as they are embodied in practices that are expressive of the nature and activity of God. It is also important to think of a corrective to Schleiermacher's tendency to see theology as primarily related to the management of the Church. Such a focus already dictates in advance what the normative expression and locus of Christian faith and action will be, rather than subjecting to critical questioning issues such as the values informing the historical development and contemporary character of the Church and associated patterns of ministry. Pastoral theology may well proceed from the assumption that the practices it studies will be conducted from the vantage-point of faith; but the forms in which that commitment is undertaken cannot be excluded from its critical agenda. Otherwise, its confessionalism becomes a closed discipline, which may be all very well for a seminary but inappropriate for a secular pluralist society and academy.

I also mentioned the work of Don Browning and congregational studies, which perhaps come closest to my understanding of pastoral theology as the critical phenomenology of praxis. For Browning, the moral praxis of a congregation is the outworking of its value-commitments; but in practice his model privileges a particular form of Christian activity over others. For him, the community is characterized by its capacity for moral reasoning and the practices he studies as indicative of its norms and ideals are ultimately *ethical principles*, which guide the decisions and ethos of the community. However, there are two chief problems with this. First, I do not think he provides an adequate epistemology for pastoral or practical *theology*, since the values embodied in his congregational praxis are essentially moral not theological precepts.

The second issue concerns his model of human subjectivity. His pastoral agents are rational, thinking subjects, and his account of practical moral reasoning at the heart of congregational praxis is one of Christians thinking their way into being or thinking virtuously. I think this is because he has inherited a kind of Weberian notion that social action is expressive of different forms of rationality (Browning, 1976). However, this ignores the extent to which individuals and believing/practising communities are shaped by non-rational concepts: dreams, stories, embodied and sensate experience, silence, space, movement and sacrament. Rosemary Ruether's comment about the necessarily symbolic and liturgical nature of Women-Church as expression of the feminist transformation of theology makes this point well:

> It is not enough to hold an ideology of criticism and social analysis as an interpretative base, nor to participate in protest and action groups and organizations of nurture ... One needs not only to engage in rational

theoretical discourse about this journey; one also needs deep symbols and symbolic actions to guide and interpret the actual experience of the journey ... to liberated humanity. (Ruether, 1985: 3)

While the legacies of Schleiermacher and Browning hint at the study of practising communities as the focus of pastoral and practical theology, therefore, I want to suggest a *fourth* image from the tradition which can guide critical interrogation of pastoral practice without privileging either the institutional Church or rational subjectivity as its focus. The 'living human document' that stands at the heart of the Clinical Pastoral Education movement points to an insistence on the pastoral encounter or event as disclosive of more than hints and helps for more effective ministry, but as an entry-point into a deeper apprehension of the very meaning of human existence. It draws on traditions of hermeneutics which regard human action as akin to texts in the way they reflect and constitute truth-claims and values. In similar ways, contemporary social theorists are identifying practice and human action, rather than metaphysical discourse, as the source of identity and meaning (Hekman, 1986; Bourdieu, 1990).

This perspective represents a recovery of Seward Hiltner's proposal that living human documents be regarded as the focus of pastoral theological study (Hiltner, 1958). However, Hiltner's understanding of that was limited to the activity of the ordained minister without placing it into any wider social or congregational context. So although his model emphasized the 'operations-centred' dimensions of theology (to distinguish it from the logic-centred fields of philosophical, historical or systematic theology) his scheme concentrated on the 'shepherding', 'communicating' and 'organizing' functions of the clergy and therefore remained within a predominantly clerical paradigm.

However, I think we should understand the living human document as standing for any instance of pastoral practice or encounter, regardless of its actual agent or locus. Living human documentary texts might be liturgies, sermons, ethnographies, or stories; but certainly, in keeping with contemporary perspectives on human personhood, we would regard those 'texts' as always already embodied, gendered and contextual. In this respect, a postmodern hermeneutics of suspicion would be useful, and the interpretative devices for reading the texts of such pastoral events would be those that offered that kind of potential: hermeneutics, phenomenology, narrative, critical theory and discourse analysis. Just as post-structuralist critics read texts with eyes sharpened towards the interplay of power and the construction of knowledge, seeing fixity of authorship and unitary meaning as achieved at the expense of the marginalization of alternative versions, so pastoral theologians might examine living human documents of pastoral practices as complex discourses, calling forth a multiplicity of accounts, never innocent of the dynamics of power and foreclosure; yet offering the possibility of disclosing the theological (the transcendent) within and beyond the pastoral (the immediate and concrete).

The notion of living human document as the primary source for pastoral theology is also profoundly incarnational, pointing to the Divine as revealed and manifested in the midst of human experience. Mindful of the traditions of liberation and mission which emphasize the kingdom, not the Church, this model would need to be inclusive and non-sectarian; so my image of pastoral agency is of it resting with no particular institutional expression but with all those who identify themselves as the people of God. Perhaps the best metaphor for such 'practising communities' is that of pilgrimage: journeying, on the move, telling and sharing stories, and occasionally visiting sacred places.

The praxis of faith-communities constitutes theology as a form of 'practical wisdom' (*phronesis*) which is mediated and embodied in the testimonies of the living human documents. It is the vocabulary through which faithful communities articulate and orientate their visions and values. The word is made flesh in the activities of care, worship, social action, formation and initiation, stewardship and decision-making, which are nothing less than incarnations of Divine purpose. The critical and constructive task of pastoral or practical theology lies in excavating and interrogating the sources and norms that inform such practices, enabling people of faith to be called to account for the central truths and values that inform collective and individual activity. Pastoral theology is, in short, the discipline that enables the community of faith to 'practise what it preaches' (Graham, 1996b: 11).

PASTORAL THEOLOGY AS TRANSFORMING PRACTICE[1]

Introduction

We live in an age of uncertainty: an age in which many of the foundations of contemporary Western culture seem to be dissolving. At the close of the twentieth century, it is said that we live in 'postmodern'[2] times, in which the 'grand narratives' of humanism, science and progress have been discredited (Lyotard, 1984). In the face of the erosion of what Edward Farley calls 'deep symbols' – questions of identity, of the common good, of truth, hope, liberation and justice – the prospects of articulating responsible Christian witness in such a world seem daunting (Farley, 1996).

Transforming Practice (1996) argues that the discipline of pastoral theology,[3] reorientated for a postmodern age of uncertainty, provides a

---

1 Since *Transforming Practice* was first published, a number of other titles have appeared which attempt to debate the nature of theological and pastoral responses to postmodernity: see Farley (1996), Lakeland (1997), Reader (1997), Ward (1997) and Goodliff (1998). I have included some insights from these works in this updated commentary.

2 The terms 'postmodernism' and 'postmodernity' are related but distinct phenomena. 'Postmodernism' denotes the cultural, intellectual and aesthetic dimensions of the postmodern age, whereas 'postmodernity' indicates the sociological, economic and political contours of late capitalism. As the ensuing discussion indicates, I believe that 'the postmodern condition' is more than a crisis of ideas, although the philosophical movements of poststructuralism and deconstruction are significant elements of my analysis.

3 In *Transforming Practice* I distinguish between the two terms 'practical' and 'pastoral' theology (Graham, 1996b: 11–12). There is still considerable disagreement about appropriate terminology, 'practical' denoting the generic activities of Christian ministry and 'pastoral' the more interpersonal levels of care. I am increasingly moved to favour 'practical theology', given my emphasis on the discipline as the study of Christian *practice*, and to locate pastoral theology as one of a number of practical theologies, but distinguished by its focus on the theory and practice of the human life-cycle. This emphasis

method for connecting theory and practice in a reconception of faithful identity. The pastoral disciplines of personal care, social action, worship and initiation are not the 'applied' offshoots of a body of propositional theory that transcends the contingency of human activity. Rather, the ways in which Christians choose to organize their ways of being in the world, of relating to one another in community, and of enacting ritual, care and spirituality, constitute the language of authentic identity. Practical theology therefore functions in order to enable communities of faith to 'practise what they preach'.

In this commentary on *Transforming Practice*, I provide a summary of the main arguments and further discussion of some of the implications of my model of pastoral theology for a postmodern age. The chief implications of *Transforming Practice* for the discipline of pastoral theology are these: its critique of the nature of an 'age of uncertainty'; its use of feminist and gender analysis to expose the fragility and inadequacy of the categories by which modernity – and the therapeutic and clerical paradigms of Christian pastoral care – constructed its core values; and its reconception of the discipline of pastoral theology as the articulation and excavation of the sources and norms of Christian *practice*.

In keeping with the postmodern spirit of 'bricolage' – enquiry which proceeds by piecing together fragments, eschewing elevated theoretical schemes, aware of the provisionality and fragility of knowledge – I suggest that the key hermeneutical criterion for a reconstructed Christian practice is the 'disclosure' of *alterity*. In practical terms, such a perspective would favour strategies that encourage empathy and solidarity with others, open up enlarged horizons of understanding and commitment and foster pastoral encounters that engender new perspectives on human experience and Divine reality. 'Disclosive practice' is, however, more than merely a procedural norm: it speaks not simply of an ecclesial communicative ethic, but serves as a metaphor for an encounter with the very nature of God.

Age of Uncertainty

> Postmodern thought ... is a series of attitudes struck in face of questions bequeathed by modernity about the nature of rationality, the nature of subjectivity, issues of rights and responsibility, and the constitution of the political community. (Lakeland, 1997: 12)

---

retains something of the interpersonal nature of pastoral care and maintains some links with conventions of pastoral care as historically conceived. For purposes of clarity, and in keeping with the terminology of this volume, I retain the original nomenclature of *Transforming Practice*.

The historical and sociological epoch known as modernity is displaced by the signs of the times of 'postmodernity' and with it comes a host of voices to destabilize Enlightenment concepts of truth, human nature, knowledge, power, selfhood and language that have informed Western thought for two hundred years (Gay, 1973; Kearney, 1994; Reader, 1997).

However, my anatomy of postmodernity does not merely conceive of intellectual debate independent of social, political and economic factors. The 'crisis' of postmodernity is not simply one of believing, but of revolutions in patterns of work and leisure, use of technology, the exercise of civic power, participation and citizenship, access to resources, relationships to the environment and the use and abuse of scientific innovations (Hall, Held and McGrew, 1992). We might also include in our analysis the growth of religious pluralism and the decline of organized religion, especially in Western Europe, as signs that patterns of believing and belonging are changing. The pre-eminence of the Christian way of life can no longer be taken for granted (Davie, 1994).

A frequent topic of debate concerns whether postmodernity is a successor epoch of modernity, or a critical corrective to it. My preference is for the latter analysis: as Richard Bernstein has it, the mood of postmodernity is a 'rage against humanism and the Enlightenment legacy' (Bernstein, 1985: x). Postmodernity exposes the *hubris* of Enlightenment optimism, tempers the excesses of literalism, objectivism and humanism, and retrieves from the margins the repressed and hidden 'Others' of Western modernity. The postmodern is where modernity is called to account, where its confident assertions are put to the test:

> Postmodernism reminds us that we are already too determined ourselves; we can never exhaustively account for the conditions which make the world, time, knowledge, the human animal, language, possible ... Postmodernism reminds modernity of its own constructed nature; the arbitrariness and instability of its own constructions. (Ward, 1997: xxvi)

Feminist thought, while in many respects a child of the Enlightenment, also exhibits a postmodern scepticism towards many of the precepts of modernity. Feminists have argued that dominant views of human nature, self, knowledge, action and value are constructed *androcentrically*: that is, they assume that maleness and masculinity are the norm for adequate accounts of what it means to be human, how I achieve a sense of self, what counts as verifiable and reliable knowledge, the relationship between thought, will and action, and the sources and norms of ultimate value, truth and beauty. Once we introduce the notion of these concepts as 'gendered', however, we gain a clearer sense of some of the ways in which Enlightenment views must necessarily be revised. The challenge of feminism thus illustrates the crisis of conventional values and the necessity of accommodating diverse and heterogenous experiences (Flax, 1990).

Transforming Pastoral Theology

Christian thought and practice has, inevitably, been touched by the intellectual and social currents of postmodernity. Despite lively debate within philosophical theology, however (Ward, 1997), much of this has ignited little interest on the part of pastoral, or practical, theology. Yet the practical question of the sources and norms that might inform Christian faithful witness in Church and world is as fundamental and problematic an issue as the purely philosophical implications of postmodernity. In the face of the collapse of the 'grand narrative' of modernity, what values of hope and obligation may now inform purposeful Christian action and vision?

One of the symptoms of postmodernity, it is said, is a resurgence of the sacred; and this opens up possibilities that go beyond either a reversion to premodern fideism or a drift into New Age eclecticism. My paramount concern is thus to remain true to the continuity of Christian witness while responding anew to the challenges of the present age. A necessary part of the critical reclamation of the 'boundaries' and 'horizons' (Oliver, 1991) of Christian identity will therefore be a robust engagement with the ambiguities of a post-secular age:

> Set free from the compulsion to talk about God, there is a new and deeper freedom to talk about God and *not* to talk about God ... In its engagement with the secular psychotherapies, neither does pastoral counselling need to lose its Christian identity as care offered in the community of faith. Set free from the compulsion to be 'religious', it has a genuine freedom to point beyond the secular to the One who is the source of all healing. (Lyall, 1995: 107)

For most of the twentieth century, the predominant model of pastoral theology has been that of the theory and practice of individual care, prominently informed by the therapeutic models of the modern psychologies. The tasks of pastoral ministry – worship, preaching, social action, personal care, Christian formation and community-building – have traditionally been regarded as the exclusive province of the ordained clergy. However, as sociological changes have precipitated a greater demand for the active participation in church life by the laity, and feminist critiques have questioned the invisibility of women's pastoral role as agents and clients of care, intensive scrutiny has been generated into the identity and aims of the pastoral task and the self-understanding of the Christian community (Graham and Halsey, 1993; Lyall, 1995).

Schleiermacher's original vision for practical theology designated the discipline as the 'crown' of theological enquiry, derivative of the higher forms of philosophical and historical theology (Schleiermacher, 1966; Burkhart, 1983). The burden of theological understanding and formulation was therefore directed towards the entirety of Christian practice, albeit within the service of ecclesial ministry, although it did effectively reduce practical theology to a deductive, or 'applied' theology. However, we may see a timely corrective to this within contemporary theologies of liberation which effectively turn Schleiermacher's system on its head. In their emphasis on *praxis* and context as hermeneutically primary, experience is thus envisaged as the origin, not the application, of theological formulation:

> the permanent self-identity of the Christian faith cannot be presupposed ... There is no purely theoretical centre of reference which can serve in an abstract, speculative way as a norm of identity. Truth does not yet exist; it cannot be reached by interpretation, but it has to be produced by change. (C. Davis, 1994: 90–1)

According to this view, therefore, pastoral theology breaks out of the 'clerical paradigm' (Farley, 1983a) and locates itself as the 'critical inquiry into the validity of Christian witness' (Wheeler and Farley, 1991: 15). The proper object of the discipline is not the moral reasoning of the congregation (Browning, 1991) or the activities of the pastor (Hiltner, 1958) or 'applied theology', but the practice of intentional communities. Pastoral theology studies the whole mission of the faith-community, as expressed in its diverse practices of ordering the faithful, engaging in social justice, communicating the faith, and administering Word and Sacrament. Pastoral theology is reconceived, therefore, as the critical discipline interrogating the norms that guide all corporate activity by which the community enacts its identity.

Practical Wisdom

Looked at from other perspectives, my proposal to reconstitute pastoral theology as the theorization of Christian practice looks promising. Contemporary feminist theories regard gender identity, relations and representations as generated by performative practices of 'gendering' (Flax: 1993), rather than derived from an ontological or biological dualism. Gender is a self-reflexive phenomenon: we experience ourselves as simultaneously the creators and creations of gendered culture. There are no transhistorical essences of gender, but only *practices* that realize or reinforce difference (Connell, 1987; Butler, 1990; Graham, 1995b).

Such a model presents identity and culture as 'performative'. Pierre

Bourdieu's concept of *habitus* – a kind of practical knowledge within which human social action enacts and constructs culture – is a synthesis of structure and agency: a 'system of structured, structuring dispositions ... constituted in practice and ... always oriented towards practical functions' (Bourdieu, 1992: 52). Such a *habitus* is also, I contend, necessarily embodied. Social structures are inscribed on bodily activity; embodied action creates tangible institutions.

As a working definition, we might therefore characterize practice as 'purposeful activity performed by embodied persons in space and time as the subjects of agency and objects of history' (Graham, 1996b: 110). Purposeful practices are the bearers of value: cultural norms are reproduced and handed down but there is also scope for creative re-rendering. Pastoral practice constitutes the *habitus* of faith; it is both inherited and indwelt but also infinitely creative: a performative practical wisdom (*phronesis*) which we inhabit and re-enact.

Thus, the core values of communities or cultures are not to be conceived as transcendent eternal realities, but as provisional – yet binding – strategies of normative action and community within which shared commitments might be negotiated and put to work. Ethics and politics therefore become processes and practices, rather than applications of metaphysical ideals.

Community and Alterity

> There is no path to utopia ... but the responsibility to seek the world 'better' or 'less cruel' persists. There may be no common human nature or human reality, but the demands of sociality continue. (Lakeland, 1997: 27)

The task of articulating binding principles out of the contingency and self-reflexivity of human practice has occupied many contemporary social theorists, and their work provides some clues for pastoral theology. Here, I turn to Jürgen Habermas' idea of 'ideal speech communities' as holding out the possibility of a 'communicative ethic' that is inclusive and pluralist yet which commands sufficient respect for rational agreement (Habermas, 1984, 1989; Bernstein, 1985). Habermas argues that the communicative ethic which informs liberative public policy has its basis in the exercise of conversational practice. Values of truth, beauty and emancipation emerge from the transactions between groupings engaged in common tasks of transformation and action.

Habermas holds out the possibility of shared rational discourse as facilitating visions of political and moral responsibility; but his feminist critic Seyla Benhabib argues that in order for such a model to be responsive to the dynamics of gender, there must be a recognition of the radical *alterity* (otherness) at the heart of the communicative encounter. Whereas the 'generalized' other stands for a universal moral claim to human integrity, the 'concrete' other reminds us that a truly ideal speech community respects heterogeneity and difference (Benhabib, 1992).

This is not a postmodern nihilism or radical relativism – which argues that truth is 'neither here nor there' (Graham, 1996b: 157). Rather, drawing on Donna Haraway's notion of 'situated knowledge' as a form of practical wisdom, I would argue that the virtues of hope and obligation are practised – inhabited and enacted – but always already from specific vantage-points. Thus, after Benhabib and Haraway, and in keeping with psychoanalytic, hermeneutic and feminist projects of recovering the unnamed, repressed and 'Other', I would argue that an adequate model of practical knowledge will exhibit a bias towards *alterity*, diversity and inclusivity. This is at the heart of an understanding of 'disclosive' practice which must take account of our situatedness (especially in terms of our embodiment), will be appropriately open to *alterity* (otherness) and is evinced by the provisional nature of both practice and the knowledge it embodies, rather than 'foreclosive' practices, exercising premature or authoritarian appeals to absolute truth.

> How do we present our views in the fullness of our embodied and perspectival commitment, without falling back into a … universalism that has rightly been criticized as expressing the will to power of those who have been able to express their views? I suggest it is not by pretending to intellectual neutrality … but rather by acknowledging and affirming the conditions of time and space, which limit our perspectives as well as giving them their distinctive perspectival power … We should not hold our views so tightly that we cannot appreciate the perspectival truths embodied in the lives and works of others. We should think of our 'truth claims' as the products of embodied *thinking* not as eternally or universally valid *thought*. (Christ, 1988: 13)

Transforming Practice

Nancy Eisland's recent work, *The Disabled God* (1994) claims to advance a 'liberation theology of disability' that models many of the criteria for pastoral theology outlined above. Eisland draws upon conventional resources of personal experience, cultural factors and Christian tradition (Tracy, 1981), although the parameters of each of these categories are subtly revised within a hermeneutic in which *alterity*, difference and the retrieval of 'stories seldom heard' (Milhaven, 1991) are privileged as having theologically disclosive authority. The validity of theological truth-claims are 'acted out' (Eisland, 1994: 95) and will be tested by their ability to animate a renewed practical wisdom for the Church: 'The struggle for wholeness and justice begins with the practices and habits of the Church itself' (ibid.: 111).

Speaking of Difference

In drawing on the *narrative experience* of two women with disabilities, Eisland refuses to render disability as if it were an ontological category. Rather, the stories bear witness to a plurality of definitions of mobility, impairment and body image. These accounts do not pathologize or victimize their narrators, but nor do they suppress the distinctive experiences of those with disabilities: 'It encompasses the recognition that disability does not mean incomplete and that difference is not dangerous' (ibid.: 47).

Hermeneutics of Suspicion

Christian teaching on disability, healing and illness is critically examined, and elements of *tradition* that portray disability as the result of sin, or suffering as a visitation from God to test the afflicted, or an opportunity for the 'able-bodied' to exercise charity, are found wanting. Instead, Eisland's criterion for theological authenticity within the tradition is one which empowers those with disabilities as theological subjects. They are affirmed as the authors of their own narratives of Divine disclosure:

> A liberatory theology sustains our difficult but ordinary lives, empowers and collaborates with individuals and groups of people with disabilities who struggle for justice in concrete situations, creates new ways of resisting the theological symbols that exclude and devalue us, and reclaims our hidden history in the presence of God on earth. (Ibid.: 86)

The symbols of faith around disability therefore have a performative power to 'create normative standards for human interaction' (ibid.: 91); Eisland advances a contextualized Christology of the 'disabled God … in a sip-puff wheelchair' (ibid.: 89).

Transforming Communities

The truth-claims of the gospel are thus incarnated in the worshipping community that seeks to embody the suffering but transfigured presence of the 'disabled God'. Eisland focuses on the significance for such communities of the Eucharist, a sacrament, not of exclusion, but a sign of the 'body broken for a people broken' (ibid.: 114). In the figure of the transfigured Christ – who retains his wounds even in a risen state – God's solidarity with suffering is realized. A vision of God embedded in human encounter and renewal animates genuinely disclosive practical wisdom: words made flesh in a community which fosters a generosity to others. Such transformative practice facilitates and encourages the exercise of the qualities of solidarity, wholeness and reconciliation, practices by which Divine disclosure can be effected.

New Horizons

The process of going *beyond* the situated and concrete towards the encounter with the Other may also serve as a metaphor for the human experience of God. It speaks of authentic faith occurring at the very point of loss of certainty and self-possession: Divine activity and presence are offered in the mystery of *alterity*. Thus, Eisland's thoroughly Christian incarnational theology understands the human and immediate as a 'sacrament' of the transcendent and Divine: 'Our bodies participate in the imago Dei, not in spite of our impairments and contingencies, but through them' (ibid.: 101).

Just as identity in the postmodern condition is contingent, performative and provisional, so theological truth-claims are to be seen as forms of *phronêsis*, or practical knowledge: faith and truth cannot be separated from practical action, which is the very vehicle and embodiment of the Word made flesh:

> Where is God? we ask. Look to the underside of history and the emancipatory struggles of oppressed peoples everywhere. Or look to the ecological quest for the wholeness and integrity of life. Or to the dialogical creation of common though shaky ground in the midst of cultural and religious differences. My thesis is that the answer to the challenge of postmodernity – how to speak meaningfully of God's presence and action in the world – is already implicit in these practices. (Hodgson, 1994: 65–6)

Can we regard authentic pastoral practice, therefore, as that which draws us into encounter with the 'Other', towards a deeper understanding of our own identity-in-relation? Pastoral theology is an interpretative discipline enabling faith-communities to give a public and critical account of their performative truth-claims. It attempts to capture glimpses of Divine activity amid human practice. Pastoral theology aims to put to the test the conviction that the imperatives of hope and obligation are enshrined in transformative practice that seeks to realize a larger vision yet to come.

12

'THE STORY' AND 'OUR STORIES'

Narrative Theology, Vernacular Religion and the Birth of Jesus[1]

This will be less of a definitive chapter than a suggestion for a research agenda. I want to locate my enquiries somewhere at the intersection of sociological studies of contemporary religion in Britain and practical theology, and to ask some questions about the ways in which religion – especially religious or sacred narratives – actually works for people. By that I mean the significance of such narratives in helping people construct worlds of meaning, perhaps in particular to make connections between their stories and the more overarching stories of faith-communities. I am, then, thinking about 'The Birth of Jesus' not just as a textual or scriptural phenomenon, not just as a point of departure for Christian apologetics or doctrine, but as a form of *cultural representation*, or *cultural practice*.

I take my empirical material not from 'high culture', as in the study of the iconography of images of the birth of Jesus in visual art, for example.[2] Rather, I have chosen to address the birth of Jesus through the phenomenon of the Nativity Play. Perhaps the nearest historical parallel might be to think about the cultural significance of mystery plays, as simultaneously expositions of theological themes and expressions of popular piety. Insofar as such cultural practices might be manifestations

---

1 This paper was originally presented at a symposium to mark the millennium, entitled 'The Birth of Jesus', Department of Religions and Theology, University of Manchester.

2 'Seeing Salvation', an exhibition at the National Gallery, London, ran from February to May 2000.

of broader social and political contexts, they might be said to reflect a kind of *vernacular* culture, if you like, that begins with a representation of the birth narrative but assumes an altogether more eclectic character.

The nativity play is, on one level, totally prosaic; but my hypothesis is that it serves to illuminate a number of important themes in the contemporary study of religion. We may regard these little events that take place in Christian churches, schools, community centres and elsewhere probably thousands of times every year, as harmless pieces of folk religion, a little sideshow for the children, fodder perhaps for the family photo or video album, but not of any lasting significance, let alone the subject of a hypothetical research agenda! I beg to differ. They consume immense amounts of person hours; in some school contexts they are treated as significant educational activities; in a church-related context, they might be treated as integral to the Christian education and formation of young children, and a crucial aspect of the worshipping community's celebration of the Christmas festival. (A subsidiary research project, on the spirituality of young children, also suggests itself at this point.)

In whatever setting it may take place, however it may be presented, there is at the heart of the nativity play an enactment of a religious narrative, albeit not necessarily in the context of public worship, nor involving (among cast or supporting crew) those who profess a religious conviction. It is more appropriately viewed as part of a general round of Christmas celebrations; but may, along with the carol service or possibly Christmas eve/Christmas morning liturgies, be the nearest many (nominally Christian) people will come to participating in an act of organized religion all year. And that's perhaps another reason for studying the nativity play as a case-study in the dynamics of 'believing and belonging' (Davie, 1994): as a microcosm of the wider meaning of the season of 'Christmas'. Of course, the phenomenon of 'Christmas' as celebrated in contemporary Britain is quite another matter from the birth of Jesus; but this observation only serves to illustrate my point. 'Christmas' is not purely a religious festival, but rather a hybrid: of Christian festival focused around birth narratives – folk religion, consumerism, pre-Christian winter festivals, post-Dickensian sentimentality, and so on. So my imaginary research begins with a question that asks, what role does the *birth of Jesus* play in popular apprehension of the holiday season, and how is this articulated?

If we were to embark on an extended study of the nativity play, we would probably come to appreciate that its textual connection to the Gospel birth narratives is a matter of great variation. In the week before Christmas 1999, I attended two such plays. One took place in the context of public worship of the Church of Scotland, which followed a synthesis of Synoptic Gospel narratives, faithfully tracing the annunciation, the journey to Bethlehem, the stable, shepherds, angels, kings and the flight into Egypt. Each scene was interspersed with a short homily by a layperson and rounded off with a short children's sermon from the minister. The second play was at a rural nursery school in the West of England, where children and staff stage an annual spectacular based on the relatively secular theme of the four seasons. Despite this non-confessional emphasis, however, the final scene draws all the participants to the manger in Bethlehem.

The contrast between these two examples already generates important questions. Do nativity plays work from a set text? Can the nativity play stray beyond the boundaries of the biblical sources? In what ways is the narrative framed? What is the purpose of the annual process of telling and retelling? Let us confine ourselves, initially, to classifying the nativity play as a type of activity, religious or quasi-religious. It might be possible to compare the nativity play with other similar events and activities which ostensibly derive from Christian festivals but which have assumed a kind of heterodox, semi-independent status, such as harvest festivals, Remembrance Sunday, or May Queen celebrations.

My supposition awaiting validation would offer the suggestion that we consider nativity plays to be of a piece with these kinds of part-religious, part-popular, events. Subsequent research might then locate nativity plays and other similar manifestations within some analytical framework or typology; something constructed by sociologists of religion, perhaps, to characterize the different patterns of religious affiliation and observance, expressions of orthodoxy/heterodoxy, institutional forms and varieties of ritual or devotional practice. A four-fold scheme might suffice: indicating a heuristic distinction between institutional, civil, popular and implicit religion, represented diagrammatically in Figure 1.[3]

Figure 1

	'OFFICIAL RELIGION'	
Institutional		*Civil*
Organized		
'Belief'		'Practice'
Popular		*Implicit*
Common		*Surrogate*
	'VERNACULAR RELIGION'	

3 Adapted from Wolffe (1993: 305–46), although the term 'vernacular' religion, denoting that of common speech, is my own addition.

This typology has been constructed on the assumption that Britain today exhibits the empirical characteristics of an indigenous Christian (or nominally Christian) majority whose formal affiliation is declining markedly (as incidentally is that of Anglo-Jewry) but with the significant presence of migrant communities from the Caribbean and South Asia who for the time being at least are retaining numerical and organizational strength. But of those who choose not to attend public worship or profess institutional membership, there is still – although the signs are that this is changing too – a great deal of non-affiliated support for religion. This phenomenon does seem to be a distinctively British manifestation in comparison to the rest of Europe and certainly to the United States – and if not universally British, then English, white, urban and working-class very markedly.

If we tried to locate the nativity play as a legitimate religious or quasi-religious event, I wonder where and according to what criteria we might categorize it within my basic typology. It might be classed as a form of *institutional or official religion* if conducted in the context of public worship in a Christian context. *Civil religion* – the use of religious rituals and language in public life, especially ceremonial associated with the monarchy, the State and civic events – also has its allure, insofar as the nativity play might be seen as an expression of community life, a ritual affirmation of a shared culture. The nativity play might also be classed as *common religion*, a wide variety of heterodox and eclectic beliefs and practices pertaining to the supernatural, some derived from official religion, some predating Christianity, especially if we were to take my earlier comments about Christmas into account. In their diversity, their capacity to mould themselves around a local context or situation, nativity plays at their most eclectic and heterodox might well exemplify some of these traits.

Invisible, implicit or 'surrogate' religion are alternative terms for a more controversial set of practices, because there is great disagreement as to whether they constitute a category with any coherence, let alone credibility. They point to activities with no explicit religious or supernatural referent, but which by some aspect of their effect on participants and observers may engender a sense of the sacred or, as Emile Durkheim would have it, of 'collective effervescence'. Football, science fiction fandom, pilgrimages to sacred sites and political rallies have all been placed in this category: corporate activities in the main, but not necessarily mass events. For its critics, implicit religion represents the triumph of form and function over substance, and many would argue that some kind of world-view or belief-system is necessary for any working definition of 'religion'. Certainly, the extent to which the nativity play retains a residual relationship to formal traditions and narratives of institutional Christianity suggests that this category is not particularly appropriate.

It is possible that a programme of participant observation of nativity plays up and down the land would in fact uncover elements of all these types; after all, my scheme is intended at this imaginary stage to be no more than a heuristic system anyway. But a research project into nativity plays might with good reason glance laterally at other contemporary phenomena which also embody elements of all these types, an empirical process which might result in significant adaptation of the theoretical construct itself. Studies of the response to the death of Diana, Princess of Wales might acknowledge that it, too, contained elements of official (formal Christian observance and liturgy), civil (the state funeral), common (the elements of popular music at the heart of the funeral service itself) and surrogate (diffuse expressions of grief in the vernacular of lighted candles and floral tributes)[4] forms of religion.

Here, perhaps, it may be most illuminating to use a heuristic scheme such as that in Figure 1 to advance an understanding of religious belief and practice in contemporary Britain as best understood as part of human cultural activity. Religion may thereby be seen as one among many 'cultural resources' (Beckford, 1992: 11–23) by which people build a world or worlds: worlds of meaning, celebration, mourning, obligation, and so on. I take my idea of human beings as builders of worlds from the work of William Paden, who argues that 'religious worlds' are the material and symbolic systems people build through ritual, through myth, through patterns of purity and pollution, through representations of their God or gods (Paden, 1994). The function of religion as cultural resource is thus one of providing means by which people can engage in the creation of what Thomas Luckmann called a 'moral universe of meaning'. While organized religion may constitute one particular external source of authority by which some kinds of moral universes are handed on, there are perhaps signs of greater latitude in the choice of moral universes that get built in a post-Christian society, as the bonds that connect people to those institutions loosen (McCarthy, 2000).

Again, to consider the proposition that nativity plays are one small cultural resource – one part of the story-telling and myth-making that is necessary for individual and collective life – might entail placing this in wider sociological context. These themes of fragmentation, of dissipation of formal narratives and teachings of official religion, to be replaced by more eclectic and personalized tools and resources, is familiar territory; but in order to introduce a little originality into the analysis, I might avoid discussion of 'postmodernity' and talk instead about mobility and fluidity as the core characteristic of twenty-first century Western societies. Geographical, social, occupational, familial and virtual[5] mobility

---

4 However orchestrated or open to suggestion they may have been by media coverage.

5 As in the use of the Internet and electronic mail to transcend distances of space and time.

means that people are much more fluid in their allegiances and lifestyles, a condition of *bricolage*, perhaps. A religious or existential mobility would be consistent with such an analysis, so that in thinking about the narratives, resources, icons, values and institutions that shape the worlds people build, it would be clear that inherited religious narratives would have to take their turn alongside other 'sacred' and exemplary stories in our culture, such as science, consumerism and the media.

I am moving gradually, intentionally, into another important area of this imagined research around the birth of Jesus and the significance of narrative, religious or otherwise. Human experience is frequently narrative experience. The key medium through which such worlds get built, how people inhabit them, how order is brought to a chaotic world, may be through the telling of stories. Narrative – whether myth, fairy tale or 'talking cure' is part of the fundamental fabric of human identity (Kepnes, 1988). A dialogue with those working in the field of narrative theology would be fruitful as we considered the relationship between people's individual story, the collective story – especially those taking place in vernacular forms such as nativity plays – and The Story, or the Christian story. For the narrative theologian, the Christian gospel is not abstract prepositional doctrine distilled from its narrative roots. The narrative is the truth, and vice versa. Hans Frei spoke of the 'indispensible narrative web' making up the texture of story, context, tellers and hearers of a story. The narrative builds a world, therefore, into which the hearer must step in order to apprehend the moral logic that underlies the story.

But for many narrative theologians, 'The Story' is Scripture, God's narrative; and these must be treated as paradigmatic, definitive for the community of faith. So The Story absorbs and corrects 'our stories'; as Gerard Loughlin has it, 'in the sense of making oneself over to its narrative in order to be made anew' (Loughlin, 1996). The Story encounters our stories and reads the human situation accordingly. But it is clear that the tradition takes precedence; as George Stroup puts it, 'revelation occurs when the Christian narrative collides with personal identity and the latter is reconstructed by means of the former' (Stroup, 1984: 124). 'To enter the world of the Scripture,' says Gerard Loughlin, 'to become a part of its story, is to enter the community that reads the Scripture as that which delineates the world of the community; it is to become a part of the community's own story' (Loughlin, 1996).

However, I want to interpose, 'but who is telling whose story, who is defending the boundaries of the community, whose voices are excluded and silenced?' I doubt that 'The Story' has the predominance or definitive status often assumed by many (not all) narrative theologians. The self-sufficiency and exclusivity of the Christian narrative for the building of worlds is, I think, misguided, for a number of reasons. First, the sociological evidence defies the self-sufficiency of religious narrative, mistakenly assumed to be independent of its context, or of Christian faith hermetically sealed from the sensibilities of folk religion. Theologically speaking, too, an incarnational faith would suggest that God's story is embodied in and through human communities who are enjoined to watch and wait for the coming of the kingdom in unexpected, even heterodox, places. Third – an obvious issue – there is the matter of the primacy and unity of The Story. After Jean-François Lyotard, we may wonder whether the idea of the metanarrative, religious or otherwise, has any purchase. For deconstructionists, no narrative is a transparent telling-forth. Meaning is elusive, deferred and problematic; all stories fragment into intertextuality and artifice.

Finally, the implied hegemony of The Story also gives concern to some. Are there absences or silences in The Story? Does The Story do violence to my story, or our stories? This is the position taken by the practitioners of many theologies of liberation, for example, who would argue that the canonical story is too exclusive to absorb and 'reconstruct' their hidden stories. Some narrative theologians take this in their stride, finding invisible witnesses between the lines and in the margin of the dominant story, and restoring them to the main text; or telling the story differently, taking issue with the boundaries of the text and changing the way it is told. Some of these writers, emphasizing the fluidity of narrative, have indeed retold elements of the nativity story, such as Heather Walton's retelling of the annunciation (Walton, 1994). While the popular nativity play is not engaged in deconstructing The Story in quite such a way, there may nevertheless be a kind of implicit negotiation underway with the original story that transforms it from the sacred sanctioned text into something that lodges more in the realm of popular affection and popular religiosity, a transposition from 'The Story' to 'our story/ies'.

Potentially, attention to nativity plays as enactments of the birth of Jesus illuminates the performative dimensions of religion, and religious narrative in particular. In a variety of settings, with a cast of thousands, year in year out, stories of the birth of Jesus are enacted by ordinary people. I have tried to indicate why we might consider the humble nativity play to be first, a kind of popular or vernacular religion, and second whether we might class it as an elementary form of narrative theology. I have suggested that nativity plays might, as a kind of thought-experiment-cum-research proposal, chart a course through some contemporary debates about the dynamics of religious believing and belonging, as well as inviting us to think about the capacity of human beings to be builders of worlds – and tellers of stories.

13

'WHAT WE MAKE OF THE WORLD'

The Turn to 'Culture' in Theology and the Study of Religion

At the end of January 2006, a message was posted on a message forum of the British Broadcasting Corporation's (BBC) website. It announced a forthcoming television production and invited readers' responses:

> There's going to be a major production on the streets of Manchester this Easter telling the story of the last days of Christ which will be shown live on BBC3. It's a modern version of the Passion featuring well-known songs by Manchester bands including New Order, Joy Division, The Smiths, Oasis and M People. Some famous Manchester musicians are being lined up to play the parts of Jesus, Mary, Judas and Peter etc. The final crucifixion scene will take place in Albert Square. What Manchester songs do you think should be in there? And who should play the main parts? How would you give the story of the Passion a modern Mancunian twist? (Manc-host2, 2006)

The programme, *Manchester Passion*, was staged in Manchester city centre on the evening of Good Friday, 14 April 2006, and broadcast live on a minority TV channel, BBC3, with an edited version shown later the same night on BBC2. The reaction to the programme on the same message forum after the screening was lively, articulate and, by and large, enthusiastic. One such contributor was 'Webstercat71':

> I'm watching Manchester Passion just now, it's fantastic!!!! A contemporary version of the story of Jesus accessible to everyone. I want to

ask if anyone was offended by the re-telling, was it wrong or blasphemous to use modern music to tell the story of the last days of Jesus?
I'm not a Christian but felt that it told the story in an interesting way
that kept me hooked. That's got to be a good thing right? I'm also
amazed that so many modern songs could be interpreted to tell the
story. (Webstercat71, 2006)

Another participant posted this message in response:

I am a Christian and I thought that the Manchester Passion was fantastic too. I thought the use of all the songs was so clever, and just
served to show the hunger and soul-search that was already there in
all of those songs. If Jesus is going to be accessible to all as I think the
play showed was his ultimate intention, then Christians need to be at
the cutting edge of engaging with contemporary culture, meeting the
culture head on with all of its questions and unresolved pain, rather
than retreating into the Church out of fear ... Good luck with your
search. In my opinion Jesus is well worth investigating. (frenchification, 2006)

In their concern that the play may have caused offence, Webstercat71
may have had in mind the way in which previous attempts by the BBC
to present religious subject-matter in the context of light entertainment
had ended in controversy. In January 2005 the Corporation's television
adaptation of the West End musical hit *Jerry Springer: the Opera* had
encountered virulent protests from many Christian groups, in particular
the conservative organization Christian Voice. The show, which features
prolific use of the F-word and depicts God, Jesus and the Virgin Mary as
a dysfunctional family appearing on a confessional daytime talk show,
was eventually broadcast but in the face – allegedly – of death threats
to the programme's producer (Plunkett, 2005; see also Branigan, 2004).
Hence the assumption, perhaps, that religious people would inevitably
be opposed to any portrayal of sacred characters or theological issues
in the performing arts, be that film, TV, popular music, musicals or live
theatre. Yet frenchification's positive reaction showed that many other
Christians regarded shows such as *Manchester Passion* to be entirely appropriate opportunities for their faith to be presented in a refreshing and
accessible way.

Clearly, there are differences between a production that uses music to
punctuate a traditional Passion narrative, and a show that deploys scata-
logical and iconoclastic devices to satirize the tendency of daytime TV to
sensationalize any human experience, however extreme or profound. Yet
these two programmes demonstrate in different ways that the contemporary encounter between religion and popular culture is both delicate

and complicated. In the days when Christianity was the predominant world-view in the West, a broad consensus would have existed between the Church and the creative and performing arts; yet this is no longer the case, due to the impact of secularization and religious pluralism. The chances are that over the next generation societies like Britain will witness a widening gulf in social attitudes between a large and increasingly secular majority, and a small but articulate minority of people of faith. The potential for misunderstanding is therefore great, and representations of religion of all kinds, in news media and popular entertainment, will become increasingly influential either as means of staking out a common ground of religious and spiritual exploration, or as contested territory on which bitter battles over freedom of expression are waged.

My main interest in this chapter lies in the theological dimensions of such engagements between religion and popular culture. What is going on when the traditional canon of Christian practices and doctrines meet the sources and resources of popular culture in all its many manifestations? Are such attempts to be celebrated as an opportunity to make the Christian faith more 'relevant' to an increasingly post-Christian (but not neces sarily post secular) society? (Crockett and Voas, 2006; Vulliamy, 2006). Or are they a risky business in which the integrity of the gospel will inevitably be undermined by the forces of commercialism and profanity?

I begin with questions of what motivations there might be for those engaging in the study of theology and popular culture, from both church and academy, and some of the chief manifestations of representations of religious and theological issues in popular culture. I will then ask what critical tools are at scholars' disposal in making sense of the encounter between theology and popular culture; and what evaluative frameworks might be deployed to enable researchers to move from 'consumption' to 'critique', and whether the theologian should be expected to advance normative judgements on popular culture.

This is essentially a line of enquiry about the ways in which popular culture might serve as a vehicle for what is sometimes termed 'theological reflection': or how everyday experience prompts engagement with the sources and norms of tradition in order to articulate the principles of faithful living (Graham, Walton and Ward, 2005). Yet there is a second dimension to the 'turn to culture' that represents further potential for an understanding of the very nature of theological enquiry itself. I shall argue that 'culture' may be viewed as the entirety of human creative activity: not just a matter of high culture or the existential search for meaning, but the whole framework of lived human experience. Culture and cultural practices thus figure as essentially both the product of, and the context for, human being, making and imagining. This, in turn, engenders new insights into the very nature of theological discourse itself, effecting a shift from theology as doctrine or belief, to theology as practice, and thus an opportunity to conceive of theological reflection as one of the activities by which human beings build worlds of meaning and significance, and experience themselves as creative, moral and purposeful beings.

Signs of the Times: Theological Motivations for Engaging with Popular Culture

At one level, an interest in popular culture may appear to be no more than a somewhat questionable search for 'relevance' on the part of academics and the churches alike. If undergraduates in theology and religious studies seem increasingly less knowledgeable about specific religious traditions, or appear reluctant to engage with written texts, then it is seductive to make use of areas of contemporary culture where they do show astonishing enthusiasm, sophistication and lucidity: visual culture, cyberspace and popular music.

Yet there are perhaps more substantial motivations stemming from a missiological or evangelistic agenda on the part of many Christians. If the churches are failing to connect with 18–24-year-olds through traditional means, then why not harness the resources of popular culture for the purposes of mission and outreach? Writing from a broadly evangelical perspective, Pete Ward has written that 'existing patterns of church fail to connect with the evident spiritual interest and hunger that we see in the UK and the US' (Ward, 2002: 3). There is no doubt that such an evangelistic impetus has contributed to a significant proportion of the literature in the field: not simply in a narrow sense of converting souls to Christ, but to establish new patterns of discipleship and church organization that correspond more closely to prevailing cultural trends.

This is part of the agenda of the various debates about 'fresh expressions' of Western Christianity, which is often but not exclusively related to the 'emergent church' movement. Just as society is moving from 'solid' to 'liquid' so too must the Christian churches adopt more flexible structures, greater informality, an emphasis on networking, on 'doing' and 'being' rather than 'believing' and 'belonging' (Ward, 2002; Cray, 2004; Carson, 2005). This includes recognizing the extent to which popular culture provides the framework through which many people's search for meaning – and thus the proclamation of the gospel – is mediated. Yet it goes beyond mere expediency to articulate the theological conviction that God needs to be apprehended not only through tradition but by reading 'the signs of the times'. The following statement by Sanctus1, a 'fresh expression' based in Manchester city centre, is typical of this understanding:

We are a welcoming Christian community and believe that God is not defined by theology. We welcome dialogue between different theological positions but also recognize that *dialogue* involves listening and real listening involves *change* ... We believe that God is already in the world and working in the world. We recognize *God's indefinable presence in music, film, arts and other key areas of contemporary culture*. We wish to affirm and enjoy the parts of our culture that give a voice to *one of the many voices of God* and challenge any areas that deafen the call of God and hence constrain human freedom. (Sanctus1, 2002, my emphasis)

However, calls for the re-establishment of a culturally sensitive and renewed Christianity are not restricted to evangelical sections of the Church. It resonates with much Roman Catholic theology after Vatican II, in which 'culture' is described both as the sum of human achievement and the milieu in which the Christian faith is necessarily proclaimed and practised (Gallagher, 2003: 121; Cobb, 2005: 8). In missiological terms, this is to say the Christian gospel must be 'inculturated' and expressed in the vernacular of local cultures. In *Virtual Faith* (1998), Tom Beaudoin extends the concept of inculturation from a cross-cultural transmission to one conceived as intergenerational. Beaudoin is especially concerned with the religious values of so-called Generation X, namely those born between about 1960 and 1980, whose outlook is characterized by a mood of disconnection from the idealism and political activism of the 'baby-boomer' generation. The Church must acknowledge the aspirations of young people if Christianity is to make any impression:

If part of the pastoral task of the Church is to communicate God's mercy and God's freedom in a way that people can understand, then you have to use the language that they're using, you have to use the metaphors and forms of experience that are already familiar to them. You can't ask people to believe in something their own experience forbids them to believe; that's just elitist ministry. We still have that going on in some places, where it's believed people need to be converted from one cultural system to the Church's cultural system. (As quoted in Nickel, 2006: 18–19)

For many, therefore, the ubiquity of popular culture has made it a primary medium for the construction of self and community and for the on-going human processes of meaning-making. This is particularly apparent in those who have focused on popular culture, as opposed to 'high' culture, such as Gordon Lynch. He defines popular culture as 'the shared environment, practices and resources of everyday life for ordinary people within a particular society' (Lynch, 2005: 14), thereby privileging the forms of expression or entertainment that are most likely to be at hand for large portions of the population. Craig Detweiler and Barry Taylor (2003) have argued that scholars of religion need to take popular culture seriously as the dominant 'canon' of literacy and information. As the institutions of organized religion recede and the incidence of active religious affiliation among the indigenous population declines, so it is argued that people turn to the sources and resources of popular culture as a means of rehearsing and examining questions of belief, meaning and spirituality. This has given rise to the contention that at a time when institutional religion and formal theology are connecting with a dwindling fraction of the population (popular) culture is one of the few shared 'matrices of meaning' within which discussion can take place and values can be debated. As institutional religion recedes, and its narratives and norms no longer furnish ordinary people with moral or existential bearings, so popular culture moves into the vacated space, offering alternative archetypes, myths, heroic figures or soteriologies to form the stories we live by. To engage with popular culture enables scholars of religion to map the fragments out of which ordinary people are piecing together their own 'vernacular' or commonplace theologies (Lynch, 2005: 166; Gallagher, 2003: 6–8).

Popular culture is conceived theologically not only as a vehicle for converting people to faith, therefore, but as a vital medium through which ultimate reality itself is mediated and revealed. Popular culture is believed to constitute a central source and resource for theological understanding. Just as in the past, philosophy or writings of classical writers may have served as a resource for theological understanding, or even a generation ago the insights of modern psychologies and psychotherapies served as windows into the human condition for pastoral theology, maybe now questions about good and evil, life and death, what it means to be human, identity and community are mediated as much through popular cultural expressions as via the voices of 'high culture'. If theology is to respond authentically to its human situation, then it must be ready to respond in kind.

Mapping the Intersection of Theology, Religion and Popular Culture

I want here to map some of the ways in which popular culture is serving to mediate understandings of the nature of religious belief and practice, or to facilitate theological reflection on the world. The following categories are intended to reflect some contemporary trends within Western culture, both in popular experience and academic debate.

Screening the Sacred

This covers the portrayal of traditional religious figures and narratives. It could refer to something as straightforward as the telling or retelling of classic biblical stories, or the reworking of enduring myths; what Lloyd

Baugh (1997) has termed the 'Jesus-Film'. Thus, biblical epics and films such as *Jesus of Montreal*, *Jesus of Nazareth*, *Last Temptation of Christ* and *The Passion of the Christ* would fall into this category. However, it could also involve the exploration of wider aspects of religious characters or controversies, such as *40 Days and 40 Nights* in which the hero abstains from sex as a wager with his friends, a scenario which parodies evangelical Christianity's campaigns on teenage chastity and virginity such as 'True Love Waits' (DeLashmutt, 2006). Yet it might also embrace more ambivalent portrayals of religious figures such as the flawed heroes in *Elmer Gantry* and *The Apostle* (Greiner, 1999).

While we may consider this genre to be essentially the telling and retelling of classic stories, clearly all these examples are 'representations' of Christ-figures rather than straightforward portrayals. For a start, the original Gospel accounts do not provide historical accounts of Jesus of Nazareth; but when comparing Pasolini's *Gospel According to Matthew*, for example, with Mel Gibson's *The Passion of the Christ*, it is apparent that they reflect very different Christologies.

Seeing Salvation

These may be cultural expressions that are essentially vehicles of encounter with the sacred, transcendent and redemptive. Such forms of popular culture may not deal with explicitly theological themes, but nevertheless may be regarded as instances of 'hierophanies of the sacred' (Eliade, 1959). They may feature a central figure who embodies redemption (Lloyd Baugh's 'Christ-Figure'), such as in *The Matrix* or *Cry Freedom*; or a strong central motif of salvation, such as *The Shawshank Redemption* (Marsh, 2004: 45–59), or *Schindler's List*.

You'll Never Walk Alone

This category considers the ways in which popular culture serves as an outlet for or expression of 'spirituality' beyond organized religion. This might furnish evidence for scholarship seeking to assess how far in spite of institutional decline religious belief and affiliation persists, albeit at the level of non-institutional, non-credal forms (Davie, 1994). Manifestations of this in popular culture might include the interest in Gothic and supernatural themes in TV series such as *Buffy the Vampire Slayer* and *Angel*; or the enormous commercial success of J. K. Rowling's Harry Potter series and despite – or because of – their implicit critiques of religion, Philip Pullman's *His Dark Materials* trilogy and Dan Brown's novel, *The da Vinci Code* (Wagner, 2003).

Other scholarship has focused on the way people appropriate familiar forms of popular culture which may not initially have been ascribed a religious association, yet develop them to refer to sacred subjects. For example, Ian Bradley's work on popular hymnody has analysed the growth in the use of popular music such as 'You'll Never Walk Alone', 'Bridge over Troubled Water' and 'Candle in the Wind' at funerals and weddings (Bradley, 2004).

Meaning of Life

This category indicates forms of popular culture which explore aspects of what it means to be human, especially in terms of ethical and existential themes (Cobb, 2005: 177–210). Examples often trace the boundaries between human and almost-human, using alien characters as mirrors against which normative and exemplary humanity is refracted (Graham, 2002a). Such examples would be *Bicentennial Man*, *Gattaca*, *Frankenstein*, or *Blade Runner* (Aichele, 2005). More broadly, the Home Box Office TV series *Six Feet Under*, set in a family-run funeral business, provided rich resources for explorations of existential issues such as death, bereavement, sexuality, religion and the nature of family relationships (Akass and McCabe, 2005).

Like a Virgin™

This category makes use of sacred themes in post-religious contexts, where many sacred symbols and cultures are available for appropriation and reappropriation. In this area of study, scholars might examine the ways in which displacement of religious imagery or references is taking place, often in ironic or syncretic-eclectic forms. Examples might include any Madonna music video; or Kevin Smith's film *Dogma* (Cobb, 2005: 22–4, 137–42).

The question is whether the ironic tone of much of this points us towards, or away from, any affirmation of theological significance. *Dogma*, for example, is hugely irreverent, and yet its purpose is to poke fun at religious bigotry and also at the Church's desperate search for relevance by assimilating to the values of corporate culture. Yet one question prompted by such material is whether its impact is essentially parasitic on a bedrock of shared religious and theological reference-points, and what happens once its audience is no longer capable of 'reading' such references.

The Empire Strikes Back

This is potentially one of the most complex and nuanced areas of religion's engagement with popular culture. It represents a seemingly paradoxical harnessing of sophisticated forms of new media and popular culture to reinforce traditional religious practice, using secular methods or technologies to pursue explicitly religious themes or causes. These may have the function to reach out to non-members as evangelistic devices, or to strengthen the cultural identity of conservative religious groups (Hendershot, 2004; Gormly, 2003). Alternatively, 'mainstream' consumerist culture becomes a means of adopting a radically counter-cultural lifestyle. One such example, from the Muslim world, is the brand *Qibla Cola*, which identifies itself explicitly as practising fair trade, but also offering an alternative to other global brands of cola and thus possibly a form of resistance to US neo-colonialism (Qibla Cola, 2003). The term 'Qibla' indicates how the faithful Muslim at prayer should be located in relation to the sacred site of Mecca; thus, by analogy, to consume this fizzy soft drink is a means of orientating oneself correctly: a way of demonstrating one's religious loyalties through the medium of the market.

Theological Discernment: Commendation and Conversation

While it is important to affirm the various ways in which religious and theological themes are mediated via popular culture, questions of discernment or evaluation cannot be ignored. How, then, might the scholar move from description to analysis? How would theologians distinguish legitimate uses of the Christian canon, or set boundaries for acceptable use of theological themes within the plethora of examples surveyed above?

One such analytical tool has been advanced by a number of scholars (Marsh, 1997; Gallagher, 2003; Lynch, 2005), who all adapt H. Richard Niebuhr's classic study, *Christ and Culture* (1951), to suggest a range of approaches to theology and culture. Niebuhr set up five different relationships between 'Christ' (the claims of the gospel) and 'culture' (the world) which were opposition, conformity, dualism, syncretism and conversion. In revisions of this, Marsh and Gallagher have both developed a similar three-fold schema, broadly tracing the alternatives of opposition, identity and mutual critique.

The first approach thus sets theology against culture, articulating the notion that there is nothing to be gained theologically from engaging with (secular) culture. There may be a number of reasons for this, such as a conservative view that Christian lifestyle is to be set apart from anything that might contradict biblical revelation, through to a more general rejection of humanistic or liberal moral attitudes. Note, however, that 'culture' is assumed to be 'secular' and that no account is taken either of the way in which Christianity informed Western culture in the first place, or of how conservative Christianity is often highly selective in its rejection or assimilation of mainstream culture.

At another level, however, such an approach may afford some degree of counter-cultural critique to the mores of media, commercialism and consumerism. Popular culture, it is argued, is inherently about triviality, celebrity, diversion; and the values of popular culture reflect a constant search for novelty, titillation and sensation rather than any serious engagement with our humanity or ultimate reality (Postman, 1985). Thus, popular culture conforms to hegemonic not gospel values: what is celebrated is strength, celebrity, individualism, wealth, competition and glamour – the antithesis of any identifiably Christian ethic. This oppositional stance may also choose to stress the transience of much of popular culture, with the resulting danger that any theological engagement will rapidly look anachronistic.

In some respects, such critical perspectives remind theologians of the contingency of any cultural expression of ultimate values. Yet while there is a sense in which God's revelation transcends human cultural expression, such a model has a relatively low doctrine of 'secular' culture and creativity as spheres of encounter with the Divine.

A second option is often represented as the polar opposite of 'hostility' between Christ and culture (Gallagher, 2003: 135), and points to an identity of revelation of God through culture and faith. In Niebuhr's terms, Christ is the fulfiller of culture, making the universal meaning of the gospel clear to all, available through the work of reason and cultural membership. We might see it as related to traditions of 'natural' theology and a very 'immanentist' model of God, or even as an affirmation of the entirety of popular culture as a form of 'implicit religion'. Yet as Clive Marsh has commented, to argue that popular culture (in this case, cinema-going) is an alternative to religious practice and affiliation is not the same as saying it is a substitute for religion. The tendency to collapse theology and culture – with their differential histories, contexts and sources – denies either any degree of autonomy, thereby preventing any critical space to emerge. Thus, while this model celebrates the presence of faith and spirituality outwith the institution, it may veer too far into what Gallagher terms 'innocent acceptance' (ibid.: 137) on the part of theology towards culture, lacking any critical edge towards mainstream cultural values.

Yet as with any kind of heuristic framework of this kind, we need to be wary of erecting typologies that distort rather than clarify empirical evidence. To my mind, these extremes serve more to sketch out critical benchmarks by which a more interactive or synthetic relationship is articulated, rather than being discrete positions in their own right. This can be demonstrated by the way in which, while some of my earlier examples may appear at first glance to inhabit the extremities, further examination reveals more dynamic factors at work. For example, the genre of 'The Empire Strikes Back' may appear to be about rejection or withdrawal from popular culture – an oppositional stance – but is in reality a complex mix of appropriation of modernity in order to effect a recapitulation of an actively counter-cultural (and in some respects pre-modern) identity.

The third dimension of this typology may therefore be closer to reality of the relationship between theology and culture, being one of conversation or dialogue in which the processes of interaction are those of mutual challenge, affirmation and critique (Marsh, 1997; Loughlin, 2005: 2–5). Theology is understood to be inescapably part of culture and shaped by its cultural contexts, yet claims to transcend the particularity of any one context or expression. At the same time, however, it allows the language of popular culture to speak on its own terms, thereby granting an intrinsic integrity to the secular.

In this respect, the history of Christian theology itself carries an important precedent, in the preaching of the apostle Paul in Athens. The story from the Acts of the Apostles has him speaking publicly at the Areopagus, or public forum, with a concern to become 'all things to all people' and stressing a universal human search for the Divine (Graham, Walton and Ward, 2005: 140–2; Gallagher, 2003: 139). While he is seeking to commend the Christian gospel to his audience (what we might term a stance of 'apologetics'), there is also a strong dialogical element to his proclamation, acknowledging the possibility that pagan culture is capable of theological discernment.

Perhaps this should commend itself to theologians as a strategy of 'responsible engagement' (Gorringe, 2004: 15). Such an approach upholds a theological conviction that the ultimate purposes of God may be discernible here and now (which grants culture an integrity of its own), yet will require Divine action to bring human affairs fully to fruition (which introduces an eschatalogical horizon into theological reflection on culture). Such a model keeps faith with the idea of an enduring 'script' of Christian narratives, symbols and meanings which constructs a normative framework, as well as the potential for popular culture to carry seeds of revelation that do not merely confirm meanings already present within the faith tradition but may offer new or corrective insights (Cobb, 2005: 72–5).

Studying 'Ordinary Theologies'

Typologies such as Niebuhr's are useful as heuristic tools, but they have limitations if they reify or over-simplify complex, shifting perspectives. The emphasis on popular culture as 'lived experience' strongly suggests that there needs to be a greater use of empirical and phenomenological approaches in order to trace the contours of 'ordinary theologies' (Astley, 2002) emerging out of the synthesis of tradition and experience. This entails scholars approaching the subject with new critical tools which enable them to take seriously the specificity of the medium they are studying. This is an important but sometimes overlooked distinction, between the study of popular culture as essentially about a critical reading of 'texts', and more ethnographically orientated methodology, which focuses on the function those 'texts' fulfil for their audiences, and the ways in which consumers of popular culture make use of them.

Examples of attempts to bring audience reception into the study of theology and film might be Clive Marsh's recent *Cinema and Sentiment* (2004), or John Lyden's *Film as Religion* (2003), which concentrate on the practices of regular cinema-goers, and the various ways in which actual film-going functions for them as a means of engaging with moral dilemmas and exploring different avenues of significance. Marsh draws analogies between this mode of study in cultural and film studies, and the emergence of 'reader-response' theories in literary and biblical studies (Marsh, 2004: 36). It is notable, however, that despite Marsh's emphasis on audience reception and the experience of movie-going as multidimensional, there is little primary research data of the kind he commends, and many of his case-studies are conducted without reference to audience response.

Nevertheless, such areas of study should alert scholars to the fact that popular culture exceeds the limits of text or visual image, while the consumption of popular culture is revealed as a far from passive pursuit. It is important to locate people's use of media and popular culture in relation to religious traditions in their own context of everyday phenomenology. This serves as a good example of how researchers need to be alert to the multiplicity of methods available. Such research is necessarily interdisciplinary, as it calls on tools of social analysis in order to offer an adequate account of religious practice in its cultural contexts. Without such interdisciplinarity, scholars risk making superficial and inadequate analyses of their field of study and are unlikely to have their work taken seriously by their academic peers.

I have argued that the focus on popular culture has rendered the lived experience of people of faith a priority for study, often via empirical or ethnographic methods. It offers legitimacy to popular or vernacular expressions of religious praxis over and against institutional, dogmatic theology. Potentially, then, this represents an important shift in our understandings of the nature of religious belief and practice. It presents a resistance to the reduction of religion to propositional belief, or of theology primarily as doctrine. This is a question to which I now return: is 'culture' simply a mode of consumption, or a set of meanings; or is it more appropriate to consider culture as a form of 'practice' or lived experience from which constructive theological reflection can proceed?

If we consider theological reflection as essentially a series of conversations between a contemporary situation and the sources and resources of faith, this 'turn to culture' offers very exciting avenues. We might consider this to be something akin to a 'theological imagination', which characterizes human religious engagement with culture in all its forms. It is because culture is always revealing something of our humanity and potentially of God. If 'talk about God' is to a large extent a human activity, the work of the human imagination, then fruits of our cultural imagination will be arenas within which God will be revealed (Loughlin, 2005: 5). This casts theology as a process of enquiry and reflection – a practice – rather than body of truth or doctrine. 'Rather than studying theological ideas as a static body of knowledge that is universally applicable, theology is better understood as a process of exploring traditional theological resources in the light of contemporary questions, beliefs, values, practices, and experiences' (Lynch, 2005: 96).

'What We Make of the World': Theology as Cultural Practice

So far, I have not offered any definition of 'culture' or 'popular culture' beyond the quotation from Gordon Lynch at the beginning of this chapter. But Tim Gorringe, in his recent book *Furthering Humanity* (2004), provides a helpful pointer in this respect. At one level, there is an anthropological definition, relating to all aspects of human activity and endeavour; and this is a profoundly materialist understanding, in which we think of the ways in which humanity transforms the raw materials of 'nature' into built environments, artefacts and activities of manufacture and exchange. But 'culture' also has associations with those more artistic, literary, symbolic expressions that constitute human creativity: as Gorringe says, the linguistic link is there between the 'cultivation' not only of fields, animals, even human bodies, but the cultivation of minds and spirits.

Famously, Clifford Geertz has represented culture as fundamentally and primarily a system of meanings: 'an historically transmitted pattern of meanings embodied in symbols, a system of inherited conceptions expressed in symbolic forms by means of which men [sic] communicate, perpetuate, and develop their own knowledge about and attitudes toward life' (Geertz, 1973: 89). As he says, human beings are creatures suspended in 'webs of significance' that they themselves have spun. But perhaps we can combine this notion of culture as a 'web of meaning' which human beings create for themselves – the stories, myths and constructions which shape our understanding of the world – with a more materialist understanding of culture as essentially the realm of human fabrication, a systematic outworking of the achievements of *Homo faber*, humanity the tool-maker, the builder of worlds. So 'culture' reflects something of our innate abilities for making, building and imagining worlds, both metaphysical and material, as well as our capacity to move adroitly between the two. For Gorringe, therefore, 'culture' denotes not so much the elevated realms of high culture, but any kind of lived experience or practice; it is, as he says, 'what we make of the world':

> Human beings, says Clifford Geertz ... are animals suspended in webs of significance that they themselves have spun. 'Culture' is the name for these webs. It is *what we make of the world*, materially, intellectually and spiritually. These dimensions cannot be separated: the Word is necessarily flesh. In constructing the world materially we interpret it, set values on it. To talk of values is to talk of a culture's self-understanding, its account of its priorities. (Gorringe, 2004: 3, my emphasis)

'Culture' is therefore more than just a realm of meaning, but is a world of material fabrication as well as one of signs, symbols and ideas. I want to emphasize this dialectic between the anthropological and the aesthetic because it gives us a very useful and theologically resonant definition of 'culture'. All is the result of human making and transforming, but it allows us to think of culture as both the exceptional, the heights of creative excellence, and the everyday, the result of the human labour that forges the material world in which we live.

In terms of theological reflection on popular culture, therefore, it is all very well to focus on ways in which popular culture elicits questions of meaning: of popular culture as a way of articulating questions about what it means to be human, the nature of the sacred, and so on. However, to consider 'what we make of the world' as a working definition of culture introduces further dimensions, which stress much more the ways in which culture as the realm of human practice serves as the environment within which religious belief and behaviour is conducted: culture not only as realm of meaning, but realm of practice.

There are parallels between the 'cultural turn' within the study of religion and theology and the renewed focus on 'practice' within the discipline of theology, especially practical theology. In its reinvention from an 'applied' discipline of clergy hints and helps to a primary discipline of the hermeneutics of theological reflection on practice, practical theology exhibits many of the same emphases as emergent trends in the study of religion and/in popular culture. Indeed, 'culture' as a category plays a significant part in contemporary practical theology as the context which generates the practical questions and challenges from which the process of theological reflection and formation stems.

The emphasis on 'orthopraxis' (or right practice) from Latin American liberation theologies, together with a sensitivity to the sociology of knowledge drawn from a range of liberationist theologies such as Black, feminist, LGBT and Third World theologies, have been key influences shaping the reinvention of practical theology as a primary theological discipline. Theology is regarded as a form of practical wisdom, enabling a critical account to be made of the values and truth claims enacted in the world by individuals and communities of faith. In its most postmodern versions, practical theology argues that theology is essentially 'performative', so that theology is not primarily or exclusively expressed in doctrinal statements or academic treatises but enacted and embodied in the liturgical, evangelistic, sacramental and practical/caring actions of faithful communities (Graham, 1996b). Methodologically, practical theologians are attuned to the extent to which all theology is necessarily contextual, and how culture, tradition and experience are inextricably interwoven.

Thus, the twin turns to culture and practice have a number of implications for the rejuvenated discipline of practical theology, many of which resemble similar trajectories in the study of religion and popular culture. First, there is a resistance to the reduction of religion to propositional belief, or of theology primarily as doctrine. Instead, the lived experience of people of faith becomes a priority for study, often via empirical or ethnographic methods. Second, practical theology is also interdisciplinary, as it calls on tools of social analysis in order to offer an adequate account of religious practice in its cultural contexts.

Third, it offers legitimacy to popular or vernacular expressions of religious praxis over and against institutional, dogmatic theology. Finally, as the institutions of organized religion recede in increasingly secular societies of the West, practical theologians look to the ways in which, in the absence of the infrastructure of formal religious affiliation, people turn to the sources and resources of popular culture as a means of rehearsing and examining questions of belief, meaning and spirituality.

There is also a strongly incarnational thread to this positive theological appraisal of the potential of culture, insofar as people's engagement with the material and aesthetic dimensions of their world provides a ready-made affirmation of the sensual, affective, embodied dimensions of human life and, by extension, the gathering up of these aspects into the life of God. It also affirms the power of the creative arts to reflect and explore aspects of the human condition, including human beings' relationship to transcendence. There is an affinity between the arts and theology because they both open up and gravitate towards questions of ultimate human concern. So the creative imagination and material culture furnish the raw materials for Divine disclosure; they both potentially represent ways in which humanity can apprehend the Divine.

This turn to culture also offers us different media through which that 'talk about God' can be made manifest, too: not just in words, or the conventions of systematic theology, but in visual arts, hymns, popular song, story, film, music, even the built environment. To see talk about God take shape in such cultural and aesthetic forms offers a different kind of theological literacy, a different medium of expression from the logic-centred mode.

So culture is what humans use to inhabit the universe, both in terms of making it physically habitable but also in making sense of things: culture is the sum total of the indivisible activities of being, making and imagining (Heidegger, 1971). Human beings are constantly moving between the material fabrication and transformation of the world, and the processes of interpretation, meaning-making about that very same world. Yet our physical transformation of the world is driven by the narratives, values and goals we have constructed for ourselves; so the objects we build – such as cathedrals, canals and computers – are dialectically connected to the concepts and values we weave around them.

This intertwining of the concrete and the imaginary tells us something about our humanity as made in the image and likeness of God. Philip Hefner's work on technology (2003) has elaborated this theme theologically, arguing that humans' need to project themselves beyond the mundane, the immediate and the concrete to imagine 'new worlds' of meaning and the imagination is an expression, theologically, of humanity's potential for transcendence. Culture, both as world of meanings and world of practices and material artefacts, thus holds the potential to disclose more about ourselves as human beings, and provides the sources and resources whereby we can contemplate fundamental and ultimate realities. Culture (material and metaphysical) like Scripture or any other conventional theological resource, becomes a source or conversation partner in theology's task of 'reading' the Divine (Loughlin, 2005: 9).

Some of this might be illustrated through a piece of testimony by Tom Beaudoin. In a recent interview with Jeremy Nickel, a documentary maker with particular interest in rock music subcultures and religion, Beaudoin reveals that his academic work in theology and popular culture is indivisible from his own involvement in music-making. He observes that often implicit in research in theology, religion and popular culture, is the researcher's own personal investment in the subject on which they are writing. Rather than seeing such personal investment as an embarrassment to be ignored or to be justified by more 'academic' reasons, it could be profitable instead to recognize the subjective basis of the work as an integral element to it.

Beaudoin provides an example of how such experiential and reflexive analysis can lead into a theological direction. He speaks of how his music assumes a 'sacramental' significance in which cultural practice becomes a vital avenue of self-expression and encounter with the Divine: 'an imaginative palette for faith', as Beaudoin puts it:

Playing in rock bands over the past 20 years has been a huge, huge part of my life. It's given me a mystical vocabulary that is also a religious vocabulary – a set of experiences that I draw upon when I do theology. For me, what gets worked out in every bass line is my own restless and searching eros, or spiritual seeking. That's what gets expressed in every creative expression on bass guitar ... To know that this practice conducts me into God's mystery is all I need ... I just need the promise. And that's all Christian theology is in a sense, and especially my own tradition, Catholic theology, we're very big on looking for those hints and we're very interested in the tastes of God here in this world. (Quoted in Nickel, 2006: 21)

Beaudoin's reflections on the 'practical theology' of popular culture – as something consumed and produced – is an articulate and profound expression of the potential of human making, building and imagining to 'speak of God' and point us towards transcendence in the midst of everyday life. Viewed this way, participation in culture – as producer, consumer and interpreter – could be understood as a form of 'theological reflection on practice': critical evaluation of one's own cultural practices sharpens one's creative awareness and serves as a glimpse into the spiritual dimensions of everyday, lived experience. This is not intended to be solipsistic or self-indulgent, but rather an experiment in self-reflexive academic enquiry, and an investigation into the ways in which the theological imagination is sparked through different forms of lived experience.

It is possible, therefore, that this renewed engagement with 'culture' as a category can go further than simply offering critiques of *Jerry Springer: the Opera* or wondering whether football is a surrogate religion, to take us to the heart of what it means to be human. Our very participation in culture – be that prosaically everyday or expressed in the creative achievements of high art, mediated through the narratives of self-acceptance and self-actualization of modern psychotherapies or in the traditions of contemplative spirituality – are all many-layered accounts of our human story which call forth interpretation in the light of God's story. It offers, I think, a way forward for us to conceive of culture as the arena of human being, making and imagining and for theology to undertake further reflection on what we make of the world, both materially and metaphysically.

Part Four

PUBLIC THEOLOGY

14

THEOLOGY IN THE CITY

Ten Years after *Faith In The City*[1]

Thirty years ago, Harvey Cox's book *The Secular City* was hailed en-
thusiastically by reviewers as a major contribution to Christian social
thought. *The Secular City* reflected an increasingly popular theological
trend of the time in its accommodation to the decline of traditional and
institutional Christianity in the West as a sign of 'humanity come of
age'. Cox's thesis was that the process of secularization liberated urban
society from ancient social ties and outdated metaphysics and enabled it
to fashion itself according to the values of reciprocity, interdependence
and mature responsibility. The secular city was for Cox a symbol for the
theological notion of the 'Kingdom of God'. 'The partnership of God and
man in history' was now made flesh in the ultimate realization of human–
Divine co-operation and co-creation, not in an other-worldly realm but
in the midst of human history; free from the anachronistic world-views of
traditional religion, the Churches could more authentically embrace the
reality of God's redemptive presence and activity in the world.

> Today, the gospel summons man to frame with his neighbour a com-
> mon life suitable to the secular city. He responds by leaving behind
> familiar patterns of life that are no longer apropos and by setting out
> to invent new ones ... The coming of the secular city is a historical
> process which removes adolescent illusions. Freed from these fantasies
> man is expected to assume the status of sonship, maturity, and respon-
> sible stewardship. (Cox, 1965: 121)

---

1 This paper was presented at an international seminar on 'Minorities' held in
Lausanne, Switzerland, between the Department of Religions and Theology, University
of Manchester, and the Faculty of Theology, University of Lausanne, in February
1995.

Cox's Utopian portrayal of the modern city as the cradle of human liberation and the triumph of liberal values of progress, enlightenment and
technological mastery is thoroughly in keeping with its time. In identifying the modern city as the triumph of human reason and agency over
superstition and tradition, and celebrating the liberating potential of
technological progress, Cox articulates the values of the liberal Enlightenment. And yet in the short space of a generation, Cox's vision has become
barely recognizable. In 1965 the secular city was the solution to human
finitude and injustice, where the anonymity and social mobility of urban
life signalled an emergent 'technopolis', where humanity would create
anew communities founded on consent, freedom and mature responsibility. In 1995 Western cities are regarded as places of decay, danger and
fragmentation; no longer centres of population growth, economic activity or cultural inspiration.

One way of looking at this contrast might be to consider Cox's arche-
typical urban dweller as exemplified in the quotation above. 'Urban man'
takes for granted the possession and exercise of autonomy, mobility and
privilege in order to achieve his dreams of 'sonship, maturity, and responsible stewardship'. Surely, the city is a delightful place – but only if
you are white, male, able-bodied, employed and wealthy. However, the
city of the 1990s is in reality inhabited by those who do not fit this speci-
fication: the unemployed, the elderly, women, the low-paid and ethnic
minorities, all of whom in various ways are excluded from or denied the
liberal dream of prosperity and independence.[2]

So Cox's vision seems hopelessly outdated, devoid of any understanding of the city as a place of marginalization and exclusion; not a place
of expansive vision and promise but instead a wasteland of decay and
impoverishment. In wholeheartedly embracing the promise of the secular
city, Cox rightly eschewed the tendency of Christian theology to deny
the material and immanent emphasis of the Christian gospel; but in so
closely associating the 'Kingdom' with 'this-worldly' communities and
values, he left no room for a more critical or 'prophetic' stance.[3]

Over the past decade, these dilemmas have grown even more acute as
the darker side of city life has become more apparent. This chapter will
attempt to assess the past decade of Christian social thought and praxis
with reference to the British urban context. It will evaluate the signifi-

---

2 Critics of the original claims of the political, intellectual and economic developments associated with the Enlightenment have commented that its version of the
rational individual, exercising choice and acting freely in the public domain actually
only reflects the aspirations of a small class of scientists, philosophers and entrepre-
neurs. Essentially, the liberal Enlightenment reflected the self-interest of a small elite
of educated, privileged white males. See Hall (1992: 1–16).

3 In many respects, Cox's vision was already obsolete by the time he wrote. By the
mid-1960s many of the nostrums of urban planning in the USA and UK were already
being called into question.

cance of the Archbishop's Commission on Urban Priority Areas, *Faith in the City*, and identify the extent to which it has marked a watershed in social theology. By focusing attention of Church and society on the inner city, urban development and local economies, by opting for preferential action on the part of marginalized and minority communities, and by registering a debt to the theologies of liberation in its analysis, the Commission signalled a new era in relationships between Church and State and stimulated new patterns and priorities for intervention and involvement by the Church in local communities.

But did *Faith in the City* herald a genuinely new way of 'doing theology in the city' as some commentators maintain? Do the methods and conclusions of the Archbishop's Commission represent a model of empowerment of the poor and marginalized or simply another variety of ecclesiastical paternalism? And what of the theological commitments of subsequent Christian thought? How influential and how lasting has been the impact of projects which, in the wake of *Faith in the City*, explicitly espouse the methods and values of liberation theology? I will conclude with an evaluation of a series of projects by the Manchester-based campaigning group, Church Action on Poverty, that has attempted to adopt new patterns of working which privilege the voices of the 'grass-roots', insisting that theology is the work of the people and not the pronouncements of church officials. It is possible that *Faith in the City* did mark a watershed in English Christian social thought; but the prospects for future faith and action are by no means clear.

To understand the context of *Faith in the City* it is important to recall the state of Britain in the early 1980s. The Conservative Government, headed by Margaret Thatcher, had been elected in May 1979 with a manifesto which attacked many of the assumptions of British 'consensus' politics after 1945. In the following years, a series of economic and political reforms were introduced which reflected the influence upon the Conservative Party during the 1970s of the so-called 'New Right' in economics and political philosophy. We can discern at least three emphases to British social and economic policy since 1979. First, the adoption of laissez-faire economics (broadly, an attempt to return to nineteenth-century classical liberalism); second, the resolve to 'roll back the frontiers of the State' – to reduce public expenditure and to liberate the citizen (or consumer) from intrusive and wasteful taxation and government intervention – which was manifested most acutely in the gradual abolition of the powers of local government; and third, an almost religious zeal to transform the cultural and social climate of Britain in the attack on many of the so-called 'progressive' causes of the 1960s and 1970s: feminism, sexual liberation, permissiveness, youth culture – all expressions of a 'socialist' creed regarded as the root of Britain's current malaise. Margaret Thatcher's celebrated comment, 'There is no such thing as society.

There are individual men and women, and there are families' (*Woman's Own*, October 1987; also quoted in Preston, 1991) reflects well both the economic and moral philosophy of 'Thatcherism': a belief that government exists primarily to enable the individual to maximize choice and that all other forms of state intervention are dangerous forms of a redundant collectivism (Clark, 1992: ch. 1).

The Government's commitment to reduce public expenditure coincided with the most acute recession since the 1930s, the most tangible effect of which was the resurgence of mass unemployment. During the 1950s and 1960s unemployment had rarely exceeded half a million; but throughout the 1980s it never fell below 2.7 million (Commission on Social Justice, 1994: 28–35).

Public concern at the effects of such trends in generating social divisions intensified following outbreaks of civil disorders ('riots') in the summers of 1980 and 1981, across the inner cities of Britain's major metropolitan areas. An enquiry into the causes of the riots in Brixton, in London, concluded that such disturbances had to be seen in the context of deepening social deprivation and economic inequality (Scarman Report, 1981).

At the same time, other social researchers were confirming the reality of widespread poverty and disadvantage in British society, employing the language of 'relative poverty': of deprivation as involving inability to participate in activities or to gain opportunities generally assumed and encouraged by the rest of society (Townsend, 1979). Poverty was therefore linked strongly with political and social alienation as well as material inequality. Whereas in 1979 at least one household in twelve of the population and one child in ten were considered to be in a household in receipt of less than half the average wage, by 1993 these figures had increased to one family in four and one child in three (Commission on Social Justice, 1994: 32).

The churches in Britain participated in responding to some of the growing concern on these issues. In 1983 the Methodist Church inaugurated a series of local projects to tackle poverty and inequality via its 'Mission Alongside the Poor' programme (Cooper, 1992) and the Church of England was also beginning to muster its resources. Following the prompting of a group of bishops from urban dioceses, the Archbishop of Canterbury established a Commission of Enquiry into the state of the inner cities.

The choice of the term 'Commission' is significant: prior to 1979, successive governments were prone to set up 'Royal Commissions' on matters of state importance. It is perhaps an indication of the distinctive approach of the Thatcher regime, and its break with much of the postwar consensus of British politics, that this practice had more or less been abandoned by 1985; so it is significant that the Church chose such a term for its enquiry. It is suggestive both of its awareness of the gravity of the issue for the nation at large, and also of the Church's responsibility to articulate a response, given its status as the Established Church in England. In this respect, the appointment of the Commission was entirely in keeping with the self-understanding of the Church as upholding those (generally Christian) values underpinning the social order, and aiming to embody in its public pronouncements such shared moral values at the heart of public life (Habgood, 1983; Moyser, 1985).

Further evidence of the Church's assumptions concerning the role and function of the exercise, and which undoubtedly influenced the approach of the eventual Report, may be gleaned from the Commission's membership. It was chaired by Sir Richard O'Brien, a retired senior civil servant, and the Secretary to the Commission was seconded from the Department of the Environment: further indications of the Commission's implicit self-understanding as a 'civil' as well as 'ecclesial' body. Its other 17 members were drawn from senior church positions, inner-city parishes, industry, academia and the voluntary and public sector (ACUPA, 1985: v–vi). [4]

During its two-year lifetime, from September 1983 to 1985, the Archbishop's Commission on Urban Priority Areas (ACUPA) received 283 submissions from voluntary and statutory bodies and individuals. It is customary for such commissions to summon written evidence; but another distinguishing feature of ACUPA was its less conventional practice of actually visiting many of the areas under discussion. Members spent time in inner-city parishes in the north-east and north-west of England, Merseyside, east London and the English Midlands. The Commission was therefore at pains to establish that this was by no means an 'arm-chair' enterprise, but one which attempted, wherever possible, to enter into the situation of those in urban priority areas (ACUPA, xiv; O'Brien, 1986: 1). Such a commitment to acquiring first-hand experience of the 'grass-roots' marks a further significant shift in the methods and theological convictions of Church pronouncements on public issues.

The Report portrays the English city as predominantly a place of economic decline, physical decay and social disadvantage. Although there are pockets of prosperity, 'for the most part opportunities for jobs, for housing and for the desired amenities of social services, shopping, schools and leisure have shifted out of the industrial city' (ACUPA: 8). Thus, alongside a prosperous, suburban or rural Britain, there are inner-city districts of multiple deprivation, comprised of populations and industries that have been 'left behind' in the changing economic circumstances of the 1980s.

It is also interesting to reflect on the ambivalence expressed by the

---

4 A further group of advisers included representatives from church-related social action/research bodies, including John Atherton from the William Temple Foundation, John Gladwin from the Board for Social Responsibility and Eric James from the pressure group Christian Action – all experienced and authoritative figures, and representative of a 'broad left' of mainstream Christian social thought.

Report about the nature of urban life. Cities are characterized as 'areas from which people and wealth depart and in which poverty and power-lessness remain' (ibid.: 3). In this respect, the Commission acknowledges a remarkably equivocal attitude in British culture towards the city: it is depicted both as the source of civilized values and the home of depravity, squalor and conflict. The Report summarizes the sources of the malaise of inner cities as follows: 'unemployment, decayed housing, sub-standard educational and medical provision, and social disintegration' (ibid.: xiv). It is interesting to note that the Commissioners relied on Government statistics for indicators of economic and social advantage and disadvan-tage, interpreted by means of a statistical device known as a 'Z-score', which correlates indices of multiple deprivation (ibid.: 21). The districts thereby designated 'Urban Priority Areas' – which may be an outer estate or inner-city district – are effectively 'a different Britain, whose people are prevented from entering fully into the mainstream of the normal life of the nation' (ibid.: 9). The Commission identified a crucial connection between the poverty of UPAs and patterns of power, opportunity and wealth in an increasingly unequal society:

> A statistical portrait of UPAs thus becomes eventually an elaborate picture of inequality. In the foreground appear the shabby streets, neglected houses and sordid demolition sites of the inner city, in the middle ground the vandalised public spaces of the peripheral estates, while in the background are the green and wooded suburbs of middle Britain. The UPAs lie at the centre of an unequal society, their poverty obscured by the busy shopping precincts of mass consumption, their bare subsistence of dole and supplementary benefit existing alongside material opulence. (Ibid.: 21)

However, the belief is that 'cities are still flourishing centres of social, economic, and political life. We confidently assert that the planned resur-gence of the British city is both possible and desirable in the immediate future' (ibid.: xvi). As we shall see, this emphasis on 'keeping faith with the city' is a strong theme of the Report, and strongly informs its insist-ence on the efficacy of ameliorative action.

The Report is candid about the dwindling status of the local church in UPAs. It acknowledges that, historically, the Church of England may well have been a significant source of such ambivalence, representing more the rural idyll than the urban Utopia; and it has long been recognized that the churches neglected the urban working-class in the years following the Industrial Revolution. The Church of England, like the city itself, was perceived as struggling, but resilient, managing to maintain a precarious existence, frequently the only organized Christian presence in the area and often the only sizeable voluntary or community-based group as well.

For this reason, proposals for the renewal of urban priority areas are addressed in equal measure to Church and nation; and the significance of *Faith in the City* rests as much in its recommendations to the local church as to national policy.[5]

Thus, the Report urges a number of reforms upon the local church in UPAs. It must reflect the diversity of its local culture, relate to the neighbourhood and overcome alienation of community to church. It must foster new forms of leadership, Christian education and worship that are appropriate to local people. There must be new patterns of ordained ministry to encourage indigenous leadership; and theological training must more fully reflect and prepare ordinands for the realities of urban ministry.

The most significant administrative proposal to the national Church concerned the setting up of a 'Church Urban Fund', which should aim to build up capital assets (£18 million) derived from central grants and diocesan fund-raising, and direct such monies to local programmes of regeneration, community development and employment opportunities.[6]

'Proposals to Government and Nation' were mainly concerned with a series of policy areas in which central and local government should devote resources to urban regeneration in partnership with the voluntary sector and in consultation with local people. This included local economic regeneration: support for small businesses in Urban Priority Areas and greater public expenditure on job creation and welfare benefit; a programme of public housing investment and new building; a more extensive programme of positive health care; affirmation of the centrality of statutory provision in social service provision; support for education and the youth service; defence of the 'rehabilitative ideal' in the criminal justice system in the face of more punitive policies.

The Report of the Commission was greeted with a ferocious attack upon its findings by senior members of the Government and their supporters in the media. It was not the first time that the Conservatives had launched a 'pre-emptive strike' on Church reports to which it took objection; but its opponents definitely went nuclear over *Faith in the City*, denouncing it as 'Marxist' (Young, 1990: 416–18). Given the 'conviction politics' of the Government, it was unlikely that the Report would have been well received; but it certainly succeeded in sparking a public debate. *Faith in the City* itself eventually sold over 50,000 copies; and a recent assessment of its significance for public policy concludes that the Report – and perhaps

---

5 It is perhaps unique among Anglican social reports to dwell so specifically on the local congregation; and again, this may be a distinguishing feature for the future, in that it recognizes the potential gulf between social responsibility reports researched and aimed at Church leadership, and the attitudes and activities of the ordinary parish churchgoer.

6 For an assessment of the work of the Church Urban Fund, with particular reference to Manchester, see Finneron (1990).

ironically, the Government's condemnation – did succeed in creating a climate of greater concern for poverty and inner-city issues, to which even government policy had eventually to concede (Clark, 1992: 105–6).

The Report opens with a (sociological) paradox: 'The Church does not have particular competence or a distinguished record in proposing social reforms; but the Church of England has a presence in all the UPAs, and a responsibility to bring their needs to the attention of all the nation' (ACUPA, 1985: xvi). The 'established' position of the Church means that, historically, it has been seen as 'the Tory Party at prayer', a predominantly middle-class church, part of the fabric of the State, emphasizing continuity, conservatism and conventional values; and yet, its very presence at the heart of the establishment, its statutory responsibility for the spiritual oversight of the whole of England and the 'cure of souls' of all people within a given geographical area, regardless of religious affiliation, also affords it unique access to every aspect of English society. This enabled the Report to argue for the Church to adopt the role of champion of those who find no representation or advocate in any other institution by nature of its comprehensive coverage of, and access to, the life of the nation.

ACUPA used this to their advantage, arguing that the parish system places the Church in a unique position to promote community and participation, because each priest and congregation has a responsibility for all the population in a district. A true and comprehensive responsibility for the whole community exhorts the Church to share its resources and opportunities for service, to pursue practical collaboration with secular agencies and other faith-communities. It envisaged that forms of 'community development' would therefore be an entirely appropriate expression of inner-city ministry. But an essential paradox presents itself here: the Church of England has universal coverage of England because of its parish system only due to its established status; but this is also being presented, not without foundation, as being the basis on which the Church can express its solidarity with the ordinary people.

> There is no reason to think that the gospel is more authentically lived out in 'comfortable Britain'. On the contrary, we have again and again found evidence of a vitality and generosity in Church life in deprived areas which is a challenge to more affluent congregations ... The failure of the Church today is not just a failure to respond to need; it is ... a failure to attend to the voices, the experience and the spiritual riches of the 'poor' in its midst. (Ibid.: 62)

The Church is thus portrayed both as marginal to the city, and yet simultaneously uniquely placed to speak on behalf of the marginalized. However, this may be a contradiction that is impossible to sustain.

Faith in the City has been criticized for its political 'naivety' by its advocacy of policy solutions which were dependent on government intervention. Critics believed that in this respect the Commission failed to appreciate, or engage with, the shift in political philosophy represented by the Thatcher administration, and the extent to which the economic and social doctrines of the 'New Right' made it reluctant to consider State intervention as an effective or appropriate vehicle of urban regeneration. Its inability to take seriously the primacy of the free market thus arguably hampered its capacity to take on government policy on its own terms; but perhaps this slowness in fully acknowledging the extent of the ideological shift to the New Right reflects a Church operating on theological presuppositions – rooted in its historically established position – which were better suited to an earlier era of 'consensus' politics (Plant, 1989; Clark, 1992: 112–13).

It has been fashionable to dismiss the theology of the Report. Although it has its limitations, however, there was much that was courageous and visionary. Underlying it are a number of important and notable commitments: that the 'facts' of a given situation are fundamental for theological reflection and action; that those with least access to power have a unique, if neglected, perspective, to which the Church must give voice; that faith is more than individual salvation, but the realization of social justice; and that theology is the articulation of the ultimate principles and values that bring such action into being (ACUPA, 1985: ch. 5).

Another feature of *Faith in the City* is the centrality of two theological concepts: 'the Kingdom of God' and *koinonia*, or community. The Report argues that the proclamation of the Kingdom of God was envisaged as a vision of human society in which worldly standards of wealth, privilege and power were to be overturned. Theological tradition testifies to a God who is concerned for the right ordering of society; and Christian social thought keeps alive the possibility of realizing a better world amid the fallenness of the present. It speaks of the priorities of the responsible acquisition and distribution of wealth, of the importance of protecting the weak and vulnerable; and of 'the existence in Scripture of a different paradigm of social and economic relationships' (ibid.: 54).

The insistence on the primacy of community also draws upon clear biblical precedent, from the Pauline emphasis on 'building up' the faithful, to the witness to all forms of *koinonia* as essential to the realization of the Kingdom. The Christian doctrine of humanity is one that necessitates mutuality, solidarity and interdependence within which 'the God-given potential of each one of us is developed' (ibid.: 59).

> A Christian community is one that is open to, and responsible for, the whole of the society in which it is set, and proclaims its care for the weak, its solidarity with all, and its values which lie beyond the mere satisfaction of material needs. (Ibid.)

Such a commitment poses a challenge to the nature of theology itself. The Western emphasis on theology as a deductive and intellectual activity is countered by the vitality of Third World approaches which emphasize the critical and practical character of theology. Liberation theology argues that knowledge reflects the concerns and interests of those who practise it; and it places in contrast with Western academic theology an alternative tradition, of theology for and by the poor. This activity has emerged from 'base communities' which sustain reflection and activity in the midst of extreme poverty and oppression. *Faith in the City* expresses a hope that parallel groups will emerge in UPAs, which would start from personal experience and story, reflecting the concerns of the community and the poor. Rather than intellectual formulations of doctrine, theological practice and profession would then be about the transformation of everyday lives. Such a shift of priorities might also be effected by new styles of Christian education and training for ministry.

Above all, the theology of the Report is an affirmation of the world – and specifically, even the neglected and marginalized realm of the secular city – as the place of encounter with the Divine:

> We believe that God, though infinitely transcendent, is also to be found, despite all appearances, in the apparent waste lands of our inner cities and housing estates … that the city is not to be shunned as a concentration of evil but enjoyed as a unique opportunity for human community; that the justice of God, as revealed in Scripture, is a standard by which all human institutions must be judged; that society, in our fallen world, cannot be purged of its imperfections by careful planning, maintenance and repair … but requires redemption through suffering and self-giving undertaken in solidarity with Christ. (Ibid.: 70)

This is a commitment to an 'incarnational' faith, therefore; and one which shares many of Harvey Cox's themes of the immanence of God, and the potential of human community and rational, creative endeavour to speak of the Divine. However, there are also subtle shifts. The unalloyed triumphs of human reason and technology, of humankind 'come of age' is now questioned; instead, ACUPA emphasizes the brokenness of the city, which is portrayed as a more muted and tragic landscape than the 'secular city'. So there is a different timbre to this particular theology of incarnation. The sphere of human agency and the fruits of freedom and progress are not signs of human perfectibility, but rather integral elements of the flawed human condition; yet they are also redolent with the salvific possibility of a creation redeemed through the suffering of the crucified Christ.

However, it is questionable whether the theology of ACUPA is prepared fully to embrace a theology of the cross. Perhaps it might have appeared too excessive to equate the conditions of the UPAs with the Passion of Christ, although much of liberation theology makes precisely this connection: that the poor are experiencing a kind of 'Calvary', that such injustice represents truly a crisis in human affairs, but that the Church is called to identify with, and bring to birth, a resurrection of love and justice.

Thus, again, we experience a fundamental contradiction at the heart of *Faith in the City*. It reflects the best of Anglican social thought, founded on a robust incarnational theology, in which God's self-identification with humanity is seen to render the things of the world – cities, human reason, social 'facts', governments, even Church Commissions – as fundamentally the channels through which God effects grace and salvation. Society is given the Church's blessing as expressing the highest human values; and theology speaks in the terms of the everyday world, articulating those 'natural' and self-evident values, just as the Church is available, unconditionally and equally for all, to assist with the pains and celebrations of life. Yet such a vision can easily become a form of theological functionalism. The status quo is believed to be thus ordained by God, particular cultural phenomena are regarded as permanent institutions of creation rather than contingent and particular products of specific human relations. While such an incarnational theology provides perfect expression for the Church of England's position in a settled, harmonious social order, and resists any tendencies towards sectarianism or withdrawal from the public or civic arena, therefore, it fares less well in providing a sharper, more distinctive profile for the Church in a world of unjust social relations and distorted human potential.

Clearly, ACUPA finds it imperative to bear witness to alternative models of human community founded not on individualism, competition and profit but upon interdependence, charity and mutuality. It also recognizes the symbolic power of local congregations living out such a witness as a prefiguration of a more perfect vision. Yet it seems to want a 'Kingdom' theology without too great a rupture of the existing order. The fact is, however, the *koinonia* and Kingdom of which ACUPA speaks are the products of a Christian vision which regarded such communities and definitive visions as radically at odds with earthly powers; as splitting asunder conventional patterns of family, state and temporal responsibility. *Faith in the City* is therefore caught theologically, as it is caught sociologically, between wholehearted identification with, and radical dissent from, the existing social order.

Despite its contradictions, *Faith in the City* has proved decisive for the development of English Christian social thought and practice. It has provided the impetus for a decade of community-based projects and initiatives alongside marginalized and disadvantaged urban communities. As well as the Church of England's own Church Urban Fund, other church-related pressure groups have adopted many of the commitments and perspectives of *Faith in the City*, reflecting its focus on grass-roots local activity and taking further its implicit debt to the 'preferential option for the poor' of theologies of liberation.

One such group is based in Manchester. Founded in 1982, Church Action on Poverty (CAP) is an ecumenical and national pressure group, concerned with studying the causes of poverty and highlighting the experiences of those who struggle against it. It organizes campaigns and lobbies of Parliament to bring attention to government policies; it seeks to influence the public debate and climate of opinion within the churches. In this respect, although it is an independent, membership-based organization, it has taken to itself ACUPA's dual responsibilities of addressing Church and Nation. Since the end of the 1980s CAP has forged an increasing emphasis on linking up with local groups and communities, of directing its campaigns towards its grass-roots membership, and co-ordinating its resources into programmes by which such locally based activities and perspectives can be brought into the public domain. In this respect, it is explicitly modelling itself on the understanding of theology as local and contextual: of developing the commitment to 'local theology' as envisaged by *Faith in the City*; and of grounding its own public statements and campaigns on an appeal to the authoritative expertise of those with direct experience of poverty. A conscious and deliberate adoption of such a method is not exceptional. Many other agencies working in areas as diverse as overseas aid, charitable and community work advocate models founded on 'empowerment' rather than paternalism; but it is instructive to examine in greater detail the steps taken by CAP to make such a commitment a reality.

An early project, *Hearing the Cry of the Poor*, consciously modelled itself on liberation theologies originating from Southern Africa and Latin America (*Kairos Document*, 1985; *Road to Damascus*, 1989). These involved ordinary Christians speaking out against the collusion of Church with oppressive State and calling for a new social order and new forms of Christian witness which explicitly embody the values of the Kingdom. *Hearing the Cry of the Poor* mirrors this style: of identifying the injustices embedded in social structures; of naming the effects of government policy; of appealing to the poor as critics of oppressive regimes and arbiters of the new; of seeking to articulate a new Christian spirituality which aligns itself with the struggle of the poor to achieve justice. The process began in 1988 with the drafting of a 'confessional statement' for consultation. CAP established a drafting process in which the phrases and sentiments of the proposed Declaration were debated and redrafted by local groups, both church-related and community-based.

Local CAP groups and community organizations debated it and it was adopted in September 1989, and launched on 4 December of that year.

It bore several similarities to *Faith in the City*. Like the earlier report, *Hearing the Cry of the Poor* also received a fair amount of press coverage; and it was also quickly condemned by Conservative ministers and their media supporters. The uncompromising social analysis of the Declaration was seen as further proof of the churches' abdication of their role as the nation's moral arbiters, and their captivity by the forces of secularism and unbelief[7] (Goggins, 1990: 4–5).

Like *Faith in the City*, the Declaration also placed great emphasis on the authority of those who spoke directly from an experience of poverty and marginalization. But here, the whole point of the Declaration was to underline the moral authority that the experience of the marginalized minority exerted on the rich majority: to stress the imperatives it placed on the many to take responsibility for the circumstances of the few.[8]

> We have heard with our own ears the cry of the poor. We have seen with our own eyes our society driven in a direction that contradicts the gospel. Wounding effects are witnessed and experienced daily. They challenge us to seek a new social order founded upon that vision and possibility of human wholeness which is contained in the Christian message and which speaks to all human experience. (Church Action on Poverty, 1991)

The structure of the Declaration has three sections: 'What Has Happened to our Common Life?' which quotes statistical evidence of worsening poverty and inequality, states that reliance on market forces favours the rich and harbours a socially divisive individualism. It admits that 'poverty did not begin in 1979', but argues that it has acquired a 'special vehemence' in that time, due to a breakdown in consensus and workings of deregulated market. The second section, entitled 'We Believe . . .'

---

7 Interestingly, despite the emphasis within the drafting process by CAP itself upon consulting local community groups and articulating their concerns, and despite the presence at the launch of representatives from CAP groups in the North-East, much of the press coverage the following day was of the nature of 'Church leaders denounce government policies'. Clearly, the media found it made more compelling and controversial news to represent the Declaration as a statement of church leadership, thus neglecting much of the effort by CAP to embody a new way of working in the Declaration. Perhaps again this reveals the tension between Church as national lobbying institution and church at local level: whereas CAP was determined to shift the focus on to the latter, and root Christian discipleship and witness as acting and speaking from margins to centre, the public impact of Church statements on national political issues still held – perhaps disproportionate – impact.

8 This had particular political significance: at the time of the Declaration, a series of statements had been made by government ministers denying the existence of poverty as a social reality; so to proclaim the continuing and worsening state of social inequality, and to present a statement emanating from the heart of poverty, was itself a radical act.

gives theological rationale for CAP's stance. Here, the centrality of the Kingdom is reiterated; but the call to discipleship has a sharper edge than *Faith in the City*. All those who follow Jesus commit themselves to the realization of the Kingdom here on earth. God's spirit speaks through the cries of the poor, restoring our social priorities and breaking the power of false illusions of money, power and status. Third, 'From Faith to Action' attempts to connect theological claims with social responsibility: 'The true end of any social order ... is to embody the Kingdom of God in human affairs.' Signs of the Kingdom will be: equal citizenship regardless of race, class or gender; hope for the future; basic needs of all are met. A renewed social vision must be informed by the 'practical wisdom' of those who seek mutuality, respect and justice.

The theology of the Declaration is perhaps less nuanced than that of *Faith in the City*, but it is intentionally designed to give the bold outlines of a moral and political stance. It is also, after all, the work of the converted. Those consulted were committed to the work of CAP, and this meant that their statements were generated from the concrete realities of marginalization and poverty, although it offers little space for equivocation or qualification. It is perhaps best regarded as essentially a credo for the anti-poverty lobby within the churches: a collective summons, a rallying-cry; and perhaps, and like the creeds of the early Church, should be taken as a statement of collective solidarity, a means of establishing the boundaries of the faithful, rather than as a substantive statement of belief.

CAP's commitment to usher to the centre of public concerns the wisdom of those on the margins was further developed in its next project, Action of the Church Towards a New Social Vision (ACTS). Again, the impetus came from the sense of an intransigent government, and a commitment to 'doing theology in the community'. Much of the development work was conducted among community groups in East Manchester, via a process of excavating and articulating their opinions on housing, health care, political participation and spirituality (Dunne *et al.*, 1993; Dale and Russell, 1993). Out of the stories and accounts of resistance and renewal would come, it was believed, the values and visions from which the marginalized communities could act to forge alternative realities.

ACTS is therefore working on a model of 'doing theology' founded on a synthesis of theology and social analysis that owes a debt to the value-commitments and methods of liberation theology and critical theory, with the intention to reconstruct theological language and the moral discourse of public policy in order that it may reflect more authentically the 'real' interests of the poor.

Thus, ACTS publications record the experiences and stories of community groups, in the belief that the everyday reveals the Kingdom. However, the process has moved on from ACUPA: by now, the institutional

Church is practically invisible, except perhaps as a penitent observer. Traditional or 'academic' theology no longer provides explicit terms of reference, although of course the values which inform the 'exercises' and consultative processes by which ACTS elicits (or constructs?) the words of its informants are implicitly those of empowerment, liberation and incarnation. However, there is a kind of mute consensus that talk of God – at least as transcendent and Other – must be banished. Any recourse to theological discourse can only refer to the respect in which life has ultimate meaning and purpose. God is only meaningful as wholly immanent: present, but seemingly synonymous, with the purposeful struggles of the poor and marginalized to 'name' their experiences and aspirations.

Critical questions may need to be asked about the extent to which, in adopting such a stance, projects such as ACTS jettison any distinctively Christian character – or indeed, whether that matters. A 'local' theology may emerge from the visions and experiences of a local community; but does it necessarily also need to bear some recognizable resemblance to the historical institutions and truth-claims of a more universal Christian community? Would it be possible for the authenticity of a 'local' theology to be assessed not simply by its faithfulness to its context but by reference to historical or biblical tradition, and still retain its integrity? There may be a danger of local theologies collapsing into a liberationist incarnationalism which cannot differentiate between world and Kingdom, not so much because of its corruption by power and establishment, but because of its total identification with specific human projects. As many commentators have noted, appeal to the notion of 'community' is often regarded as self-evidently wholesome; but it can also conceal self-interest and introversion. Without wishing to decry the value and scrupulousness of the ACTS endeavour, therefore, it seems important to ask whether a local theology needs a point of reference beyond the horizons of its own community so as to avoid itself becoming a self-serving 'ideology'.

ACTS's successor project, Local People, National Voice (LPNV) further exemplified the commitment to grass-roots campaigning and solidarity with those most badly affected by poverty. It aimed to collect evidence and insights from local contexts in advance of convening a national 'hearing' on poverty, to be held in 1996. It is envisaged that campaigns will take place at three levels of action: local groups, regional meetings and national.

Once more, there is emphasis on the creation of partnerships between people from different sections of society – of listening to people in the midst of poverty, of gaining accurate information and creating the right circumstances in which the powerless and silenced can gain a voice. However, the initial campaigning literature of LPNV seems more clearly directed towards the churches; its aim appears one of prompting Christian responsibility to act in response to 'the cry of the poor':

> The structures of power, wealth creation and distribution must be changed so that the rights bestowed on us all, by virtue of being created in the image and likeness of our God, are restored to each and everyone. This challenge is just as strong today and should lead us actively to align ourselves with the low-paid, unemployed, homeless and other oppressed groups ... We will become truly Christian as we work in partnership, to proclaim good news to the poor. (Church Action on Poverty, 1993: 1)

Another local initiative to Greater Manchester whose origin lay in the response to *Faith in the City* is an organization called Linking Up, which came into existence in 1989. The aim of Linking Up is 'to help the churches play a more effective role in regenerating the economic life of Urban Priority Areas'. It does this by providing a variety of services for local 'self-help' projects: training, financial advice, organizational development, business planning and commercial sponsorship.

As a project promoted by the Church Urban Fund, Linking Up represents two significant departures or developments from *Faith in the City*. First, Linking Up does not work exclusively with the Christian churches, but with a variety of faith-communities throughout the UPAs of Britain.[9] The second point to note is the extent to which the assumptions of ACUPA in the mid-1980s, that the economic regeneration of UPAs would be largely the responsibility of central or local government, has been superseded. In the 1990s, the agents of the Church Urban Fund – such as Linking Up – seem to work quite happily within a very different economic environment, in which local initiatives are very publicly promoted as 'community partnerships' between businesses, local authorities and voluntary funding. In this respect Linking Up is much more typical of urban regeneration activity in the British city of the 1990s, and reflects a greater degree of collaboration between the voluntary sector – including the churches – local authorities and private enterprise than *Faith in the City* ever envisaged.[10] So the Church Urban Fund, as the main project agency of *Faith in the City*, has concentrated on programmes

---

9 It works with a Muslim project in Bradford providing literacy and information technology training for young Muslim women; another project in a Hindu temple in Leeds promotes a variety of educational and business schemes. Further material available from Linking Up, 27 Blackfriars Road, Manchester M3 7AQ.

10 One project that has gained assistance from Linking Up is based at St Wilfrid's Church in Hulme, a public housing estate on the fringes of the University of Manchester. 'Firmstart' is a managed workspace house in a redundant Roman Catholic church of small business units, employing local people and offering training and financial support for new enterprises.

that direct resources to local communities and enable them to build up initiatives that equip local people with skills and resources which will – it is hoped – take them from dependency to empowerment.[11] Meanwhile, however, the decade since *Faith in the City* has been one of a growing socio-economic divide. While the better off members of society have increased their share of national wealth, the poorest are now worse off. The gap in earnings between richest and poorest in Britain is wider now than at any time since records began in 1886 (Commission on Social Justice, 1994: 28).

Since Augustine, Christian social thought has always had to compromise between the earthly city and the City of God, of seeking ways of affirming the world as the arena of Divine revelation and salvation while retaining some critical distance. Theologies of the city risk endorsing the 'signs of the times' without fully appreciating the provisionality and partiality of even such secular visions – as the anachronism of Harvey Cox's vision now show. Yet for those Christian communities who do see their vocation as one of solidarity with wider society, the challenge remains of how to maintain a credible and authentic presence in wider society without compromising a distinctive and authoritative Christian perspective on human destiny and social organization. One criticism of *Faith in the City* was that it failed to recognize the extent of the breakdown of social consensus by 1985; not only did it overestimate the government's will to intervene, but it also held a mistaken and wildly inflated estimate of the ability of the Church itself to construct a viable alternative to free-market models of urban renewal. However, other evidence suggests that *Faith in the City* was received warmly by many urban priority communities, and that the 'residual religiosity' of the English remained sufficiently strong to ensure that the Church still retains a credibility and influence in relation to the contemporary city (ACAGUPA, 1990; Clark, 1992: 105–6). Yet the contradictions of ACUPA still persist: an established Church whose active membership stands at less than 1 per cent of the urban population; an institution that owes its very existence to political and civil compromise espousing a radical vision of an alternative human community; a Church which regards itself as an advocate of the poor and yet owes its financial security to the management of a sizeable investment portfolio; a theology that speaks the language of scandal, vulnerability and kenosis translated into policies relevant to government and nation; a Church struggling to articulate a distinctive theology rooted in the specific life and context of a local community, simultaneously claiming that interfaith dialogue is the most important and fruitful challenge for the urban Church. Such contradictions may ultimately either signal the death of the

---

11 However, the Church Urban Fund has been criticized for colluding with programmes of urban regeneration without being sufficiently critical of wider economic policies. See James (1991).

institutional Church, or else herald the birth of new forms of (Christian) faith and practice in UPAs.

Christian social thought must always be dynamic, forged at the intersection of economic and social reality and Christian faith and practice. *Faith in the City* represents one such response to a changing context, even though at times it founders on the contradictions of a State Church, predominantly middle-class in membership, attempting to 'keep faith' with those most badly hit by an increasingly polarized society. Whatever the fault-lines of division and fragmentation, whatever the scale of contrast between wealth and dispossession, the city of the year 2000 will still be a place of ambivalence and contradiction, and certainly a place where the old certainties and institutions no longer hold sway. The question is whether contemporary social theology and Christian praxis has the resources and commitment to make a difference in that context.

15

PUBLIC THEOLOGY IN AN AGE OF 'VOTER APATHY'

Introduction

On the weekend after the last British General Election, most newspapers gave prominence to pictures of Tony and Cherie Blair and their children posing happily outside No. 10 Downing Street. There was good reason to celebrate; the government had been re-elected for a second term, a feat not achieved by any other Labour administration in the party's history. What is more, a Commons majority of 167 represented another 'landslide' victory for the party, an unprecedented pattern of success.[1]

Closer analysis of the inside contents of these same newspapers, however, told a slightly different story, suggesting that the outcome of Campaign 2001 might have been something of a hollow victory. The so-called 'landslide' could hardly be said to represent a popular mandate, given that only 59 per cent of the electorate had bothered to vote, the lowest turnout since 1918. Labour's own share of the vote stood at 40.7 per cent.[2] No wonder commentators referred to the result as an 'Apathetic Landslide' (Hertz, 2001). A particular cause for concern in many quarters was the lack of interest among younger people: less than four in ten

---

1 A landslide is a majority of 100 seats or more, and although 13 out of 26 of twentieth-century results qualified as such, not even Margaret Thatcher at her peak could deliver successive parliamentary victories of the magnitude of 1997 and 2001.

2 Some of the mismatch between the size of the majority and the low turnout is due to the peculiarities of the (Westminster) system of first-past-the-post election. In terms of net gains and losses, there was relatively little change in the overall standing of the parties between 1997 and 2001. Labour lost six seats overall, the Conservatives increased by one, the SNP lost one seat and the Liberal Democrats gained six. See Norris (2001a: 17, table 3).

of those aged 18 to 25 cast their vote. And in some inner-city constituencies ('old' Labour's traditional heartland), little more than one-third of those registered to vote actually did so.[3]

Opinion is divided, however, as to the significance that can really be attached to so-called 'voter apathy'. Some analysts identify specific factors about Campaign 2001 that failed to generate enthusiasm, and argue that despite low turnout on this particular occasion, the electorate's commitment to the political system is undiminished. Others, however, trace emergent patterns throughout the West which suggest an unprecedented and widespread loss of faith in public institutions: not only a disaffection with the organs of the State (parliament, legal system, civil service) but also a withdrawal from voluntary and community activity, including trade unions, community associations and organized religion. The implications of this, they argue, are serious for the health of participatory democracy.

Even though a more considered examination of 'voter apathy' which follows in this chapter sketches a quite complex and subtle picture, such research still raises important questions not only for political debate in general but for the discipline of public theology in particular. On one level, the increasing fragility of many civic institutions may confirm fears about 'the withering of public hope' (Forrester, 1997: 198), a symptom of the fragmentation of moral discourse that has preoccupied public theology and social ethics since Alasdair MacIntyre's *After Virtue*. Yet while public trust in the institutions of participatory democracy may rest to a large extent on moral agreements concerning *procedural* norms by which matters as human rights, democracy, freedom and the rule of law may be debated, it also requires us to think about the *iterative* processes by which individuals connect to the wider social order. It concerns not only what kinds of values need to inform the public domain, but also the very infrastructure through which the fabric of the State, public institutions and civil society is maintained. But in a changing context, increasingly one of rapid globalization, it is not simply a matter of defending 'politics as usual', but of looking at how institutions facilitate the common good and respond to the challenge of social exclusion.

Such developments have an impact on the discourse of public theology, not only because Christian churches have traditionally been actively engaged in politics at many levels – from practical service delivery through to moral debate – but also because any contraction of the public domain could radically affect the kinds of contributions deemed acceptable or legitimate. Amid such problems, however, new opportunities emerge, not least in the shape of New Labour's encouragement of faith-

---

3 Glasgow Shettleston constituency had a turnout of 38.8% of the electorate; Liverpool Riverside, 33.8%.

communities' participation in urban regeneration and welfare services, and the insistent question of the role of organized religion in relation to the conduct of civil society. Public theology in the twenty-first century will need to address these fundamental changes and realignments taking place in the political process, and work to articulate a rejuvenated theological discourse capable of addressing the complexities and divisions of contemporary society.

Voter Apathy

Two key sources may serve as initial indicators of what really happened in the British General Election: MORI's survey of a sample of the electorate during and after election 2001 (MORI, 2001), and a qualitative study of Basildon in Essex, carried out between 1992 and 1997 (Hayes and Hudson, 2001). A third source, analysis of comparative electorates in the West, also helps to put British evidence in context (Norris, 2001b; Newton and Norris, 1999).

MORI's research was carried out on a sample of 18,000 people in two phases, covering a period early in the election campaign 9–15 May (Phase 1), and one immediately after the election itself 9–18 June (Phase 2). The questions covered public attitudes towards voting, the campaign itself and the electoral process in general. The survey found marked variation in reported voter participation, especially by age, the lowest rates being among the younger age groups. Of 18–24-year-olds interviewed 39 per cent had voted, rising to 59 per cent (the national average for the electorate as a whole) among 35–44-year-olds, to levels of 65 per cent among 45–54-year-olds, and 69 and 70 per cent respectively for 55–64 and 65-plus.

Participation also varied across socio-economic groups, ranging between 68 per cent among professionals, to 53 per cent among unskilled workers. The differentials are similar depending on type of housing tenure: those who own their house outright were recorded at 68 per cent, mortgage homeowners at 59 per cent (again, the UK average) to council tenants and private tenants at 52 and 46 per cent respectively.

Given Labour's lead in the opinion polls throughout the campaign, and the size of the Commons majority it was defending, it was perhaps unsurprising that many people decided that there was little at stake in the campaign. Certainly, only 36 per cent agreed with the proposition that 'voting would make a difference' (MORI, 2001: 1). However, the survey finds little evidence of this being a symptom of endemic cynicism with democracy, and concludes that the campaign itself was the cause of most lack of interest. In Phase 1, for example, 65 per cent of respondents reported being actively interested in politics; but by Phase 2, even 61 per cent of that sample admitted they had not found the election campaign interesting.

MORI's research was sponsored by the Electoral Commission, who made much in its commentary of the fact that two-thirds of the electorate still believed that voting makes a difference, even if they were sceptical about Campaign 2001 itself. Its report concluded: 'civic duty and habit are key motivations to voting ... people have positive attitudes towards voting ... Interest in politics has remained very stable over the past three decades' (ibid.: 5). Turnout could easily be improved, it went on, by the introduction of new methods of voting, for example by mobile phone or over the Internet: 'Voter engagement is an issue, rather than apathy ... declining turnout is not a function of declining interest in politics or elections but rather a failure of the campaign to connect with the electorate' (ibid.: 1).

These conclusions may allay many of the worst fears about 'voter apathy'. Yet given that the voter attitudes survey did not delve more deeply into evidence of wider political activity beyond the ballot box, it is difficult to speculate much further on the significance of this evidence. There is, however, a hint of a mismatch between the importance people attach in principle to the entitlement to vote and the sentiment that the electoral system exercises very little effective accountability over the government of the day. The size of Labour's lead notwithstanding, this report offers small glimpses of a deeper dislocation in the political process: 32 per cent of the sample stated that 'none of the parties stood for policies I would like to see', and 38 per cent that there was 'little difference between ... the main parties'. Predictably, perhaps, those who did not vote were inclined to be more negative about the value of voting, the policies of the main parties and the quality of the campaign. And arguably, the most serious dimension of voter apathy extends beyond mere boredom or frustration with election coverage to manifest itself as abstention from the democratic process itself. Among the non-voters of the MORI sample, 15 per cent did not do so because they had never registered, a figure that stood at 27 per cent of Black non-voters sampled, and 29 per cent of 18–24-year-olds.

Attitudes, and a sense of popular investment in the political process, are thus a crucial factor in influencing behaviour, something the Commission itself concedes. New practical measures may prompt a few more to cast their vote, but 'equally important are ... the perceptions people have of the political process in the long term' (MORI, 2001: 5). Other surveys of voter attitudes represent a more complex, and less reassuring, picture, however, and serve to substantiate rumours of gradual disengagement from public institutions and democratic processes.

Basildon, a new town in Essex, has been called 'a barometer for the mood of the nation' (Hayes and Hudson, 2001: 3). That may be too expansive a claim, although Basildon's electoral history throughout the 1980s and early 1990s casts it as a model example of the fortunes of post-war social democracy, especially the ability of Thatcherism to steal working-class votes from Labour and to remodel the aspirations of many of the electorate away from 'tax and spend' economics and state intervention towards the ideals, if not the realities, of home ownership, lower taxes and private enterprise. In their surveys of Basildon between 1992 and 1997, however, Hayes and Hudson chart the gradual disaffection with the Conservatives and with it a decisive disengagement from the political process itself. The overriding feature of Basildon's political culture was, they concluded, 'a profound detachment from all forms of collective political process or social agency' (ibid.: 11). However peculiar to its local context – a migrant town, predominantly skilled working-class, created within the very dispensation that brought the Welfare State into being after 1945 – it suggests that the patterns of 2001 may have significant, and inauspicious, antecedents.

For example, Hayes and Hudson produce evidence to suggest that voter disengagement is part of a wider pattern of withdrawal from public association altogether. Those interviewed in Basildon identified themselves overwhelmingly as working class, yet eschew affiliations to trade unions or other labour organizations. This is reflected in national trends: between 1955 and 1995, membership of trade unions in Britain fell by 30 per cent.[4] In other words, the cultural and social context – through which political engagement, public debate, community organization and neighbourhood activism have traditionally been expressed – has atrophied:

> All the evidence of our survey suggests a disengagement from the political sphere and perhaps more importantly from all the intermediary and mediating institutions through which public discussions about priorities used to be conducted. (Ibid.: 65)

When questioning people about habits outside the workplace, a similar pattern emerges. 'Family' is the overwhelmingly most popular focus of allegiance; an obvious choice, perhaps, but standing in contrast to the paucity of alternative foci of association. Basildonians are not disposed to join voluntary associations, clubs, or political movements. Leisure preferences outside the family tended to be a session at the gym or the shopping mall; although to share social space with others in these pursuits is more 'an accident of timing' (ibid.: 29) than a conscious search for collective assembly. 'The quality of public life is not sustained merely by resource provision but through participation and active adherence to a public agenda. In Basildon this seems to be largely absent' (ibid.: 37).

Even allowing for Basildon's special features, Hayes and Hudson's

---

4 Although a key factor in this would also have been the decline in the manufacturing sector over the same period.

anatomy of the town provides evidence of a far more radical level of dis-affiliation from a range of collective organizations than simply boredom with one unspectacular campaign. The people of Basildon do not hold out much hope for government, indeed anybody outside themselves, for delivering long-term improvement to their lot. There is little confidence in any external agency or institution: only education, as a means of self-improvement, is the preferred vehicle of personal aspiration. In short, 'these voters have very little faith in anything other than themselves' (ibid.: 59).

A comparative perspective on voter attitudes, from a series of surveys of the so-called 'trilateral democracies', provides a further context. For a start, it serves as a reminder that concern for the erosion of public trust in democratic organizations is not new (Crozier *et al.*, 1975: 2). But it also allows us to extrapolate further from 'voter apathy' towards broader questions of confidence in parliamentary processes, the quality of civil society and so on. Norris and Newton's evidence suggests that disillusion with government is more acute than other measures of investment in public institutions, such as trust of fellow citizens, involvement in voluntary and community organizations, or faith in private companies. This has similarities to the mood evoked by Hayes and Hudson, in that Norris and Newton argue that the key to strong democratic institutions is the abundance of 'social capital', especially that represented by civil society.[5] Voluntary and community bodies perform a vital function in linking individuals and communities to local and national decision-making processes, which in turn fosters confidence in government performance and credibility (Newton and Norris, 1999: 10–12).

After Politics?

What emerges from these studies? While voters' basic motivation does seem harder to stimulate, this may be due to the more fluid nature of political commitment, or the phenomenon of 'social dealignment' (Norris, 2001b: 11) among electorates throughout the West. Voters are more likely to make decisions on a specific and conditional basis, which may in some circumstances suggest a more critical and discerning electorate. Yet the danger is that it may signal a more fragmented political process, as people cast aside group loyalties (such as social class) in favour of more short-term or sectional interests.

Two issues really stand out, however. First, the greatest drift away from political engagement – in terms of participation in parliamentary elections – is occurring among younger people, poorer socio-economic groups and ethnic minorities. This is consistent with research suggesting

---

5 Civil society is that part of the public domain independent of the market or the State. For ideas about 'social capital', see Putnam (2000).

that 'social exclusion' encompasses a network of economic, cultural and political factors, such that 'deprivation results in a constraint on citizenship' (Barnes *et al.*, 2001). However, the rhetoric of 'joined-up government' as redressing the multiple and connected indices of disadvantage is seldom matched by the reality of measures to combat social exclusion, which have tended to focus on the job market at the expense of other strategies (Graham, 2000). Whether non-participation in elections is regarded as self-imposed exclusion, or part of a more general syndrome of alienation, therefore, a commitment to social inclusion requires attention to the dynamics of political participation and civic involvement – necessitating a 'thick' notion of *active citizenship*.

Second, even though respondents to the various qualitative surveys reviewed above seem to retain a principled belief in the right to vote, there seems to be growing scepticism that it will actually make any difference. This may reflect a lack of faith not so much in democracy in theory as in the processes of governance in practice; a loss of confidence in the ability of the State to deliver better welfare provision and economic growth through fiscal management and wealth distribution; and an unravelling of the post war social democratic manifesto – responsible for the conception of Basildon itself – in which rational centralized government planning was regarded as the means to build a better society. In this respect, the *Observer* newspaper's judgement immediately after the UK General Election on low voter turnout corresponds quite closely with Hayes and Hudson's analysis of Basildon: 'People don't turn out to vote, not because they already know who will win, but because they don't believe that politicians will deliver' (Hertz, 2001).

Some of this is reflected in the uncertainty among politicians themselves at the ability of national governments to control their economies given the power of transnational corporations and the fluidity of labour, capital and production in a global economy (Plant, 1999: 32). Not to mention the large-scale, long-term problems such as climate change and technological innovation which far exceed the fiscal or political powers of national governments.

The legacy of neo-liberal economic and social politics during the 1980s and 1990s may also have contributed. While it would be facile to assume a golden age of mass participation, evidence suggests a gradual 'privatization' triggered by an unravelling of the infrastructure of collective association during the 1980s and 1990s. The elevation of the market and dismantling of many intermediate organizations such as local government and trade unions, privatization and the effects of neo-liberal individualism have worn away the warp and weft of civil society:

Thatcherism has left no legacy in the shape of prominent individuals or new institutions that could carry forward its key tenets. But one achievement did endure: it dealt a death-blow to important forms of collectivism in society ... What has emerged in the late 1990s is a landscape in which individuals stand out in isolated relief, without much reference to each other and with only minimal relationships to other institutions and organizations. (Hayes and Hudson, 2001: 42)

For some, however, this is not a short-term aberration that can be redressed by a change of government, because such attenuation of the public domain is an inevitable result of the economic logic inherent in global capitalism (Bauman, 1994). Modernity's emphasis on personal responsibility founded on self-authenticating powers of inherent reason – once a powerful counter to the heteronomy of tradition and deference – weakens the bonds of social solidarity based on common interest. The 'discontinuous, fragmentary, episodic, consequences-avoiding life' (ibid.: xx) is ultimately incompatible with communities built on long-term planning, security and continuity.

At the heart of this, is a kind of social atomism – Basildon's loss of faith in anything beyond themselves – which, Geoff Mulgan writes, 'has eroded our capacity to think in terms of common interests and fates, contributing to the decay of an active culture of political argument and action' (quoted in Bauman, 1994: i). Nor do attempts by local policy-makers to connect with the electorate seem significantly to have animated local politics in places like Basildon. Their solutions seem to be about more efficient delivery of 'politics as usual' rather than any means of rebuilding the formal and informal community links – the 'social capital' of local democracy – through which the democratic process has traditionally been mediated: tenants' associations, local ward parties, voluntary organizations (including the churches), and which carried authority by virtue of belief in their ability to represent the local community. 'We are left with characteristically top-down policy-making, devoid of any sense of community involvement or social partnership' (Hayes and Hudson, 2001: 12).

Anyone exercised by the future of democracy – at least in its parliamentary manifestations – is therefore presented with a 'puzzle over how to recreate and renew the civil and political institutions that are the backbone of a thousand towns like Basildon' (ibid.). Enabling people to vote by mobile phone, as the Electoral Commission recommends, will not address the introversion infecting the political process. Governments cannot simply rely on greater sophistication of technocratic measures without also engendering more robust forms of self-government and consent. Attention to the theory and practice of citizenship, of what Tom Bentley calls not joined-up but 'grown-up' government (Bentley, 2000), will necessitate a root-and-branch reconstruction of the very fundamentals of the body politic. Any constitutional reform aimed at restoring trust in the processes and legitimacy of governance 'must be created with the active participation of the people. It must empower people and give them a sense of belonging. It must protect difference and diversity. It must allow us to claim our rights and protect us from arbitrary authority. It must be based on equality' (Charter 88, 2000: 7).

The 'end of politics' may be not so much about its demise, therefore, as an opportunity to rethink the fundamental objectives, or ends, that constitute the public domain.

Public Theology and the Renewal of Civil Society

By establishing a link between a vigorous culture of involvement in local associations which generate 'social capital' and public trust in institutions such as Parliament, civil service and legal system, commentators such as Hayes and Hudson, and Newton and Norris invoke the contemporary debate about 'civil society'. Some of this is close to the 'Third Way' politics which attempts to find an alternative to State socialism or neo-liberal market economics. It seeks to reconfigure the relationship between individuals, communities and the State by emphasizing the importance of strong intermediary organizations – and in particular, the voluntary sector – for fostering citizenship and directing delivery of welfare services.

It is intriguing to see how religious groups have found themselves centre-stage in this new dispensation, both in the UK and the US (Curti, 2001; Harris, 2001). It is clear, however, that a very wide spectrum of opinions and political philosophies is at work here. To involve faith-communities in public life may mean the scaling-down of public expenditure and the promotion of faith-based welfare schemes in its place, as in the right-wing thinking of Marvin Olasky, an adviser to George W. Bush. More towards the centre-ground, though, are a number of commentators and politicians who would regard faith-communities as ideal examples of civil society working in partnership with local and national government. Speaking at a rally organized by the Christian Socialist Movement in Westminster in March 2001, Tony Blair expounded a very typical version of this view:

> Community action has always been a central mission of the churches and other faith groups. Looking outwards to the needs of others, beyond your own immediate members, is perhaps the prime expression of how you express your own faith and values. And in carrying out this mission you've developed some of the most effective voluntary community organizations in the country. In many cases you meet urgent social needs directly. In others you work in partnership with central and local government to give a special character to the delivery of public services, which state funds would otherwise have to provide directly. (Quoted in Haslam and Dale, 2001: 12)

Note how this touches on the distinctive qualities of faith-communities' contribution: how it emphasizes the fostering of a volunteer ethic; how it touches on the significance of local knowledge and provision; how it synthesizes values with practical service-delivery. In this, Blair captures perfectly the hopes of those who see the various components of civil society as capable of complementing state provision but also promoting social cohesion, trust, civic duty and responsible citizenship.

All well and good, but perhaps the spectre of the more right-wing version serves as a reminder that we are looking for a model of civil society which fosters an emergent new form of political establishment that is locally based and values-driven, and not something that allows further unravelling of the links between communities and the State. At one level, the encouragement given by the Blair administration is a genuine acknowledgement of the difference made by religion to public life, and the need to find 'stakeholders' whose activities and organizations can help rejuvenate political participation. In other ways, however, it does little to address the two crucial factors mentioned earlier: a more structural understanding of what makes society tick, and how to meet the growing challenge of social exclusion, especially if civil society only embraces the interests of those sufficiently motivated to participate in the first place. A public theology that tries to be genuinely comprehensive and inclusive, therefore, will need to move beyond an equation of civil society with service delivery on the cheap. Clearly, voluntary action has a complementary role to State provision: but the problem with the churches and civil society is precisely that it precludes public theology from engaging with the values and structures of the State and the market. Civil society must promote the local economy, sustainable regeneration and employment and not be limited to voluntary action alone (Lowe, 2000).

Public Theology

> But is it possible any longer for *religious* images to be reborn, for a religious account of hope to become once more influential? Can the Christian faith any longer sustain a living and relevant hope in cold times? (Forrester, 1997: 256–7)

So is there a task for public theology in an age of 'voter apathy'? The climate of public opinion towards the democratic process suggests that people's faith in politics is increasingly conditional upon government being perceived as responsive and effective; and yet at the same time, the dynamics of globalization make the task of governmental management more complex. Renewal of trust in the democratic process must also encompass a robust theory of justice, empowerment and inclusion if it is not to fail those on the margins.

These questions go to the heart of public theology. Contemporary writers in the discipline have addressed themselves to a number of related issues: the terms on which shared moral discourse might be conducted in the context of 'the conspicuous absence of unifying narratives that generate moral consensus ... and the consequent difficulty of generating shared values or common assumptions about the nature of "reality"' (Brown, 2001: 103; see also Stout, 1988; Markham, 1994), and whether narratives of faith can effectively contribute to moral and political debate into the twenty-first century. There has also been attention to the ways in which theological insights might contribute to the constitution of public policy such as equality (Hicks, 2000), criminal justice (Forrester, 2001) and economics (Long, 2000); or how church-sponsored social action and local partnerships might constitute a form of 'practical divinity' (Atherton, 2000: 3), a kind of performative public theology that clearly owes much to liberationist traditions of *orthopraxis*. Clearly, all these strands of public theology and social responsibility implicitly concern themselves with questions of social justice, and represent a heterogenous set of traditions in public theology concerning the nature of theological interventions in the public forum.⁶ The key question is whether public life that is increasingly secular and pluralist is able any longer to connect with the historic insights of Christianity, and whether by clinging to the 'fragments' of that tradition the latter can make a meaningful contribution.⁷

In terms of the future of participation, empowerment and the nature of governance, these debates certainly interrogate the terms on which the various interest groups in an increasingly plural society are prepared to enter and invest in the institutions and procedures on which civil society is deemed to rest – principles of justice, the rule of law, equality, distribution and growth, and so on. Much of this literature assumes

---

6 See Sedgwick (1997) for an overview of different theological traditions within twentieth-century social ethics.

7 Duncan Forrester's contention that public theology can only contribute 'fragments' of the tradition to public discourse (Forrester, 1997: 3), vividly evokes the loss of Christianity as pre-eminent narrative of Western civilization, and warns the theologian against commenting on public debates 'as if their linkage with Christian beliefs will be self evident' (Atherton, 2000: 13). However, it also conjures up an image of the theologian as 'scavenger', picking over the detrius of a post-Christian culture, unable to salvage more than a few bits and pieces. Forrester is not saying that the Christian tradition itself is now composed of nothing but fragments, but merely that its correspondence with an increasingly secular culture will be fragmentary and partial. The danger is, however, that the correlation is between the fragments of the (religious) past and the perspectives of the (secular) present. The reality is, though, that theology is more than a recycling of the fragments of the past. It is reshaped in interaction with its changing context. Public theology understood as 'dialogical' does not claim superiority rooted in integrity and coherence unbroken by the fractures of postmodernity, but nor does it abandon the disciplines and continuities of faithful practice. It is better rendered as faithful *praxis* evolving in response to the imperatives of present and future.

implicitly, I think, that 'the public realm' is axiomatic, and that questions of operation, participation and governance are secondary to the primary task of finding a sufficiently 'thick' discourse of moral reasoning by which common consent may be reached. Yet this fails precisely to consider practical and strategic measures for the renewal of social capital.

Universal or Preferential?

A further fault-line within contemporary public theology is also worth introducing into our discussion because it relates directly to the objectives of a renewal of the public realm, and the values informing commitments to social inclusion. On the one hand, we are presented with the challenge of the fragility of the public realm. This invites a reconstruction of the very idea of a common polity, to notions of the common good – the very values seemingly at risk in many of the attitudes expressed above. Yet I would also contend that public theology is faced with the challenge of helping to articulate accounts of polity that are capable of enhancing the 'social capital' of community cohesion, and especially mindful of those at risk from exclusion from the democratic process itself.

In the context of an exploration of inequality and social ethics, Douglas Hicks considers how public theology consistently encounters just such a tension. He illustrates this through the notion of 'social solidarity'. For Hicks, God's actions as creator and redeemer – forming all people in God's image and adopting the human condition in the person of Jesus – guarantee human self-apprehension as uniquely loved; but this also underwrites a fundamental commitment to human equality. This is reminiscent of the work of Gutiérrez, who maintains the primary task of liberation theology is to proclaim the essential and irreducible *humanity* of all people in the face of dehumanizing structures of poverty and oppression (Gutiérrez, 1983: 58). However, extremes of inequality or exclusion represent a threat to the fundamental concept of human unity under God by virtue of their deleterious effect on community cohesion, or social solidarity.

Hicks thus identifies two important emphases within the notion of solidarity which ostensibly appear paradoxical. An emphasis on the *universality* of human organizations reflects a concern for the common good of all, regardless of status; but a *preferential* attention to the needs of those at risk from exclusion, and a commitment to take their side, is an essential benchmark for the quality of that very community (Hicks, 2000: 168–76).

These ideas are relevant to a consideration of the nature of public faith in collective organizations and institutions of civil society, the State and politics. On the one hand, 'solidarity' as an achievable objective of faith-based involvement in the political process might be said to relate to a sociological tradition dating back to Auguste Comte, whereby religion is held to articulate the shared moral values that underwrite social cohesion. The role of religion is here to provide the opportunities for individuals to express symbolic obligation to the shared moral order, thereby sealing the bonds of the collective once more. As critics of this kind of functionalist social theory have observed, however, such an equation of the social order with a common moral universe emphasizes the virtues of consensus and hierarchy and obscures the extent to which appeals to 'national unity' or 'traditional values' are often expressions of sectional self-interest masquerading as universal welfare (Bauman, 1994: 30).

Public theology has in the past had many champions who have valued the importance of certain forms of ecclesial dispensation being 'representative' of the nation (Habgood, 1983). The danger is that in an age of endangered democratic institutions such an arrangement is attenuated into a thin form of civil religion, colluding in anachronistic notions of Church and State that only serve to perpetuate public alienation from national symbols. A theologically derived faith in symbols of transcendence as invoking a reality larger than individual or sectional self-interest is powerful, but not if it serves to sanctify nostalgic imaginings of community that do not adequately reflect the complexities and exclusions of the contemporary polity.

Yet alongside the established traditions of Christian churches in these islands, there is a parallel dissenting strand as well (Forrester, 2001). This alternative dimension of solidarity articulates a more partisan tradition of social theology 'from below', in which the faithful are called to identify with God's purposes in history as representing what the meeting of the Conference of Latin American Bishops at Medellín in 1968 termed 'the preferential option for the poor'. This public theology, and the acts of advocacy and solidarity that embody it, eschews any call that the Church remains neutral or disengaged from the political fray.

This tension, between the *universal* and *preferential* dimensions of public theology, needs to be taken into consideration when we consider the role of Christian social thought and practice in the renewal of civil society and political culture. For example, there is still a legitimate issue as to whether religious narratives, symbols and values might be capable of furnishing concepts of common sociality that genuinely animate people's understanding of a civil order to which they can claim allegiance. How might common institutions be embodied and represented in the public imagination? How would national events be marked in a post-Christian, post-secular age?[8]

---

8 It is possible that the United Kingdom now inhabits a post-Christian, and post-secular age: that the pre-eminence of the Christian West is over and the mainstream churches in Britain struggle to maintain members, viable ministerial deployment and institutional structures. Yet the signs also are that religion and spirituality endure, albeit in heterodox forms. See Percy (2002).

On the other hand, Western theology is still learning of the implicit biases it has imported into its own canons that have served to silence the voices of the excluded and the powerless (Althaus-Reid, 2001). A 'preferential' public theology places itself in an explicitly partisan role, as advocate, whose objective in seeking solidarity is not to silence the voices of dissent but to hear the cry of the poor. Public theology in liberationist mode is necessary also in order to introduce structural analysis – something Christians find difficult – and to think beyond individual voter or consumer behaviour as personal 'choice' but as embedded in a web of privatization, poverty and alienation that are systemic and purposeful. 'Perhaps the theologian's task here is not so much to take part in elegant academic games ... as to articulate the cry of the oppressed, and speak for the dumb' (Forrester, 1997: 226).

These are important when we think about implications for renewal of the 'public' sphere. Where is public theology located and embodied? Who are its agents, where are its resources, its convictions, actually located? By what criteria are the effectiveness and legitimacy of public institutions to be judged?

Reconstructing Citizenship

> There is no going back to the old institutions. But it is equally artificial to suppose that they can be invented or declared from above ... Such priorities cannot be established without a shared framework for public decision making, in which the performance of public services is contextualised ... Without finding new ways to engage the latent social and public concerns of these people, better, more efficient delivery of public services is unlikely to make much different [sic] to the quality of their lives. (Hayes and Hudson, 2001: 67)

A difficult tension maybe, but perhaps public theology in theory and practice needs to embrace the paradox of these two forms of social solidarity as the twin poles on which debate about a just society might be conducted. This will involve grass-roots partnerships in urban regeneration, working for capacity-building in communities impoverished – in multiple senses – by generations of unemployment and dispossession. Yet it also encompasses the more traditional functions of public theology, one that enshrines the theological values at the heart of government. However, it is important to remember that such participation cannot ignore the fact that in many cases the very institutions of the State, local democracy and civil society through which churches have learned to participate are the very mechanisms that are diminished and faltering. As Hayes and Hudson's research demonstrates, therefore, the very nature of governance and participation will change because the context is changing. Perhaps the most useful lessons might come from consultations between faith-communities and the State which have given consideration to the nature of constitutional reform and national identity. One obvious recent example is the role of the Scottish churches in debates about constitutional reform, national identity and devolution (Church of Scotland, 2001).

Rethinking the nature of citizenship is no longer simply a national dilemma, however. Any renewal of democratic forms needs to acknowledge the global nature of commercial, fiscal, ecological and technological decision-making. It will also need to be flexible and adaptive, ready to engage comprehensively and effectively with the complexities of twenty-first century society. The political process must be capable of addressing such complexities. The acceleration of digital and biotechnological innovation, and their effects on our economic, medical, environmental – even existential – reality will only continue (Graham, 2002a). This will require extra or supra-national agencies and may need transnational legal bodies, as the current debate about human cloning indicates. So public theology will need to be comprehensive, capable of embracing and addressing the complexities of globalization. '[T]he inexorable movement towards a global economy and its interaction with a series of dominating global challenges requires the development of a Christian faith sufficiently *capacious* to engage its nature and extent' (Atherton, 2000: 2).

With the practical agencies, however, must go an adequate theological method capable of discerning the signs of the times and articulating these in terms accessible to ecclesial and secular audiences. Public theology should consider expanding its concerns, in order to engage not only with political and constitutional matters, but the influence of popular culture as well. The power of rapidly proliferating and ubiquitous media will assume an even higher profile and exert an ever greater power over public opinion and popular aspirations – including attitudes to social trust, political processes and global issues.

Conclusion

Measures of ordinary people's engagement with the democratic process call everyone to account because they test the adequacy of our core values and institutions. While surveys of attitudes among electorates in the UK and internationally do not fully endorse charges of 'voter apathy', there is evidence to suggest that the processes of participatory democracy require more than passive consent, and that the legitimation of the 'public' domain is itself an iterative phenomenon. The reconstruction of political will requires a dynamic infrastructure of active citizenship.

In responding to future debates about the nature of participation and democracy, public theology's objective must be to speak about God-in-the-world, *to* the world. So long as public theology prizes the health of public institutions, its contribution will need to adopt a functional *and* sacramental role. That is to say, it will assume material expression in the form of involvement in community, strategies of solidarity and local partnership (Atherton, 2000; Chester *et al.*, 1999). Yet on the other hand, such activity also points beyond itself, as a sign of Divine redemption in the midst of human culture. That is nowhere more plain than in the creative interplay between two dimensions of public 'solidarity', the universalist and preferential: while affirming the integrity of human energies, there is also a drive towards their transformation. And so public theology into the twenty-first century will embrace both the vision of a cohesive shared polity in which all participants are treated with equal regard, as well as the conviction that the very legitimacy of such governance rests on the authenticity of their claims to equity, inclusion and justice.

16

POWER, KNOWLEDGE AND AUTHORITY IN PUBLIC THEOLOGY

Introduction

In his *Theses on the Philosophy of History* the Marxist philosopher Walter Benjamin famously called for historians to 'read against the grain' of history which had hitherto been written from the perspective of the victor and not centred on the sufferings of the vanquished (Benjamin, 1974: VII). Benjamin was reflecting on the fact that what passes for authoritative knowledge in most cultures is the product of the experiences and perspectives of the powerful. A generation ago, one might have said the same thing about Christian theology; but in the light of the emergence of so-called 'theologies of liberation', theologians are now aware of the extent to which new voices, representing the life and faith of those on the margins of Church and society, are reshaping many of the core features of theological debate.

Does public theology have a responsibility to join this trend? Many public theologians have been influenced by theologies of liberation, and would regard part of their work as enabling the dispossessed to take a more active role in secular decision-making. But should public theology also consider a parallel, potentially more radical, process of theological empowerment alongside one of political change? In this chapter I argue that the issue of power in theology goes beyond addressing questions of power in Church and society, and extends to what might be termed theological epistemology: or how theological understanding is articulated, to reflect these emergent voices and aspirations of the poor and marginalized. It represents a shift from the centre to the margins in terms of the 'ownership' of theological discourse. How public theology could actually contribute to such a process of theological formulation is the subject of the second half of the chapter: just as an academic researcher needs to be mindful of the methods by which they gather their data, ensuring that their research strategy is such as to generate knowledge that is both reliable and responsible, so too should public theologians attend to matters of how such new theological voices can be brought into the public domain, and the uses to which such knowledge might be put.

Knowledge and Power in Christian Theology

In *Power and Christian Theology* Stephen Sykes argues that issues of power concern theologians in three ways (Sykes, 2006). First, there is what he calls 'the power of God' (ibid.: 12), which relates to the imagery of the nature of God and God's action in the world. Sykes asks whether the use of language depicting God as almighty and all-powerful provides a transcendental justification for structures and relationships of hierarchy rather than mutuality.

Second, there is the question of 'the power of the Church', concerning the way in which Church as a political institution engages with or intervenes in wider society, a matter which is at the heart of public theology. Third, Sykes speaks of 'power in the Church' concerning 'the distribution and exercise of power by various members of the Church' (ibid.: ix) and how internal relations of authority, decision-making and participation are exercised.

However, there is another dimension that Sykes omits to acknowledge, and which forms the topic of this chapter. It is the issue of power in the very shaping of theological discourse itself: questions of whose voices, whose perspectives are incorporated into theology; and by implication, whose voices and experiences are absent. This question has come to the fore in liberation theology, which originated in Latin America at the end of the 1960s. In championing the rights of the poor and dispossessed in a context of economic and political polarization, many Christians, and especially portions of the progressive Roman Catholic Church, found themselves thrown into active political engagement. In this respect, liberation theology served to 'politicize' the churches, along the lines of Sykes' second category. Yet there was a twin ramification of liberation theology which has proved, potentially, just as radical. By rooting itself in the experiences and voices of the poor and marginalized, by placing the resources of theological reflection on practice in the hands of those groups, liberation theology served to 'democratize' theology.

Liberating the Poor, Liberating Theology

A central principle within Latin American liberation theology which is crucial for our discussion of power is taken from its materialist reading of Scripture and its claim that all theological interpretation and practice should be guided by the fundamental hermeneutic of 'God's preferential option for the poor'. But is this an option that manifests itself in terms of a theology *for* the poor, or one that proceeds *from* the poor? Liberation theologians are in no doubt that the balance must be struck towards the latter; and this is the key to its claim to be a new way of doing theology:

> The gospel read from the viewpoint of the poor, the exploited classes, and their militant struggles for liberation, convokes a church of the people. It calls for a church to be gathered from among the poor, the marginalized ... In other words, it calls together a church that will be marked by the faithful response of the poor to the call of Jesus Christ. It will spring from the people, this church. And the people will snatch the gospel out of the hands of their dominators, never more to permit it to be utilized for the justification of a situation contrary to the will of God who liberates. (Gutiérrez, 1983: 21)

Liberation theology began with a response to the experiences of marginalization and injustice. Church-based grass-roots movements, working alongside those living in desperate poverty, were concerned to identify the root causes of poverty and engaged in a critique of the structural dynamics of inequality using tools of social analysis, such as 'dependency theory' (Gutiérrez, 1999: 22). For the progressive Roman Catholic Church in 1960s and 1970s Latin America, this also became a question of aligning themselves with the oppressed rather than the establishment. Similarly, there was an understanding that the task of theology is to proceed from the experiences of such marginalization and resistance to oppression – often expressed as addressing the factors which reduce people to 'non-humans' and finding the theological language that restores people to full humans in the sight of God:

> A good part of contemporary theology seems to have arisen from the challenge of the nonbeliever. The nonbeliever questions our religious world, and demands a purification and profound renewal. Dietrich Bonhoeffer took up that challenge and formulated the incisive question we find at the origin of so many of the theological efforts of our day: How can one proclaim God in a world become adult, a world grown up, a world come of age?
> In Latin America, however, the challenge does not come first and foremost from the nonbeliever. It comes from the nonperson. It comes

from the person whom the prevailing social order fails to recognize as a person – the poor, the exploited, the ones systematically and legally despoiled of their humanness, the ones who scarcely know they are persons at all.

Hence the question here will not be how to speak of God in a world come of age, but rather how to proclaim God as Father in a world that is inhuman. What can it mean to tell a nonperson that he or she is God's child? (Gutiérrez, 1983: 57)

It turned much of traditional theology on its head in that it sought to do more than simply relating 'tradition' or 'doctrine' to practical issues as some kind of 'applied theology'. In contrast it advocated a process of 'theological reflection' on practice with a view to generating principles that serve to guide further action in the form of transformative and faithful practice. Yet if that reflection on experience is to be genuinely liberating, it must speak from the situation of those whom it wishes to serve:

Who are the agents of liberation, those who carry it out? Not the ruling classes ... Not the State ... Not the Churches, either ... Those who bring about liberation are the impoverished themselves, with their allies, becoming conscious of their oppression, organizing themselves, projecting their vision of society and struggling for their freedom ... If the oppressed do not take up the cause of their own liberation, it will not come from anywhere. This is the basic conviction of liberation theology. (Boff, 1988: 8)

So the theological compass turns to the marginalized, the excluded, the silenced as both the focus of theological priority – it is authenticated by its answer to the question, will it liberate? – but also to revaluing the origins and authorities of theological formulation, away from the privileged towards the poor. The preferential option for the poor thus works at two levels: of politicizing the church, of regarding its mission as to free the captive, to remove the endemic economic, political and cultural structures of systematic dehumanization. Yet the other level is also about power and transforming conventional understandings of the vocation of theological discourse: to place at the centre of theological discourse the experiences and voices and interests of those from 'the underside of history' (Kristenson, 2005).

Institutionally, especially in Latin America, this was exemplified in the formation of thousands of basic ecclesial communities (CEBs) in which the practice of reflection becomes a democratic and participatory exercise. This is especially the case in relation to the way such groups engage in study of the Bible. In its move to place Scripture back into the hands of the people, the formation of the CEBs mirrors, in many respects, the attempts by Protestant Reformers and biblical translators to render the Bible 'in the vernacular' in an effort to place salvation and access to God's Word in the hands of ordinary believers. As Leonardo Boff comments, this means that 'commentary on the word of God has been taken over by the people themselves, producing a new view of faith, less abstract and dogmatic, more historical and tied to the ethical demands of justice and solidarity' (Boff, 1988: 8).

Liberation theologies of all varieties therefore take the experiences of the marginalized and silenced groups in society – those traditionally excluded from articulating theology and exercising ecclesial leadership – and adopt them as the starting-point and foundation of biblical interpretation and theological reflection. It represents an explicit commitment to claiming the authority and agency of 'the little ones' or those 'on the underside of history' as the basis of theological understanding. It represents a challenge to move from a theology *for* the poor to a theology *of and from* the poor.

For 'professional' biblical interpreters and theologians, therefore, the task is not so much one of translating or disseminating the results of their scholarship to a wider (possibly popular) audience, but one of aligning themselves as advocates and interpreters of the stories of struggle and survival from the grass-roots. Theologies of liberation emphasize the importance of listening to the stories and honouring the experiences of the oppressed. For Gustavo Gutiérrez, theology 'should help us to understand the life of faith and the urgent need to build a society that is humane and just' (Gutiérrez, 1999: 29) and in order to do so, it must represent the hopes and needs of the poor.

Excavating the Politics of Knowledge

The next step is to ask whether, if theology is shaped by its human authors and contexts, the introduction of new hitherto unheard voices might actually serve to reshape understandings not only of who speaks, and from where, but how that might shape what theology says and how. I would like to identify three motifs that characterize theologies of liberation once they begin to examine the conditions of their own claims to knowledge: the political imperative of excavating hidden lives; the cathartic and existential power of giving voice to experience; and the need for theology to speak in the authentic language and culture – the 'vernacular' – of the poor.

1 Searching for lost coins

A memorable example of this process is Alice Walker's essay, 'Looking for Zora' (1975). The womanist writer Alice Walker speaks of her quest to reinstate the literary reputation of the African-American novelist Zora Neale Hurston, who was a celebrated figure during the so-called 'Harlem renaissance' of the 1920s but who died in poverty and obscurity (see Hurston, 1937; Hogan, 1995). Walker goes to Zora Neale Hurston's home town in Florida, where she is reputed to be buried (in what at the time of Hurston's death in 1960 was a segregated cemetery), in an attempt to find out more about her.

With the aid of a local guide, Rosalee, Walker sallies forth into the cemetery ground, beset by weeds, insects, snakes and other hazards. Eventually, by scouring through the undergrowth, of trying to get her bearings without a map to orientate herself, of persisting with the search, finally she stumbles – almost literally – upon her goal.

> Finding the grave seems positively hopeless. There is only one thing to do:
>
> 'Zora!' I yell, as loud as I can (causing Rosalee to jump). 'Are you out here?'
>
> 'If she is, I sho hope she don't answer you. If she do, I'm gone.'
>
> 'Zora!' I call again. 'I'm here. Are you?'
>
> 'If she is,' grumbles Rosalee, 'I hope she'll keep it to herself.'
>
> 'Zora!' Then I start fussing with her. 'I hope you don't think I'm going to stand out here all day, with these snakes watching me and these ants having a field day. In fact, I'm going to call you just one or two more times.' On a clump of dried grass, near a small bushy tree, my eye falls on one of the largest bugs I have ever seen. It is on its back, and is as large as three of my fingers. I walk toward it, and yell 'Zo-ra!' and my foot sinks into a hole. I look down. I am standing in a sunken rectangle that is about six feet long and about three or four feet wide. I look up to see where the two gates are.
>
> 'Well,' I say, 'this is the center, or approximately anyhow. It's also the only sunken space we've found. Doesn't this look like a grave to you?'
>
> 'For the sake of not going no farther through these bushes,' Rosalee growls, 'Yes, it do.'
>
> 'Wait a minute,' I say, 'I have to look around some more to be sure this is the only spot that resembles a grave. But you don't have to come.'
>
> Rosalee smiles – a grin, really – beautiful and tough.
>
> 'Naw,' she says, 'I feels sorry for you. If one of these snakes got ahold of you out here by yourself I'd feel *real* bad.' She laughs. 'I done come this far, I'll go on with you.'
>
> 'Thank you, Rosalee,' I say. 'Zora thanks you too.' (Walker, 1984: 105)

Walker's account of retrieving what is buried beneath the accumulated overgrowth of years of neglect is a vivid metaphor for the process of recovering a life and a reputation that has been buried underneath years of forgetfulness and indifference. Walker's act to commission a headstone for Zora Neale Hurston is both a gesture of respect for the dead but also a statement of intent to restore her to the literary mainstream.

In similar fashion, we can see how a theology of liberation such as feminist theology is engaged in 'searching for lost coins' (Loades, 1987). It has traditionally appealed to 'women's experience' as both critical and reconstructive resource: first, to expose the historical exclusion of women from positions of ecclesial power and leadership, and their invisibility as authors and mediators of theological understanding; and second to provide a creative vantage-point from which the tradition can be renewed and reformed. This is best exemplified by the Roman Catholic feminist historian and theologian Rosemary Ruether, when she challenges the assumption that feminist theology has been unique in claiming a basis in 'women's experience' (Ruether, 1993: ch. 1). All codified tradition, she argues, has its source in experience; it is simply that feminist theology exposes the partial and value-laden nature of appeals to experience as universal.

> The uniqueness of feminist theology lies not in its use of the criterion of experience but rather in its use of *women's* experience, which has been almost entirely shut out of theological reflection in the past. The use of women's experience in feminist theology, therefore, explodes as a critical force, exposing classical theology, including its codified traditions, as based on *male* experience rather than on universal human experience. Feminist theology makes the sociology of theological knowledge visible, no longer hidden behind mystifications of objectified Divine and universal authority. (Ibid.: 13)

By drawing on submerged traditions which place at their centre the critical principle of promoting the full humanity of women, Ruether proposes to introduce a fresh hermeneutic of interpretation which can reconstruct the theological canon in a more inclusive direction.

2 Hearing ourselves into speech

So if certain voices have been submerged, historically, this introduces a second theme: that of retrieving and revaluing the hidden perspectives. But how to 'bring to speech' that which has been systematically silenced? From writers such as the African-American feminist theologian and therapist Nelle Morton, and the Brazilian educator and activist Paulo Freire, we see further how the process of finding a voice necessitates a politics of empowerment which at root is about recovering the agency of formerly oppressed groups.

The process of consciousness-raising or 'conscientization' is associated above all with the work of Paulo Freire, who was formative in the development of the first generation of grass-roots organizing in Latin America that led to the establishment of CEBs. Freire championed a learning process in which education is envisaged not so much as a matter of filling empty vessels with information, as enabling participants to name their own experience. It is possible to see Freire's pedagogical method as a critical corrective to the Marxist concept of ideology, which argues that world-views that purport to be neutral and objective actually reflect and serve the dominant interests of the powerful. It is the journey from false consciousness – of accepting as inevitable, maybe even God-given, the hegemonic ideology – towards a more critical exposure of the way their lives have been shaped by the logic of inequality and exclusion, that characterizes the process of conscientization of the poor.

> Whenever men [sic] make God responsible for intolerable situations, for oppression, then the dominating structures help to popularize that myth. If God is not the cause, they whisper, then destiny must be. Human reason at this level easily becomes fatalistic; it sits back and sighs: 'Nothing can be done about it.'
>
> Sometimes another scapegoat is found, and it too is a myth spread by the dominating structure: the helplessness of the oppressed. The dominated mind looks inward and decides that it is totally unable to cope with its misery: it concludes that it is impotent ...
>
> For the critical mind, though, for the mind that conscientizes itself, beyond this situation there is the future, what we must do, the thing we must create, the historical futurity we have to bring into being; and to do that, we must change whatever it is that prevents the humanization of our fellow humans.
>
> As we examine the structures and the reasons why they are so intolerable, as we expose the oppressive situation, we are forced to a decision: we either commit ourselves or we don't – but we will have to answer to our consciences for our choice. The process of conscientization leaves no one with his arms folded. It makes some unfold their arms. It leaves others with a guilty feel, because conscientization shows us that God wants us to act.
>
> As I conscientize myself, I realize that my brothers who don't eat, who don't laugh, who don't sing, who don't love, who live oppressed, crushed and despised, who *are* less each day, are suffering all this because of some reality that is causing it. (Freire, 1972)

In a fusion of existentialism and Marxism, Freire argues that the poor, once conscientized and able to name and analyse their own experience free of the cloak of ideology, can then be free to act upon and change their situation. Conscientization is both a critical and transformative process, a constant 'spiral' of reflection and action.

There are parallels, too, with Nelle Morton's frequently cited motif of 'hearing one another to speech' which has assumed iconic status within feminist thought. It is celebrated as the quintessential quality of feminist consciousness-raising, of providing a supportive space in which the faltering voices and experiences of women, long stifled by the structures of patriarchy, can come forth.

> Hearing of this sort is equivalent to empowerment. We empower one another by hearing the other to speech. We empower the disinherited, the outsider, as we are able to hear them name in their own way their own oppression and suffering. In turn, we are empowered as we can put ourselves in a position to be heard by the disinherited ... to speaking our own feeling of being caught and trapped. (Morton, 1985: 128)

What is interesting about Morton's analysis, however, is that it is invariably quoted out of context. It is assumed that this is an account of a feminist consciousness-raising or therapy group, in which the empathy and solidarity of women engenders the empowerment. But in fact Morton frames this within a theological understanding of the process. Her discussion of finding a voice emerges out of a protest against the constant invisibility of women in church life, either as preachers or teachers. Their absence from pulpit, seminary and sanctuary is an indication of the institution's denial of their vocation and their exclusion as authentic or authoritative bearers of the theological tradition.

For Morton, however, the hearing to speech is not simply a human phenomenon, but one which occurs because of a prior Divine hearing and listening. In defiance of some theological conventions that place God's activity wholly in the realm of speech, Morton asks, 'Could it be that *Logos* deified reduces communication to a one-way relationship – that of *speak-ing* – and bypasses the far more radical divine aspect of *hearing*?' (ibid.: 54). Morton argues that women need to claim an understanding of the Divine act as 'hearing to speech rather than speaking to hearing'. We are able to hear one another into speech (and thus, perhaps, into full humanity) because we are first heard by 'a prior great Listening Ear ... an ear that hears ... our own' (ibid.: 55). It is by virtue of that Godly acceptance and encouragement that the words are able to come; and Morton equates this with the experience of Pentecost (ibid.: 128), of the work of the Spirit as one of 'hearing before speaking' and thus giving birth to a 'new language' of liberation:

> Women know hearing to speech as powerfully spiritual, and know spirit as movement and presence hearing us until we know and own the words and the images as our own words and our own images that have come out of the depth of our struggle. (Ibid.: 129)

3 'Theology in the vernacular'

Following two decades after the landmark report of Anglican public theology, *Faith in the City* (1985), the Commission on Urban Life and Faith returned to the question of urban poverty and marginalization to enquire again after the state of the UK's cities and towns, to evaluate the role of faith-based organizations in contributing to civil society and asking, 'What makes a Good City?' (CULF, 2006). Twenty years ago, *Faith in the City* set as its task to address Church and nation from Christian principles, and drew heated controversy with its forthright criticism of the monetarist economic policies of the Thatcher administration. Intriguingly, it invoked Latin American liberation theology in its theological chapter, arguing that its recovery of the biblical principle of the preferential option for the poor meant that Christians should see their task as challenging structural economic injustice as well as preaching personal morality (ACUPA, 1985). According to Sykes' categories, therefore, *Faith in the City* 'politicized' the Church; and many commentators have argued that its publication marked the end of the Church of England's characterization as 'the Tory party at prayer' (Clark, 1993).

Yet it has long been my contention that despite critics' denouncing *Faith in the City* as 'Marxist', liberation theology made relatively little impact on the thinking of the Commission, and that its opposition to the divisive policies of Thatcherism were informed more by a social liberal concern for 'the common good' than a coherently worked socialist analysis (Graham, 1996a). Twenty years on, however, *Faithful Cities* set as its task to address the additional dimension of power in theology, by asking what would happen to urban theology and to the Church's practice if it really heeded the commitment of theologies of liberation to 'hear the cry of the poor' and bring forth an urban theology that genuinely reflected the aspirations of those most deeply affected by poverty, inequality and marginalization:

> When *Faith in the City* declared that listening to the voices of local communities enabled the Commissioners to discover authentic 'faith in the city', we recognized that it was articulating a valuable truth. This was that it is not enough simply to develop a theology *for* the poor,

but that we have to make space for the development of a theology *of* and *from* those experiencing poverty ... In our enquiries, therefore, we have emphasized the stories, insights and experiences that emerge from urban communities of faith. We have tried to be attentive to what these understandings may have to say to the world at large. It is our way of genuinely exposing ourselves to 'the gospel of the poor' – of fostering voices 'from the underside' and encouraging the rest of the Church to acknowledge these voices as gifts to the wider Church. (CULF, 2006: 15)

The very format of the report – interspersing analysis with narrative, case studies, living examples from local communities – is an attempt to embody a commitment to what *Faithful Cities* calls a 'theology in the vernacular': that is, a theology that speaks the everyday language of ordinary people rather than the grand styles of the academy. Theology need not always speak in a propositional, philosophical register, but may also find expression in forms of narrative, even visual imagery, art, song and poetry in order to give voice in its own way to the experiences of hope out of despair, of resilience, of regeneration and the transformative power of faith:

We have called these 'everyday theologies', referring to the popular, the language of the streets, the vernacular, or what ... Jeff Astley terms 'ordinary theology' (Astley, 2002). We have tried to follow the work of theologians such as Robert Beckford (1998) and Anthony Reddie (2003) who seek to merge liberation theology with 'black expressive cultures'. We are therefore looking for signs of new liturgies and expressions of spirituality and ways of exploring the person of Christ which speak more authentically from, and to, the lives of those in our urban areas. (CULF, 2006: 15)

Church Action on Poverty (CAP), a national ecumenical campaigning organization, has since its inception in the early 1980s worked on a strong model of advocacy whereby people living in poverty are equipped to speak for themselves and to engage actively with church leaders and policy-makers. In 1996 CAP held the first of its national 'Poverty Hearings' which featured 12 people giving first-hand accounts of what it meant on a day-to-day basis to live in poverty.

One of the participants, Millicent Dews, remembered the importance of her involvement in the process:

At the hearing, I talked about how devalued I felt to be without work since I qualified [as a nursery nurse]. I wasn't as poor as a beggar on the street but it was difficult to find money to buy food and pay bills

... I went on the dole. While I was standing in the queue one day looking at so many miserable faces I felt physically sick to have been left in this position without work ... People in poverty must not be afraid to speak out and find as much information as possible on how to improve their lives ... The key to getting out of poverty is training and skills. (B. McCarthy, 2006)

Ten years after the first hearing, CAP convened another Poverty Hearing, at which anti-poverty campaigners, faith groups, trade unions and politicians heard the testimonies of ordinary people living in poverty calling for a statutory fair wage, affordable housing, better financial support for asylum seekers and an end to child poverty. Once again, the process modelled the hope that those in poverty need not be invisible, and embodied the conviction that those in power ought to be confronted with the human face of problems that are too frequently reduced to mere statistics (Mackay, 2006).

Critique

In the concern to excavate the voices and perspectives of those formerly silenced, it is sometimes claimed that theologies of liberation make too much claim for the liberative potential of speaking from 'experience'. Clearly, this is a category that needs careful investigation: what is it about 'hearing ourselves into speech' that is liberating? Is the speaking forth of experience *ipso facto* cathartic, liberative and empowering; or does it require other factors (audience, interpretation, action) to enable it to be authentic? Freire might argue that it is a question of identifying one's own experience and agency with the emancipatory trajectory of history. Gutiérrez might say it is about bringing the non-person into full humanity and therefore into the realm of God's liberating purposes, which is, ultimately, for liberationists, what makes 'experience' theologically significant. Similarly, feminist theology has often been accused of adopting a naive universalism in its appeal to 'women's experience', although it has moved towards a more sophisticated grasp of the complexity of race, class, gender, dis/ability and other factors (K. McCarthy, 1996; Pui-lan, 2005: 53–60).

Is theology to validate all insights emerging from marginalized communities, even if such views are politically unacceptable or theologically unorthodox? Along with the need for nuanced accounts of the nature and significance of 'experience' must also go an honesty about a tendency to romanticize the lives of those experiencing poverty. Yet from the start, Gutiérrez argued against romanticizing either poverty or the poor – although there is still, I believe, a tendency, especially in Gutiérrez, to treat 'the poor' more as a rhetorical than an empirical category. Yet for him, those living in poverty are characterized by grace and sin, like any other person. God's *preference* for the poor should not imply exclusiveness, or that such people are perfect. God's love is *universal*, but the primary concern is for the most vulnerable and the least powerful, and that determines the *preferential* dimension.

There are also challenges from postmodernism, especially concerning the transparency of 'experience' in the formation of subjectivity. In *Changing the Subject* Mary McLintock Fulkerson (1994) is critical of many of the knee-jerk assumptions of feminist theology to presuppose what it knows to be liberating or the correct consciousness of liberated women. She argues that women's subjectivity is formed by many complex processes, and that what counts as 'liberating' is not a constant. In her ethnographic study of women in three conservative Protestant congregations, she examines how there may be many different ways of religious practice – interpreting Scripture, taking on roles of leadership, negotiating gender roles – which serve to shape these women's identities and prospects. They all have ways of winning limited space for themselves, and affirming their autonomy and dignity often in the face of negative or limiting theological messages. Fulkerson's study deploys ethnographic research, in which the 'outsider' enters into the world of the 'insider' via a process of participant observation. Yet she warns against the dangers of imposing on others a framework of interpretation that they would not share. Rather than being a fully blown feminist theology, the women's experience is more complex and contradictory, more a question of claiming limited space or voice within the parameters of what remains a quite traditional world-view (Clark-King, 2005).

Furthermore, while some would argue that 'the truth will set you free', other perspectives eschew any such notion. The historian and cultural critic Michel Foucault argues that knowledge itself is so thoroughly infused by the interests of domination and ideology that there is no such thing as 'emancipatory' (as if neutral) truth. Knowledge certainly carries its own power dynamics, according to Foucault; but its complicity with disciplines of surveillance and classification renders it an imperfect medium.

There is also a danger of tokenism, by which while lip-service is paid to the epistemological revolution of valuing 'narrative' or 'voices from the margins', in other respects it is 'business as usual'. Kwok Pui-lan asks whether there is still a hierarchy within feminist scholarship or discourse, such that: 'Third World feminists merely talk about stories of their lives, while First World feminists do theory' (Pui-lan, 2005: 74). In this way, another pattern of (neo)colonialism is reproduced: that of the Third World exporting the raw materials in order that Western experts can 'examine, analyse, and theorize' (ibid.). A division of labour still persists: narrative or immediacy of experience is never enough, and must be abstracted or processed into a more acceptable 'finished product'.

So there are questions here about what kind of knowledge 'matters'. Can local insights 'travel' effectively and make a difference cross-culturally? How can we preserve the integrity of the specific and the local while drawing out significant insights for a more universal discourse?

4 Issues for public theology

How might the public theologian, as researcher or activist, attend to some of these issues? Is there a possibility of adopting some methods of study and enquiry that address questions of power and authority in the production and reproduction of knowledge?

Susan Thistlethwaite addresses the problem of how those with power and privilege from the academy can work alongside those at the grassroots, while eschewing any accusation of 'theological tourism' – of finding ways of researching 'the other' without objectification or misrepresentation. She asks, 'How do I come to know the otherness of other people in a way that neither collapses their subjectivity into mine or makes them an exotic other?' (Thistlethwaite, 1994: 6). Any process of coming to know another human being carries with it philosophical, psychological and epistemological questions. Knowing another person across the boundaries of power and difference also bears political and ethical issues. As Thistlethwaite asks, 'how do we describe what it means to become humans together when the real, material differences between human beings are made central?' (ibid.: 10).

This question of a seemingly unbridgeable gulf between persons and communities, and whether indeed we can find ways of becoming humans together, is illustrated quite graphically by Duncan Forrester. He begins his book *On Human Worth* with an encounter he had in India with a beggar, Munuswamy. He wonders how he, as a privileged Western academic, can do justice to Munuswamy's plight. Their shared humanity represents a moral and theological imperative for Forrester to demonstrate solidarity; but the structural and intransigent nature of Munuswamy's absolute poverty renders that virtually impossible. So what courses of action are open to Forrester? His solution is that of 'speaking truth to power' and adopting an advocate's role, providing a framework through which the anger and passion of those on the margins can be expressed. This is something he also embodied at the Centre for Theology and Public Issues in Edinburgh: of designing public seminars about matters such as crime and punishment, poverty, welfare, constitutional reform and mental health in which those on the receiving end of public policy came face to face in order to 'speak truth to power' (Cary *et al.*, 1955). While these were never comfortable encounters, they were an attempt to embody a dialogue in which theology served as 'honest broker', bringing a voice to ordinary communities.

We might characterize the task of bridging the gulf of power and bringing voices from the underside into the public domain as essentially one of *representation*. This has two aspects: first, there is the question of how the experience of a particular group is portrayed. How can the lives and aspirations of formerly unrepresented lives be reported authentically without misrepresentation or romanticization? No account can ever be neutral, and reflects to some extent the standpoint of those who record and report. All experience, however mediated, is therefore in part a matter of 'construction' of knowledge: so it is a matter of representation rather than portrayal or description. Yet in part, this is an issue faced by anyone researching human subjects, especially in the field of qualitative research: how to represent the lives of one's subjects reliably?

But representation also calls forth, of course, a second, political dimension: as in who represents whom, within the public domain, and whose version of events is given public voice and recognition. This is more a matter of activism, of ensuring that the liberation of such voices can make a difference.

It is not new to consider how the dual act of representation involves questions of power. As John Swinton and Harriet Mowat point out, the tradition of action-research is explicitly located in a recognition that the production of knowledge, and the researcher's task, is never neutral. Action-research, as 'a method of enquiry and practice which encourages controlled and focussed change using the knowledge and expertise of those involved in the research setting' (Swinton and Mowat, 2006: x) may therefore be regarded as bearing strong affinities to the praxis model from liberation theology in which reflection on experience generates knowledge that facilitates transformation. But action-research also frames the subjects of research – its informants – as agents in the generation of their own knowledge, and not simply 'objects' to be investigated or 'consumers' of research disseminated in a top-down fashion.

Jeffrey Heskins also speaks of listening to 'unheard voices' in the context of the debate about gay and lesbian sexuality in the Church (Heskins, 2001). He writes from the context of an Anglican parish in Charlton, South London, which has established itself as sympathetic space for those wishing to celebrate a same-sex partnership in church (this research was conducted before it was legally possible to conduct a civil partnership for same-sex couples). Heskins is concerned to record and articulate the voices of all members of the congregation as they think through the theological dimensions of this controversial aspect of their ministry: 'this is a book which records everyday Christian people thinking about what they are doing in pastoral action and how they are able to draw images of God from it. This is practical theology done in a practical way' (ibid.: 17). In the process, Heskins relies on the very traditions of contextual and liberation theology that I have been outlining; and how the business of 'telling one's story' is an essential part of articulating identity, of reflection on practice, of a theology of experience. He implicitly privileges what he calls the 'unheard voices' over and against 'the same old voices' as a piece of action-reflection: the Church is already committed to such liturgies, but believes that

> it is only when a community begins to *tell* its story that the community comes to understand something of its identity, nature and mission ... If this theory of story-telling proves true, then in telling its story any local church community will not only reveal how it sees itself in the larger parish community, but it is likely to make impact at other levels of the Church as well. The power of story-telling then lies in enabling a community to exert influence beyond itself. (Ibid.: 45–6)

Such research, therefore, serves to make visible the implicit values of a community so that it can be more transparent about its own core values, the better to give an account of itself. Is this qualitative research (and especially a method that emphasizes hearing the voices and telling the stories) as apologia?

Swinton and Mowat stress the importance of recognizing hidden power dynamics within the research process. They ask whether it is possible to design genuinely participatory research that does not objectify others, but establishes them as subjects of knowledge: an issue for anyone researching human subjects, either through ethnography or other qualitative means. Swinton and Mowat cite the example of research into the spiritual needs of people with learning disabilities to consider how a model of truly participatory research might be designed and implemented. The use of an advisory group containing people with learning disabilities, and deployment of a variety of research methods including in-depth one-to-one interviews, focus groups and direct observation, ensures that the issues will be explored from a range of perspectives. Questions of consent are also paramount. But by involving the subjects in the design and management of the research itself, such a method attempts to be accountable to its informants.

These issues are of course all the more acute when the research relates to vulnerable groups, such as children, adults with learning disabilities or illness which is a factor in the research, or anyone whose status might be affected by the outcomes of the research. But there are also the researcher's own obligations to consider. Will you have the means to maintain appropriate confidentiality? Are you creating false hopes or expectations? Will you maintain contact with your informants when the research has been completed? What right of reply will your subjects have?

But clearly, as with any research, there are ethical considerations to be borne in mind. The principle of informed consent is important, and those taking part should be told that they are participating in research, and what the research is for; what the investigative procedures will be; the terms and conditions of their participation, how confidentiality will be assured, how the research will be used, and how data will be stored and reported.

It is also interesting that Swinton and Mowat conclude that the values informing the model of participatory research flow over into lessons of how one might build an inclusive church community. This is consistent with the commitments of action-research in which research is not simply about gaining new knowledge but about 'enabling new and transformative action' (Swinton and Mowat, 2006: 255).

All these examples show how research methodology and design in public theology might aim to align itself with principles of empowerment and participation of groups who for whatever reason often operate outside the mainstream. I might also add other approaches that have proved useful in hearing others (and ourselves) into speech – and here, perhaps the device of using personal testimony as a vehicle of speaking of God in public may be relevant. Public theologians might explore using journalling, or narrative, or the creative arts, either with individuals or groups, as ways of giving voice to experience, or in forging what we call 'the living human document' (see Graham, Walton and Ward, 2005: ch. 1). This may also reinforce the conviction that theology may not necessarily find expression in academic treatises but in other, more 'performative' styles, such as liturgy, creative writing, drama or music.

As we can see, therefore, there is a very real sense in which, in public theology, knowledge *is* power. How those wishing to intervene in the public domain, either to effect change in policy or in public opinion, need to be aware of whose voices are heard, and those seeking to represent or make space for formerly silenced voices need to think about how that process comes about. For many working in public theology, a commitment to the perspective of those who experience poverty and dispossession is an integral part of their vision; and public theology may even be seen as a form of what is known as 'linking' social capital. Social capital refers to the range of values, resources and assets that any group in civil society may have at its disposal not only to work for change and achieve its objectives but to strengthen the fabric of civil society itself: to mobilize protest, effect political change or enhance social cohesion, for example (Field, 2003). Social capital is often characterized as effecting 'bonding, bridging and linking' – the first two indicating intra- and inter-group horizontal cohesion respectively, and the latter expressing capacity to bring about vertical connections between different groups, perhaps within a social or political hierarchy. So 'linking' social capital may offer an avenue whereby the voices of the marginalized can find expression in the public domain, thereby connecting less powerful communities with sites of public discourse and decision-making (Wood, 2003; MacRoberts, 2003). The public theologian as researcher, bringing forth the hidden voices, and activist, as ensuring the voices are placed on the political and moral agenda, may thus have a decisive contribution to make.

Conclusion

All research, as the task of representing 'the living human document' of human and social life carries ethical and political implications, and public theology is no exception. This is clear when we seek responsible ways of representing others' (and our own) experiences that for whatever reason have struggled to find their way into the mainstream. So questions of who speaks from where, who speaks for whom, and how 'experience' can be trusted and authenticated, let alone the uses to which our knowledge is put, are all essential questions of good public theology (as in reliable and trustworthy, but maybe also ethically unimpeachable). Public theologians need to be clear about their objectives and the difference they believe that knowledge can make to the world, as well as striving to find appropriate methods by which such knowledge can be generated and passed on.

17

'WHAT MAKES A GOOD CITY?'

Reflections on the Commission on Urban Life and Faith

Introduction: 'New Commission on Urban Life and Faith Launched'

In February 2004, the following press release was issued by the Church of England:

> The Archbishops' Commission on Urban Life and Faith [CULE], launched today in the House of Lords, will promote a vision of urban life which analyses and addresses the realities of its delights, injustices and its needs. It will spotlight work, especially by faith communities, that makes a difference in disadvantaged areas.
>
> Working in an innovative and creative way, the Commission will listen to and reflect on the experiences of individuals in urban communities. Reporting at the end of 2005, having held conferences, consultations and festivals up and down the country, its findings will be available to inform government views on urban issues. The government's own report, *The State of our Cities and Towns,* is also due to be published in 2005. The Commission was initiated by the House of Bishops of the Church of England and is timed to coincide with the twentieth anniversary of *Faith in the City,* the groundbreaking urban poverty study. (Church of England, 2004)

I was a member of that Commission, between February 2004 and the publication of its eventual report, *Faithful Cities: A Call for Celebration, Vision and Justice,* in May 2006. As the press release indicated, CULF was established to mark the twentieth anniversary of an earlier groundbreaking report of the Church of England, *Faith in the City* (published in 1985), and the relationship between the two reports and their respective contexts will form a major part of this chapter. But in focusing on three particular themes emerging from *Faithful Cities*, I also want to consider its significance for the evolving tradition of public theology in the UK. In its attempt to get to grips with the changing nature of the 'urban', in its bold claims for the distinctiveness of faith-based contribution to urban regeneration, and in its call for theology to emerge from the 'vernacular' (or everyday) faithfulness of local communities, *Faithful Cities* embodied some important principles for public theology. But did those principles prove convincing; and will their long-term legacy be as decisive as that of *Faith in the City*?

Then and Now

It should be clear that the work of the Commission on Urban Life and Faith did not take place in a historical vacuum. In the words of its press release, it promised 'innovative and creative' work; but it also deliberately placed itself in a very formidable tradition of Anglican social thought by marking the twentieth anniversary of the report of the 'Archbishop's Commission on Urban Priority Areas', *Faith in the City*, considered by many to represent the high watermark of twentieth-century public theology in the UK. When it was published in December 1985 *Faith in the City* provoked a storm of controversy, invoking the wrath of the Conservative government of the day; but nevertheless it has become recognized as landmark document in urban theology.

Faith in the City emerged in part to the urban riots in some northern English cities of the early 1980s, and to concerns among the urban bishops of the Church of England about the effects of unemployment and the re-structuring of the welfare state on many of the most marginalized communities. It highlighted the growing number of neighbourhoods – so-called 'urban priority areas' – that were experiencing disadvantage and exclusion in society, and criticized government policies to reduce state expenditure on basic social services at a time of growing economic crisis.

As part of their work, the Commissioners actually visited many of the worst-hit areas, believing that first-hand experiences of these so-called 'urban priority areas' was a necessary part of their work:

> In the course of a series of visits we saw something of the physical conditions under which people in the UPAs are living, and we listened to their own accounts and experiences at open public meetings and in smaller invited groups. We also spent many hours with representatives of local government, the police, social workers, the various caring agencies and the local churches themselves. (ACUPA, 1985: xiv)

One crucial aspect of *Faith in the City* was its emphasis on the significance of the specifically *urban* as a locus of political intervention and
theological reflection. The state of the cities was judged to be a critical
indicator of the extent to which Britain could call itself a just and equitable society; but it was also a space of theological epiphany:

> Each of us has faced a personal challenge to our lives and life styles: a
> call to change our thinking and action in such a way as to help us to
> stand more closely alongside the risen Christ with those who are poor
> and powerless. We have found faith in the city. (Ibid.: 360)

That intention to endorse the manifestations of 'faith in the city' has
continued ever since, in the continuing financial commitment on the part
of the Church of England to make special provision for urban ministry
and mission, in particular in the form of the Church Urban Fund, as an
enduring strategy for the upkeep of its urban presence through personnel,
buildings and community-development.

What does *Faith in the City* say about public theology? We might
regard it as reflecting the voice of the Established Church, and the Church
of England's self-understanding of itself as representing a wider body of
public opinion, acting almost as the 'conscience of the nation'. *Faith in
the City* portrayed the Commission as upholding 'those basic Christian
principles of justice and compassion which we believe we share with the
great majority of the people of Britain' (ibid.). This was, perhaps, the root
of the antipathy between the Church and the Conservative government:
in presuming to address Church *and* nation, the ACUPA was casting the
Church as a kind of 'unofficial opposition' to the conviction politics of
Thatcherism (Clark, 1993).

Chapter 3 of *Faith in the City* was devoted to a theological analysis of
urban poverty, and it is here that the source of its controversial reception
probably lies. By denouncing the Report as 'Marxist', a leading government minister guaranteed that *Faith in the City* rocketed to the top of
the best-seller lists; but he may have had in mind the references to Latin
American liberation theology, and the inevitable mix of politics and religion that it signalled in popular opinion. Yet it is debatable whether the
writers of this section ever intended to endorse Marxist analysis in such
a blatant way. Rather, the chapter reads as a call for any urban theology
to integrate the influence of structural factors, such as government economic policy, on the lives of urban priority areas, and to acknowledge
that politics and economics are the moral province of the churches as
much as issues of conversion or personal behaviour. In that respect, the
politics of *Faith in the City* were to espouse a determination to move
beyond simply ameliorating problems or delivering welfare provision,
to active engagement in their structural causes; but implicitly, of course,

this still amounted to a strong repudiation of the public values underlying Thatcherism.

So on the one hand, *Faith in the City* articulated a 'preferential option to the poor' that was beginning to infiltrate public theology; yet on the other, it still remained firmly rooted in a strong model of Establishment, albeit one of speaking 'truth to power' (Cary *et al.*, 1955). But at the heart of *Faith in the City* is a huge paradox: it reflects the sensibilities of a middle-class Church that finds itself championing marginalized urban communities in areas where levels of church attendance were often no higher than 1 or 2 per cent of the population. The paradox is resolved, I believe, by looking less to the traces of liberation theology and emphasizing instead the geographical realities of the parish system (Graham, 1996a). As the national Church, the Church of England had, by law, the responsibility for the cure of souls of every square metre in the country; when other agencies (government, business, and others) were abandoning the urban priority areas, the Church stayed put, and became the leading advocate of the UPAs more by accident than design.

Twenty Years On

Faith in the City created a political climate within the Church of England (and other denominations to a lesser extent) which prioritized urban ministry and physical presence, despite continuing institutional decline. ACUPA's successor, the Commission for Urban Life and Faith, emerged out of those two decades of commitment to urban ministry; and, charged to 'discern and promote a positive vision of urban society and the churches' presence and witness within it', it set out to evaluate some of the strategies adopted by churches and other faith-based organizations towards the renewal of urban communities.

Times had changed over the intervening decades, however – a realization that conditioned the thinking of the second Commission from the start. Not only were we unlikely to provoke the kind of controversy engendered by *Faith in the City*, but we were dealing with a radically different political, economic and religious context. As we have seen, *Faith in the City* had been, in part, a reaction to the seismic changes of deindustrialization in the 1980s, such as the decline of heavy manufacturing and the rise of retail, service and information-based jobs. Twenty years on, while these trends had left their mark, the physical and economic landscape of most English cities had changed out of all recognition, prompted by the policies of urban regeneration which began in the 1990s and continued to the present day. Many UK cities, like many others around the world, pursued strategies such as the conversion of city-centre factories and warehouses into luxury housing designed to attract a new generation of residents, mainly young professionals. Cities such as Glasgow and Liverpool have reaped the benefit of the European Union's 'cities of culture' initiative, in which tourism, performing arts, heritage and sport are targeted as the drivers of local economic revival and civic pride. Manchester's revival during the 1990s was due in part to the activities accompanying the 2002 Commonwealth Games (Peck and Ward, 2002). Cities once wracked by structural economic decline in the 1980s were by the early 2000s no longer abandoned husks of post-industrial decay, but hubs of vibrant economic and cultural activity. This extends, as well, to the recognition of the impact of globalization, where a city's global dimensions are apparent not only in the faces of people on the streets but in the names and logos of the companies doing business in the factories and offices of our major urban areas.

The religious demography of British cities had also changed over the intervening two decades. On the one hand, the numerical decline of organized religion, especially mainstream Christianity, already apparent in the 1980s, showed no sign of abating. Yet Britain, even urban England, is far from secular or irreligious; and *Faithful Cities* acknowledged, and celebrated, the fact of religious pluralism – such as the growth of British Islam and other non-Christian faith-communities, or the emergence of African and African-Caribbean Christian congregations. Yet the paradox at the heart of *Faith in the City* – of an Established Church claiming to speak to the government on behalf of the nation while representing only a tiny minority of the population – had become ever more unavoidable. The Commission was therefore taxed with the delicate task of speaking from a perspective of faith in the context of public discourse in which faith no longer had an automatic place. However, the core proposition of *Faithful Cities* was that despite religious pluralism and the fragilities of many local faith-communities, religion could be counted as a force for good, and was often the source of vibrant new partnerships and initiatives.

In 1985, *Faith in the City* referred to 'the arrival in our cities of large numbers of adherents of other faiths', but did not anticipate the implications of cultural and religious pluralism or the role of a broad range of faith communities.

In contrast, this Commission is keenly aware that our analysis of urban life and faith must reflect, and respond to, this greater diversity. We argue that not only the churches, but all people of faith, are engaging with urban society. This is manifest in countless examples of action which counter and transcend the fragmentation, impoverishment and despair that still haunt our cities. For this reason from the beginning our Commission included people from a wide range of Christian denominations and from Islamic and Jewish perspectives. (CULF, 2006: 11)

The legacy of *Faith in the City* constituted a 'presence and engagement' with many of the most disadvantaged urban communities thanks to a concerted strategy of maintaining staff and resources in urban priority areas. Yet increasingly a mood of opposition to government was being replaced by a context of partnership, beginning with regeneration initiatives in the early 1990s and continuing with the election of New Labour in 1997. It was to this changing climate that the Commission for Urban Life and Faith addressed itself at the beginning of 2004.

Faithful Cities: Key Themes and Findings

The main thesis of *Faithful Cities* can be summarized as follows. Despite the gains of urban regeneration over the past 20 years, and the undoubted improvement in quality of life and economic prospects of many English cities – especially the post-industrial northern cities – market forces had still failed to narrow the gap between rich and poor. If unemployment was the watchword of inequality in the 1980s for many urban communities, people in those areas continued to be disadvantaged by a combination of factors such as low wages, chronic indebtedness (often to loan sharks), and lack of affordable housing. *Faithful Cities* therefore questioned whether economic models of regeneration had delivered greater social equity, since rising levels of prosperity did not appear to be 'trickling down' to those in greatest need. Similarly, despite the increased prosperity of urban areas, statistics also suggested that – in common with other major Western societies – the UK's greater wealth did not necessarily breed more happiness.

Faithful Cities argues, therefore, that the material signs of regeneration and prosperity need to be augmented by quality of life, a sense of purpose, good relationships and a value-system, faith or world-view which includes a commitment to something beyond serving one's individual needs:

> Strategies for regeneration frequently coalesce around four key principles of a good or successful city: economics; environment and infrastructure; politics and governance; and culture. These four 'pillars of regeneration' relate to questions of physical resources, wealth-creation, sustainability and political structures. What they don't do is to take into account less quantifiable questions such as quality of life, well-being – happiness even – what we might term the 'human face' of the city. We have to ask questions about the *soul* of the city as well, and how faith communities can help develop this. (Ibid.: 5–6)

To consider a spiritual dimension to a city's well-being as, potentially, the 'fifth pillar' of regeneration offers intriguing possibilities. Yet such a sensitivity to the language of values and spirituality is by no means the exclusive province of the theologian or faith-community. A generation of urban theorists, such as planners, sociologists and geographers, were eschewing rationalist, forensic and quantitative analyses in favour of 'insurgent', narrative and holistic approaches. Some members of the Commission had been greatly influenced by the new wave of urban geography, through the work of scholars such as Edward Soja, Doreen Massey and Leonie Sandercock, who have challenged the rationalism and reductionism of modernist urban planning in favour of a bottom-up, grass-roots approach, in which participatory models of urban design and community development are preferred to the centralized, technocratic planning of an earlier generation. Sandercock in particular has stressed the 'spiritual' dimension of such a project, drawing upon the insurgent struggles of indigenous and first peoples in Australia and Canada, for whom the sacredness of land becomes the expression of oppositional values based on the sanctity and integrity of the natural environment, the memory of place, the politics of vision and the practice of hope (Sandercock, 2003; CULF, 2006: 56–65).

It was this kind of urban praxis that prompted us to pose the question, 'What makes a good city?' and to attempt in *Faithful Cities* to go beyond the statistical and target-driven to value the meanings and stories people invest in their actual inhabitation of space and place. It was also a way of registering the deeper questions of value necessary for the underpinning of urban regeneration strategies, and the importance of faith perspectives in fuelling such debates rather than mere delivery of services.

Faithful Cities argued that such a broad-based and holistic analysis could best be encapsulated in the shape of a (deceptively simple) question: *what makes a good city?* In the process, the Commission saw itself as undertaking a traditional task of public theology, by undertaking public debate on economic, moral and social concerns on an open and inclusive basis. Earlier generations of Anglican social thought conducted public theology in the shape of 'middle axioms', which sought to construct guidelines for responsible public policy out of broad moral principles which might be derived from theological tradition yet could also be translated into values accessible to a wider audience. In similar terms, Heinrich Bedford-Strohm has argued for the necessity for public theology to be 'bilingual', in terms of being 'eloquent in its own biblical and theological language' and yet also in 'a language that can be understood by the public as a whole' (Bedford-Strohm, 2007: 38).

While the invitation to participate on common ground in this case is represented not by a statement of value but a question, certainly the invocation to discuss 'what makes a good city?' is intended to reflect the understanding that the work of the Commission was not addressed at the churches alone, but was intended as a catalyst for the churches to involve a range of policy-makers, government, civic and corporate institutions in a wide-ranging debate – a clear statement of intent to do theology 'in public'. This is reiterated throughout *Faithful Cities*; public theology should be prepared to defend the foundations of its own principles while ensuring that its own internal discourse is accessible and comprehensible to a wider constituency. 'While theology provides the vocabulary of faithful action, it can never be simply the private language of a sectarian few, and it should be prepared to engage critically and constructively with alternative points of view' (CULF, 2006: 15).

Fundamentally, therefore, *Faithful Cities* argued that cities were, quintessentially spaces of meaning: places where human values are embodied in material culture. The built environment is a tangible sign of a culture's deeper ideals and aspirations, and any process of exposing the deeper values underpinning the tangible substance of our urban contexts represents an important public theological task. This may, as *Faithful Cities* argues, be apparent within the language of regeneration: the Report talks about the 'secular doctrines' surrounding regeneration, and what views of human failure and pride, sin and salvation, of redemption, undergird the rhetoric of urban renewal. What, amid the rhetoric of regeneration and renaissance, are the agents of transformation choosing to elevate as their ultimate objects of worship? As Tim Gorringe argues, 'The spirituality of a culture expresses itself in, and therefore shapes, ethics, but also art, literature, music, religion, cuisine, and building – the whole of everyday life' (Gorringe, 2002: 243).

Faithful Cities begins with a very arresting image, a visual image of the London Eye, to accompany a quotation from the Chief Rabbi, Dr Jonathan Sacks. He asks what the physical appearance of a city like London tells us, when we adopt a 'birds-eye view' in terms of identifying its most significant and influential institutions. The values and priorities of a particular society Sacks calls its 'moral sense'. The types of buildings on the skyline of London, he argues, certainly speak of the centrality of economics and wealth creation and politics or governance to our society; but he also makes a plea for the value of faith-communities, represented by the tangible presence of mosques and churches and temples and gurdwaras on the horizon of any urban panorama:

> Imagine that you are taking your nephew or niece for a ride on the giant ferris wheel on the bank of the Thames, the London Eye, and using the occasion to say something about the structures of society. The first thing you both see are the great buildings of Westminster and Whitehall. These, you say, are the homes of government, and government is about the concentration and distribution of power. Next you see shops and offices, and in the distance the Stock Exchange. These, you explain, are the home of the market, and the market is about the

production and distribution of wealth. Then your nephew or niece notices the dome of St Paul's and the various church spires still visible between the tower blocks and asks, 'What are those?' You explain that they are houses of worship. 'And what,' he or she asks, 'do they produce and distribute?' Our first inclination might be to say that they are not that sort of place at all. This, I want to suggest, would be an error, but no mere error. In a certain sense it is a defining error of our culture. (Wilson and Sacks, 2002: 15; see CULF, 2006: 1)

This introduces a second theme running throughout *Faithful Cities*, which stresses the distinctive contribution of faith to the city, and how religion and religious organizations might promote the 'soul' of the city. Religion remains a vital part of the culture of our major cities and continues to be recognized as a key element of community life and public policy. In May 2006, shortly before the launch of *Faithful Cities*, the Archbishop of Canterbury introduced a debate in the House of Lords on the theme of 'Churches and Cities', largely anticipating the publication of this report. What marked that debate was the way in which speaker after speaker rose to affirm the value of the contribution of faith-based organizations: not only in urban regeneration and community renewal, but in areas as diverse as health care chaplaincy, racial justice and social enterprise.

Yet part of the argument of *Faithful Cities* was that the resources of organized religion in many urban areas have gone unrecognized. This may be partly due to government misunderstandings of the real nature of many faith-based organizations – what is beginning to be called 'religious literacy' (or lack of it) within the public and statutory sector. Some of this may be due to the dominance of the secularization thesis within the social sciences, which means that the construction of racial and ethnic identities (and their policy implications) has been discussed with little or no reference to or comprehension of, religious affiliation (Smith, 2004: 187).

Faithful Cities offers dozens of local case studies which tell of congregations intimately involved with the affairs of their local community. These stories tell of countless initiatives, ranging from service provision for families, young people and the elderly, to ambitious programmes of community capacity-building and neighbourhood regeneration. The cumulative impact of all these stories was to demonstrate how the values of faith provide a powerful and enduring motivation for believers to work actively for the well-being of their communities.

In this report, we argue that despite its ambivalent history, and its capacity to incite hatred and conflict, religious faith is still one of the richest, most enduring and most dynamic sources of energy and hope for cities. Faith is a vital – and often essential – resource in the building of relationships and communities. In the values they promote, in the service they inspire, and in the resources they command, faith-based organizations make a decisive contribution to their communities. (CULF, 2006: 4)

Another central concept of *Faithful Cities* is to be found in that of 'faithful capital', as a means of expressing the contribution that is made by faith-based organizations to the enhancement of social networks which contribute to a healthy civil society. The discussion of faithful capital derives from Robert Putnam's work on 'social capital', as an index of the quality of people's ability to connect and work together towards common objectives via the processes that strengthen social bonds, transactions and institutions (Putnam, 2000). Putnam describes it as 'connections among individuals – social networks and the norms of reciprocity and trustworthiness that arise from them' (Putnam, 2000, 19). Through these connections, which are further defined as 'bonding' (close-knit relationships based on family, ethnicity or class), 'bridging' (outward-looking relationships between diverse groups) and 'linking' (relationships which connect people to networks outside their normal peer groups), Putnam believes people are enabled to develop the skills and virtues necessary to build healthy civil society.

Faithful Cities built on this analysis, to argue that 'faithful capital' is distinguished from social capital by its 'moral sense', rooted in beliefs about God as the source of life, about each person being made 'in the image of God' and therefore of unique worth and dignity, and about humanity being intended to live in relationship with God and each other, in lives of 'mutuality, love and justice' (CULF, 2006: 2). These beliefs are the wellsprings of love of neighbour, care for the stranger, giving voice to the voiceless, a striving for human dignity and social justice, and a quest for personal and communal transformation. They inspire acts of hospitality, an important aspect of faithful capital, which goes beyond mere tolerance, deeply enshrined in biblical tradition, of welcoming the stranger or sojourner, of entertaining Christ in one's care for the prisoner, the homeless and dispossessed (ibid.: 3). It is by virtue of faithful capital that faith-based organizations play a vital role in regeneration, its 'major dividend' being people motivated to engage in their community by the conviction that 'other people and their circumstances matter' (ibid.: 66–75).

The concept of 'faithful capital', therefore, is intended to encapsulate the motivations and practices of faith-in-action, and as such, can be used to affirm and challenge the role of faith-based organizations, and to bring to the notice of the government the contribution such groups make. The implication is that it causes faith-based organizations to operate in a distinctive way, with a 'people-centredness', that is often at odds with the economically driven goals and working styles of commercial and statutory organizations with whom they enter into fruitful, but critical, partnerships.

> If the dominant idea of much urban regeneration is one of 'delivering a good city to the people', then faith traditions offer alternative understandings ... Cities, as human dwelling places which somehow prefigure and point to the presence of God within them, are always 'under construction', and need the active and continuing participation of all parts of the community to fulfil their potential. (Ibid.: 4)

So *Faithful Cities* also warned against the way that the resources and the energy of faith communities could be co-opted by the authorities, or the capacities and skills of local people undervalued in the process of regeneration. *Faithful Cities* argues that faith is often misunderstood by policymakers and those steering regeneration projects, arguing for a grass-roots approach to decision-making and community participation that place values of human flourishing and a rounded sense of what makes a good city, as opposed to narrowly economistic criteria, as well as models of wealth creation that pay attention to matters of equity and fair distribution.

While the reserves of faithful capital are practically and tangibly put to work in generating practical outcomes, the bearers of such resources represent an independent and critical voice that cannot simply be co-opted by expediency or sectional interest, since it should derive from independent values from the tradition of faith. While *Faithful Cities* endorses the importance of a critical solidarity with other planning and regeneration agencies, it also stresses that it is one in which faith-based organizations also interpose alternative priorities, perhaps with a different time-frame and more holistic values (Furbey and Macey, 2005: 95–116).

As the Archbishop of Canterbury put it in the House of Lords debate:

> [Communities of faith] speak of a commitment and availability of social capital that is not likely to be withdrawn when things get difficult. In a world of time-limited grants and often desperate scrambling to create leadership and management structures that will survive the somewhat breathless rhythms of funding regimes, they allow a longer view. (Hansard, 2006: col. 502–3)

So religious congregations are places where the skills and capacities for social renewal are nurtured; and *Faithful Cities* calls on local and national government to acknowledge that faith-based organizations are well placed to help many of our urban neighbourhoods to flourish, materially and spiritually.

A final theme of *Faithful Cities* concerns its theological method. The Commission believed that its claims for the distinctive contribution of faithful capital as the embodiment of particular values required its report to be more explicit right from the start about the religious or theological foundations of those values. *Faithful Cities* therefore opens with a general expression of its core convictions, careful to stress its rootedness in an identifiable faith tradition:

> What we have to say grows out of three convictions: ... what we understand about the nature of God; ... what it means to be human; and ... how humanity should live in community together.
>
> First, we understand God to be source of all life from whom all creation draws its purpose and character. Second, we understand that to be human means that we are made 'in the image and likeness of God', and that ... each person possesses an innate and irreducible dignity. Thirdly, our traditions speak of humanity being called into relationship with God and that human purpose and destiny is fulfilled in relationships of community, mutuality and justice ...
>
> Our 'moral sense' of society tells us that *life itself* is sacred, that our *individual lives* are interconnected and our *common life* should be constructed to enable all people to flourish. This is the wellspring of faithful capital. (CULF, 2006: 2)

Once again, the 'bilingualism' of the Commission's public theology comes to the fore: it seeks to ground its core values in a broadly Trinitarian theology, while also acknowledging the shared responsibility of seeking 'the good city'.

CULF also set itself the task of elaborating a style of doing theology that built on some elements of *Faith in the City*, but which was more explicitly rooted in subsequent developments in Christian social ethics and practical theology. First, it stresses the 'practical' nature of all theology, arguing that it is the discourse that enables the Church to 'practise what it preaches' in order to guide the praxis of faith. 'Talk about God' is most authentic when it is embodied in the faithful actions of worship, outreach and pastoral care: essentially, about words becoming flesh. It also means that faith (the theology) and practice are indivisible in an essential unity of belief and action. This also implicitly challenges the frequent claim that the churches' involvement in social action is a distraction from its devotional practices:

> The stories, scriptures, songs, prayers, rituals and teachings that form the everyday life of religious faith (the 'habits of the heart') are not some anthropological curiosity. They are the sources of the values which prompt action on behalf of those who are marginalized. The practices of faith and the actions on behalf of their neighbour cannot be separated. (Ibid.: 82)

Second, if *Faith in the City* used motifs from liberation theology to politicize the Church, calling it to address structural injustices, then *Faithful Cities* extended that to argue that liberation theology is also no less 'political' in its intention to give voice to those on the margins and to value the experiences of those at the grass-roots (Graham, 2007).

> Our struggle for God's reign involves acting as advocates for those whose voice is rarely heard, and empowering the excluded. We are compelled to stand alongside them and to form alliances with them and with others who work for the same purposes. (CULF, 2006: 67)

This is consistent with the emergence of Black, feminist and post-colonial theologies over the past 20 years which privilege the ways in which ordinary people – often on the margins of Church and society – are articulating important theological values in their own ways, in their own words. *Faithful Cities* therefore talks of 'theology in the vernacular', adopting the 'everyday' or popular speech; of listening to those at the grass-roots and of paying testimony to the vitality of expressions of faith to be found at the margins. It also meant that the physical format of the report itself embodied a variety of printed styles, combining paragraphs of analysis with pictures and text-boxes of case studies, pictures and anecdotes. It was deliberately designed to be more accessible to the general reader and to honour the Commission's commitment to give voice to perspectives that are often marginalized by official accounts, be they the 'top-down' and deadline-driven agendas of regeneration programmes, or even the institutional Church.

Critiques of *Faithful Cities*

What has been the critical reception of *Faithful Cities*? Predictably, perhaps, it has not incited the same degree of controversy as its predecessor, possibly reflecting the less polarized and febrile nature of British society and political debate in general. Yet for some critics, *Faithful Cities* is too sanguine about the excitement and vitality of urban life, and the implications of the growing divisions between rich and poor over the past 20 years; too preoccupied with the impact of gentrification at the expense of those who remained invisible and marginalized; and failed to comment sufficiently on issues around crime, fear of crime, and law and order. The report failed to foresee the rise of incidents of gun crime in some English cities; and pressures of its publication schedule prevented a sufficiently detailed response to the bomb attacks in London on 7 July 2005 with corresponding agonizing about the future of British Islam.

The central notion of 'faithful capital' has also received critical attention. For some critics, such terminology reflects too much of an attempt to prove the 'usefulness' of religious groups, playing into the hands of local and national government which – especially in the wake of moral panics about 'furious religion' after 7/7 – are desperate to find alternative sources of social cohesion in urban communities. Andrew Davey has argued that making the practice of faith a 'quantifiable product or commodity to attract attention or additional resources' has its dangers, and questions the use of the economic term 'capital', seeing little theological precedent for what he sees as moving beyond metaphor to reify 'the resources and assets of faith' (Davey, 2007: 16).

The true capacity of faith-based organizations actually to deliver services when they themselves are fragile or in terminal decline is also clearly a stringent test of the long-term viability of the language of faithful capital. Yet current interest in the capacity of faith-based organizations to deliver government policy and to be agents of the less tangible values of social cohesion is open to criticism. Greg Smith challenges the assumption that

> 'faith communities' have a large army of 'community leaders' poised to give their time to support the government's projects ... [which] seems wedded to a traditional Anglican concept of the role of the Church, where a vicar with time on his/her hands is happy to work uncontroversially for the welfare of the whole community. However, the reality of religious life in the inner city is more likely to be one of over-stretched clergy, groups relying on lay (and socially excluded) leadership, faith that makes priorities of spiritual rather than social agendas, and sectarian or communal competition for scarce resources. (Smith, 2004: 195)

What of the theology of *Faithful Cities*, and its insistence on an inductive, contextual approach? Arguably, this was honoured more in principle than in practice. Lack of a consistent editorial position in the writing of the report meant that the good intentions of a 'theology in the vernacular' ultimately appeared fragmented, anecdotal and piecemeal, rather than a fully executed theological method. The lesson to be learned appears to be that while it may be desirable to do theology collaboratively, it is less easy to do it by committee.

A further criticism of *Faithful Cities* has been its perceived failure to address questions of mission, evangelism and congregational life. This is, in part, an institutional question about the very survival of the urban church itself, insofar as it is ultimately dependent on the long-term viability of local congregational life in urban priority areas. It also raises the question of the relationship between faithful capital and mission in the sense of evangelism – does conversion to Christ, leading to the personal transformation of individuals and seen by some as a necessary part of community transformation, have any place within the concept? (Cox, 2006).

For some critics, the inclusive nature of the Commission's public theology falls far short of the imperatives of proclamation and evangelism. *Faithful Cities* claims that faithful capital, and the dividend it represents in terms of local activism, are grounded in shared convictions about the nature of God and what it means to be human. Yet many would argue that if, for Christians, the revelation of God in Christ is unique to their understanding, no such spiritual dimension of faithful action can be sustained if it cannot be nurtured by a common programme of prayer, worship or 'explanation of the faith that motivates us ... if we are not in agreement about that faith' (ibid.: 4). This does raise questions about the viability of partnership, a feature central to faithful capital, and how faithful capital can be built, sustained, and 'confessed' when people involved in the same project come from different faiths and none. This effectively places debate about faithful capital within the ongoing debate surrounding 'service versus proclamation', social action versus evangelism, in the ministry of the Church (Leech, 2006) – but of course, it is a matter of opinion as to whether those different dimensions are incompatible or complementary.

However, I believe that the inclusive and 'bilingual' nature of *Faithful Cities* can be defended. The hallmark of 'doing theology in public' is not a matter of choosing between tradition and dialogue, but of holding them in creative tension. Arguably, engagement and dialogue with traditions other than one's own takes place out of a deepened, rather than an attenuated faith: in adopting a metaphor from the prophet Isaiah, the Commission argued that if the breadth of one's vision of truth is extended, then that requires the deepening of the roots of one's faith:

> To withdraw [from collaboration] on the grounds that partnerships involve compromise and getting our hands dirty, only leaves the field open to those to whom getting their hands dirty is less of a problem. To withdraw behind the walls of places of worship, speaking only to one another, is to ignore the divine claim on the whole of creation and the divine invitation to become partners in the redemption of the world. But, if the Church is not to be compromised by its partnerships, it must stay true to the core beliefs of its Christian vision. If it is, to use a metaphor of the prophet Isaiah (54.2), 'to lengthen its ropes' through partnership with others, then it must also 'strengthen its pegs' by attention to worship, which touches the heart as well as the mind. (CULF, 2006: 75)

Less easy to defend, in retrospect, is the Commission's failure to reflect the decisive shift in urban ministry and theology represented by evangelical churches and movements. They have moved into cities in the 20 years since *Faith in the City* and combine practical projects with distinctive Christian witness: groups such as Eden, Faithworks and Urban Presence, as well as the growing prominence of Black-majority church traditions, both African and African-Caribbean. *Faithful Cities'* lack of attention to that dimension means that we did not really address the question of what it means to preach and live the gospel in the midst of increasingly diverse urban life. 'Especially how [sic] is the gospel of Christ life transforming, in a personal way today for the poor and marginalized, as well as for the comfortably off. Christian discipleship must be more than a pseudo ethnic affiliation or a mere consumer choice in the hypermarket of spiritualities and religious cultures on offer' (Smith, 2006).

Conclusion

Posing the question, 'What makes a good city?', *Faithful Cities* identifies religious faith as one of the 'most dynamic sources of energy and hope for cities'. It argues that 'In the values they promote, in the service they inspire, and in the resources they command, faith-based organizations make a decisive difference to their communities' (CULF, 2006: 4) and it suggests that those values and resources can be drawn together within a single defining concept, faithful capital, which churches and other faith groups invest in the community in numerous different ways as they tackle local issues and seek to contribute to the well-being of their neighbourhoods. It expresses a 'performative' theology with roots in the theologies of liberation which, in their commitment to God's 'preferential option for the poor' and to social change being 'as much an integral part of the Church's mission as personal conversion', emphasized orthopraxis above orthodoxy (Graham, Walton and Ward, 2005: 170–1). It is a concept that sees faith and practice as indivisible and, as such, provides a way of drawing the link between people's values and their actions.

Faithful Cities makes a lot of the importance of valuing the experiences and aspirations of ordinary people, but also criticizing the extent to which the agenda of urban regeneration is not driven with those interests at its heart. It is evident in what we say about the importance of 'theologies from below' and of listening to the stories, hopes and achievements of local communities of faith; and it is also there in our analysis of the way the 'regeneration industry' is often driven by considerations that do not reflect long-term grass-roots interest, although projects would often be more sustainable if they did. And this is linked to the question of harnessing and valuing the 'social capital' or 'faithful capital' of such communities, because social/faithful capital is an effective means of capacity-building.

What of the long-term prospects of the report? Like its predecessor, two decades earlier, *Faithful Cities* may also end up embodying an unexpected paradox, for despite its attempts to break the vestiges of the Establishment mould of public theology, *Faithful Cities'* best chance for enduring impact may rest in a quite traditional Anglican solution, namely the intervention of its bishops in public life. In November 2006, Stephen Lowe, a member of CULF and already area bishop of Hulme, in inner-city Manchester, was appointed 'Bishop for Urban Life and Faith', and was charged with implementing CULF's 11 various recommendations, which ranged from supporting appropriate forms of urban ministry, promoting new styles of theological education and contextual theology, sponsoring the debate about values via the question of 'what makes a good city', and fostering greater 'religious literacy' on the part of government at all levels. Bishop Stephen's advocacy gives a focus and energy to the after-life of *Faithful Cities* which is probably its best chance of influencing policy and practice into the future. So the work continues, and the debates show no sign of abating, for despite the many changes that have taken place over the past 20 years, *Faithful Cities* provides compelling evidence of the enduring presence, and decisive impact, of 'faith in the city'.

Part Five

NEW TECHNOLOGIES AND POST/HUMAN FUTURES

18

POST/HUMAN CONDITIONS

The issues that technological culture throws into sharp relief are those of values, and the value judgements on which decisions about ends and the restrictions (if any) on the means to achieve those ends, have to be taken. More particularly, at the heart of the problem of value judgements is the issue of the nature of the person. What does it mean to be human? is a question that has taken on a new urgency in a culture where behaviour can be manipulated by increasingly sophisticated technology. (Brown and Wesson, 1991: 22)

Introduction

Having decreed 'the end of history' some years ago, the political scientist and commentator Francis Fukuyama has now turned his attention to the future of human nature. *Our Posthuman Future*, published in 2002, considers the implications of the biotechnological revolution, and in particular the prospects of cloning, genetic modification and other biotechnologies on our understandings of what it means to be human. However, discussion of the so-called 'posthuman condition' (Halberstam and Livingston, 1995: 19) had already attracted attention from scholars in areas as diverse as cultural theory, science and technology studies, bioethics and philosophy of technology.

Although philosophical speculation about the relationship between humanity and technologies has a long history, and current thinking can be placed in a long legacy of debate (Scharff and Dusek, 2003), certain advances over the past half-century – most particularly the construction of the world's first stored-memory computer in 1948 and the identification of DNA in 1953 – do seem to represent an unprecedented intensification of technoscientific potential. Talk of the posthuman thus evokes a highly technoscientific[1] world in which, thanks to cybernetics, artificial intelligence, virtual reality, plastic surgery, gene therapies and assisted reproduction, biological humans are everywhere surrounded – and transformed – into mixtures of machine and organism, where what we call 'nature' has been significantly reshaped by technology, and technology, in turn has become assimilated into 'nature' as a fully functioning component of organic life itself.

In current writing, this has become a shorthand metaphor for talking about a number of interrelated issues. First, it denotes the scientific and medical prospects for enhancement of human physical and intellectual powers by means of cybernetic implants or genetic modification, including increased longevity, resistance to congenital or other illnesses, improved cognitive skills (Warwick, 2002; Kaku, 1998). Second, as a corollary to this, the posthuman has come to be identified for many with the emergence of a new phase of human evolution, albeit technologically driven (and the result of human choices) rather than as a series of adaptive processes within non-human nature (Stock, 2002; Mazlish, 1993). Third, these two strands have been taken up by writers within cultural studies, the philosophy of technology and critical theory as an opportunity to think anew about enduring issues to do with the relationship between humans and their environments, artifacts and tools (Latour, 1993; Haraway, 1997; Gray, 1995).

Yet if the future is one of augmented, modified, virtual, 'post-biological' humanity, and if – as Fukuyama claims – any basis for a political, legal or moral appeal to a notion of our shared humanity will soon become redundant, then what will be the implications? How will we talk about what it means to be human when we are more dependent on what Gregory Stock calls 'human self-design' than the accidents of nature? Who is likely to be included and excluded from any future vision of posthumanity? What can be learned from the hopes and anxieties engendered by the technologies that surround us – and are these technologies likely to lead to human well-being or to our extinction?

Using critical perspectives drawn from Michel Foucault, Donna Haraway and Bruno Latour, as well as studies of science fiction, feminist theory and bioethics, *Representations of the Post/Human* (Graham, 2002a) examines how advances in medical, reproductive, genetic and

---

1 Use of the term 'technoscience' is frequently attributed to Bruno Latour, whose work on the social contexts of scientific research implicitly refutes any notion of the separation of science and technology into 'pure' and 'applied' forms of knowledge. The priorities of practising scientists are shaped by wider cultural factors, not least the availability of funding; and the logic of technological developments often exert defining influences over cultural institutions and behaviours (Latour and Woolgar, 1986), not least in the harnessing of scientific endeavours to corporate commercial interests (Haraway, 1997: 3–4).

information technologies are currently calling into question the very meaning of 'human nature' itself. I argue that contemporary technologies carry ethical and metaphysical, as well as material, implications, and the book weaves these concerns together in an extended study of the kinds of discourses – political, scientific, ethical, even theological – that will shape our understandings of what it means to be human into the next century. For embedded in the various representations of our posthuman future emergent in new technologies are crucial issues of identity, community and spirituality: what it means to be human, who counts as being fully human, who gets excluded and included in definitions of the (post)human – as well as what visions of the future are idealized, and idolized, in the name of technoscientific aspiration.

The Posthuman Condition

The possible effects of twenty-first-century genetic, cybernetic and digital technologies are numerous and might be summarized into the following themes:

1 The mechanization of the human and the technologization of the natural

The AbiCor artificial heart, constructed from plastic and titanium and powered by external batteries, is one example of a new breed of cybernetic devices, self-regulating mechanisms that mimic physiological functions. The AbiCor mechanism was implanted into a patient called Robert Tools in July 2001, and although Mr Tools was not expected to survive more than a month, he eventually died on 30 November 2001, five months after surgery. More rudimentary medical implants, such as heart pacemakers and cochlear implants, are becoming more commonplace, at least in the West; but in all cases, 'natural' processes are reproduced or enhanced by technological means with a view to rectifying abnormalities, replacing lost faculties or assisting depleted physical functions.

Forms of assisted reproduction, made possible by a variety of biotechnological processes, are also having a significant impact on Western culture, as children are conceived via *in vitro* fertilization, and procedures such as ultrasound, amniocentesis and genetic screening of foetuses are a regular aspect of medical prenatal diagnosis (Casper, 1995). Yet this has proven to be a particularly rich area of critique on the part of feminist and queer theorists, who point to the liberatory potential resulting from the separation of procreation from heterosexual intercourse (Halberstam and Livingston, 1995), but also to the 'medicalization' of childbirth inherent in greater degrees of technological intervention (Shildrick, 1997).

Once the province of military experiment and science fiction, therefore, 'cyborgs' (mixtures of organic and cybernetic) are now moving
from fantasy into reality (Gray, 1995). The term 'cyborg' was first used
in a paper published in 1960 by two aeronautics experts, Manfred Clynes
and Nathan Kline. Their paper speculated how technological adaptations
of physical functioning might enhance human performance in hostile environments such as outer space (Clynes and Kline, 1995). Subsequently,
cyborg technologies have been developed to restore impaired functions
(such as prosthesis or implants), or modify existing capabilities, enhancing bodies into stronger, better, faster systems.

Cyborgs thus inhabit a world simultaneously 'biological' and 'technological'. A living fusion of the human and non-human animal, the human
and the mechanical, and the organic and the fabricated, the cyborg exposes the collapse of taken-for-granted boundaries between species and
categories (Haraway, 1991: 152–3). However, for many the cyborg occupies a larger, metaphorical place in social theory, symbolizing the increasing interconnections between humans and technologies, a kind of
'thought experiment' in our understanding of being human in an age of
advanced technologies.

For Donna Haraway, the cyborg represents the potential for a *renewed*
relationship between humanity and what have been characterized as
nature and technology, a greater intimacy and complicity with environment and artefact, a true interdependence in which human nature is no
longer characterized through mastery and exclusion of its designated
others. Others are more mindful, however, of the classic Sci-Fi cyborg,
such as *Terminator* or *Robocop*:[2] the hypermasculine fighting machine,
who is rendered invulnerable (and *inhuman*) by technological enhance-
ments and modifications.

2 *Blurring of species boundaries*

The development of 'transgenic' procedures – the practice of transplant-
ing genetic material from one species into another – creates *hybrids* whose
genetic composition is no longer 'born' but 'made'. Similarly, discoveries about the nature of the human genome have stressed the amount of
shared genetic material common both to *Homo sapiens* and the chim-
panzee. We may ask, what makes us distinctively human in the face of
such information; and what characterizes the boundaries between any
one species and another?

A graphic illustration of this is the figure of what Donna Haraway has
called 'OncoMouse™' (Haraway, 1997), a laboratory mouse bred especially to carry a carcinogenic gene to assist research into breast cancer.

---

2 Although I have always regarded the latter as a parody of this.

However, when we ask, 'What is OncoMouse™? Where does she belong in the taxonomy of species?', we discover she occupies a variety of categorical and discursive spaces. She is simultaneously mammal, scientific object, transgenic species and biotechnological commodity (Haraway, 1997: 38ff.); and as the offspring of technologized and commercialized biology, OncoMouse™ straddles the boundaries of science, business and nature, defying categorizations that depend on ontological purity and discreteness (Haraway, 1997: 119).

So OncoMouse™ is a living being, but also a lucrative commodity, a piece of patented information harnessed by corporate biotechnology in its fight to achieve a therapeutic 'good', namely a cure for cancer. An example, then, of the hybrid and uncertain status of many of the products of biotechnological intervention; but also a signal that we are dealing with a world not only of material technologies, of the manipulation of the physical world, but a world compromised by ethical and political decisions and replete with meanings and myths.

And we can begin to get hints of the way in which new technologies are not only material artefacts, but also objects of philosophical, ontological, ethical – even theological – speculation, from the manner in which Onco-Mouse™ is portrayed as the bearer not only of scientific exploration but deeper narratives, about human suffering and salvation. In the rhetoric of ameliorative medicine, argues Haraway, this little rodent is elevated to a redemptive status:

> Although her promise is decidedly secular, s/he is a figure in the sense developed within Christian realism: s/he is our scapegoat; s/he bears our suffering; s/he signifies and enacts our mortality in a powerful, historically specific way that promises a culturally privileged kind of salvation – a 'cure for cancer'. Whether I agree to her existence and use or not, s/he suffers, physically, repeatedly, and profoundly, that I and my sisters may live. (Haraway, 1997:79)

Thus, OncoMouse™ is not only an empirical or material phenomenon, a product of scientific experimentation, but a cultural icon too, embodying moral, emotional, even theological resonances.

3 Blurring of bodily boundaries

Yet another blurring takes place at the boundaries of the human body. Whereas it was appropriate to think of tools such as the knife, the hammer and the water-pot as simple instruments of extension and containment, in the highly technologized societies of the twenty-first century we are increasingly engaging with technologies that actually reshape the very boundaries and contours of the human body itself.

We might think of two dimensions to this: first, the ways in which prostheses, implants and synthetic drugs are internalized by the organic body, so that technology is not an extension or appendage to the human body, but is *incorporated*, assimilated into its very structures. In the words of Stelarc, the Australian performance artist who specializes in installations that depict human fusions with technologies, 'The skin has been a boundary for the soul, for the self, and simultaneously a beginning to the world. Once technology stretches and pierces the skin, the skin as a barrier is erased' (Atzori and Woolford, 1995).

A second characteristic of the digital and biotechnological age – alongside that of incorporation – is its *immersive* nature, as new habitats for the containment and circulation of communication are created. The epitome of this, of course, would be the creation of digitally generated virtual realities. The philosophical question here is how 'real' such 'imaginary' environments are: whether they represent a flight from embodiment, or a continuation of corporeal and physical extension and augmentation already available via technologies such as the telephone.

4 Creation of new personal and social worlds

Digital technology will soon be of such sophistication as to be capable of synthesizing an entire virtual environment, creating cyberspace into which a person can be sensorially if not physically assimilated. In their capacity to engender new immersive worlds that authentically mimic organic reality, digital technologies have become not so much *tools* – extensions of the body – as total *environments*. (Poster, 1996: 188–9)

Virtual reality allows the user to project a digitally generated self into cyberspace, synthesizing new spatial and temporal contexts within which alternative subjectivities are constructed. Digitally generated virtual worlds thereby offer new forms of 'post-bodied' activity, and the unitary face-to-face self is superceded by the multiple self – the simulated, fictive identity of the electronic chatroom or the multi-user domain. So just as the boundaries between humans, animals and machines erode, so do the distinctions between the virtual and the real.

Enslavement or Liberation?

It is perhaps worth commenting at this stage on some underlying issues already emerging from this analysis of the 'posthuman condition'. First, it is interesting to note that the impact of advanced technologies on our experiences of being human are greeted by a range of reactions, from optimism to anxiety. Some reactions articulate sentiments close to technophobia; epitomized, perhaps, in the epithet of 'Frankenstein Foods' (Newton *et al.*, 1999; Turney, 1998). Reports in the 1990s about the impact of genetic modification of crops was accompanied – and fuelled – by media references to 'Frankenstein Foods' (Newton *et al.*, 1999; Wood, 1999). Even Monsanto, the multinational biotechnology corporation, saw fit to counter what it regarded as the negative publicity this occasioned (Monsanto Corporation, 1999). Such associations with mad scientists and monstrosity evokes a reaction of horror and suspicion – of creation turning on its creator who dares to 'play God'. The alliterative quality of the term adds to its impact; but in comparison to more neutral terms such as 'genetically modified crops' we are presented already with a powerful set of allusions and associations. Note again, as with OncoMouse™, how science and popular culture/myth are interwoven in the way these issues are framed.

By contrast, Kevin Warwick's *I Cyborg* (2002) tells the story of his own quest to become a living 'cyborg' by means of a miniature radio-transmitter implanted in his arm and capable of sending and receiving signals between his nervous system and a computer program. Warwick's speculation over the potential of such experiments exemplifies a mild form of what is often known as 'transhumanism': the belief that digital, cybernetic, genetic and biomedical technologies are the instruments of the next phase of human evolution, in which *Homo sapiens* will mutate into *Homo cyberneticus* or *Techno sapiens* (Jackelén, 2002):

> In the future, I believe, we will be able to send signals to and from human and machine brains. We will be able to directly harness the memory and mathematical capabilities of humans. We will be able to communicate across the internet by means of thought signals alone. Human speech and language, as we know it, will become obsolete. Ultimately, humans will become a lower form of life, unable to compete with either intelligent machines or cyborgs. (Warwick, 2000: 1)

This popular, highly technocratic, form of posthumanism suffuses much of technoscientific and corporate research, as well as dominating the work of scientific popularizers such as the mass-circulation journal *Scientific American* (Graham, 2002a: 156) and writers such as Warwick, Gregory Stock (2002), Lee Silver (1998), Michio Kaku (1998), as well as the more extreme manifestations of transhumanism such as the Extropians, Max More and Nick Bostrom (Graham, 2002a: 154–75; 2003; Bostrom, 2003). Yet there is a parallel and altogether more critical corpus of analysis on the nature of the posthuman which attempts to move beyond the polarizations of expansiveness and fear, technophilia and technophobia, towards an interrogation of the very terms underpinning the evocation of the 'posthuman' – what Bart Simon terms 'critical posthumanism' (Simon,

2003) and thriving in disciplines such as cultural theory (Lyotard, 1991; Gray, 1995; Hayles, 1999; Badmington, 2000), science and technology studies (Latour, 1993; Haraway, 1997), and feminist, gender and queer theory (Halberstam and Livingston, 1995; Haraway, 1991). The latter is concerned not only to evaluate the material impact of new technologies on economics, communications, sexuality and reproduction, embodiment and so on, but to raise the question of the kind of values at work in these various discourses of 'fear' and 'hope' in the face of new technologies. Writers such as Katharine Hayles, Neil Badmington, Scott Bukatman and Bruno Latour argue that these popular accounts still tend to operate within a framework of liberal humanism on to which we merely 'graft' something called technology. Rather, it is necessary to question that, and to see that what are also changing are the very criteria by which we think about 'human nature'. It is not simply a matter of projecting the humanist subject into the future, therefore, but to ask what kinds of definitive criteria for being 'human' are actually circulating in these many and varied reactions (Simon, 2003; Badmington, 2003).

'Critical posthumanism' therefore argues that digital, cybernetic and genetic technologies have not only material but existential impact, in their ability to question the boundaries and categories by which we have always delineated 'human nature'. In their own ways, many of the models of what 'technology' is doing to 'us' still entertain traces of humanist subjectivities. They also assume that technologies are neutral instruments, whereas they exercise a transformative power over their users. The image of the pristine humanist subject untouched and unpenetrated by invasive technologies, the hyper-macho invulnerable techno-hero or transhumanist sublime, all suffer from what I called an 'ontological hygiene' with respect to human nature, refusing to recognize how the very distinctions between the organic and technological, nature and artefact, human and machine are coming under pressure.

Bruno Latour and Donna Haraway both assume that in a digital and biotechnological age, it is impossible to speak of a pristine, unadulterated 'human nature' without considering the ways in which humans have always, as it were, co-evolved with their tools and technologies. Thus, in her essay, 'A Cyborg Manifesto', first published in the mid-1980s (Haraway, 1991) Haraway famously argued that in the face of new technologies, we have to realize – and celebrate – the accompanying erosion of many of the boundaries by which we have set the limits of normative or authentic human nature. For Haraway, the 'blasphemy' of the cyborg rests in its refusal to observe the essentialist categories of species, gender, nature and ontology, and in whom 'the boundaries of a fatally transgressive world, ruled by the Subject and the Object, give way to the borderlands, inhabited by human and unhuman collectives' (1992a: 328). Latour puts it this way: 'we have never been modern' (Latour, 1993); ontological hygiene was a condition of a particular phase of scientific enquiry and categorization, but a recognition of the hybridity of the 'posthuman condition' enables us to consider that the delineation of human nature is more a question of boundaries than essences (Graham, 2002a: 33–7).

It is these very questions that lie at the heart of *Representations of the Post/Human*, for the significance of the posthuman is not simply as a means of examining the material impact of new technologies on human bodies, communications, family structures, reproduction, economy and so on, but in the way they expose the very discourses and values informing our assumptions about what it means to be human. For me, therefore, the use of the *oblique* in my terminology of 'post/human' reflects this wish to insert a kind of critical interval in our talk of the post/human. The critical task is to gain some analytical grasp on how the fault-lines are established – not simply as *material* factors (for example, the 1 per cent of genetic material which supposedly differentiates human beings from chimpanzees), but the *discursive technologies* which demarcate humans from nature, non-human animals, machines. My chosen means of framing the condition of post/humanity, therefore, is to say that it is concerned with the blurring of boundaries, an exposure of the ontological hygiene by which for the past three hundred years Western culture has distinguished the 'human' from the non-human, monstrous, abject or alien.

As Neil Badmington observes (Badmington, 2004: 56), the use of the oblique between 'post' and 'human' is intended to draw attention to the function and meaning of both terms in mutual interaction. As the many contested visions of the posthuman condition indicate, whether or not the 'post' denotes a humanity superceded or enhanced depends entirely on our assumptions about the role of technologies in advancing or compromising human integrity – however that is conceived. It alerts us to the element of human agency, rather than technological determinism, entailed in the conception, design and implementation of such technologies: the political choices inherent in the use of all technologies, to the values beneath the choices that get made, and who gets included and who gets excluded by 'the posthuman condition'. It prevents us from reading the 'posthuman' as a simplistic indication that we are merely talking about a successor species whose future trajectory and ultimate characteristics are already known, without asking *whose version* of normative and exemplary humanity is assumed to be engaging with technologies. I do not regard the 'posthuman' as an inevitable condition, therefore, so much as an *interrogation* into the terms by which Western culture has defined what it means to be human (Graham, 2002a: 37).

What is at stake, supremely, in the debate about the implications of digital, genetic, cybernetic and biomedical technologies is precisely what (and who) will define authoritative notions of normative, exemplary, desirable humanity into the twenty-first century. It is also a question of how such visions will be enshrined in the design of technologies and built environments; how they will shape political and policy choices about scientific funding; and how they will inform scientific theories and metaphors. It is not so much about the end of the human or the advent of the superhuman, therefore, as whose visions will fuel the technoscientific developments that contribute towards the realization of any such futures. (Ibid.: 11)

So in talking about the era of the post/human, I would want to stop and query the axiomatic use of such a term if it prevents us from thinking critically. And thinking critically on two levels: first, to recognize the diversity of human engagements with and reactions to our tools, technologies and artefacts; and second, to realize that the power of technologies to reshape our worlds and indeed our very selves is a matter of human agency and choice, rather than technological inevitability.

Posthuman Monsters

In search of critical tools, therefore, my book develops a two-fold approach, by drawing on the tradition of 'teratology', or the study of monsters, and the genealogical critique of Michel Foucault.

The significance of monstrosity takes us back to my earlier comments about figures such as OncoMouse™ and the recurrent references to Frankenstein which punctuate popular reception of genetically modified foods (Turney, 1998). These remind us of the symbolic meanings accruing to technological endeavour, and the way in which such innovations excite philosophical, ethical and theological speculation over and beyond their material impact. This is reminiscent of an older tradition of teratology, or the study of monsters.

In Haraway's analysis of the multiple meanings which surround OncoMouse™, her fascination derives largely from the creature's hybrid, uncertain location amid a number of discourses. In her position at the cutting-edge of gene therapy, she becomes for us more than a laboratory experiment, assuming a quasi-iconic status with Christ-like healing properties. Similarly, 'Frankenstein Food' evokes responses of horror and fear in the face of misbegotten progenies of transgressive science. It is their very ambivalent status, their refusal to be adequately pigeon-holed (neither animal nor artefact, the products of 'unnatural' processes) which both repels and attracts, compelling us to struggle with the disruption of taken-for-granted categories which once served to order the world around us.

Similarly, in the ancient world, a fascination with the conditions of monstrosity – real or imagined – served a moral and aetiological purpose.

The monster was literally a 'showing forth' of the non-human or almost-human as spectacle, forming a great warning to its audience; in its deviation from the acceptable norm, it served to remind others of the proper limits of normality. Teratology thus makes possible a critical purchase on the processes of definition and exclusion by which the boundaries of what it means to be (authentically) human are drawn. What we are seeing are not essentialist doctrines of 'human nature' therefore, but the discourses and devices by which they are articulated. For every assertion of the definitively 'human' there is a refracted 'other' – the almost-human, the monster, the alien – who shows the workings of the principles by which normative and exemplary humanity is defined.

Similar processes are at work in a very different context, that of Michel Foucault's theory of 'genealogy', yet which also seeks to disrupt fixed and essentialized accounts of the human subject. Foucault denied that there has ever been such a thing as 'human nature'; rather, it has been produced discursively via a range of 'technologies of the self': regimes or epistemologies which embody in their practices of therapy, diagnosis, incarceration or social control particular understandings of what it means to be human (Davidson, 1986). Genealogical critique reveals the artifice of that presumed to be 'natural', rendering 'the strange familiar and the familiar strange' (Muesse, 1999) and asking how the familiar and axiomatic are actually created via networks of power and social relations. Through his studies of the discourses of transgression and pathology (crime, madness, confession, homosexuality), Foucault's analysis exposed how the production of the *fully or normatively human* is dependent on the production of categories of the *non-human* (Foucault, 1991).

If Foucault wrote about modern technologies of the self as emanating from the processes and institutions of the confessional, the asylum, the prison and the clinic, in *Representations* I suggest that 'posthuman' technologies of the self might now be contested in twenty-first century sites such as cyberspace, AI laboratories and IVF clinics (Graham, 2002a: 13). The 'genealogical' task for the posthuman is thus to ask how these material and discursive occasions engender powerful normative understandings of what it means to be human (Graham, 2002a: 38–60).

For example, Foucault's concept of 'biopower' has relevance for the social impact of many new reproductive technologies: IVF, genetic screening, even cloning. However, at the same time as new medical techniques open up new and multiple possibilities for reproduction and parenthood, effectively separating heterosexual intercourse from reproduction, moral and legal discourses limit access to such opportunities by non-traditional groups, such as gay and lesbian parents, people with disabilities, and so on. Artificial impregnation, surrogacy and other forms of assisted reproduction are represented as assisting and embellishing 'nature', rather than bypassing it – a way, according to many commentators, of resisting the potentially 'queering' or 'post-biological' effects of new reproductive technologies (Halberstam and Livingston, 1995; Graham, 2002a: 111–23). Feminists have long argued that, far from liberating women from the burdens of pregnancy and childbirth, new reproductive technologies can be merely pretexts for the medical profession to exercise intrusive control over women's bodies (Shildrick, 1997). Yet as Elizabeth Sourbut argues, whereas the *cultural* logic of the technologies is to circumvent heterosexual reproduction and nuclear family structures, the accompanying medical, moral and legal rhetoric serves to reinforce the continuity with an imagined discourse of *natural* processes:

> The discourse of biological destiny defines infertility within the terms of biological science. Heterosexuality and the nuclear family are presented as natural. Only procreation through heterosexual intercourse within marriage is seen as producing legitimate parenthood. This, of course, is profoundly disrupted by the new reproductive technologies, which not only bypass heterosexual intercourse, but often involve third-party donations of gametes. This contradiction can only be contained by rigid discursive conventions which privilege genetic inheritance over all other forms of parent-child ties. (Sourbut, 1996: 236)

Similarly, just as the implementation of new reproductive technologies, genetic manipulation of plants and animals and innovative transgenic procedures presupposes the permeability of species boundaries and the assimilation of the human with the non-human, so the discursive representation of such innovations – especially in transhumanist or technocratic accounts – reiterate the continuing dominance of the human over the non-human. For such techniques to be possible, what is 'natural' can have no intrinsic or sacred quality; and yet, in celebrating the manipulation of nature in pursuit of humanist ideals, the superiority of human intentions is upheld and the boundary between the human and the non-human is reinscribed.

It is intriguing to note how critical posthumanism also involves a further blurring of supposedly impermeable boundaries: that between scientific objectivity (the world of fact) and that of cultural representation (the world of fiction). Not only my book, but Katharine Hayles' *How We Became Posthuman*, Noreen Herzfeld's recent book on AI, *In Our Image*, and Scott Bukatman's *Terminal Identity* draw on popular culture as an important measure of the values informing reception of new technologies, and influential sources for the cultural imagination.

As Katharine Hayles argues, 'culture circulates through science no less than science circulates through culture' (Hayles, 1999: 21) – in itself, perhaps, a postmodern acknowledgement of the constructedness of scientific theories, a contention that science does not report on or portray an a priori reality, but is dependent on wider cultural metaphors to weave a narrative about the world – and that this will often draw on images, analogies, other narratives, to achieve rhetorical effect. Thus, the human genome project as a search for the 'holy grail' or the 'code of codes'; Francis Bacon's discourse of science as the male appropriator seizing nature and forcing her to relinquish her secrets; the continuing potency of the Frankenstein myth in informing public reception of genetic technologies – all of these suggest a creative interplay between science and culture. But similarly, popular culture (Sci-Fi especially) has functioned as both advocate and opponent of science and technology.

But that intertwining of literature and science – forming a kind of transgenic union of its own – serves as a pointer, I think, to the power of popular culture and imaginative fiction (and Sci-Fi in particular) as enduring resources through which Western societies portray their hopes and fears about futuristic humanities, the implications of technology, life on other worlds, and so on. And so it is to *Star Trek*, *Star Wars*, *The X-Files* and other science fiction, literature, TV and movies, to which we can turn for clues as to the kinds of thinking being done in the face of new technologies. *Representations of the Post/Human* is not unique in drawing upon debates about technologies from both science and popular culture (Hayles, 1999; Herzfeld, 2002; Bukatman, 1993). However, I am sensitive to the presence of religious and theological referents and undercurrents in informing visions of post/human. Are these in some sense now secular narratives of awe and wonder, life, death, fall and redemption?

Post/Human Theologies

The idea that a fascination with technology is actually an expression or a resurgence of a kind of *spirituality* provides an intriguing avenue for analysis of the post/human, and demands a critical and reconstructive position from theologians. Clearly, even in a supposedly secular age, prevailing concepts of God and spirituality still impinge on the kinds of normative and exemplary models of Divine and human nature that fuel our technological dreams.

In *Representations*, I identify a number of ways in which appeals to religion inform visions of the posthuman future. It is intriguing to see how religious language is constantly evoked: Hans Moravec speaks of the 'transmigration' of consciousness from the 'meat' of living bodies into computer programmes; David Noble argues that scientists have long regarded technology as an 'instrument of deliverance' (Noble, 1999); and Erik Davis characterizes emergent virtual communities as 'techno-pagans', regarding technologies rather than nature as redolent with sacred power (Graham, 2002a: 165–75; 2002b). What they seem to share is that they are shaped by appeals to a neo-Platonic ideal of 'transcendence', or the drive to use human creative energies to abandon the physical world – as in the quest for outer space, or the wish to transform embodied experience into pure information, as in the human genome project or characterization of cyberspace as the 'heavenly city' free of the encumbrances of the flesh.

> Although today's technologists, in their sober pursuit of utility, power, and profit, seem to set society's standard for rationality, they are driven also by distant dreams, spiritual yearnings for supernatural redemption. However dazzling and daunting their display of worldly wisdom, their true inspiration lies elsewhere, in an *enduring, other-worldly* quest for transcendence and salvation. (Noble, 1999: 3, my emphasis)

So some of the more intriguing representations of the post/human are those which consciously deploy religious metaphor, in terms of regarding technologies as Noble's 'instruments of deliverance', apocalyptic devices which promise to consummate human dreams of immortality, freedom from the flesh, the powers of demiurgic creation and ascent into a kind of Gnostic realm of pure information – 'cyberspace as sacred space' (Graham, 2002a: 169; Graham, 2002b). The implications of this, however, are disturbing, not least because such a representation of humanity's religious quest through technoscientific endeavour rests on a distorted appropriation of the notion of 'transcendence'. It is taken to mean the final attainment of the Cartesian split between body and mind, the ultimate detachment of posthumanity from contingency, embodiment, finitude and particularity.

Yet as such it bears no relation to the more materialist doctrines of creation, incarnation and salvation within Christian theology. For what might be called the *technological sublime* actually rests upon an unexamined identification of 'religion' with a flight from contingency and materialism, and a spirituality that seeks fulfilment in union with a 'transcendent' deity entirely removed from the immanence of this mortal world. The presumption is that the quest for technological advancement is at some level an expression of the *imago Dei*, and that this entails a necessary mastery over creation, heedless of the fragility and interdependence of life – ambitions which have in the past been used as rationalizations for dominion over non-human nature, and even colonized peoples. Its predilection for the qualities of detachment, omniscience, immutability and incorporeality promote disdain for embodied contingency and foster technologies that are obsessed with cheating death, vulnerability and finitude. To represent religion in this way, therefore, is to see it as providing the ideological underpinning for many of the dualisms that have fuelled modernity and technoscientific innovation (Jantzen, 1998a, 1998b; Carrette and King, 1998).

Yet there are alternative aspects of the notion of humanity as created in the image of God which serve as a vital theological corrective to all this. Certainly, an understanding of *human* creativity as participation in *Divine* creativity affirms the goodness of our inventive abilities: and I would wish to celebrate our capacity to be 'builders of worlds', tool-makers and tool-users, and see this as part of what makes us distinctive as a species. Yet the materialist and incarnationalist nature of Christianity also teaches that the God in whose image we are made is not only transcendent but also immanent in the world, in history, in human affairs. 'Transcendence' is not about God's absence from history, or God's antipathy to matter, as some of the quasi-gnostic evocations of cyberspace as sacred space seem to suggest. Rather, it means that God is never reducible to this world, and is inviting creation into its final transformation that surpasses creation as it can presently be known; and this is a necessary reminder that our technologies are ultimately not our own, that our inventions, like the created order, only make sense when offered up as part of God's larger purposes. They cannot simply be reduced to the objects of human self-interest; and the 'Divine horizon' of talk about God serves to orientate us to the view that humans are part of a wider web of creation and relatedness that is not, ultimately of their making. Creation – including human participation in its transformation – is gift and grace, guarding against the hubris of too much power, of our seeking to 'play God', of remaking the world in the image of our own desires at the expense of other members of the human community or the rest of (non-human) nature. So while theology affirms the dignity of humanity's role as *(co)-creators* it also recalls us, crucially, to human *creatureliness*; to a dependence on the ultimate reality we call God and an interdependence with the rest of the created order of which we are a part.

Just as we need to rethink our understandings of human nature and the *imago Dei* in the light of advanced technologies, however, we should beware of erroneous and damaging constructions of the nature of God that attempt to insulate us from the realities of our interdependence and hybridity with non-human nature. Christianity has often invoked the 'transcendence' of God in the name of an other-worldly sensibility that seeks to deny the material and embodied nature of experience (Jantzen, 1998: 209). This is, however, erroneous. Transcendence is not to be equated with invulnerability and disengagement from material existence, but may simply indicate the irreducibility of the Divine to human self-interest.

Appeals to the 'transcendence' of God in order to evoke an other-worldly sensibility that seeks to deny the material and embodied nature of experience is, however, erroneous. Transcendence may simply indicate the irreducibility of the Divine to human self-interest. As such, it would serve as an important antidote to the narratives of hyper-humanism in which the 'will to power' is used as the rationalization for aggrandizing versions of corporate interest and transhuman superiority. 'Transcendence' needs therefore to be linked with materialist rather than Gnostic doctrines of creation, signalling an understanding of humanity made in the image of God which, far from being granted licence to conquer and subdue, recognizes that human *creativity* is always already framed by human *creatureliness* and finitude.

Post/Human Futures

> If my nightmare is a culture inhabited by posthumans who regard their bodies as fashion accessories rather than the ground of being, my dream is a version of the posthuman that embraces the possibilities of information technologies without being seduced by fantasies of unlimited power and disembodied immortality, that recognizes and celebrates finitude as a condition of human being, and that understands human life is embedded in a material world of great complexity, one on which we depend for our continued survival. (Hayles, 1999: 5)

Narratives of technologies as 'enslavement or liberation' (Cooper, 1995) assume that we are either helpless puppets in the face of remorseless technological determinism, or that technologies are mere instruments at the disposal of the liberal humanist ego. Yet we cannot essentialize technologies as if they existed outside social contexts, political and economic choices, or even human agency. Rather, we need to adopt a *reflexive* understanding of technologies (Feenberg, 1991): that they emerge from, and reflect, social, political and economic priorities in terms of design and deployment (and are not neutral) but that in turn, technoscience shapes our very engagement with the world, and potentially our very ontology.

> To conceive ... of technologies as reflexive phenomena is to see them as both products of our own creative energies as well as possessing the capacity to shape, in turn, the environments and cultures we inhabit. Yet it also reminds us that important value-judgements – what kinds of humans we wish to become, questions of access, equity and distribution, how humanity will use the natural resources, commodities and artefacts at its disposal – lie at the very heart of our engagement with technologies. (Graham, 2003: 43)

But if we can regard technologies as 'full of human labour' (Latour, 1993), imbued with political and ethical choices, capable of facilitating particular visions of what it means to be human, then the question is, how do we – can we – still judge which of those representations or visions is more or less desirable, authentic, or sustainable? For if the advent of the post/human is about recognizing the constructedness of the fault-lines by which we have in the past delineated the boundaries of the normatively human, then we can hardly revert to fixed categories of 'human nature' as a basis of our moral judgements.

However, the sense that humans and machines are increasingly assimilated, that it is not so easy to separate human beings from their tools and artefacts (either as objects of fear or as tools of mastery), may not be such an unthinkable notion of where we are in a digital and biotechnological age. It is also a profoundly materialist understanding, because it refuses to think either that we can retreat to some pure unadulterated 'human nature' independent of the world we have made; or that we can use technology to transcend bodily finitude and limitation. It is thus from within, always already immersed in the material conditions of our own creation, that we make ethical and political decisions. I am arguing, effectively, in *Representations* for an ethics not of purity, but hybridity and complicity. We cannot divorce ourselves from the worlds we have made through technologies and tools; and nor do we need to be afraid of our complicity with technologies, or fear our hybridity, or assume that proper knowledge of and access to God can only come through a withdrawal from these activities of world-building.

Conclusion

Representations of the Post/Human argues that the debate about what it means to be human in a digital, cybernetic and biotechnological age is not only the province of academic and scientific debate. It is also, crucially, addressed in the realms of popular culture and the creative arts, where a proliferation of representations of the 'posthuman' serve as *refractions* of what it might mean to be human, examining the possibilities – and the limits – of the relationship between humans, their tools and technologies. Yet while the challenges of twenty-first-century 'posthumanity' may have their own distinctive dimensions, there is also a continuity throughout Western history with the question of what it means to be human, and with the prospect of a blurring of boundaries between the human and the almost-human. I would argue that contemporary concerns for the post/human are but the latest in an enduring fascination with the relationship between humans and their own inventions, material and imaginary, and that the persistence of fantastic and monstrous creatures from earliest myth, religion and literature through to many forms of popular culture today testifies to the continuity of such enquiry into the implications of human creative endeavour. From the myth of Prometheus, the Jewish legend of the Golem, the Gothic horror of Frankenstein's monster, to contemporary postmodern science fiction, a gallery of fantastic creatures haunt Western myth, religion and literature. They serve to connect contemporary debates with enduring concerns about the potential, and the limits, of human creativity.

> Monsters, aliens and others ... function as important monitors and mediators of understandings of what it means to be post/human, not least in their indeterminacy, their eschewal of ontological purity, and their attention to human nature as defined by boundaries rather than essences. They embody the disturbing reminders of difference at the heart of unitary identity, and they suggest that any post/human ethic can be neither an escape into technocratic invulnerability nor a retreat into the imagined purity of organic essentialism. Rather ... it will be about the pleasures and risks of multiple allegiances, contingent identities and nomadic sensibilities. Fantastic encounters with representations of the post/human offer important insights into the many meanings of being human, but they are also devices by which new worlds can be imagined. (Graham, 2002a: 234)

19

'BIG BROTHER' OR 'NEW JERUSALEM'?

Anti-Utopia and Utopia in a Virtual Age

The movie *eXistenZ* (1999), directed by David Cronenberg, is one of a number of cinematic explorations of humanity's encounter with information and communication technologies during the past decade. *eXistenZ* explores the implications of digitally generated multi-sensory 'virtual reality' (VR), its title referring to the name of a software program that runs a complex interactive role-play game. It is intriguing to see how the two main characters, one male and one female, are made to represent two very different reactions to technology. The 'heroine', Allegra Geller, a games designer, loves the exhilarating rush of entering the virtual domain, and sees it as a stimulus to the imagination and the intellect. In a neat reversal of gender stereotyping, it is the male character, Ted Pikel, who expresses the greater anxiety – close to hysteria – when asked to undergo his first journey into cyberspace, fearing a loss of personal integrity and control when 'under the influence' of the digital program.

I like *eXistenZ* because throughout the film these two approaches are held in tension. *eXistenZ* deliberately plays with that ambivalence, switching between euphoria and dislocation as it shifts from one virtual world to another.

We are presented here, in fictional form, with two contrasting representations of the effects of information and communication technologies on the way we live, work and communicate. Reactions to the impact of technologies on human society frequently polarize on the question of 'liberation' or 'enslavement' (Cooper, 1995), ushering in either a Utopian 'new Jerusalem' of unlimited prosperity and wealth or the dystopia of a panoptic, 'Big Brother'-type society.

In truth, this polarization is more realistically a continuum of responses, embracing a variety of philosophies of technology, of social change and even doctrines of human nature (Graham, 2002a); but such a stark coincidence of fear and fascination is a vivid indication of our uncertainty as to the future trajectory of human engagement with technologies. We find ourselves asking, therefore, what choices and opportunities are implicit in the hopes and anxieties engendered by new information and communication technologies: not only choices to do with access and distribution; but also what kind of human beings we will be in such a technological future. These present themselves as questions about interpersonal encounter, about community, about the body politic; yet, as we shall see, implicit within the debate about information and communication technology (ICT) is a level of discourse about human nature often ignored by secular humanism. For there is a strong religious subtext at work, especially in some writers' expansive pronouncements on the mystical and metaphysical dimensions of cyberspace, their equation of new technologies with a kind of demiurgical power, and their expectations of technologies effecting the liberation of the human race from the limits of embodiment, finitude and mortality.

'New Jerusalem': Digital Utopia

The Net makes a type of equation: Data = information = knowledge = wisdom = truth = freedom. (Interrogate the Internet 1996: 126)

One of the most frequently occurring models of ICT, and especially the Internet, is that they are inherently powerful democratic media, serving to create a global virtual forum, free of restraint, in which freedom of expression will reign. It is argued that ICTs are democratic by virtue of their accessibility for ordinary people: they circumvent mediating processes that may distort or divert the authentic wishes of the people, and they draw more people in to participate by virtue of their immediacy of impact. ICTs thus provide the technological means to deliver mass participation in the political process, free of the bureaucracy and conservatism of party machinery, circumventing the manipulation of conventional news media or institutional parliamentary protocol. Email and the World Wide Web thus put into the hands of ordinary citizens powerful and effective means of communication (and influence) which were formerly the property of a wealthy elite. For example, new information and communication technologies have been suggested as one means of attracting groups of voters currently alienated by politics. After the election in the UK in 2001, it was suggested by the Electoral Commission itself that voting might take place in future by mobile telephone (MORI, 2001).

Such an optimistic view finds echoes in scholarly literature and research, especially in the United States, where the 'new frontier' of ICT is often likened to the early days of the American nation (Kapor, 1993) in which new democratic forms are enabled to flourish unconstrained by forces of tradition or entrenched political interests. New media offer ideal opportunities to create genuinely democratic communities, albeit based in virtual, rather than geographical constituencies. It is not that new technologies are eroding people's ability or willingness to participate, but merely providing new patterns of democratic access (Rheingold, 1991).

Such a vision of the on-line Utopia of the New Jerusalem reflects broadly 'technocratic' views. These are single-mindedly positive about the ability of technological advance to facilitate problem-solving and advance human interests. ICTs do not threaten or render human activities obsolete, but simply free our human creativity to achieve new limits. In that respect, too, there is what we may term an 'instrumental' attitude to technologies, in that they are regarded as quintessentially neutral, neither good nor bad, merely instruments for achieving purposes and values enshrined elsewhere. Underlying this is a version of Enlightenment humanism in which the rational subject, uninhibited by the external constraints of superstition, fear or conservatism, is enabled to scale new heights of intellectual and technological achievement. And this link with secular humanism is, I believe, quite significant when we come to consider the theological dimensions to this.

> The Net has ... become a simulacrum of a possible libertarian world: an unregulated plenitude where technological wizardry and a clean hack can overcome the inertia of embodied history, where ossified political and economic structures will melt down into the liquid flow of bits. (E. Davis, 1998: 115)

There are, however, at least two objections to the Utopian vision of the digital new Jerusalem. First, when it comes to mustering resources to influence public opinion or make a political intervention by establishing a presence on the Internet, then it is the corporate interests rather than private individuals or pressure groups who will have the requisite financial resources. Research suggests that the economic inequalities already present in other media – TV, radio, newspapers, billboards and so on – will simply be reproduced on-line (Norris, 2001b: 95–111).

> The language of cyberspace is English and cyberspacetime itself is a Western, post-industrial and specifically American creation. For most people on the planet, this reconstruction of reality is far from being of paramount importance or relevance. It remains to be seen what effects

this reality gap will have on relations between the West and the Rest, and on humanity's ability to deal with the very real problem of earthly scarcity and limitations: resources, population, pollution. (Nguyen and Alexander, 1996: 104)

Second, although the number of outlets for expression has increased exponentially, our ability to access them does not necessarily increase at the same rate, if at all. If most people are selective in what they can absorb, then research suggests that we tend to gravitate towards sources that already confirm our views. Indeed, there is evidence that those participating online are activists already involved in politics, rather than a significantly broader constituency (Norris, 2001b: 18–19). Similarly, the law of diminishing returns may also apply; that is, as more information is generated, the chances of any of it making any significant impact are reduced.

This suggests that rather than helping to create an accessible, coherent polis, electronic media will actually serve to fragment public debate and political intervention. The populist nature of media such as the Internet comes about because there is very little gate-keeping; but we know that it is also very indiscriminate and varied in quality: 'the ability simply to surf a vast unstructured web of material which both expresses and provokes an enormous variety of tastes and interests gives scope to mere congruence rather than co-ordination' (G. Graham, 1999).

'Big Brother': Virtual Dystopia

Gordon Graham has characterized resistance to new technologies, and the Internet in particular, as 'a neo-Luddite reaction' on the part of those who forecast that the ubiquity of computers and electronic media will herald the death of the book, contribute fatally to the dumbing-down of culture as our attention spans shorten and individuals retreat into the atomistic solipsism of virtual reality (G. Graham, 1999: 7).

Within this framework, digital technologies are both the cause of social fragmentation and also a sanctuary from the resulting anomie and alienation. Indeed, many commentators derive their critiques from a kind of digital Marxism, in which the ideological superstructure (cyberspace) is parasitic upon the material – 'real' – infrastructure of organic life, physical bodies and face-to-face interaction. Thus, Jean Baudrillard argues that digital technologies such as virtual reality represent a kind of technological substitute or prosthesis for reality (Baudrillard, 1983). The shift from the real to what Baudrillard terms 'the hyper-real' takes place when representation (of a presumed pre-existent reality) is displaced by simulation: popular culture pre-empts the exchange of symbols between individuals, introducing another layer of experience that undermines the subject's ability to define and to grasp the truth. Electronic mediation cripples the modern system of representation, folding it into a new mode of signification in which signs are divorced from their referents in the object world, becoming reorganized into a 'hyperreality' of screen surfaces (Poster, 2001: 133).

This blurring of the real and the unreal marks Baudrillard's analysis of postmodern space and place wrought by the development of cyberspace and electronic communications. The Internet is a virtual community in the way Disneyland is virtual, capable of existing only insofar as it is a simulacrum, a simulation; but in faking reality it distracts us from realizing that the community it simulates actually no longer exists anywhere. It feeds us the vision of inclusive community, personal liberty, freedom of speech, unlimited information as a strategy of 'deterrence' – in Marxian terms, an ideology – against the fact that these things have in fact dissolved. In *Le Crime Parfait* (1995), Baudrillard speaks of the 'theft' of truth by the simulacrum, in which the idea of the real has been stolen by the virtual, which then takes its place as the semblance of reality (see Kroker, 1996).

Many critics argue that the disembodied nature of cyberspace and ICT is responsible for the erosion of conventional patterns of association, for which networked, on-line communication is a poor substitute. On-line, there is autonomy and freedom; yet ICTs serve to erode traditional networks of association, so that we have more communication with friends via email than our next-door neighbours. Having lost their moorings in physical association, our politics begin to dissolve, to become as 'fragile, airy, and ephemeral' (Heim, 1993: 68) as cyberspace itself. And for some, the fragility of cyberspace and the virtual communities it engenders has something to do with its essentially disembodied nature:

> Our virtual life in cyberspace paralyses our bodies. Cyber-spacetime promises us liberation from the constraints of space, time and materiality. However, without the experiences of our bodies, our thoughts, our ideas, our ethics and politics must all suffer. We know ourselves and our world mainly because we live and move in the world through our bodies ... In cyberspace we no longer need to face and live with the presence of others. What then becomes of our ethical and political consciousness? (Nguyen and Alexander, 1996: 117–18)

While some commentators warn against the panoptic nature of ICTs, arguing that our every movement will soon be tracked electronically, that we cannot help but leave digital traces of ourselves wherever we go in a networked world, others argue, more prosaically, that any need for coercive, external surveillance is obviated by the fact that we are all too prepared to collude in our own oppression and passivity.[1] Who needs 'Big Brother' the surveillance technology, when we have Big Brother reality TV?

Before the television monitor, the individual participates in a new cultural space in which the definition of truth is altered. No longer a correspondence to reality, no longer posing the critical question ('What relation does what I see bear to what I know?'), televisual epistemology asks rather, 'Does what I see hold my attention or urge me to switch channels?' (Poster, 2001: 24).

Technological Re-enchantment/Disenchantment

Fundamentally, these are questions of whether an essential human nature will be compromised or consummated through new technologies. But underlying the discussion too are questions of the re-enchantment or disenchantment of the world; for it is intriguing to see how much of the utopianism towards new technologies and especially the Internet evokes themes of spirituality and transcendence. For many, new technologies are demiurgical devices, enabling humanity to transcend physical limits, such as bodily finitude, illness and mortality, or to transport their users to a higher plane of existence. For others, the very existential and spiritual integrity of human beings is threatened by the encroachment of rationalization. Despite the assumptions about the incompatibility between science and religion, therefore, these new explorations into what it means to be human in a digital, cybernetic and information age call forth theological deliberations. But these, too, reflect the Utopian and dystopian pairings of the more politically driven debates.

Cyberspace as Sacred Space

> Technologies of communication are always, at least potentially, technologies of the sacred. (Davis, 1998: 8)

One strand of futuristic speculation captures the trend towards the 're-enchantment' of public discourse often associated with a move into postmodernity at the end of the twentieth century. This sensibility is strongly optimistic about the prospects for technologically enhanced and assisted development; but it dwells on the spiritual opportunities offered by the digital age – cyberspace as 'sacred space'.

Erik Davis has argued for a strong continuity between users of ICT with ancient traditions of spirituality, especially Hermetism and Gnosticism

---

1 This view is perhaps best expressed by Postman (1987; 1993).

(Davis, 1998). Despite the secular, technical-rational nature of modernity, the potential of information and communications technologies for reawakening dormant instincts for the spiritual is widely celebrated. He maintains that advanced technologies are a means of realizing Utopian dreams, apocalyptic fantasies and drives towards infinite knowledge and immortal existence. Davis calls this new movement 'techno-paganism': like neo-paganism, a characteristically modern movement, but one inclined to equate the sacred with technology rather than nature. In regarding the tangible, material world as an elaborate cipher for Divine power, in which the codes and bytes of digital information serve as the vehicles of transport into a higher reality, many adepts continue the arts and practices of earlier magi and demiurges. In this respect, Davis suggests that techno-paganism may be regarded as a continuation of early modern Hermetism; although we may also trace elements of more ancient Platonic, even Gnostic, tendencies, in which the fallen, prosaic, material – and illusory – world is but a pale shadow of a higher, secret, spiritual realm of perfect order and information (ibid.).

Michael Heim renders this Platonic connection most explicit, when he argues that our fascination with cyberspace is a function of a perennial erotic drive to transcend the material world in search of 'a sensationless world of pure ideas' (Nguyen and Alexander, 1996: 115). What we are pursuing are the Platonic forms themselves, drawing the mind away from the meat of the body into its realm of perfection. 'With an electronic infrastructure, the dream of perfect FORMS becomes the dream of inFORMation' (Heim, 1993: 82). This sacralizing of the technological extends to other activities: the Internet is teeming with religious activities, from the staging of virtual rituals to the posting of cyber-shrines and digitalization of sacred texts in cyberspace (Brasher, 2001), and the celebration of the noosphere, a vast, global intelligent system encompassing the earth like a benevolent Spirit (Davis, 1998: 280).

Once more, this contradicts interpretations which regard science and religion as antipathetic, for here are new technologies as – in David Noble's words – instruments of deliverance (Noble, 1999): the tangible, material means by which humanity can manipulate elemental and hidden powers, thereby ascending into a sacred realm of 'transcendence', no longer inhibited by the inconveniences of embodiment. Cyberspace invites us, therefore, to consummate the timeless human quest to transcend the physical world in search of perfection and immortality; but note how this vision is heavily infected with a startling dualism of mind and body: 'The animating archetype of the information economy, its psychological spunk, lies in a gnostic [sic] flight from the heaviness and torpor of the material earth, a transition from the laboring body into the symbol-processing mind' (Davis, 1998: 115).

Disenchantment

> We are the moths attracted to flames, and frightened by them too, for there may be no home behind the lights, no secure abode behind the vast glowing structures. There are only the fiery objects of dream and longing. (Heim, 1993:86)

Just as there are those who speak of technologies as facilitating spiritual as well as political enlightenment, there are those who regard them as anathema to human spiritual flourishing. Such technological pessimists believe that the intensification of new technologies can only degrade human uniqueness. While his reflections on the trajectory of modern culture's fascination with technology predated computers, the Internet and cyberspace, Martin Heidegger (1889–1976) articulated some prescient themes which have provided powerful material for later commentators (Heim, 1993; Myerson, 2001).

In *The Question Concerning Technology*, written towards the end of his life, Heidegger links what he regards as nihilistic tendencies of technology with earlier themes about the nature of authentic human existence. Heidegger claimed that 'technology's essence is nothing technological' (1993a: 4): in other words, not to be understood or approached through its design or function, or even in terms of productive processes, but rather in its potential to yield or 'enframe' the inner essence of Being. Technology thus assumes for him an ontological status; more than a mere instrument, or manufactured tool, it is the means by which potential being is brought forth (*aletheia*) into tangible form. So technology is not something created or forged by human activity, but the manifestation or unconcealing of a ubiquitous, elemental force.

Thus technology becomes an overarching system, a way of understanding and relating to the world as a whole; but a system that ultimately masters and determines all human activities. Everything, including human labour, is reduced to 'standing reserves', or mere raw materials awaiting disposal according to the inexorable trajectory of technological manufacture. Technology is insidious in its effects, which will be to distort and impoverish humanity's openness to the richness of their existence (in his terms, an openness to Dasein, or Being). The imperatives of technology now serve to determine the ways in which the world is revealed to us, and the nature of our engagement with it. Eventually the logic of technological framing is so dominant that it obscures other more authentic revelations of the nature of Being. Humanity may believe that it is in control of technology in an instrumental sense, but Heidegger's warning was that technology as an ontological force is potentially all-encompassing, at the expense of authentic and spontaneous human apprehension of the world.

The danger of technology lies in the transformation of the human being, by which human actions and aspirations are fundamentally distorted. Not that machines can run amok, or even that we might misunderstand ourselves through a faulty comparison with machines. Instead, technology enters the inmost recesses of human existence, transforming the way we think and know and will. (Heim, 1993: 61)

The chief danger of the effects of technology, for Heidegger, lay in its engulfing of the human spirit and its capacity to distort human intentions and actions. It was the ability of technology to transform humanity from within, and not so much a fantasy of assimilation as ontological transformation (as in the amalgam of human and machine in the figure of the cyborg), that constituted technology's fundamental alteration of the essence of human experience. In a technological age, human labour has become so contaminated by the demonic forces of reification that the inner truth of artefacts is obliterated by (to use a rather more Weberian term) technical-rational instrumentality. The solution is a reinvigoration of spiritual values (a *poesis*) and a return to a more organic medium in which humanity is not alienated from its own existence. As Heidegger puts it, 'Only a god can save us' (1976).

Heidegger's concerns echo those of other philosophers and sociologists of modernity (such as Max Weber and Karl Marx) in his presupposition that the essence of modernity is to be found in its underlying characteristics of rationalization, bureaucratization, disenchantment and reification of human labour and commodities alike. However, one of the problems with Heidegger's model of technology is that, like modernization, it is a monolithic and ahistorical phenomenon independent of human agency or cultural and historical variations. Inevitably, perhaps, this means that Heidegger's concept of technology is one of an impersonal force against which human beings are merely passive, helpless victims: 'Technology is often treated as unitary both from the favourable perspective of toolmaking and progress and from the negative standpoint of degradation and loss' (Poster, 2001: 34).

In thinking about the nature of technology and its impact on our lives, however, it is important to consider how, empirically, it has developed and how in different circumstances economy, culture and technology will interrelate. Indeed, the history of one of the most pervasive and fundamental technologies of contemporary times, the Internet, is a good example of this. Developed originally as a means of communication for use in the event of nuclear war or other total catastrophe, electronic and web-based communication have now evolved in far more populist and diverse directions (Ross, 1991: 75–100). Technological development can have unexpected consequences, a reminder that histories of technology do not simply conform to patterns of unbroken and progressive innovation

(Pinch and Bijker, 2003 [1987]). It is valuable to preserve Heidegger's insight that technologies are more than neutral tools and instruments, but rather possess the power to reconstitute human relations in which they are embedded; but other aspects of his evocation amount to a somewhat deterministic and abstract model of the impact of technology on human experience. Under Heidegger, technology reifies into destiny, and his retreat into eco-spirituality as the only option descends into mystification and abstraction.

Posthuman Thinking

Viewed all together, therefore, we can perceive a crucial fault-line running throughout. Do new ICTs represent promise or endangerment, mastery or extinction? This is a question regarding the future trajectory of human engagement with technologies: whether new communications technologies foster greater interaction, nurturing new forms of democratic participation and freedom of information, creating vibrant, networked, global communities, or whether they represent an attentuation of healthy political and civic association, a narrowing of cognitive horizons encouraging introverted individualism which substitutes 'virtual' relationships for their 'real' counterparts; whether they expand our lexicon of space, time and place or remove us from embodied, face-to-face authentic living. But what does it mean to be human, if our very humanity has itself been so transformed, so circumscribed, by new ways of technological living?

The impact of new technologies blurs many of the taken-for-granted categories of space, place and time; the boundaries of the body; the interface of machine and human. In the case of the Internet, it collapses physical distance, transcends national boundaries, reinvents conventions of text and reading, transforms human interactions into the flow of information, creates new artificial environments and machinic intelligences. This necessarily calls forth some radical rethinking of what it means to be human in an age some call the 'posthuman': 'We need to re-question the uniqueness of that which is human, and to redefine differences between human and animal, human and machine. This is, in a sense, the age-old investigation into the nature of mind and body, reason and intelligence' (Nguyen and Alexander, 1996: 113).

Notions of the posthuman argue powerfully not simply for the power of new technologies on our economic, cultural and political existence, but as an ontological force, too. For certain we cannot disinvent the technologies but, at a more fundamental level, nor can we conceive of 'human nature' untouched by our engagement and interdependence with our tools, artefacts and environment. This is perhaps most lucidly expressed in Donna Haraway's seminal essay, 'A Cyborg Manifesto', first published in 1985 (Haraway, 1991). In a high-tech world, she argues, the only political and ethical vantage-point to make any sense is one in which we regard ourselves as 'cyborgs', fusions of flesh and machine, human and cybernetic. This means we cannot ground our ethics on the high ground of essential humanity, uncorrupted spirit or pristine body. 'Bodies can no longer serve as the last outpost of a vanishing world of finite spacetime and bounded order' (Nguyen and Alexander, 1996: 121). Instead, we need to learn to think ethically, politically, even theologically, from a position of complicity with the technologies. That means refusing the polarities of instrumentalism or determinism, because both deny human agency, the heterogeneity of technologies and the reflexive nature of human engagement with our tools, artefacts and technologies.

Both instrumentalism and determinism maintain a rigid dualism of agents and tools, action and fabrication (Kaufman-Osborn, 1997). On the one hand, instrumentalism conceives human agency in relation to technologies to be supreme, unlimited; the material world of tools and artefacts, not to mention non-human nature, is relegated to mere matter to be manipulated according to the will of human self-aggrandizement. On the other, human agency seemingly plays no constructive part in the building of worlds; the 'essence' of human distinctiveness is somehow conceived as independent of the processes of invention and fabrication.

While we may wish to argue that technology transforms what it means to be human, that there is no extra-cultural human essence independent of material culture, therefore, it is necessary to articulate an alternative approach which would attribute a radically different place to the role of human agency in the making and remaking of humanity, nature and culture, and one which attends to the vagaries of specific technological activities and forms. Andrew Feenberg has argued that theories of technology fall into one of two major categories: the instrumental theory and the substantive theory. The instrumental theory, exemplified by the technocratic model surveyed above, 'offers the most widely accepted view of technology. It is based on the common sense idea that technologies are "tools" standing ready to serve the purposes of their users. Technology is deemed "neutral", without valuative content of its own' (Feenberg, 1991: 5).

The substantive model of technology, by contrast, understands technologies as embedded in, and emerging to shape, social, cultural and economic conditions. Technology needs to be regarded as a form of social practice (Pinch and Bijker, 2003 [1987]); so to assume, as the technocratic perspective does, that technologies can be conceived independently of context or implementation, is to deny the extent to which economic interests, scientific world-views and cultural values are embedded in the design and utilization of tools, artefacts and other technologies, not to mention their portrayal back to us as instruments of mastery or extinction. It is also to evade questions of access, power and distribution.

The issue is not that machines have 'taken over', but that in choosing to use them we make many unwitting cultural choices. Technology is not simply a means but has become an environment and a way of life: this is its 'substantive' impact (Feenberg, 1991: 8).

No Place for No-Place

In their different ways, Baudrillard and Heidegger are, in their protest against the illusory or ideological nature of technologies, pointing towards the danger of their being elevated above their origins in material contexts, social conventions and human labour. The 'reflexive' model of technological design and deployment, similarly, reminds us of technologies' very embeddedness and complicity in such processes, and defies notions of instrumentalism or determinism that invite us to 'bracket out' questions of human agency in relation to technologies.

> It is fine to want to defend the claims of the suffering body and human warmth against the cold universality of scientific laws. But if universality stems from a series of places in which warm flesh-and-blood bodies are suffering everywhere, is not this defence grotesque? Protecting human bodies from the domination of machines and technocrats is a laudable enterprise, but if the machines are full of human beings who find their salvation there, such a protection is merely absurd. (Latour, 1993: 124)

Reflexivity calls attention to the origins, interests and applications inherent in the design and use of new technologies; that, in the words of Bruno Latour, our machines are already full of human labour. In other words, human beings cannot be considered to be the sole actors or agents in a world of interdependent humans, machines and nature where all are mutually constitutive.

In virtual reality participants merge with a computer-generated world; object and subject combine and interact; the boundaries of the body become indeterminate. Similarly, whereas when machines became predominant for the means of production, as for example in the manufactories of the industrial age they were part of a fixed, quite inflexible system of production, supply and demand dedicated to the manufacture of particular commodities, in the information age they are interactive, inserted into a network of non-hierarchical communications with no overarching plan of production, amounting to 'combinations of machines and humans in surprising and unanticipated configurations' (Poster 2001: 27).

Within such a reflexive, hybrid (posthuman) model of our engagement with technologies, the boundaries between object and subject, determinism and agency, enframing and Being, are irrevocably blurred. Our response can no longer be the protest against the distortion of an essential humanity by invasive, instrumental machines, but a question of acquiring appropriate knowledge concerning the most equitable means of configuring humans, nature and machines, of living alongside and intermingled with our tools, technologies and artefacts: a truly 'cyborg ethic'. And there seems nowhere better to begin this critical process than with the very notions of Utopia and dystopia themselves, and whether these alternative visions are themselves working according to the assumptions of instrumentalism and determinism or by a more reflexive, substantive model.

The tradition of Utopian thinking goes back to Plato's *Republic* (350 BC) in which he speculated on how a perfect society might be ordered. But ever since, writers have been conjuring up imaginary good societies (Utopias) and bad ones (dystopias, anti-utopias, negative Utopias) as a recognizable exercise in imagining new worlds. But it is Thomas More's *Utopia* (1516) which first uses the word, taken from two other Greek terms: *eutopia*, the good place, and *outopia*, no-place (Pringle, 1997: 11–14). The conflation of these two terms intrigues me. As a good place, Utopia performs a didactic purpose, suspending reality through the exercise of imagination, the better to serve as critical lens to its own day. But this 'fantastic' function of the fictional, non-existent 'no-place' is a far cry from the creation of an imaginary place that bears no relationship to anywhere else. To visit the 'no-place' of the imagination (or virtual domain) without any intention of building the 'good place' to which it points is, arguably, to sell Utopia short on its ethical or political substance.

Yet in relation to cyberspace as good/bad space or no-space, therefore, it seems to me that much of the Utopian appeal of cyber communities and communications rests in their very inability to reproduce the complexities of gender, race, dis/ability, thus freeing participants to play with personal identity, to suspend reality: but this is not so much a transcendence of these issues of power and difference, as a bracketing out. The fatal choice, however, is to behave as if the virtual world were not connected to other worlds in any way at all – in other words, to absolutize that world, to seal it off from any political interventions or moral debate: to refuse to see that world as, in fact, 'full of human labour'.

It may be more appropriate, therefore, to acknowledge that humans are capable of building and inhabiting all kinds of worlds – some material, others virtual – but that they are all bound by the relations of their production, albeit working according to different conventions. So when Kevin Robins says that 'I think it is time that this real world broke in on the virtual one' (Robins, 1995: 137), I hear this not so much as a return to Baudrillard's rather rigid distinction between the virtual and the real nor necessarily a denial of cyberspace as a legitimate sphere of operation so much as a plea to regard the creation of new synthesized domains, however seductive, as always requiring accommodation within a 'political economy of cyberculture' (Escobar, 2001: 58).

Theological Reflection

Neither a deterministic model of technological development, which affords little scope to human agency or choice, therefore, nor an instrumental understanding, which assumes human freedom to transcend material limitations to be absolute, are consistent with a theological anthropology that understands humanity in the image of God as bounded, finite and relational.

First, I think we can affirm the creative activity represented by human engagement with its tools and technologies, an understanding of science and technology as entirely consistent with traditional notions of the *imago Dei* (Herzfeld, 2002). As Ted Peters puts it, humanity cannot not be inventive and innovative (Peters, 1997: 15); yet he maintains that an understanding of creativity and personhood as relational and responsible would preclude the treatment of nature as a mere commodity to be manipulated at will. To place human creativity – including new technologies – within the context of its Divine giftedness (Peters' notion of 'created co-creators') fosters a different sensibility in which such activity is afforded an alternative horizon other than expediency. It argues that human will is, ultimately, bounded by the integrity of Others; that natural resources, non-human animals and subordinated human groups are not to be reduced to 'standing reserves' for our disposal. Rather, everything retains its own purpose, to be routed back into the life of God; and human self-sufficiency – secular or merely self-regarding – is fatally fragile.

> Should we play God? No, we should not play God in the promethean sense. But we should play human in the imago Dei sense – that is, we should understand ourselves as created co-creators and press our scientific and technological creativity into the service of neighbour love, of beneficence. (Peters, 1997: 161)

This links back to my discussion of Utopia. To pretend that our building of worlds – material, literary or virtual – bears no relationship to questions of how we live in these worlds is unacceptable because it is a denial of their necessary interdependence. We can regard technological endeavour as that which results in the 'concealment' of the political and economic interests, human labour and social conventions that go into their construction; or as that which serves to reveal the artefactual nature of technologies, their role in bringing human creativity into material and tangible form.

Amid the discussion of technological innovation as a legitimate sphere of human creative activity, therefore, it is also necessary to recognize the limits of such discourse. The notion that humanity can seek redemption via technocratic means alone – whether this be the inhabitation of a perfect, pure virtual environment or the achievement of bodily perfection via genetic modification, cybernetic or prosthetic enhancement, even social engineering – represents the ultimate in the pursuit of human perfection as the apotheosis of our technological, moral or political endeavours. I have already argued that to talk of humanity as in some degree self-constituting via its own technologies, of being capable of influencing the course of its own development is to fall prey to what we might term 'hyper-humanism': a distortion of modernity's faith in the benevolence of human reason, producing the hubristic belief that humanity alone is in control of history. Hyper-humanism may even be regarded, in theological perspective, as a kind of idolatry: the elevation of human, finite creation as ultimate reality; a confusion of the fabricated with the ineffable. To affirm humanity as simultaneously creative and creaturely is one corrective to this, as a counterweight to the self-interest of technocratic humanism as, for example, in the tendency of the global elite to manufacture technological visions in its own image and self-interest, to the neglect of wider questions of equity and distribution.

Similarly, we have seen how celebrations of the 'technological sublime' as facilitating human ascent from material embodiment into the ideal realm of disembodied, detached omniscience are regarded by some as the outworking of humanity's eternal, enduring and universal 'religious' instincts. Yet these ideals betray only a predilection for qualities of detachment, omniscience, immutability and incorporeality, motivated by 'fear of death, loathing of the body, desire to be moral and free of error' (Mazlish 1993: 218). A theological anthropology, by contrast, sees things differently, not least in its eschewal of a symbolic of transcendence premised on omnipotence, individualism and immortality. Rather than regarding the immanent, embodied, material world as an impediment to genuine spirituality, or – reminiscent of Gnostic world-views – as the profane, flawed, pale reflection of the authentic Divine world, this vision sees it as the very realm of Divine-human encounter. This is perhaps best encapsulated theologically in a distinction between 'magical' and 'sacramental' action.

I have already alluded to the similarities between ideas of cyberspace as sacred space and Gnostic world-views. This teaches that underlying external, material reality there is an inner, spiritual world perceptible only through access to a higher knowledge or superior consciousness.

The material world is but a shroud for the spiritual realm, which is the true home of higher beings and cosmic energies. As with the Hermetic world-view, however, signs and symbols are tangible manifestations of the higher powers: thus numerology, the movements of the stars, mysterious configurations of the alphabet, can all give access to the deeper, hidden world of the sacred. Such esotericism represents a flight from the body, but also an enduring fascination with what is seen as the magical nature of information and communication technologies, in that the use of digital data, bytes and codes is seen as a hermetical device to unlock the vital, hidden, energies of creation.

By contrast, a sacramental understanding of matter and spirit regards the physical world as the outward form that communicates inner grace; but it does not seek 'transcendence' so much as 'transformation' of matter in order to experience the sacred. Once again, the attitude towards embodiment is revealing:

> Both ... the spiritualized Divine and human body, and the noncorporeal existence of humans allied to cyberspace, picture the body not in terms of fallen corporeal 'nature' requiring transformation, but in terms of a necessary transcending of the gory messiness of the flesh in a technologically or spiritually rarefied version. (Oliver, 1999: 343)

In sacramental activity, the mundane, even the profane is taken and transformed, via human labour, into something that can be considered a Divine epiphany. Yet this does not discard, but essentially sacralizes, the material in order to point to the spiritual; and it does this by being reordered, rather than destroyed: 'We do not encounter God in the displacement of the world we live in, the suspension of our bodily and historical nature' (Williams 2000: 207). The significance of sacraments, as Rowan Williams argues, is not to mimic the power of the Divine but to make humans holy through their interaction with the material world. This is not achieved, however, by discarding, but by embracing material, contingent and embodied experience for these ends. Yet in embracing it, we discover too, that it evades our grasp: that the world of representation and world-building (physical or symbolic) is always inadequate fully to express the Divine. So again, far from being infused in themselves with Divine or supernatural powers, signs and symbols, material objects and practices rather point away from themselves to a reality they can never capture. This is reflected in theological traditions that speak of the non-representability of the Divine, the impossibility of speaking the name of the Holy One; and the injunctions against believing that human creative powers can ever rival those of God. In an age when all energy, reality and information is becoming digitalized – the flesh becoming word – it is perhaps important to remember that language, that quintessential mark of Divine (and human) creativity, will always fall short of what it attempts to signify. Hence the intriguing detail in the Jewish legend of the Golem, in which a clay man is animated via the magical powers of incantation, but where the artificial being, once given life, heralds its essential imperfection – its artefactual rather than creaturely status – by being unable to speak (Graham, 2002a: 92–4). Made through words and signs, it remains outwith the economy of language by virtue of its human and not Divine origins. This is an understanding that, while human creativity can reflect that of the Creator (and in particular by calling existence into being through the Word), human invention is always contingent, bounded and flawed.

Conclusion

> At the highest level, public life involves choices about what it means to be human. Today these choices are increasingly mediated by technical decisions. What human beings are and will become is decided in the shape of our tools no less than in the action of statesmen and political movements. The design of technology is thus an ontological decision fraught with political consequences. The exclusion of the vast majority from participation in this decision is the underlying cause of many of our problems. (Feenberg, 1991: 3)

In surveying the range of responses to the impact of ICT on personal identity, patterns of community and the public domain, we have seen how the information age is regarded as simultaneously 'threat' and 'promise' to human integrity. Yet crucially, this only serves to illuminate implicit philosophies of the relationship between human agency and creativity, and its products: our tools, artefacts and technologies. An insistence on the determinative – but not deterministic – nature of technologies, and the importance of the political and economic choices imbuing human design and interaction with technologies, provides an alternative to models of technology as monolithic, impersonal and instrumental. To conceive, instead, of technologies as reflexive phenomena is to see them as simultaneously products of our own creative energies and possessing a capacity for shaping, in turn, the environments and cultures we inhabit. It also reminds us that important value-judgements lie at the very heart of our engagement with technologies: what kinds of humans we may become, how humanity will use the resources, commodities and artefacts granted to it, questions of access, equity and distribution. These are, ultimately, questions of how we use our creative abilities – abilities to build and inhabit all kinds of worlds, material, virtual and imaginary; but worlds which, nevertheless, can either enhance or diminish the image of God within all of us.

20

BIOETHICS AFTER POSTHUMANISM

Natural Law, Communicative Ethics and the Problem of Self-Design

Introduction

Over the past decade, a new term has entered our vocabulary, that of the 'posthuman'. On one level, it self-consciously evokes talk of the 'postmodern', as in Halberstam and Livingston's homage to the title of Jean-François Lyotard's famous monograph in their discussion of the 'posthuman condition' (Halberstam and Livingston, 1995). At its simplest level, the posthuman reflects the extent to which in an increasingly technological age, human bodies (and minds) are subject to enhancement, repair and modification of many kinds. 'Nature' is increasingly merging with technology, either in the way for example in which the human genome is codified and translated into bioinformatic data as a result of the mapping of the Human Genome Project; or how cybernetic and other mechanical devices (such as heart pacemakers and cochlear implants) are incorporated into the body; and how physical and biochemical functioning is adapted and reconstituted via various techniques of genetic science[1] and new generations of pharmacological treatments.

The concept of the 'posthuman' thus evokes a world in which humans are mixtures of machine and organism, where nature can be modified

---

1 As, for example, prenatal genetic screening; recombinant DNA procedures such as gene therapy or enhancement (germ-line or somatic); synthesis of artificial chromosomes; transgenic modifications; forms of assisted reproduction such as IVF; cloning; as well as associated areas of biotechnology such as the sequencing and patenting of human genetic information.

by technology, and technology has become assimilated into 'nature' as a functioning component of organic bodies, by means of cybernetic implants or genetic modification (Warwick, 2002; Fukuyama, 2002). The posthuman also describes a condition in which the boundaries (formerly assumed to be discrete and secure) between the natural/artificial, technological/biological, real/virtual are apparently dissolving.

What Karl Bayertz terms the 'technological contingency of human nature' (Bayertz, 2003: 131) is for some commentators simply the inevitable outworking of scientific and medical potential for enhancing human physical and intellectual powers, which in themselves are considered relatively value-neutral. Others, however, regard such developments in more radical, ontological perspective. Technologically driven modifications will engender a new phase of *human evolution*, superseding the adaptive functions of natural selection: a realization of the dreams of science-fictional visions of technologically enhanced minds and bodies, the prolongation of life (sometimes to the verge of immortality), the human physique rendered indifferent to pain, disease or finitude, the transport of the human mind and soul into the limitless horizons of cyberspace.

In my view, however, talk of the posthuman is not simply a marker of an inevitable process of succession, nor even a clearly defined set of characteristics, so much as an invitation to consider how cybernetic, digital and genetic technologies call into question the deepest assumptions underlying our notions of normative and exemplary humanity (Graham, 2002a, 2002b).[2] In this respect, the posthuman might also be conceived as a kind of 'thought experiment': an opportunity to think anew about the relationship between humans and their environments, artefacts and tools in a digital and biotechnological age. We might, therefore call this term 'critical posthumanism' (Simon, 2003: 2), or 'a general critical space in which the techno-cultural forces which both produce and undermine the stability of the categories of "human" and "nonhuman" can be investigated' (Waldby, 2000: 43).

Yet if critical posthumanism asks the question, 'What does it mean to be human in an age of technologies?' can it be confident of receiving a clear answer? As Gerhold Becker argues, biotechnologies hold the potential to elevate humanity to demiurgical status, with god-like powers to manipulate and redirect nature. But the risk is, when humanity itself becomes the object as well as the agent of such procedures, and human nature is no longer seen as immutable, inviolable and sacrosanct, our notions of human distinctiveness begin to dissolve:

Has biotech just opened a new chapter in the long history of the scientific conquest of nature, or has it effectively closed the old volume

---

2 For this reason, I adopted the notion of 'post/human' to indicate that I wished to place the very term itself under interrogation.

and begun to write the first lines of an entirely different story? ... Can we utilize its potential and carry on with our familiar worldviews and religious interpretations of the world, or is biotechnology in itself some sort of new ideology which challenges our traditional place in nature? Is it endowing us with the creative powers of God, or rather reducing us and the mystery of life to mere genetic components at the molecular level? (Becker, 1996: 5)

If *Homo sapiens* is to be succeeded by *Techno sapiens* (Jackélin, 2002), therefore, what happens to the human subject, and in particular the basis on which we might ascribe it a moral status? In a world populated by living beings who are not so much 'born' as 'made', whose inherent characteristics are the result not of evolutionary adaptation but 'human self-design' (Stock, 2002: 3), what is left to guarantee human dignity and distinctiveness? In the face of the alleged dissolution of any normative concept of human nature, how are criteria for differentiating between legitimate and illegitimate biotechnological procedures to be articulated?

These are matters not only of academic debate, but of popular concern too; and this chapter is concerned to examine the recent work of three well-known writers – two of whom are better known for their work in political philosophy than bioethics – whose work is seeking to communicate to a wider audience some of the ethical dilemmas inherent in contemporary biotechnology. In surveying 'the posthuman future' and 'the end of human nature', a variety of constructive proposals are made concerning the possible basis of a normative 'human nature' on which a renewed moral discourse might be based; and this chapter also hints at further ways forward, to what I term a 'critical realist' model of what it means to be human in an age of biotechnology.

Francis Fukuyama

Perhaps the clearest endorsement of the significance of the posthuman and all that it represents is the intervention of the political scientist Francis Fukuyama. Having proclaimed the 'end of History' and the redundancy of political ideology after the collapse of the Soviet Union, Fukuyama now argues that the power to shape human destiny has passed to contemporary biotechnologies. He focuses on four dimensions of this: new insights into the genetic and neurological basis of human behaviour; developments in neuropharmacology; advances in molecular biology to increase human life-expectancy; and genetic engineering, both somatic and germ-line modification. Such techniques promise to alter the very foundations of human nature, a challenge that necessarily demands fresh ethical and political solutions: 'The aim of this book is to argue ... that the most significant threat posed by contemporary biotechnology is the possibility that it will alter human nature and thereby move us into a "posthuman" stage of history' (Fukuyama, 2002: 7).

For example, the prolongation of life via gene therapies and other measures will create unprecedented social problems resulting from a disproportionately older population, with concomitant impact on voting behaviour, employment and family structure. The danger of a genetic 'class war' as a result of inequality of access to reproductive technologies also represents a threat to social stability (ibid.: 57–71). At the heart of Fukuyama's analysis is the contention that the human impact of new technologies cannot be limited to their ethical or legal implications, but are also fundamentally questions of *ontology*:

> the most significant threat posed by contemporary biotechnology is the possibility that it will alter human nature and thereby move us into a 'posthuman' stage of history. This is important ... because human nature exists, is a meaningful concept, and has provided a stable continuity to our experience as a species. It is, conjointly with religion, what defines our most basic values. Human nature shapes and constrains the possible kinds of political regimes, so a technology powerful enough to reshape what we are will have a possibly malign consequence for liberal democracy and the nature of politics itself. (Ibid.: 7)

Fukuyama's fear is that biotechnology threatens to engineer a dystopia in which the material and biological basis of our common humanity has been bred out of us, engendering a 'Brave New World' of unregulated experimentation, half-human monsters and profaned nature. He thus argues that our very discourse of human rights must be replenished in order to forestall dystopia, and his solution is a restoration of a universal concept of human rights founded upon the bedrock of enduring human instinct and adaptability:

> The connection between human rights and human nature is not clear-cut, however, and has been vigorously denied by many modern philosophers who assert that human nature does not exist, and that even if it did, rules of right and wrong have nothing whatever to do with it ... It is my view that this turn away from notions of rights based on human nature is profoundly mistaken, both on philosophical grounds and as a matter of everyday moral reasoning. Human nature is what gives us a moral sense, provides us with the social skills to live in society, and serves as a ground for more sophisticated philosophical discussions of rights, justice, and morality. What is ultimately at stake with biotechnology is not just some utilitarian cost-benefit calculus concerning future medical technologies, but the very grounding of the human moral sense, which has been a constant ever since there were human beings. (Ibid.: 101–2)

Fukuyama's reconstitution of natural law as the foundation of his ethic of human dignity is informed by the recent resurgence of neo-Darwinian biological science which has seen fit to challenge social constructionist understandings of human behaviour. While acknowledging cultural variation, Fukuyama maintains that human nature is universal, immutable and irreducible; a sure sign, he argues, that human beings are hard-wired by evolution to express certain constant traits which form the basis of all that is normative and exemplary in human nature. We have to 'live according to our nature', 'defer to the natural order of things' – and this will mean taking the unnatural step of framing legislation to limit genetic modification.

> What is it that we want to protect from any future advances in biotechnology? The answer is, we want to protect the full range of our complex, evolved natures against attempts at self-modification. We do not want to disrupt either the unity or the continuity of human nature, and thereby the human rights that are based on it. (Ibid.: 172)

However, the contradiction lies in Fukuyama's attempt to forge a theory of human rights rooted in an understanding of 'nature', the very category revealed to be malleable in an age of advanced biotechnology. Furthermore, the very concept of 'nature' itself has a complex history. Even the tendency to regard nature as fixed, unchanging and subject to scientific observation and manipulation is a comparatively modern idea. So while 'human nature' may for Fukuyama signal something constant, this may not necessarily be the case. Arguably, we only know 'nature' as it is culturally mediated to us; and to be human is to be cultural – Fukuyama's model of unchanging human traits is questionable, as any cultural anthropologist would tell us. What we assume to be 'natural' may therefore be more a work of rhetoric than observation.

To be 'human' has often been equated with a capacity for reason – the mind, preferably free of the encumbrances and distractions of the flesh and the sense, is the source of true knowing. Paradoxically, however, Fukuyama argues that human dignity is quintessentially rooted in those aspects of human nature that *transcend* reductionist science: emotion, consciousness, morality – which only for the most thoroughgoing sociobiologist would have a purely genetic base. So we have an account of human nature that is presumed to be genetically based, but which turns out to rest in qualities which, while identifiably human, have a less secure foundation in straightforward biology. Insofar as Fukuyama seems to be talking more about human capacity to exhibit emotion, intelligence, moral value, and so on, this would seem to be the emphasis of his thinking. Yet all of these, arguably, could still be properties of a species which had, to some degree, undergone genetic modification. Ultimately, there-

fore the special qualities Fukuyama prizes turn out not to be as 'natural'
– in the sense of being purely genetically derived or biologically based,
or even resting in the integrity of an unmodified body – but in something
less tangible which is founded, paradoxically, on our very capacity to
transcend biological contingency or physiological subsistence; in effect,
to transform 'nature' into 'culture':

> We are begotten, we have parents and thus there is a history of our
> species. And yet our being does not end with these moments. In a way
> that exceeds all these moments, humans perceive themselves as crea-
> tures of liberty, of intelligence, with a relation to transcendence. These
> perceptions build the basis for our ability to act against our 'natural
> determinations', without complete necessity of following our instincts.
> (Löw, 1996: 153)

We may also need to read Fukuyama's understanding of human nature
through the lenses of his earlier work on *The End of History*, in which he
proclaimed the superiority of capitalism as a form of political economy
over other kinds of systems such as state socialism. When he argues that
human nature is a constant, therefore, he is (in part) arguing that it is
immune to forms of social engineering or political modification; but the
same value-commitments are then displaced into his judgement on the
futility of altering human genetic arrangements:

> Whatever academic philosophers and social scientists may think of
> the concept of human nature, the fact that there has been a stable
> human nature throughout human history has had very great political
> consequences. As Aristotle and every serious theorist of human nature
> has understood, human beings are by nature cultural animals, which
> means that they can learn from experience and pass on that learn-
> ing to their descendants through nongenetic means. Hence human
> nature is not narrowly determinative of human behavior but leads to
> a huge variance in the way people raise children, govern themselves,
> provide resources, and the like. Mankind's constant efforts at cultural
> self-modification are what lead to human history and to the progres-
> sive growth in the complexity and sophistication of human institutions
> over time. (Fukuyama, 2002: 13)

Despite these problems, Fukuyama nevertheless advances some important issues. First, he insists that the logic of posthuman evolution is not
inevitable or inexorable simply by virtue of the existence of certain kinds
of technology. Rather, such developments arise from policy choices that
are, at root, politically driven. As we shall see, this constitutes a significant attempt to reinsert notions of human agency and choice into the

debate about our posthuman future. Fukuyama also wishes to protect human genetic diversity from becoming subservient to short-term imperatives such as commercial advantage or passing fashion. (This is in fact one of the criteria upon which resistance to the Human Genome Project has been based, in the name of ensuring that the appropriation of genetic information by commercial biotechnology corporations does not jeopardize human genetic diversity.)

Gregory Stock

Gregory Stock, the only practising biological scientist among the three, is unimpressed by the prospect of permanent modification of the human body by artificial implants or prostheses when, as he sees it, enhancement of cognitive, intellectual or physical powers can be achieved just as effectively with miniaturized cybernetic devices that require no surgery.[3] Stock's preferred route to the posthuman condition, however, is via biotechnology, and in particular germ-line therapies, such as the insertion of auxiliary chromosomes, and the programming of genetic information that is capable of 'shutting down' senescent cells and thus slowing the ageing process. Such therapies will correct many commonplace ailments, from infertility, to ageing to congenital disorders. However, since germ-line genetic modification alters human stem-cells, such alterations can be transmitted to one's offspring. Parents could, regardless, decide on a child's behalf to have certain treatments, usually to furnish the child with greater advantage in life (Stock, 2002: 37–49).

> These developments will write a new page in the history of life, allowing us to seize control of our evolutionary future. Our coming ability to choose our children's genes will have immense social impact and raise difficult ethical dilemmas. Biological enhancement will lead us into unexplored realms, eventually challenging our basic ideas about what it means to be human. (Ibid.: 2)

In considering the ethical implications, Stock is sanguine about the future. Certainly he foresees widespread cultural implications, not least in the potential complications arising from the exercise of parental choice. However, Stock argues that the challenges inherent in the adoption of sophisticated biotechnological methods are not novel. Qualitatively speaking, they may be regarded as simply extrapolations of cultural trends already

---

3 Stock prefers to talk of 'fyborgs' (functional cyborgs) – organic humans interfacing with discrete technologies – rather than hybrids of biological and mechanical. In his view, most people with access to new technologies are already living as fyborgs, with very little adaptation needed. The radical transformation, and the bridge to the posthuman, he argues, will come with genetic modification.

in evidence, such as the popularity of cosmetic surgery. He is therefore pragmatic about our capacity to manage the choices through what he terms 'Germinal Choice Technology' (ibid.: 110) and assures his readers that values such as openness to public scrutiny, freedom of information and the integrity of the scientific establishment will afford sufficient protection. Whatever genetic changes may occur to human beings, there is a constancy to human nature in our shared instinct for invention and self-improvement that unites us all:

> The only constant in a future of rapid biological manipulation would be evolutionary change itself. What could unite us in this future would be our common participation in this fluid, self-directed process rather than any transitory similarities in form. Seen in this light, strange as future humans may become if germline manipulation achieves its promise, they will still remain *human*. (Ibid.: 183)

Despite the complexities arising from biotechnologies, therefore, Stock is confident that human reason will find its own equilibrium; and in this respect, he articulates an essentially humanist perspective. The continuity underpinning the persistence of humanity – and presumably, the essence by which we define human dignity – rests in our capacity to innovate, to invent, to take responsibility for our future evolution. Stock's solution is a version of Kantian humanism in which benign reason, rather than revelation or natural law (which is Fukuyama's preference), becomes the faculty by which right actions are guided. Whatever our genetic constitution, this enduring faculty will safeguard our posthuman integrity and welfare.

> When we imagine Prometheus stealing fire from the gods, we are not incredulous or shocked by his act. It is too characteristically human. To forgo the powerful technologies that genomics and molecular biology are bringing would be as out of character for humanity as it would be to use them without concern for the dangers they pose. We will do neither. The question is no longer whether we will manipulate embryos, but when, where, and how. (Ibid.: 2)

This is a very thin account of human becoming through technology; it asserts rather than argues a doctrine of human nature. It is also, effectively, a somewhat simplistic form of technocracy. Stock does not consider what might be driving the development of biotechnologies: human common sense or corporate interests and the commodification of human genome. Stock insists that government regulation of biotechnologies will be unnecessary, arguing 'the free market is best suited to determine their use' (ibid.: 59), an attitude consistent with his liberal humanist outlook, but betraying a naivety towards the extent to which biotechnologies are embedded within the networks of global capitalism; the free market may serve to ration (and thus limit) questionable or dangerous treatments, but it also simply exacerbates existing inequalities in health care provision, access to new technologies and consumer choice. Such a disregard for the *political economy* of technologies is reminiscent of Fukuyama's call to impose stringent international controls on genetic experiments, which seems equally unrealistic in a context where the power of statutory agencies is overshadowed by private corporations' quest for scientific and commercial advantage.

Jürgen Habermas

The critical theorist and social philosopher Jürgen Habermas has recently entered the debate, with the publication of a series of lectures originally delivered in Marburg, entitled *The Future of Human Nature*. Like other commentators, he considers the prospect of human genetic self-design and modification to represent a profound disjunction in human history and human nature: 'more and more of what we are "by nature" is coming within the reach of biotechnological intervention' (Habermas, 2003: 23).

> To the degree that the evolution of the species, proceeding by random selection, comes within the reach of the interventions of genetic engineering and, thus, of actions we have to answer for, the categories of what is *manufactured* and what has *come to be by nature*, which in the lifeworld still maintain their demarcating power, dedifferentiate. (Ibid.: 46)

Like Fukuyama, Habermas is concerned to find a response to the de-stabilization of concepts of human nature, and thus our moral self-understanding by restating a notion of a core account of what it means to be human. Unlike Fukuyama, however, Habermas relies on his previously worked theory of 'communicative action' to articulate an understanding of human nature that is derivative of their participation in moral discourse and communities. So this value does not rest in inherent 'human nature' granted by biology; rather, it is derived from the ascribed self-image and value attributed to the human species. It is a dialectic, effectively: our moral status as persons is actually a function of our participation in the collective, 'species-ethical' experience of humanity as a whole.

At the root of this lies the dignity of being permitted to be the author of one's own destiny, and in this instance of one's own genetic history. It is an abuse of another's inherent autonomy to choose their genetic constitution, as might a parent seeking genetic enhancement or selection for their offspring. For Habermas, this constitutes an unacceptable breach of the unborn child's right to self-determination. To be the product of such interventions would be to be less than human: an object of another's ambition and design, rather than the subject of one's own life-story.

> For as soon as adults treat the desirable genetic traits of their descendants as a product they can shape according to a design of their own liking, they are exercising a kind of control over their genetically manipulated offspring that intervenes in the somatic bases of another person's spontaneous relation-to-self and ethical freedom. This kind of intervention should only be exercised over things, not persons. (Ibid.: 13)

This is significant: the manipulation of another's genome effectively renders them an object, displacing them into 'the realm of artifacts and their production' (ibid.: 12) rather than, for Habermas, where they belong by virtue of their very humanity, which is the sphere of public discourse and communicative action. We must draw the line at 'obliterating the boundary between persons and things' (ibid.: 13). The individuality and freedom of that enhanced embryo will grow up feeling diminished by the fact that her 'nature' has been assembled according to the will of others, and so such genetic intervention undermines the fundamental relations of human beings with one another, since there is then no possibility of our encountering each other as equals.

This kind of argument may actually assume too much significance for alterations to the genome in determining someone's life-chances. After all, genes only carry information which instructs other physiological functioning; and the outcome of genetic predispositions is, except in a very few cases, still dependent on other factors such as nutrition, environment and non-genetic medical interventions. *Contra* genetic determinism, we might argue that the dynamics of poverty, racism or other social and economic inequalities already condemn many children to a life of disadvantage even before they enter the world, to a far more acute degree than any genetic modification. Mothers can influence the well-being of their unborn babies by monitoring diet or stopping smoking; parents can select a good school for their child, or subject them to intensive training from an early age in order to accelerate their intellectual development. So why should Habermas object to genetic intervention when it may be no more powerful than other biological or even social forces?

Habermas' position is further complicated by his concession to allowing some genetic treatments in special circumstances, conceding that certain interventions may be acceptable in cases where the outcome will unquestionably improve the person's quality of life, on the assumption that the individual concerned would have given informed consent had they been in a position to do so. But he still needs clearer criteria as to who determines how far to go in such therapeutic interventions. Might it be the case that to intervene on another's behalf, however much one might believe it to be in their best interests, is simply a form of paternalist benevolence which still deprives that person of the ability to choose for themselves?

It might be the case that prenatal genetic modification could enhance, or expand, rather than reduce or predetermine, a child's life-choices. Who could deny their child these privileges; and where does the line come between pre-emptive repair of genetic dysfunction which might result in a disability, and other modifications which enhance opportunity? The fact remains, that in a market economy, some therapeutic options may be available to some and not others; and the benefits accruing will bring differential economic and social life-chances. The only solution would be to make all potential treatments available to everyone.

Equally, what do we think, morally, about the position of a neo-natal so severely disabled as to require constant care for the rest of their lives. How much 'autonomy' and independence awaits this person? Here, we encroach on the territory of the ethics of disability, and on what terms those with profound learning disabilities, for example, or those in permanent vegetative states, may be attributed 'personhood'. Habermas' analysis takes us no further into resolving these questions: a eugenicist solution would be to propose genetic therapies in order to 'edit out' such impairments, whereas ethicists such as Tom Shakespeare would robustly oppose genetic intervention in the name of human diversity. Similarly, the very availability of such techniques 'insidiously shift the ground towards what has been variously called "tentative pregnancy" or "the perfect baby syndrome" or the "supermarket syndrome", by which I mean the expectation that medical expertise will deliver a baby free from impairment or illness' (Shakespeare, 1998: 666). Nevertheless, Shakespeare would acknowledge that there is a world of difference between a society in which one is able to live a full and viable life as a person with disabilities, and of merely existing with no possibility of anything approaching a real life at all. One counter-argument is that such individuals are persons not simply by virtue of their own cognitive abilities but insofar as they are the recipients of care, attention and unconditional positive regard from another.

Is Habermas basing his doctrine of human nature on an Enlightenment notion of self-determination (cf. feminist critiques of autonomous individualism), or is he suggesting that human dignity is dependent upon cultural (communicative) recognition, in which the very human capacity to create culture/community is the very basis of human value?

As germ-line treatments become more feasible, important questions are raised which, arguably, require a robust model of the body politic capable of supporting the kinds of moral and political debates which such interventions call forth: our responsibilities to future generations, questions of access and consent, not to mention the limits of proportionate risk in the face of biotechnological advance. Habermas' evocation of communicative action is an important element in considering not only how moral discourse might be conducted in an age of posthumanism, but also what kinds of criteria might underpin moral judgement, since it reminds us that the very well-springs of collective and personal sociality rest on mutual, inclusive dialogue and the possibilities of normative agreement. It also suggests that any right to self-determination on the part of the individual cannot be separated from wider questions of how to organize our common life in ways which make possible an equitable and dignified level of participation for everybody.

Discussion

I have been arguing that bioethics grounded in axiomatic notions of human nature are looking fragile in face of 'posthuman' technologies such as genetic modification, cloning and other interventions.

Fukuyama has been said to advance a version of 'natural law' in his defence of human dignity, although I consider it to be a very insipid version of this doctrine. His insistence on an enduring human essence can ultimately be revealed to be as much 'cultural' as 'natural'. Certainly, it is important to be mindful that human activity is always to some degree dependent on biological processes (and humans are part of a wider ecology of non-human nature and living things which we ignore at our peril); but equally, 'nature' is always mediated to us through 'culture'. We may be biological beings, but our moral values derive from our possession of qualities such as agency, imagination and self-consciousness, none of which can be said to derive purely from evolutionary or genetic imperatives.

Paradoxically, Fukuyama does a better job by wishing to resist reductionist accounts of what it means to be human, which attempt to identify an abstract 'essence' or continuity of human nature within biological or evolutionary continuity, failing to do justice to the complexity of what makes us human. We need 'thicker', more pluralist accounts, which appreciates the extent to which 'human nature' is actually a compound of the two terms: it is *both* about being distinctively and uniquely human, largely through our capacity for culture, fabrication and imagination; *and* natural, insofar as our survival is dependent on our interdependence and affinity with all living things.

Second, Gregory Stock's important insistence on the self-regulating benevolence of human reason has long been a staple of Enlightenment humanism. However, we have to have reasonable discourse both of

307

human potential and human contingency or finitude. Human self-interest alone cannot be the sole arbiter of moral reasoning, not least because any adequate account of what it means to be human would need to take account of the ambiguity of human experience:

> On the one hand, advances in evolutionary theory allow us to say that the use of our freedom, language and symbols do help us to change and configure our nature. On the other hand, they warn us not to be too optimistic about the outcome of our conscious will, bound as it is to all sorts of constraints resulting from a haphazard evolutionary history ... Human nature is marked by a capacity for violence and destructiveness as well as a capacity for justice and creativity ... Perhaps this realism will more adequately equip us for the task of seeking justice in an unjust world. (Cruz, 2002: 184)

In Habermas' arguments, we saw something of this insistence that human becoming is cultural and technological as well as biological/genetic. We might read his theory of communicative ethics as a suggestion that human value and distinctiveness rests on our abilities to bring worlds of culture, imagination, symbol, narrative and religion into being, as well as our fabrication of technological worlds of canals, cathedrals and computers. Peter Scott's understanding of humanity as 'un/natural' encapsulates for me much of Habermas' wish to locate his account of human dignity in our very sociality, as creatures capable of inhabiting different worlds at once: as self-determined beings whose very humanity also rests in being part of a community of language and meaning; as *Homo faber* responsible not only for the fabrication of material and technological worlds – such as the built environment or manufactured goods – but also as creatures who inhabit worlds of symbol, myth, narrative and religion. In that respect, we may be drawing close to some kind of working definition of what it means to be human: those who exhibit qualities of 'immanence' and 'transcendence', those who seek meaning and value in the world around them and for whom autonomy and community, individuality and mutuality, are equally vital for true personhood to flourish.

The idea of a distinctive moral status to human nature is of course nothing new, and we have already discovered three different perspectives on this. But does our concept of human nature have to be fixed and immutable in order to have moral substance? Just because it is 'technologically contingent' doesn't mean to say human beings and human nature have dissolved completely. Rather, the task would be to articulate a theory of normativity out of a model of human nature as emergent and relational – as 'co-evolving' out of our interactions with other humans, non-human nature as well as our tools and technologies.

When we speak of 'human nature', therefore, we need perhaps to realize the need to stress the *first* as well as the second half of that phrase – or, as Peter Scott's recent book puts it, to consider the 'un/natural' status of human beings: 'the nature of social humanity, its natural and cultured relations to nature, its use of nature' (Scott, 2003: 29). This term reflects human nature as simultaneously a part of nature and other than nature, and affirms our transformative agency towards, and our creaturely co-dependency with, the world of non-human nature, our tools and technologies.

Perhaps this, ultimately, is what it means to be (fully) human: a facility to move beyond the actual to the imagined, whether it is by transforming raw materials into an artefact or tool, or by ascribing value to our actions. The very fact that we search for meaning amid our technological endeavours points to our tendency both to be creatures of our environment and physical reality, and to be creators of new worlds of imagination and vision. This ability to explore, extend, to exceed our own programming is part of human creativity; and within a theological perspective, such a transcendence of the empirical and material into the imaginary would be termed 'spirituality': a sense of connectedness, a denial of reductionism, and a commitment to 'the acknowledged dimension of what is not immanent, inner-human, inner-worldly' (Löw, 1996: 154), a call towards a horizon of otherness towards which we strive and against which we measure our limits.

Such a posthuman ethic has yet to be fully developed, but it would necessarily give a 'thick' and non-reductionist account of what it means to be human in a biotechnological age – a kind of 'critical realism' (Russell and Wegter-McNally, 2002)[4] perhaps, which recognizes the provisionality of any truth-claims regarding the absolute 'essentials' of human nature, choosing instead to integrate a number of considerations in assembling normative criteria: concern to alleviate individual suffering while aware of personal accountability to wider, collective social goals; commitment to human well-being alongside that of the integrity of non-human nature and the physical environment as essential for the flourishing of all living things; celebration of the fruits and potentials of human achievement, tempered by a realist's appreciation of human frailty. But I would want to speak the language of 'a universe of grace' – that ultimately, our own human nature, the powers granted us, and the worlds we build and inhabit are worthy of respect as 'gift' and 'mystery'.

---

4 'Like science, theology is ultimately realist in character: it makes claims about reality. Also like science, however, theological "theories" can yield only partial, revisable, and abstract knowledge of the world and its relationship to the Divine or sacred. Religious beliefs, much like scientific theories, are expressed through "metaphor", open-ended analogies whose meaning cannot be reduced to a set of literal statements' (Russell and Wegter-McNally, 2002: 25).

21

IN WHOSE IMAGE?

Representations of Technology and the 'Ends' of Humanity

Introduction

> [T]he question can never be first of all 'what are we *doing* with our technology?' but it must be 'what are we *becoming* with our technology?' (Hefner, 2003: 9)

Thinking about the impact of new technologies on what it means to be human brings sharply into focus the question of relationship between technological activity and 'human becoming'. What is at stake in seeking to evaluate the significance of human engagement with its tools and technologies? Is technology a neutral instrument, an epiphenomenon to human nature? Or is it an integral part not only of the formation of human material culture, but of our very ontology? In this chapter, I want to consider some of the debate surrounding the advent of the so-called 'posthuman condition' (Halberstam and Livingston, 1995: vii) and in particular, how the theme of *human dignity*, its endangerment or rejuvenation, features in relation to the impact of digital, biomedical and cybernetic technologies.

I will argue that technologies and the work of material fabrication are indeed a substantive, and not simply an incidental, part of being human. This is most evident in the ways in which in contemporary debates, advanced technologies are both heralded as the means by which humanity might attain its most fundamental aspirations – the *end* of humanity – and perceived as constituting an urgent threat to human dignity: the end of *humanity*.

But this also implies that technological endeavour, if part of our humanity, needs to form part of our theological anthropology. In what ways might theology engage, both in critical and reconstructive terms, with some of the dominant representations of the posthuman as they permeate not only scientific discourse but Western culture as a whole?

The challenge of the posthuman condition for theological anthropology has attracted the attention of a number of contemporary commentators (Cruz, 2002, Jackelén, 2002, Murray, 2003). Regardless of whether many of the more expansive technological developments ever materialize, the anticipated emergence of 'Techno sapiens' (Jackelén, 2002) is already shaping the Western cultural and scientific imagination, not to mention the research and policy priorities of corporate and academic interests. It would therefore seem important to trace some of the underlying values informing such visions of the technological future, what kinds of exemplary and normative understandings of the 'posthuman' are circulating in Western culture, and what happens when these are subjected to critique. In particular, I shall argue that aspects of theological anthropology – particularly traditions which speak of humanity as *imago Dei*, as made in the image and likeness of God – point us towards a framework of values, priorities and criteria by which the proper *ends of humanity* might be adjudicated. Yet in some respects, this chapter can only set an agenda for further work in this direction, since our concepts of what it means to be human – like our very humanity itself – may not be fixed or absolute, but themselves in process, defined iteratively in relation to particular technological and cultural contexts.

Endangerment or Promise?

The impact of new technologies has had a profound impact on Western culture; but the terminology of the 'posthuman' attempts to capture the extent to which material innovations call forth the possibility of deeper, metaphysical transformations. Yet in all three of these dimensions of the posthuman future, we can discern a recurrent theme in reactions and predictions. Broadly, it is possible to trace strong threads of both 'technophobia' and 'technophilia': technologies as bearers of human diminishment, or as heralds of a brave new world of unlimited human capabilities. Three issues in particular demonstrate how particular aspects of human experience correlate with anxieties and expectations about the very future of 'human nature': embodiment, autonomy and subjectivity.

1 Post-biological embodiment

If much of the debate about the impact of new technologies concerns their power either to facilitate a better quality of life or unleash Promethean powers which threaten our very humanity, then much of that attention and anxiety has come to be focused around the integrity of the body. Opinions polarize around whether it is appropriate to dream of transcending the frailties of the flesh to embrace new physical forms, or whether the end of our embodiment would fatally compromise our essential humanity.

For some commentators, the advent of new technologies will protect us against physical disease and vulnerability. Technologies, long having been the means of enabling humanity to compensate for physical limitations by providing instruments of comfort and utility, now offer the opportunities to overcome the limitations of the flesh entirely. This gives rise to the possibilities for achieving a 'post-biological' existence, as in the incorporation of artificial organs or prosthetic limbs or our transformation into 'post-bodied' individuals as we go on-line or experience virtual reality.

Such processes are often signalled as the emergence of 'cyborgs', or 'cybernetic organisms', as hybrids of biological and technological components, but this raises wider questions about the integrity of embodiment as a distinctive marker of personal identity, and whether computer-mediated media (such as the Internet and virtual reality) represent a valuable extension to the limits of human community, or a pale imitation of face-to-face interaction.

In describing his own (temporary) transformation from organic human to cyborg via the implantation of a silicon chip transmitter in his forearm, Kevin Warwick is expansive in his speculations about the potential of such technological enhancement. 'Might it be possible for humans to have extra capabilities, particularly mental attributes, and become super humans or, as some regard it, post humans [sic]?' (Warwick, 2002: 175). His enthusiasm encapsulates perfectly the vision of those who see the promise of cybernetic technologies as going beyond mere clinical benefits to embrace nothing less than an ontological transformation. Warwick sees no limit to the transcendence of normal physical and cognitive limitations, an achievement that for him signals nothing less than a new phase in human evolution (2002: 295–6).

Similarly, the impact of computer-mediated communications can be traced in the way it changes taken-for-granted categories of space, place and time, the boundaries of the body and the interface of machine and human. In the case of the Internet, it collapses physical distance, transcends national boundaries, reinvents conventions of text and reading, transforms human interactions into the flow of information, creates new artificial environments and machinic intelligences. For some, this offers unprecedented opportunities of freedom of information and communication, the creation of a global forum of exchange and interchange. For others, the disembodied nature of virtual technologies such as the Internet represents a fundamental loss of moral grounding. Despite the many benefits of computer-assisted communication, it is feared that the lack of face-to-face contact will lead to the dissolution of human community, as individuals descend into what Andrew Feenberg characterizes as a 'new narcissism':

> The collapse of public life and the decline of the family seem to cut indi-viduality loose from its institutional moorings and sources of meaning. No longer concretized through real bonds and obligations, the person becomes a discontented spectator on his or her own life, engaged in strategies of manipulation and control directed towards the self and others alike. (Feenberg, 1991: 98)

2 Trajectory of technologies

One recurrent motif of modern science fiction has been that of 'creation out of control', or the fear that machines will rebel against their human masters, with catastrophic results. This anxiety is reflected in a strong and influential strand in the philosophy of technology which argues that technology has assumed a deterministic character, insofar as the impera-tives of efficiency, rationalization and mass production have engulfed the priorities of human welfare. The sense is that technological imperatives are not dependent on human design, and have an autonomous status in determining economic, personal, cultural and moral priorities. Technol-ogy has moved from being an instrument or tool in the hands of human agents, or even a means to transform the natural environment, and be-come a series of processes or interventions capable of reshaping human ontology. It also raises the question of whether as cybernetic systems such as artificial intelligence become more sophisticated, technologies might acquire the facility to become self-programming.

Jacques Ellul speaks of the degradation of creative production to the routinization of mere 'technique' (Ellul, 1965); Martin Heidegger argues that technology has a particular way of 'revealing' the world to its users which obscures all possibilities other than that of 'standing-reserve' – essentially, an objectification of nature which reduces everything to a commodity (Heidegger, 1993: 307–42).

For Albert Borgmann, similarly, technologies have colonized everyday life to such an extent that they have become virtually invisible. The con-veniences of processed food, television, text messaging and labour-saving gadgets have displaced more traditional skills and pastimes which may have involved more effort but which also constituted the essential fabric of daily life. By removing technologies from their human creators and from any sense of connectedness to their social or cultural contexts of production, Borgmann argues that we have emptied their accompanying activities of meaning. Technologies have ceased to become benevolent aids to human comfort and now serve as the taken-for-granted matrix through which all experience is mediated:

> The peril of technology lies not in this or that of its manifestations but *in the pervasiveness and consistency of its pattern*. There are always occasions where a Big Mac, an exercycle, or a television program are unobjectionable and truly helpful answers to human needs. This makes a case-by-case appraisal of technology so inconclusive. It is when we attempt to take the measure of technological life in its normal totality that we are distressed by its shallowness. (Borgmann, 1984: 224)

As well as developing Heidegger's perspective on technologies' ability to reveal or conceal aspects of the world, Borgmann's analysis also carries traces of Feuerbach's and Marx's concept of 'alienation'. Technology, as the product of human labour, has itself become reified and now assumes a deterministic quality in which humans regard themselves as the objects of technological imperatives, rather than its subjects. The everyday familiarity of technologies blunts our sense of wonder at their complexity and dulls our curiosity towards their origins in the actual processes and relations of production, and their ubiquity serves as an ideological opiate to dull our moral and political sensibilities. The solution for Borgmann is to restore a sense of the origins of technologies in the human practices of fabrication and sociability, thereby returning them to the status of 'focal things' (Borgmann, 2003: 27).

Borgmann thus sees ways of affirming technologies in relation to human existence, despite his foreboding. However, other accounts of the future are altogether more unequivocal, regarding technologies as the benign tools of human self-actualization. Rather than envisaging the effacement of human agency, or endangering our capacity to participate in authentic existence, these more technocratic analyses are single-mindedly positive about the ability of technologies to facilitate problem-solving and advance human interests. Humans will continue to be the masters of their technological inventions, and this will enable them to dominate, subdue and eventually transcend the forces of non-human nature as well.

An example of such a perspective would be the philosophy of technology known as transhumanism. Transhumanists advocate the use of advanced medical, prosthetic and genetic techniques to extend the human life-span, enhance human intellectual powers and improve physical and psychological capabilities. The World Transhumanist Association describes transhumanism as 'an interdisciplinary approach to understanding and evaluating the possibilities for overcoming biological limitations through technological progress' (Bostrom, 2003: 4). The possibility of the distinction between humans and machines dissolving altogether is also contemplated, as in Hans Moravec's dream of uploading human intelligence into computer software and then downloading it into an artificial environment, such as virtual reality or robotic hardware (ibid.: 17–18).

Underlying this vision is a version of Enlightenment humanism in which the rational subject, uninhibited by the external constraints of superstition, fear or conservatism, is enabled to scale new heights of intellectual and technological achievement. Technologies are regarded as quintessentially neutral, neither good nor bad, merely instruments for achieving purposes and values enshrined elsewhere. They do not threaten or render human activities obsolete, but simply free human creativity to achieve new limits: 'Buried in the murk of the human self lies an unformed golden core, and with technology ... we can tap and transform this potential' (Davis, 1998: 128).

While many of transhumanists' proposed technological developments are yet to be realized, it may be more appropriate to regard transhumanism, like all other posthumanist thinking, as a kind of 'thought experiment', which, like fictional representations of technologized humanity, serve to illuminate and refract deeper hopes and fears. What makes transhumanism such a vivid example of such posthuman thinking is the way in which it articulates a particular set of humanist ideals and transposes them into the technological sphere. Transhumanists deliberately harness the aspirations of Enlightenment humanism and individualism as a philosophical underpinning for their endeavours. In its endorsement of human self-actualization unconstrained by fear, tradition or superstition, transhumanism exhibits a secular scepticism towards theologically grounded values, arguing that these serve to rationalize passivity and resignation in the face of human mortality and suffering.

No mysteries are sacrosanct, no limits unquestionable; the unknown will yield to the ingenious mind. The practice of progress challenges us to understand the universe, not to cower before mystery. It invites us to learn and grow and enjoy our lives ever more (More, 2003).

Yet this is not a human distinctiveness grounded in embodiment or even rational mind per se so much as a set of qualities enshrined in a human 'spirit' of inventiveness and self-actualization:

> It is not our human shape or the details of our current human biology that define what is valuable about us, but rather our aspirations and ideals, our experiences and the kinds of lives we live. To a transhumanist, progress is when more people become more able to deliberately shape themselves, their lives, and the ways they relate to others, in accordance with their own deepest values. (Bostrom, 2003: 6)

Yet in that respect transhumanism represents something of a paradox, in that to become posthuman – to be radically dependent on technology for future evolution and survival – actually entails the erosion of the very categories of bodily integrity, autonomy and personal subjectivity that define liberal 'human nature'. Furthermore, in its 'realized eschatology' of immortality and escape from biological contingency, transhumanism embraces a dualistic – one might say Cartesian – anthropology, in that the continuity of individuals and the human species is equated with the continuation of consciousness rather than any notion of embodied self-hood. Theologically, as Brent Waters has argued, Christian doctrine has envisaged that the griefs and limitations of the human condition takes place not via a denial of death but via its embrace, but ultimate defeat, through cross and resurrection. In other words, the betterment or per-fection of humanity does not occur by the negation of the body but by embracing and redeeming corporeal humanity (Waters, 2004).

In addressing the claims of transhumanism, therefore, it is important to recognize its implicit truth-claims regarding normative and exemplary human nature. It is perhaps the starkest example of a posthuman doc-trine seizing upon selected aspects of cultural understandings of what it means to be human – in this case Enlightenment liberal individualism – and projecting these as universal and inevitable aspirations of techno-logical endeavours. Yet as Katharine Hayles argues, the dilemma is to affirm the beneficial potential of technologies without being seduced by their Gnostic or Platonic tendencies:

> If my nightmare is a culture inhabited by posthumans who regard their bodies as fashion accessories rather than the ground of being, my dream is a version of the posthuman that embraces the possibilities of infor-mation technologies without being seduced by fantasies of unlimited power and disembodied immortality, that recognizes and celebrates finitude as a condition of human being, and that understands human life is embedded in a material world of great complexity, one on which we depend for our continued survival. (Hayles, 1999: 5)

3 The death of the subject?

A fundamental fault-line exists at the heart of all these perspectives on technology. Does the 'posthuman condition' represent promise or threat, mastery or extinction? If 'critical posthumanism' is asking the question, 'What does it mean to be human in an age of technologies?' where is it to look for an answer? If *Homo sapiens* is to be succeeded by *Techno sapiens*, what happens to our accounts of human subjectivity, and in par-ticular the basis on which we might ascribe it a moral status? In the face of the alleged dissolution of any normative concept of human nature, how are criteria for differentiating between legitimate and illegitimate technological appropriations to be articulated?

These are questions regarding the future trajectory of human engagement with technologies, and whether the transition from *Homo sapiens* to *Techno sapiens* will propel humanity towards greater knowledge and prosperity, or diminish human uniqueness to the point of obsolescence. Yet how seriously should we take these posthuman claims that technology is reshaping our deepest experiences and understandings of what it means to be human?

Post/human Technologies

> It is ... not enough to ensure that a technological activity or product is examined in its context, exposing the human and environmental implications and even, asking questions about its purpose: it has to be acknowledged that technologies *are* the context. Technology is itself shaping the value judgements we are making about it. (Conway, 1999: 109)

Although philosophical speculation about the relationship between humanity and technologies has a long history, and current thinking can be placed in a long legacy of debate (Scharff and Dusek, 2003), certain advances over the past half-century – most particularly the construction of the world's first stored-memory computer in 1948 and the identification of DNA in 1953 – do seem to represent an unprecedented intensification of techno-scientific potential. The shift into a so-called 'posthuman' sensibility thus signals a recognition that technology as 'other' to human existence is now assimilated into everyday human functioning: in a literal sense, in terms of the possibilities of devices such as cochlear implants, intraocular lenses, heart pacemakers and other artificial organs or prostheses becoming a permanent part of human physiology, and in a more existential sense, insofar as most of the population of the First World are completely dependent on technologies such as computer-mediated communications, broadcasting media, transport infrastructure and generation of power.

Talk of the posthuman in this respect thus evokes a world in which, thanks to cybernetics, artificial intelligence, virtual reality, plastic surgery, gene therapies and assisted reproduction, biological humans are everywhere surrounded – and transformed – into mixtures of machine and organism, where what we call 'nature' has been significantly reshaped by technology, and technology, in turn has become assimilated into 'nature' as a fully functioning component of organic life itself.

The posthuman has thus become a shorthand metaphor for talking about a number of interrelated issues. First, the scientific and medical prospects for *enhancement of human physical and intellectual powers* by means of cybernetic implants or genetic modification, including increased longevity, resistance to congenital or other illnesses, and improved cognitive skills. Second, as a corollary to this, the posthuman has come to be identified for many with the emergence of a *new phase of human evolution*, albeit technologically driven (and the result of human choices) rather than driven by the forces of natural selection.

However, as Bart Simon points out, it is helpful to differentiate between these first two, which he terms 'popular posthumanism' and a third strand, which he terms 'critical posthumanism' (Simon, 2003). The latter is concerned not only to evaluate the material impact of technologies on economics, communications, sexuality and reproduction, embodiment and so on, but to raise the question of *the kind of models of human nature* at work in the various discourses in the face of new technologies.

Simon's point is that popular posthumanist perspectives emanate from a taken-for-granted assumption that sometime before the advent of biomedical, cybernetic and genetic technologies the boundaries between the human/non-human, natural/artificial, organic/technological were fixed and axiomatic, and to be human rested on a clear 'ontological hygiene' (Graham, 2002a) of essential qualities. Yet, as many critics argue, the boundaries have always been contested, and attempts to define the 'human' in relation to the 'non- human' is a work of exclusion, a denial of our entanglement, our complicity, with the world of our tools, technologies and environments. In a digital and biotechnological age, therefore, it is impossible to speak of a pristine, unadulterated 'human nature'. Yet this may be no more than a reminder that as the creators of material cultures, via the processes of transforming or constructing the world, humanity cannot but re-fashion *itself* as integral elements of that world.

> For what does it mean to say that our context is *now* posthuman? What does it mean to say that the human is intertwined with nonhumans *as never before*? When was the human *not* inextricably entwined in material, technological and informational networks? When was the human ever just 'itself'? (Braun, 2004: 271)

There is a tendency to regard 'technology' as merely synonymous with advances in computing, genetic engineering and the industrial age. But the root of the word, the Greek *techne*, or 'craft' or 'skill' reminds us that technologies are both more basic and more ubiquitous within human culture. Indeed, they may be the very facility that distinguishes human beings from other non-human animals, insofar as they make possible sophisticated cultures, enable human beings to sustain long-term inhabitation of difficult environments, as well as being the very medium through which cultural achievements – such as language, visual arts, material culture, economic production, exchange and consumption, as well as religion – are embodied. Technology is thus both a body of knowledge, in terms of accumulated know-how, and the material instruments and machines through which such knowledge is practised.

All human societies may be said to be 'technological', therefore, inso-far as they deploy tools, devices and procedures to assist human living. Such technologies also actually fuel human evolution, as humans adapt to changing conditions by inventing technologies that enable us to maxi-mize our chances of survival and development in previously hostile or problematic contexts. Yet those technologies, arguably, are more than mere appendages to autonomous human reason. They actually affect our experiences and apprehensions of what it means to be human so that we cannot conceive of ourselves independent of our tools and technologies.

Cyborgs Unbound

Both Bruno Latour and Donna Haraway have argued that the ubiquity and sophistication of technologies necessitate that the world – nature, culture, technology and human nature itself – be understood as existing in various states of 'hybridity'. For example, in her essay, 'A Cyborg Mani-festo' (1991), Haraway famously argued that in the face of new technolo-gies, we have to realize – and celebrate – the accompanying erosion of many of the boundaries by which we have set the limits of normative or authentic human nature. For Haraway, the 'blasphemy' of the cyborg rests in its refusal to observe the essentialist categories of species, gender, nature and ontology, and in whom 'the boundaries of a fatally transgres-sive world, ruled by the Subject and the Object, give way to the border-lands, inhabited by human and unhuman collectives' (Haraway, 1992: 328). Yet in a culture profoundly driven and shaped by technologies, human beings cannot remain immune from this breaching of boundaries and categories, and the impact of critical posthumanism's perspective is precisely to argue that no such hegemony can be maintained.

In my view, therefore, talk of the 'posthuman' is not simply a marker of an inevitable process of succession, nor even a clearly defined set of characteristics, so much as an invitation, as Bart Simon suggests, to con-sider how cybernetic, digital and genetic technologies call into question the deepest assumptions underlying our notions of normative and ex-emplary humanity. This strand of 'critical posthumanism' might best be described as indicating the *reconstitution* of the subject. Like much of post-structuralism, which exposes the artifice of modernist constructions of the subject, 'post' unsettles its suffix, serving to betray its fictional and contingent status. The posthuman condition is one in which the bound-aries of humanity are interrogated; not so much a singular epoch, then, or a particular evolutionary vision, but more a critical lens. The post-human is less a 'condition' than an *interrogation*; and for this reason, I have chosen to adopt the notion of the 'post/human' – the forward-slash or oblique serving as a reminder that our delineation of human nature may be more a question of *boundaries* than essences (Graham, 2002a).

319

As we encounter anew ourselves and others, so we embark on theoretical realignments on issues such as identity, subjectivity, embodiment, reproduction, life, death, human creativity. Given the blurring of human/machine (as in the figure of the cyborg, or the multiple, role-playing virtual self, dependent on computer communications for its realization) we can no longer define just what exactly constitutes the human subject that might be enhanced or propelled into cyberspace; in fact we cannot ontologically separate humanity from its technological medium. 'Human nature' ceases to be a fixed category and re-emerges as a constantly changing set of possibilities and configurations. The post/human banishes hopes of a purity of species, in which:

> nostalgia for a humanist philosophy of self and other, human and alien, normal and queer is merely the echo of a battle that has already taken place. This argument is not a truth-claim but ... an open invitation to engage discursive and bodily configurations that displace the human, humanism, and the humanities. (Halberstam and Livingston, 1995: vii)

Within such a reflexive, hybrid, post/human model of human engagement with technologies, the boundaries between object and subject, determinism and agency, human and non-human, are irrevocably blurred. Our response can no longer be a protest against the distortion of an essential humanity by invasive, instrumental machines or a celebration of the so-called 'technological sublime', but a question of situated knowledge concerning the most equitable means of configuring humans, nature and machines, of living alongside and intermingled with our tools, technologies and artefacts: a truly 'cyborg ethic'.

In thinking about the future of human nature in a technological age, therefore, it may be more appropriate to acknowledge that humans are capable of building and inhabiting all kinds of worlds – some material, others virtual – but that they are all bound by the relations of their production, albeit working according to different conventions. Who and what 'we' are or become is thus intimately linked to the conditions under which we engage with technologies, and to what end. Neither the 'transcendence' of the technological sublime nor the 'determinism' of disenchantment fully captures the complexity and reflexivity of the necessarily hybrid nature of post/human experience.

In Whose Image?

I have identified some of the questions about what it means to be human which are fuelling the anxieties and hopes surrounding the emergence of cybernetic, genetic and digital technologies. Despite the predominance of secularism in modern science, it is intriguing to identify a number of ways in which religious discourses still imbue many of the considerations of what should constitute our post/human future. This does not simply apply to those who regard technologies as responsible for the *disenchantment* of the world in the name of spiritual values (Borgmann, 2003), but also to those who deploy theological language to justify technologically driven human evolution. Yet the ways in which religion is evoked to support this project are also problematic, as critical dialogue between some of these tendencies and Christian theological anthropology will indicate.

Narratives of transcendence, disembodiment and mastery, masquerading as eternal, enduring, universal 'religious' instincts, are elevated as exemplary ideals. Hence my reference earlier to the aspirations of transhumanism as a form of 'realized eschatology', despite the movement's antipathy to religion. In assuming that the end of humanity (as in its ultimate destiny) is to become like God, or the gods, however, an apparently secular doctrine of humanity continues to draw on a traditional theological motif: that of the *imago Dei*. Humans must seek to overcome those elements of their nature that are not Divine (mortality, embodiment, contingency) in order to aspire to the true marks of Divinity. Yet in fact this implicit religious vision bears little relation to many of the conceptions of the *imago Dei* that Christian theology has traditionally developed.

While there are many strands to the Christian notion of humanity made in the image or likeness of God,[1] it is perhaps in relation to God as creator that alternative themes in relation to human *techne* and technological endeavour might be made: values which do not deny the significance of human inventiveness, but which locate the *telos* of any such activity in a very different set of Divine – and therefore human – attributes.

It is certainly important to see *techne* as spiritually and theologically worthwhile, and to affirm that a quintessential aspect of our very humanity is realized in and through our relationships with our tools and technologies. Technologies may be regarded as tools by which our capacity to create is brought to fruition, a way of resolving problems, of extending human capabilities and meeting needs (Hefner, 2003: 43); yet technologies are not merely means to the ends of faster communication, greater crop yields or secure dwellings: they are objects of beauty as well as utility, artefacts and creations in their own right. They are thus both the vehicles and the expressions of human creativity, an integral part of our very human nature; or in the words of Philip Hefner, a necessary means

---

1 Such as, for example, thinking of humanity as possessing certain qualities or capabilities (such as creativity or rationality), as essentially relational beings (after Trinitarian understandings), or as called to particular responsibilities and activities (such as stewardship), all of which are human expressions of Divine nature. See Herzfeld, 2002.

of 'human becoming' (ibid.). In that respect, human beings may be said to be enacting the image or likeness of God when engaging in technological innovation, and the possibility of human evolution continuing through technologies is not to be rejected.

For example, Philip Hefner has recently begun to explore a thesis that locates as one of the key hallmarks of human nature the facility to create and inhabit metaphysical as well as material worlds: a capacity for 'self-transcendence' via 'worlds' of the imagination similar to the capacity to build worlds that extend physical potential by extending our bodily faculties or creating devices for storage or containment (ibid.). So, too, at a more abstract level, through language, story, myth and visual art humans can imagine alternative worlds that do not exist in a strictly scientific sense. And material technologies are, of course, the media through which such worlds can be conjured and communicated. This means we can talk about ourselves as builders of 'worlds' of the imagination as well as worlds of material technologies, and that through the interplay between the two we ascribe meaning and value to our material fabrication, as well as being able to realize our abstract dreams and aspirations in more concrete forms.

So on the one hand, it is important to see technologies not simply as mere instruments of doing and making, but as vehicles of human development and self-realization. This is, after all, what the post/human is pointing to, in terms of human beings themselves becoming the objects of their own self-design, or biological life being modified and engineered in ways that 'transcend' or surpass the workings of unassisted nature. Some further qualifications may therefore be necessary in relation to the potential and limits of human creativity.

One approach within Christian theology would be to affirm human inventiveness while arguing that it is akin to Divine creativity only by analogy. Humans are not capable of creating the universe *ex nihilo*, even though they may be capable of creating life by biological and technological means. This image of humanity as 'created co-creators' (Hefner, 2003: 260) expresses it well, not least because it encapsulates a theological anthropology of likeness and affinity to Divine activity, yet limits any notion of humanity's complete or literal equivalence to God. Humanity is both creator and creature, affirming yet also limiting claims to the autonomy of human self-design. It suggests that the final ends of creation cannot be subsumed either to technological imperatives or contingent human ambitions (Scott, 2003).

Thus, *imago Dei* cannot be used to justify narratives of the ascent of superhuman beings to become omniscient, omnipotent immortal demigods. This kind of rhetoric actually rests upon an unexamined identification of 'religion' with a flight from contingency and materiality, and a spirituality that seeks fulfilment in union with a 'transcendent' deity entirely removed from the immanence of this mortal world. This is both a misrepresentation of what 'image' and 'likeness' indicate, as well as a distortion of the very concept of 'transcendence' in relation to the nature of God and its equation of aspirations towards 'becoming Divine' with attainment of absolute power. A Christian theological anthropology, by contrast, sees things differently, not least in its eschewal of a symbolic of transcendence premised on omnipotence, individualism and immortality. Rather than regarding the immanent, embodied, material world as an impediment to genuine spirituality, or – reminiscent of Gnostic world-views – as the profane, flawed, pale reflection of the authentic Divine world – this vision sees it as the very realm of Divine-human encounter. 'Whatever it is, salvation will be an affirmation of the essential finitude of human nature, not an escape from it' (Kelsey, 1998: 144).

Thus, the *imago Dei* in theological anthropology is an expression of the potential of human beings to grow into likeness of God in Christ, and of Christ as the model for the perfection of humanity. Yet to aspire to *imago Dei*, to see human fulfilment in the image of God as revealed in Christ, properly leads to humility rather than self-aggrandizement. To 'become Divine' in Christian terms is to follow a pattern of Divine *kenosis* in Christ, an acknowledgement of the unconditional, parental love of the creator, and a commitment to absolute trust in the values of the Kingdom and not of those of earthly powers. Again, this is not to argue for a rejection of technologies per se, but to recognize that if they are to be fully a part of human ends then they are necessarily complicit in activities that build worlds of moral value as well as those of material objects – worlds that take account of human existence in wider contexts of responsibility and mutuality with one another, with animals, the environment and other living organisms. This is in part because if humans are *created* beings, then they share that status with the rest of non-human nature; but an acknowledgement of such a common affinity grounded in creatureliness is inconsistent with human engagement with nature, non-human animals and technologies based on principles of mastery, control and appropriation.

Similarly, it is not necessarily fatalism or passive resignation to admit the finitude of creation or human links to nature and responsibility. This is where cyborg anthropology differentiates itself from transhumanism. The recognition of the hybridity of humanity in an age of technology, and the interdependence of nature, humanity and technology, come from a sense that we can evade neither our biological origins nor our technological ambitions. Rather, an ethical responsibility begins with that very ambivalence and complicity, whereas, as I have argued, transhumanism seeks to escape all limits of scarcity, the consequences of human actions on non-human nature and questions of access and distribution.

In that respect, there is nothing to prevent Christian anthropology from speaking, as does transhumanism, of the capacity of humanity for perfection. The difference lies, however, in the source of the benchmark for our ideals of human potential and human dignity. Whereas the latter speaks of that as limited only by the boundaries of human imagination or capability, the former roots its ideal of human potential and growth in *imitatio Christi*. Transhumanism tends to identify perfection with physical and intellectual functioning: freedom from vulnerability, even mortality; but theological anthropology stresses wisdom, compassion and self-emptying.

In fact, Antje Jackelén suggests that a significant dimension of Christian anthropology as *imago Dei* should be that of *imperfection*, a trait not normally associated with God as timeless, omnipotent and transcendent. Such an interpretation may appear incongruous; yet Jackelén is arguing from an eschatological perspective rather than seeking to allude to some Gnostic notion of a flawed demiurge. The focus on an eschatological dimension to creation and to human history thus offers a reminder – suggestive of much contemporary work in science and religion – that creation may occur through 'irregularity, instability, disturbance, and sudden inflation' (Jackelén, 2002: 299). Importantly, such an eschatological understanding of creation places human agency within a wider perspective: just as creation itself began with Divine invocation, so its ultimate fulfilment and end rests in Divine gift rather than human choice. This also offers an antidote to models of the dispassionate watchmaker God, suggesting instead a Divine creator who continues to be involved in the unfolding of creation which is still in the process of completion. Such a way of talking about God places limits on claims to the autonomy of human self-design and suggests that the final ends of creation cannot be subsumed either to technological imperatives or contingent human ambitions.

There are other respects in which humanity in the image of God might offer normative criteria in the area of human dignity. If human identity is rooted in Divine likeness, then in some respects it evades absolute categorization. Just as God is mystery, so too an element of the ineffable remains about human nature. Such an understanding could serve as a regulative ideal against some tendencies to adopt reductionist accounts of what it means to be human.

For example, many critics of post/human technologies have argued that developments in biotechnology have opened the way to a range of therapeutic techniques which radically threaten the autonomy or self-determination of the individual. This lies behind much of the opposition to the genetic diagnosis and selection of human embryos prior to implantation, for example, in cases where parents could adjudicate the fate of a pre-implanted embryo conceived by IVF on the basis of its providing a match for a terminally ill sibling. The concern is whether such a child has been brought into the world for its own sake, or as a means to an end. At the root of this lies the dignity of being permitted to be the author of one's own destiny in fellowship with God. However benign the motive, it is an abuse of another's inherent autonomy to choose his or her constitution, as might parents seeking genetic enhancement or selection for their offspring. To be the product of such interventions would be to be treated as less than human: an object of another's ambition and design, rather than the subject of one's own life-story. The manipulation of another's genome effectively renders them an object, displacing them into 'the realm of artifacts and their production' (Habermas, 2003: 12) rather than ascribing them value simply by virtue of their status as human beings.

In sum, concerns about the eugenic implications of genetic screening or genetic modification are founded on the risks of the commodification or instrumentalization of human life; a loss of choice and autonomy for an individual which represents a fundamental dehumanization. In other ways, too, critics of much of the rhetoric of the Human Genome Project have argued that it fuels fantasies of capturing the essence of humanity in a bioinformatic database: a kind of genetic reductionism (Hubbard and Wald, 1997). Similarly, critics speak of the 'geneticization' of human nature, in which all aspects of human experience are seen to be governed by genetic factors to the exclusion of social, environmental or behavioural influences: a kind of genetic determinism (Peters, 1997: 161). To speak of humanity created by God, in the image of God, thus provides an alternative horizon by which human value is located as transcending human utility or objectification and restored to a deeper irreducibility.

Such talk of humanity as in some degree self-constituting via its own technologies, of being capable of influencing the course of its own development is to fall prey to what we might term 'hyper-humanism': a distortion of modernity's faith in the benevolence of human reason, producing the hubristic belief that humanity alone is in control of history. According to this model of technology and human becoming, humanity comes to consider itself the supreme source of value without reference either to its common origins in nature, or of its relationship to a horizon of otherness – such as a Divine creator. The notion that humanity can seek redemption via technocratic means alone – whether this would be via genetic modification, cybernetic or prosthetic enhancement, even social engineering – represents the ultimate in the elevation of human perfection as the apotheosis of our technological, moral or political endeavours. Hyper-humanism may even be regarded, theologically speaking, as an attempt to elevate humanity to the status of gods by confusing human artefacts with Divine creation.

Technology is to be done as a form of service to our fellow human beings and to natural creation. This means that we are to develop technology in such a way that the blessings, riches, and potential God has put in creation are allowed to flower ... Second, our technological activity should reflect love for God and neighbor by expanding, not constricting, the opportunities for men and women to be the loving, joyful beings God intends them to be. Our technological activity should increase opportunities for us to freely choose and act, [and] thereby contribute to society. (Monsma, 1986: 8–9)

A *sacramental* understanding also emerges from strong doctrines of the materiality of creation. It offers intriguing new directions for thinking about humanity's relationships with its tools and technologies. Traditionally, sacraments have been understood as 'the outward and tangible expressions of inward grace'; but not in the sense that they resemble mere visible vessels for invisible, Platonic realities. Just as we may need to rethink the language of 'transcendence' and 'immanence' in order to move away from spatial or physical referents, towards understandings of contingency, finitude and ultimate being, so too the language of 'inward' and 'outward' may need some rethinking. Rowan Williams has said that sacraments are all about 'making humans holy' (Williams, 2000: 197); and if we are to begin to understand the Divine dimensions of human creativity, then it will not be by withdrawing from the fruits of our labours into nostalgic evocation of a world gone by; but neither can it be simply an uncritical baptism of technocratic solutions. I would suggest, rather, that a sacramental understanding both of human creativity and of technologies enables us, on one level, to affirm the goodness of human agency. Sacraments have the potential to sanctify the human capacities for tool-making and world-building by identifying cultures and artefacts, and not simply 'natural' processes or phenomena, as potential epiphanies of the sacred. In their 'outward' form, technologies are objects of utility and function; but insofar as they also point us to human creativity as resting in the nature of God, their 'inwardness' points away from their immediate significance and utility to the need to locate their proper use in activities of right relationship. Once again, therefore, the material and the metaphysical coexist.

To speak of humanity created by God, in God's image, thus provides an alternative horizon by which human value is located as transcending human utility or objectification and restored to a deeper irreducibility. It also propels us towards a theological anthropology which talks of human creatureliness, a dependence on our common origin in Divine purpose rather than self-design.

Conclusion

If 'the posthuman condition is upon us' (Halberstam and Livingston, 1995: vii), then the significance of this goes beyond the impact of specific technologies to embrace deeper questions about the future of humanity itself. In surveying the range of responses to the post/human, we have seen how the cybernetic, biotechnological and digital age is regarded as simultaneously 'endangerment' and 'promise' to human integrity. Yet crucially, this only serves to illuminate implicit philosophies of the relationship between human agency and creativity, and its products: our tools, artefacts and technologies.

I have emphasized how different perspectives on the nature of technologies reflect alternative understandings, and in particular the contrasting visions of 'enslavement or liberation' within their visions of the post/human future (Cooper, 1995: 7–18). I have argued, however, that neither a model that envisages humans as helpless puppets in the face of technological determinism, nor that which regards technologies as mere instruments at the disposal of the liberal humanist ego, are adequate to describe the relationship. We cannot essentialize technologies, either *reifying* them as possessing powers beyond our control, or *deifying* them as the sure means to our future salvation, as if they had been created outside social contexts, political and economic choices, or even independent of human agency. Instead, I have argued for a rather more *reflexive* understanding of technologies (Feenberg, 1991), insofar as they emerge from, and reflect, social, political and economic priorities in terms of design and deployment, and are therefore never culturally, morally or politically neutral. We return instead to the fundamental issue at the heart of critical post/humanism: technologies are not neutral tools or instruments, but shape our very engagement with the world, and potentially our very ontology.

This serves to remind us that important value-judgements lie at the very heart of our engagement with technologies: what kinds of humans we may become, how humanity will use the resources, commodities and artefacts granted to it, questions of access, equity and distribution. These are, ultimately, questions of how we use our creative abilities – abilities to build and inhabit all kinds of worlds, material, virtual and imaginary; but worlds which, nevertheless, can either enhance or diminish the precious commodity of human dignity.

I have argued that the notion of humanity as created in the image of God provides a useful benchmark for thinking about the future of human nature in a technological world. An understanding of *human* creativity as participation in *Divine* creativity affirms the goodness of our inventive abilities: and it is important to celebrate our capacity to be 'builders of worlds', tool-makers and tool-users, and see this as part of what makes us distinctive as a species. Yet to conceive of the 'transcendence' of God does not necessarily imply a flight from the material. Rather, 'transcendence' is that which surpasses and exceeds the material, without denying or suppressing it. It may be more appropriately regarded, perhaps, as the

327

inverse of reductionism, an expression of 'the irreducibility of the divine to human self-interest' (Graham, 2004: 25). As such, it would serve as an important antidote to the narratives of hyper-humanism in which the 'will to power' is used as the rationalization for aggrandizing versions of corporate interest and transhumanist superiority. 'Transcendence' needs therefore to be linked with materialist and incarnational, rather than quasi-Gnostic, doctrines of creation, signalling an understanding of humanity made in the image of God which, far from being granted licence to conquer and subdue, recognizes that human *creativity* is always already framed by human *creatureliness* and interdependence. In turn, this offers a necessary reminder that our technologies are ultimately not our own, that our inventions, like the whole of creation, only make sense when offered up as part of a larger, Divine purpose.[2]

Yet the very hybridity of human being simply compounds the difficulties of making appeals to human dignity on ontological grounds. Human nature is not 'a template untouched by social contingencies and historical becoming' (Scott, 1998: 261); indeed, theological anthropology calls for an incarnational, relational, performative model of human personhood that regards the material world and history as the proper sphere of creation and redemption, and of humans as 'created co-creators'. It also means, I think, that we cannot afford to be afraid of our complicity with technologies, or fear our hybridity, or assume that proper knowledge of and access to God can only come through a withdrawal from these activities of world-building. What it means to be human, what is happening to the material world, are not matters that divert us from the true task of spiritual reflection and Christian living, but their very preconditions.

---

2 See Scott, 2003 for a discussion of how an eschatological understanding of creation also redirects discussion of human *telos* in a technological age, in that creation cannot be brought to fruition by human effort alone, but awaits Divine completion.

EPILOGUE

22

WORDS OF ENCOURAGEMENT FROM ONE PILGRIM TO ANOTHER

For Stephen Lowe on the occasion of his commissioning as Bishop for Urban Life and Faith, Manchester Cathedral, 12 November 2007

Who are we, who call ourselves pilgrims on the journey of life and faith?
Maybe your journey began with a call: a call to faith, to turn away from the old path and choose a new way. Maybe you have always been on this journey, the path rising ahead of you, the route map vivid and clear. But for others, the road twists and turns, encountering unknown dangers and difficult obstacles.

Look around you:
Remember that others have taken this path before you. See those ahead, who have come this way in generations past. Consult the Scriptures: and remember, with the writer of the letter to the Hebrews, that we are part of a long and illustrious procession of faith led by our forebears. Or fix your eyes instead on the communion of saints, going before us, calling us to follow in their footsteps. Even so, each generation starts from its own place of departure, and must make its own way to the heavenly city. On the journey, like all pilgrims, we share our burdens and tell our stories. Such words of encouragement are a vital part of the path we take. You are not alone on the journey of life and faith.

Does your pilgrimage take you through pleasant fields, quiet suburbs and restful parks? Or do you find yourself in the midst of the city, with all its noise, confusion and turmoil: caught up in the rat race of the business quarter; stranded in the waiting room at the hospital, the asylum, the detention centre? Can you afford to ride business class; or are you required to take public transport, where the sights, sounds and smells of your fellow passengers are inescapable?

Look around you:
In the faces of your travelling companions, you will see a wisdom and strength born of suffering. And in the face of the Other, you glimpse the irreducible dignity of the person who bears the stamp of divinity. In the stories of dislocation and exile, you hear the refrain of the human spirit unquenched. And in the faces of those who have known and endured the hard road, you will see the flame of life that is stronger than death.

Look around you:
In the energy of human beings fully alive, in the wonders of the city, are mirrored all the glories of creation. You are not alone on the journey of life and faith; and sometimes, you may feel the guiding hand of the living God at your elbow.

Maybe your journey has been one that has taken you from despair to hope; from dispossession to empowerment; from decline to regeneration. You have spoken truth to power; you have overturned huge majorities; you have told stories of famous victories over profiteering and exploitation.

Look around you:
In the faces of your fellow travellers you see the passion of the prophets, and those who find true worship in the making of right relations. In the restlessness of those who never break their journey, you see the ones whose vision of the heavenly city yet to come leads them unceasingly onward.

Where do you stop to worship along the way? Perhaps you prefer the roadside shrine, the little local gods of the hedgerow – or the manicured, sanitized, wide-open spaces of the exclusive country club. Maybe you come to visit the monuments to the property-developers, to marvel at the gated communities, to be a spectator at the lives of the rich and famous. Or perhaps, as you pass the temple, you see the iconoclasts overturning the gaming tables of those who bring their casinos on to sacred ground. And you ask if true peace can possibly be found among all these false gods?

Look around you:
Amid the outward signs of regeneration you glimpse a hunger for the deeper things: justice, sustainability, well-being, and the things of the spirit. And see, in that passion for justice, the One whose love knows no limits, who offers us unconditional grace, who brings new life out of death, and who challenges us to take the risk of asking, what makes a good city?

But now, pause for a moment on your journey and sit for a while at the heart of the city. There, in the public squares, the streets and the marketplaces, look around you. You will see pilgrims arriving from four corners of the earth. All creeds and colours are congregating; and in their happy chatter, you will hear their stories of hazards shared and overcome; you will hear prayers of thanksgiving for safe arrival; you will hear greetings to friends, old and new.

Look around you:

As you stop to break bread, share your food with your companions, and remember how the risen Christ appeared to pilgrims in need of rest and refuge. Take the hospitality offered you by those who have been waiting for your arrival – who were preparing a welcome even before you set out. And you will know that here, for a short time, the Kingdom of Heaven is at hand. And you will know that you are not alone.

BIBLIOGRAPHY

ACAGUPA (Archbishop of Canterbury's Advisory Group on Urban Priority Areas), 1990, *Living Faith in the City*, London: Church House Publishing.

Ackermann, Denise, 1998, 'A Voice was Heard in Ramah': A feminist theology of praxis for healing in South Africa, in D. Ackermann and R. Bons-Storm, eds, *Liberating Faith Practices: Feminist Practical Theologies in Context*, Leuven. Peeters, pp. 75–102.

Ackermann, Denise and Riet Bons-Storm, eds, 1998, *Liberating Faith Practices: Feminist Practical Theologies in Context*, Leuven: Peeters.

ACUPA (Archbishop's Commission on Urban Priority Areas), 1985, *Faith in the City*, London: Church Information Office.

Addy, Hazel, 1993, Suffering in Silence, in E. L. Graham and M. Halsey, eds, *Life-Cycles: Women and Pastoral Care*, London: SPCK, pp. 80–90.

Aichele, George, 2005, Artificial Bodies: *Blade Runner* and the Death of Man, in E. C. Christiansen, P. Francis and W. R. Telford, eds, *Cinéma Divinité: Religion, Theology and the Bible in Film*, London: SCM Press, pp. 137–48.

Akass, K. and J. McCabe, eds, 2005, *Reading Six Feet Under: TV to Die for*, London: I. B. Tauris.

Alexander, V., 1996, 'A Mouse in a Jungle': the Black Christian Women's Experience in the Church and Society in Britain, in D. J. Macauley, ed., *Reconstructing Womanhood, Reconstructing Feminism*, London: Routledge, pp. 85–108.

Alliaume, K. T., 1998, The Risks of Repeating Ourselves, Reading Feminist/Womanist Figures of Jesus, *Cross Currents: The Journal of the Association for Religion and Intellectual Life*, 48(2), 198–217.

Allison, M., ed., 1990, *Christianity and Conservatism*, London: Hodder & Stoughton.

Alternative Service Book, 1980, Oxford: Mowbray.

Althaus-Reid, Marcella, 2001, Review of C. Rowland, ed., *Cambridge Companion to Liberation Theology*, *Political Theology* 4, 119–21.

Alvarez, S. E., 1990, Women's Participation in the Brazilian 'People's Church': a Critical Appraisal, *Feminist Studies* 16(2), 381–408.

Archer, J. and B. B. Lloyd, 1982, *Sex and Gender*, Harmondsworth, Middlesex: Pelican.

Arnold, M., 2006 [1869], *Culture and Anarchy*, edited by J. Garnett, Oxford: Oxford University Press.

Astley, Jeff, 2002, *Ordinary Theology: Looking Listening and Learning in Theology,* London: Ashgate.

Atherton, John R., 2000, *Public Theology for Changing Times,* London: SPCK.

Atzori, P, and Woolford, K., 1995, Extended-Body: Interview with Stelarc, *Ctheory,* [online], 6 Sep. Available at http://www.ctheory.com/a29extended_body.html [Accessed 14 July 1999].

Badmington, Neil, ed., 2000, *Posthumanism: Readers in Cultural Criticism,* London, Routledge.

Badmington, Neil, 2003, Theorizing Posthumanism, *Cultural Critique* 53.

Badmington, Neil, 2004, Post Oblique, Human, *Theology and Sexuality,* 10(2), 56–64

Baker, R., 1996, *Sperm Wars: Sexual Conflict and Bedroom Battles,* London: Fourth Estate.

Barker, F., P. Hulme and M. Iversen, eds, 1992, *Postmodernism and the Re-reading of Modernity,* Manchester: Manchester University Press.

Barnes, M., A. Knops, J. Newman and H. Sullivan, 2001, Participation and Exclusion: Problems of Theory and Method [online]. Economic and Social Research Council, Democracy and Participation Programme. Available at http://www.shef.ac.uk/~pol/ Projects/proj1wp1.htm [Accessed 31 July 2001].

Baudrillard, Jean, 1983, *Simulations,* New York: Semiotext(e).

Baudrillard, Jean, 1995, *Le crime parfait: collection l'espace critique,* Paris: Galilee,

Baugh, L., 1997, *Imaging the Divine: Jesus and Christ-Figures in Film,* Kansas City: Sheed & Ward.

Baum, Gregory, 1987, *Theology and Society,* New York: Paulist Press.

Bauman, Zigmunt, 1989, *Modernity and the Holocaust,* Cambridge: Polity Press.

Bauman, Zigmunt, 1994, *Alone Again: Ethics after Certainty,* London: Demos.

Bayertz, K. 2003, Human nature: how normative might it be? *Journal of Medicine and Philosophy* 28(2), 131–50.

Baynes K., J. Bohman and T. McCarthy, eds, 1987, *After Philosophy: End or Transformation?* Massachusetts: Massachusetts Institute of Technology.

BBC (British Broadcasting Corporation), 2006, The Manchester Passion [online]. 13 April. Available at http://www.bbc.co.uk/manchester/content/articles/2006/04/ 10/140406_manchester_passion_event_feature.shtml [Accessed 5 July 2006].

Beaudoin, Tom, 1998, *Virtual Faith: The Irreverent Spiritual Quest of Generation X,* San Francisco: Jossey-Bass.

Becker, G. K., 1996, Biotechnology: The new ethical frontier, in G. K. Becker, ed., *Changing Course: The Ethical Challenge of Biotechnology,* Hong Kong: Hong Kong University Press, pp. 1–14.

Beckford, James A., 1992, Religion, Modernity and Post-modernity, in B. Wilson, ed., *Religion: Contemporary Issues: The All Souls Seminar in the Sociology of Religion,* London: Bellew, pp. 11–23.

Beckford, Robert, 1998, *Jesus is Dread: Black Theology and Black Culture in Britain,* London: Darton, Longman & Todd.

Beckford, Robert, 2005, *Jesus Dub: Faith, Culture and Social Change,* London: Routledge.

Bedford-Strohm, Heinrich, 2007, Nurturing reason: the public role of religion in the liberal state, *Ned Geref Teologiese Tydskrif* 48(1–2), 25–41.

Begbie, Jeremy, 2002, *Sounding the Depths: Theology Through the Arts,* London: SCM Press.

Benhabib, Seyla, 1992, *Situating the Self: Gender, Community and Postmodernism in Contemporary Ethics*, Cambridge: Polity Press.

Benjamin, Walter, 1974, On the concept of history, in Benjamin, W. *Gesammelten Schriften* 1, Frankfurt am Main: Surkamp Verlag.

Bentley, T., 2000, *It's Democracy, Stupid: An Agenda for Self-government*, London: Demos.

Bernstein, Richard J., 1985, *Habermas and Modernity*, Massachusetts: Massachusetts Institute of Technology.

Berry, Pippa and Andrew Wernick, 1992, *Shadow of Spirit: Postmodernism and Religion*, London: Routledge.

Bhaskar, R., 1989, *Reclaiming Reality: A Critical Introduction to Contemporary Philosophy*, London: Verso.

Birke, Linda, 1982, Cleaving the mind: speculations on conceptual dichotomies, in The Dialectics of Biology Group, *Against Biological Determinism*, London: Allison & Busby, pp. 60–78.

Boff, Leonardo, 1988, What are Third World Theologies? *Concilium* 1988(5), 3–14.

Boff, Leonardo and Clodovis Boff, 1986, *Introducing Liberation Theology*, London: Burns & Oates.

Bons-Storm, Riet, 1996, *The Incredible Woman: Listening to Women's Silences in Pastoral Care and Counseling*, Nashville: Abingdon.

Bons-Storm, Riet, 1998, Putting the Little Ones into the Dialogue, A feminist practical theology, in D. Ackermann and R. Bons-Storm, eds, *Liberating Faith Practices*, Leuven: Peeters, pp. 9–26.

Borgmann, Albert, 1984, *Technology and the Character of Everyday Life*, Chicago: University of Chicago Press.

Borgmann, Albert, 2003, *Power Failure: Christianity in the Culture of Technology*, Grand Rapids, MI: Brazos.

Borrowdale, Ann, 1989, *A Woman's Work: Changing Christian Attitudes*, London: SPCK.

Bostrom, Nick, 2003, The transhumanist FAQ: a general introduction, version 2.1 [online]. Available at: http://transhumanism.org/index.php/WTA/faq/ [Accessed 9 April 2005].

Bourdieu, Pierre, 1990, *The Logic of Practice*, Cambridge: Polity Press.

Brackenbury, M. C., 1964, *Women and Religion*, Boston: Beacon Press.

Bradley, H., 1989, *Men's Work, Women's Work*, Cambridge: Polity Press.

Bradley, I., 2004, *You've Got to Have a Dream: The Message of the Musical*, London: SCM Press.

Braidotti, R., 1989, The Politics of Ontological Difference, in T. Brennan, ed. *Between Feminism and Psychoanalysis,* London: Routledge, pp. 89–105.

Braidotti, Rosi, 1991, *Patterns of Dissonance*, Cambridge: Polity Press.

Braidotti, Rosi, 1994a, *Nomadic Subjects: Embodiment and Sexual Difference in Contemporary Feminist Thought*, New York: Columbia University Press.

Braidotti, Rosi, 1994b, What's wrong with gender?, in F. van Dijk Hemmes and A. Brenner, eds, *Reflections on Theology and Gender*, Kampen, Netherlands: Kok Pharos, pp. 49–70.

Branigan, T., 2004, Tale of rape at the temple sparks riots at the theatre, *Guardian*, 20 December [online]. Available at: http://arts.guardian.co.uk/print/o,,5089359-110427,oo.html [Accessed 16/12/06].

Brasher, Brenda, 2001, *Give Me That Online Religion*, San Francisco: Jossey-Bass.

Braun, B., 2004, Querying posthumanisms, *Geoforum* 35, 269–72.

Brennan, J. H., 1967, Pastoral theology, in W. J. McDonald *et al.*, *New Catholic Encyclopedia*, New York: McGraw-Hill, pp. 1080–4.

Brewin, Kester, 2004, *The Complex Christ: Signs of Emergence in the Urban Church*, London: SPCK.

Brock, Rita Nagashima and Susan Brooks Thistlethwaite, 1996, *Casting Stones: Prostitution and Liberation in Asia and the United States*, Minneapolis: Fortress Press.

Brown, Malcolm, 2001, Plurality and globalization: the challenge of economics to social theology, *Political Theology* 4, 102–16.

Brown, P. and L. Jordanova, 1982, Oppressive Dichotomies: the Nature/Culture Debate, in E. Whitelegg, ed., *The Changing Experience of Women*, Oxford: Martin Robertson, pp. 389–99.

Brown, R. A. and Wesson, A. J., 1991, Technology and theology: co-operation or conflict? *Modern Churchman*, new series 22(5), 16–23.

Browning, Don S., 1976, *The Moral Context of Pastoral Care*, Philadelphia: Westminster.

Browning, Don S., 1982, The Estrangement of Pastoral Care from Ethics, *Concilium* 156, No 6, 10–17.

Browning, Don S., 1985, Practical Theology and Political Theology, *Theology Today* 42(1), 15–33.

Browning, Don S., 1991, *A Fundamental Practical Theology: Descriptive and Strategic Proposals*, Minneapolis: Fortress Press.

Browning, Don S. and Francis S. Fiorenza, eds, 1992, *Habermas, Modernity and Public Theology*, New York: Crossroad.

Bryant, Chris, ed., 1993, *Reclaiming the Ground: Christianity and Socialism*, London: Hodder & Stoughton.

Buckley, S., 1994, A short history of the feminist movement in Japan, in J. Gelb, M. Lief, eds, *Women of Japan and Korea: Continuity and Change*, pp. 150–86.

Bukatman, Scott, 1993, *Terminal Identity: The Virtual Subject in Post-modern Science Fiction*, Durham: Duke University Press.

Bunch, C., 1992 [1983], Not by Degrees: Feminist Theory and Education, in Maggie Humm, ed., *Feminisms: A Reader*, Hemel Hempstead: Harvester Wheatsheaf.

Burck, J. R. and R. J. Hunter, 1990, Pastoral Theology, Protestant, in R. J. Hunter, ed., *Dictionary of Pastoral Care and Counseling*, Nashville: Abingdon, pp. 867–72.

Burdick, J., 1993, *Looking for God in Brazil*, Berkeley: University of California Press.

Burkhart, J. E., 1983, Schleiermacher's Vision for Theology, in D. S. Browning, ed., *Practical Theology: The Emerging Field in Theology, Church and World*, San Francisco: Harper & Row, pp. 42–60.

Butler, Judith, 1990, *Gender Trouble: Feminism and the Subversion of Identity*, London: Routledge.

Butler, Judith, 1997, *Excitable Speech*, London: Routledge.

Campbell, Heidi, 2005, *Exploring Religious Community Online*, Bern: Peter Lang.

Campbell, K., 1992, Matters of theory and practice, or: We'll be coming out the harbour, in K. Campbell, ed., *Critical Feminism: Argument in the Disciplines*, Milton Keynes: Open University.

Caplan, A., 2002, Revulsion is Not Enough, *American Journal of Bioethics* 2(3), 57–61.

Carmody, Denise, 1994, *Responses to 101 Questions about Feminism*, London: Geoffrey Chapman.

Carrett, J. and R. King, 1998, Review-Article: Giving 'Birth' to Theory: critical perspectives on Religion and the Body, *Scottish Journal of Religious Studies* 19:1, 123–43.

Carson, D. A., 2005, *Becoming Conversant with the Emerging Church*, Grand Rapids, Michigan: Zondervan.

Cary, S. G. *et al.*, 1955, Speak Truth to Power: A Quaker Search for an Alternative to Violence [online], American Friends Service Committee, Available at http://www.quaker.org/sttp.html [Accessed 19 December 2006].

Casper, M. J., 1995, Fetal Cyborgs and Technomums on the Reproductive Frontier: Which Way to the Carnival?, in C. H. Gray, ed., *The Cyborg Handbook*, London: Routledge, pp. 183–202.

Charter 88, 2000, *Unlocking Democracy*, London: Charter 88.

Chester, M., M. Farrands, D. Finneron and E. Venning, eds, 1999, *Flourishing Communities: Engaging Church Communities with Government in New Deal for Communities*, London: Church Urban Fund.

Chopp, R., 1996, Theological Methodology, in L. M. Russell and S. Clarkson, eds, *Dictionary of Feminist Theologies*, Louisville: Westminster John Knox, 180–2.

Christ, Carol P., 1988, Embodied thinking: reflections on feminist theological method, *Journal of Feminist Studies in Religion* 5(1), 7–15.

Chung, Jae-yeon, 1997, Haunted lives: caring for 'comfort women' in transition, Unpublished paper, International Academy of Practical Theology, Seoul, Korea.

Church Action on Poverty, 1991, *Hearing the Cry of the Poor*, Manchester: Church Action on Poverty.

Church Action on Poverty, 1993, *Local People, National Voice*, Manchester: Church Action on Poverty.

Church of England, 2004, New Commission on Urban Life and Faith Announced [online], 2 February. Available at http://www.cofe.anglican.org/news/new_commission_on_urban_life_and_faith_launched.html [Accessed 3 February 2004].

Church of Scotland, 2001, Church and Nation Committee [online]. Available at http://www.churchofscotland.org.uk/boards/churchnation/churchnation.htm [Accessed 31 July 2001].

Clark, Henry, 1993, *The Church Under Thatcher*, London: SPCK.

Clarke, R. L., 1986, *Pastoral Care of Battered Women*, Philadelphia: Westminster Press.

Clark-King, Ellen, 2005, *Theology By Heart*, London: SCM Press.

Clebsch, W. A. and C. R. Jaekle, 1964, *Pastoral Care in Historical Perspective*, Englewood Cliffs, New Jersey: Prentice Hall.

Clynes, M. E. and Kline, N. S., 1995, Cyborgs and Space, in Gray, C. H., ed., *The Cyborg Handbook*, London: Routledge, pp. 29–30.

Cobb, Kelton, 2005, *The Blackwell Guide to Theology and Popular Culture*, Oxford: Blackwell.

Collins, P. H., 1991, *Black Feminist Thought*, London: Routledge.

Commission on Social Justice, The, 1994, *Social Justice: Strategies for National Renewal*, London: Vintage.

Connell, R. W., 1985, Theorising Gender, *Sociology* 19(2), 260–72.

Connell, R. W., 1987, *Gender and Power: Society, the Person and Sexual Politics*, London: Polity Press.

Conway, R., 1999, *Choices at the Heart of Technology: A Christian Perspective*, Harrisburg, PA: Trinity Press International.

Cooey, Pamela M., 1994, *Religious Imagination and the Body*, Oxford: Oxford University Press.

Cooper, D. E., 1995, Technology: Liberation or Enslavement?, in R. Fellows, ed., *Philosophy and Technology*, Cambridge: Cambridge University Press, pp. 7–18.

Cooper, Niall, 1992, *All Mapped Out? A Critical Evaluation of the Methodist Mission Alongside the Poor Programme*, Manchester: William Temple Foundation.

Coote, A. and B. Campbell, 1982, *Sweet Freedom*, London: Picador.

Cotter, Jim, 1988, *Prayer at Night: A Book for the Darkness*, Sheffield: Cairns Publications.

Couture, Pamela D., 1991, *Blessed are the Poor? Women's Poverty, Family Policy and Practical Theology*, Nashville: Abingdon.

Couture, Pamela D., 1996, Weaving the Web. Pastoral Care in an Individualistic Society, in J. S. Moessner, ed., *Through the Eyes of Women: Insights for Pastoral Care*, Philadelphia: Augsburg Fortress, pp. 94–104.

Couture, Pamela D. and Rodney J. Hunter, eds, 1995, *Pastoral Care and Social Conflict*, Nashville: Abingdon.

Cox, Harvey, 1965, *The Secular City*, London: SCM Press.

Cox, S., 2006, Review of *Faithful Cities* [online], *Fulcrum*. Available at http://www.fulcrum-anglican.org.uk/news/2006/20061015cox.cfm?doc=146 [Accessed 24 October 2006].

Crawford, J. and M. Kinnamon, eds, 1983, *in God's Image: Reflections on Identity, Human Wholeness and the Authority of Scripture*, Geneva: World Council of Churches.

Cray, Graham, ed., 2004, *Mission-Shaped Church*, London: Church House Publishing.

Crews, Frederick C., 1993, The Unknown Freud, *New York Review of Books*, 18 Nov., 55–66.

Crockett, A., and D. Voas, 2006, Generations of Decline: Religious Change in Twentieth-Century Britain, *Journal for the Scientific Study of Religion* 45(4), 567–84.

Crozier Michel, Samuel P. Huntington and Joji Watanuki, 1975, *The Crisis of Democracy*, New York: New York University Press.

Cruz, Eduardo, 2002, The Nature of Being Human, in T. Peters and G. Bennett, eds, *Bridging Science and Religion*, London: SCM Press, pp. 173–84.

CULF (Archbishops' Commission on Urban Life and Faith), 2006, *Faithful Cities: A Call for Celebration, Vision and Justice*, London: Methodist Publishing House.

Curti, E., 2001, God and Government, *The Tablet*, 1 July, 10.

Dale, J. and C. Russell, eds, 1993, Experience encounters faith: action of the Church towards a new social vision, *Christian Action Journal* Spring 1993.

Daly, Mary, 1968, *The Church and the Second Sex*, Boston: Beacon Press.

Davey, Andrew, 2007, Faithful Cities: locating everyday faithfulness, *Contact: The Interdisciplinary Journal of Pastoral Studies* 152, 8–20.

Davidson, A. I., 1986, Archaeology, Genealogy, Ethics, in D. C. Hoy, ed., *Foucault: A Critical Reader*, Oxford: Blackwell, pp. 221–34.

Davie, Grace, 1994, *Religion in Britain Since 1945: Believing without Belonging*, Oxford: Blackwell.

Davis, Charles, 1994, *Religion and the Making of Society*, Cambridge: Cambridge University Press.

Davis, Erik, 1998, *Techgnosis: Myth, Magic and Mysticism in the Age of Information*, London: Serpent's Tail,

Davis, K., 1997, Embodying theory: beyond Modernist and Postmodernist readings of the body, in K. Davis, ed., *Embodied Practices: Feminist Perspectives on the Body*, London: Sage, pp. 1–23.

Davis, K., ed., 1997, *Embodied Practices: Feminist Perspectives on the Body*, London: Sage.

Davis L. K., 1994, Korean women's groups organize for change, in J. Gelb and M. L. Palley, eds, *Women of Japan and Korea: Continuity and Change,* Philadelphia: Temple University Press, pp. 223–39.

Dawson, Rosemary, 1986, 'And all that is unseen': A New Look at Women's Work, London: Church Information Office.

de Beauvoir, Simone, 1949 [1988], *The Second Sex*, translated and edited by H. M. Parshley, London: Picador.

de Beauvoir, Simone, 1987, quoted in M. A. Simons and J. Benjamin, 'Simone de Beauvoir: an Interview', *Feminist Studies* 5, 330–45.

de Haardt, M., E. Maeckelberghe and M. van Dijk, eds, 1998, *Geroepen om te Spreken: Over verbeelding en creativiteit im theologie en pastoraat*, Kampon: Kok Phoros, pp. 100–14.

DeLashmutt, Michael, 2006, The Sexualisation of Popular Culture: Towards a Christian Sexual Aesthetic, *Crucible* July–September, 34–41.

Detweiler, Craig and Barry Taylor, 2003, *A Matrix of Meanings: Finding God in Pop Culture*, Grand Rapids, MN: Baker Academic.

Diprose, Rosalind, 1991, A 'genethics' that makes sense, in R. Diprose and R. Ferrell, eds, *Cartographies: Poststructuralism and the Mapping of Bodies and Spaces*, Sydney: Allen & Unwin, pp. 65–76.

Diprose, Rosalind, 1994, *The Bodies of Women: Ethics, Embodiment and Sexual Difference*, London: Routledge.

Doehring, Carrie, 1992, Developing Models of Feminist Pastoral Counseling, *Journal of Pastoral Care* 46(1), 23–31.

Douglas, Mary, 1966, *Purity and Danger,* London: Routledge & Kegan Paul.

Dowell, Sue and Jane Williams, eds, 1994, *Bread, Wine and Women: The Ordination Debate in the Church of England*, London, Virago.

Doyle, J. and M. Paludi, 1992, *Sex and Gender: The Human Experience,* California: W. Brown and Co.

Dudley, Carl, ed., 1983, *Building Effective Ministry*, San Francisco: Harper & Row.

Duffy, R. A., 1983, *A Roman Catholic Theology of Pastoral Care*, Philadelphia: Fortress Press.

Duffy, R. A., 1990, Roman Catholic Pastoral Care, in R. J. Hunter, ed., *Dictionary of Pastoral Care and Counseling*, Nashville: Abingdon, pp. 1093–5.

Dunne, M. *et al.*, 1993, *Stitched up! Action for Health in Ancoats,* Manchester: Church Action on Poverty.

Durber, Susan and Heather Walton, eds, 1994, *Silence in Heaven: A Book of Women's Preaching,* London: SCM Press.

Edwards, R. B., 1989, *The Case for Women's Ministry*, London: SPCK.

Eisland, Nancy L., 1994, *The Disabled God: Toward a Liberatory Theology of Disability,* Nashville: Abingdon.

Eisland, Nancy L., 1998, Things not seen: Women with physical disabilities, oppression and practical theology, in D. Ackermann and R. Bons-Storm, eds, *Liberating Faith Practices: Feminist Practical Theologies in Context*, Leuven: Peeters, pp. 103–28.

Eliade, M., 1959, *The Sacred and the Profane: The Nature of Religion*, translated by W. R. Trask, London: Harcourt.

Ellul, Jacques, 1965, *The Technological Society*, translated by J. Wilkinson, with an introduction by R. Merton, London: Jonathan Cape.

Englander, D. 1993, Integrated but insecure: a portrait of Anglo-Jewry at the close of the twentieth century, in G. Parsons, ed., *The Growth of Religious Diversity: Britain from 1945*, London: Routledge, pp. 95–131.

Escobar, Arturo, 2001, Welcome to Cyberia, in D. Bell and B. M. Kennedy, eds, *The Cybercultures Reader*, London: Routledge, pp. 56–76.

Evans, J., 1995, *Feminist Theory Today: An Introduction to Second-Wave Feminism*, London: Sage.

Fageol, Suzanne, 1991, Celebrating Experience, in St Hilda Community, *Women Included: A Book of Services and Prayers*, London: SPCK.

Farganis, S., 1986, *The Social Reconstruction of the Feminine Character*, Totowa, New Jersey: Rowman & Littlefield.

Farley, Edward, 1983a, *Theologia: The Fragmentation and Unity of Theological Education*, Philadelphia: Fortress Press.

Farley, Edward, 1983b, Theology and Practice Outside the Clerical Paradigm, in D. S. Browning, ed., *Practical Theology: The Emerging Field in Theology, Church, and World*, San Francisco: Harper & Row, pp. 21–41.

Farley, Edward, 1996, *Deep Symbols: Their Postmodern Effacement*, Minneapolis: Fortress Press.

Farley, Margaret S., 1975, New Patterns of Relationship: Beginnings of a Moral Revolution, *Theological Studies* 36, 627–46.

Fausto-Sterling, A., 1985, *Myths of Gender: Biological Theories About Women and Men*, New York: Basic Books.

Feenberg, Andrew, 1991, *Critical Theory of Technology*, Oxford: Oxford University Press.

Field, John, 2003, *Social Capital*, London: Routledge.

Field-Bibb, Jacqueline, 1991, *Women Towards Priesthood: Ministerial Praxis and Feminist Politics*, Cambridge, Cambridge University Press.

Finneron, Doreen, 1990, Church involvement as a development agency in the community, M. Phil Manchester: University of Manchester.

Flax, Jane, 1990, *Thinking Fragments: Psychoanalysis, Feminism, and Postmodernism in the Contemporary West*, Berkeley: University of California Press.

Flax, Jane, 1993, *Disputed Subjects: Essays on Psychoanalysis, Politics and Philosophy*, London: Routledge.

Forrester, Duncan B., 1994, Can Liberation Theology Survive 1989? *Scottish Journal of Theology* 47, 245–53.

Forrester, Duncan B., 1997, *Christian Justice and Public Policy*, Cambridge: Cambridge University Press.

Forrester, Duncan B., 2001, *On Human Worth*, London: SCM Press.

Foucault, Michel, 1970, *The Order of Things*, London: Tavistock.

Foucault, Michel, 1977, *Discipline and Punish: The Birth of the Prison*, translated by A. Sheridan, London: Penguin.

Foucault, Michel, 1980, *Power/Knowledge: Selected Interviews and Other Writings*, edited by C. Gordon, New York: Pantheon Press.

Foucault, Michel, 1991, Nietzsche, Genealogy, History, in P. Rabinow, ed., *The Foucault Reader*, London: Penguin, pp. 76–100.

Frank, Arthur W., 1990, Bringing bodies back in: a decade review, *Theory, Culture and Society* 7, 131–62.

Frank, Arthur W., 1991a, *At the Will of the Body: Reflections on Illness*, Boston: Houghton Mifflin.

Frank, Arthur W., 1991b, For a Sociology of the Body: an Analytical Review, in M. Featherstone, M. Hepworth and B. S. Turner, eds, *The Body: Social Process and Cultural Theory*, London: Sage, pp. 36–102.

Frank, Arthur W., 1995, *The Wounded Storyteller: Body, Illness and Ethics,* Chicago and London: University of Chicago Press.

Freire, Paulo, 1972, *Pedagogy of the Oppressed*, Harmondsworth: Penguin.

frenchification, 2006, Manchester Passion, message 14 (online), 15 April, Available at: http://www.bbc.co.uk/dna/england/F2770282?thread=2090395andphrase=Manchester [Accessed 12 December 2006].

Freud, Sigmund, 1986 [1925], Some psychical consequences of the anatomical distinction between the sexes, in A. Freud, ed., *The Essentials of Psychoanalysis*, translated by J. Strachey, London: Penguin.

Freud, Sigmund, 1971, *The Complete Introductory Lectures on Psychoanalysis*, edited and translated by J. Strachey, London: Allen & Unwin.

Friedan, Betty, 1963, *The Feminine Mystique*, Gollancz.

Fukuyama, Francis, 2002, *Our Posthuman Future: Consequences of the Biotechnology Revolution*, London, Profile Books.

Fulkerson, Mary McLintock, 1994, *Changing the Subject: Women's Discourses and Feminist Theology,* Minneapolis: Fortress Press.

Fulkerson, Mary McLintock, 1996, Changing the Subject, Feminist Theology and Discourse, *Literature and Theology* 10(2), 131–47.

Fuller, R. C., 1986, *Americans and the Unconscious*, Oxford: Oxford University Press.

Furbey, Rob and Marie Macey, 2005, Religion and urban regeneration: a place for faith? *Policy and Politics* 33(1), 95–116.

Furlong, Monica, 1991a, A 'Non-Sexist' Community, in St Hilda Community, *Women Included: A Book of Services and Prayers,* London: SPCK.

Furlong, Monica, 1991b, *A Dangerous Delight: Women and Power in the Church*, London, SPCK.

Gallagher, M. P., 1984, Imagination and Faith, *The Way* 24, 115–23.

Gallagher, M. P., 2003, *Clashing Symbols: An Introduction to Faith and Culture*, 2nd edn, London: Darton, Longman & Todd.

Garma, JoAnn M., 1991, A cry of anguish: the battered woman, in M. Glaz and J. S. Moessner, eds, *Women in Travail and Transition: A New Pastoral Care*, Minneapolis: Fortress Press, pp. 126–45.

Gatens, Moira, 1991, *Feminism and Philosophy*, Cambridge: Polity Press.

Gay, Peter, 1973, *The Enlightenment: An Interpretation, Volume I: The Rise of Modern Paganism*, London: Wildwood House.

Geertz, Clifford, 1973, *The Interpretation of Cultures*, New York: Basic Books.

Gill-Austern, B., 1996, Love understood as self-sacrifice and self-denial: what does it do to women? in J. S. Moessner, ed., *Through the Eyes of Women: Insights for Pastoral Care*, Philadelphia: Augsburg Fortress, pp. 304–21.

Gladden, Washington, 1898, *The Christian Pastor and the Working Church*, Edinburgh, T&T Clark.

Glaz, Maxine and Jeanne Stevenson Moessner, eds, 1991, *Women in Travail and Transition: A New Pastoral Care*, Philadelphia: Fortress Press.

Glendenning, C. and J. Millar, eds, 1992, *Women and Poverty in Britain in the 1990s*, Hemel Hempstead: Harvester Wheatsheaf.

Goggins, Paul, 1990, Standing on the firing line: the launch of the CAP Declaration, in H. Russell, ed., *From Faith to Action*, London: Christian Action Journal, pp. 4–5.

Goodliff, P., 1998, *Care in a Confused Climate: Pastoral Care and Postmodern Culture*, London: Darton, Longman & Todd.

Gormly, Eric, 2003, Evangelizing through Appropriation: Toward a Cultural Theory on the Growth of Contemporary Christian Rock Music, *Journal of Media and Religion* 2(3), 251–65.

Gorringe, Tim, 2002, *A Theology of the Built Environment*, Cambridge: Cambridge University Press.

Gorringe, Tim, 2004, *Furthering Humanity: A Theology of Culture*, London: Ashgate.

Graham, Elaine L., 1989, The Pastoral Needs of Women, *Contact: The Interdisciplinary Journal of Pastoral Studies* 100, 23–5.

Graham, Elaine L., 1990, Pastoral Theology, Feminism and the Future, *Contact* 103, 2–9.

Graham, Elaine L., 1993, The Sexual Politics of Pastoral Care, in E. L. Graham and M. Halsey, eds, *Life-Cycles: Women and Pastoral Care*, London: SPCK, pp. 210–24.

Graham, Elaine L., 1995a, From 'Space' to 'Woman-Space', *Feminist Theology* 9, 11–34.

Graham, Elaine L., 1995b, *Making the Difference: Gender, Personhood and Theology*, London: Mowbray.

Graham, Elaine L., 1996a, Theology in the City: Ten Years after *Faith in the City*, *Bulletin of the John Rylands Research Institute* 78(1), 179–97.

Graham, Elaine L., 1996b, *Transforming Practice: Pastoral Theology in an Age of Uncertainty*, London: Mowbray.

Graham, Elaine L., 1997, Feminist Theology: 'Myth', 'Mystery' or 'Monster'?, in Elizabeth Stanley, ed., *Knowing Feminisms*, London and California: Sage, pp. 109–19.

Graham, Elaine L., 1998, A view from a room: feminist practical theology from academy, kitchen or sanctuary?, in Ackermann, D. and R. Bons-Storm, eds, *Liberating Faith Practices: Feminist Practical Theologies in Context*, Leuven: Peeters, pp. 129–52.

Graham, Elaine L., 2000, Good News for the Socially Excluded? Political Theology and the Politics of New Labour, *Political Theology* 2, 77–100.

Graham, Elaine L., 2002a, *Representations of the Post/Human: Monsters, Aliens and Others in Popular Culture*, Manchester: Manchester University Press.

Graham, Elaine L., 2002b, 'Nietzsche Gets a Modem': Transhumanism and the technological sublime, *Literature and Theology* 16(1), 65–80.

Graham, Elaine L., 2003, Frankensteins and Cyborgs: Visions of the Global Future in an Age of Technology, *Studies in Christian Ethics* 16(1), 29–43.

Graham, Elaine L., 2007, Power, Knowledge and Authority in Public Theology, *International Journal of Public Theology* 1(1), 42–62.

Graham, Elaine L. and M. Halsey, eds, 1993, *Life-Cycles: Women and Pastoral Care*, London: SPCK.

Graham, Elaine, Heather Walton and Frances Ward, 2005, *Theological Reflection: Methods*, London: SCM Press.

Graham, Elaine, Heather Walton and Frances Ward, eds, 2007, *Theological Reflection: Sources*, London: SCM Press.

Graham, Gordon, 1999, *The Internet: A Philosophical Inquiry*, London: Routledge.

Grant, J., 1993, *Fundamental Feminism, Contesting the Core Concepts of Feminist Theory*, London: Routledge.

Gray, C. H. ed., 1995, *The Cyborg Handbook*, London: Routledge.

Greeley, A., 1993, Religion in Britain, Ireland and USA, *British Social Attitudes, 9th Report 1992/3*, Brighton: Gower.

Green, G., 1999, *Imagining God: Theology and the Religious Imagination*, Grand Rapids, MN: Baker Academic,

Greiner, Carl, 1999, The Apostle: A Psychiatric Appraisal [online], *Journal of Religion and Film* 3(2), Available at http://www.unomaha.edu/jrf/greinart2.htm [Accessed 12 December 2006].

Gribbin, M. and J. Gribbin, 1998, *Being Human: Putting People in Evolutionary Perspective*, 2nd edn, London: Phoenix.

Griffis, J. E., 1985, Theology and Pastoral Care, in J. E. Griffis, ed., *Anglican Theology and Pastoral Care*, Wilton, CT.: Morehouse-Barlow.

Grosz, Elizabeth, 1989, *Sexual Subversions: Three French Feminists*, Sydney: George Allen & Unwin.

Grosz, Elizabeth, 1990, A note on essentialism and difference, in S. Gunew, ed., *Feminist Knowledge: Critique and Construct*, London: Routledge, pp. 332–44.

Gutiérrez, Gustavo, 1983, *The Power of the Poor in History*, London: SCM Press.

Gutiérrez, Gustavo, 1988, *A Theology of Liberation*, 2nd edn, Maryknoll, NY: Orbis.

Gutiérrez, Gustavo, 1999, The Task and Content of Liberation Theology, in C. Rowland, ed., *The Cambridge Companion to Liberation Theology*, Cambridge: Cambridge University Press, pp. 19–38.

Habermas, Jürgen, 1971, *Knowledge and Human Interests*, Boston: Beacon Press.

Habermas, Jürgen, 1984, *The Theory of Communicative Action*, Vol. 1, *Rationality and Rationalization*, translated by T. McCarthy, Boston: Beacon Press.

Habermas, Jürgen, 1987, *The Philosophical Discourse of Modernity*, Cambridge: Polity.

Habermas, Jürgen, 1989, *The Theory of Communicative Action*, Vol. 2, *Lifeworld and System: The Critique of Functionalist Reason*, translated by T. McCarthy, Boston: Beacon Press.

Habermas, Jürgen, 2003, *The Future of Human Nature*, Cambridge: Polity Press.

Habgood, John, 1983, *Church and Nation in a Secular Age*, London: Darton, Longman & Todd.

Halberstam, J. and I. Livingston, eds, 1995, *Posthuman Bodies*, Indianapolis: Indiana University Press.

Hall, C. E., 1968, Some contributions of Anton T. Boisen to Understanding Psychiatry and Religion, *Pastoral Psychology*, 40–8.

Hall, M. P. and I. V. Howes, 1965, *The Church in Social Work: A Study of Moral Welfare Work Undertaken by the Church of England*, London: RKP.

Hall, Stuart, 1992, Introduction, in S. Hall and B. Gieben, eds, *Formations of Modernity*, Cambridge: Polity Press, 1–16.

Hall, Stuart and B. Gieben, eds, 1992, *Formations of Modernity*, Cambridge: Polity Press.

Hall, Stuart, D. Held and T. McGrew, eds, 1992, *Modernity and its Futures*, Cambridge: Polity Press.

Halmos, P., 1965, *The Faith of the Counsellors*, London: Constable.

Hampson, Daphne, 1990, *Theology and Feminism*, Oxford: Blackwell.

Hampson, Daphne, ed., 1996, *Swallowing a Fishbone? Feminist Theologians Debate Christianity*, London: SPCK.

Hampson, Daphne and Rosemary Radford Ruether, 1987, Is there a Place for Feminists in a Christian Church? *New Blackfriars*, January, 7–24.

Hanish, C., 1969, The Personal is Political, in S. Firestone and A. Koedt, eds, *Notes from the Second Year*, New York: Radical Feminism.

Hanmer, J. and M. Maynard, eds, 1987, *Women, Violence and Social Control*, London: Macmillan.

Hansard, 2006, Churches and Cities debate [online], House of Lords, 19 May. Available at http://www.publications.parliament.uk/pa/ld200506/ldhansrd/vo060519/text/60519-01.htm#60519-01_heado [Accessed 21 May 2006].

Haraway, Donna, 1991, A Cyborg Manifesto: Science, Technology, and Socialist-Feminism in the Late Twentieth Century, in D. Haraway, *Cyborgs, Simians and Women: The Reinvention of Nature*, London: Free Association Books, pp. 149–82.

Haraway, Donna, 1992a, Ecce Homo, Ain't (Ar'n't) I a Woman, and Inappropriate/d Others: The Human in a Post-Humanist Landscape, in J. W. Scott and J. Butler, eds, *Feminists Theorize the Political*, London: Routledge, pp. 86–100.

Haraway, Donna, 1992b, The Promises of Monsters, in L. Grossberg, C. Nelson and P. Treichler, eds, *Cultural Studies*, New York: Routledge, pp. 295–337.

Haraway, Donna, 1997, *Modest_Witness@Second_Millennium.FemaleMan_Meets_OncoMouse™*, London: Routledge.

Haraway, Donna, 2004, Otherworldly Conversations; Terran Topics; Local Terms, in D. Haraway, ed., *The Haraway Reader,* London: Routledge, pp. 125–50.

Harding, Sandra, 1986, *The Science Question in Feminism*, Milton Keynes: Open University Press.

Harris, Margaret, 2001, Civil society and the role of UK churches: an exploration, Birmingham: University of Aston Business School, unpublished paper.

Haslam, David and Graham Dale, eds, 2001, *Faith in Politics,* London: Christian Socialist Movement.

Hassan, Ihab, 1977, Prometheus as Performer: Toward a Posthumanist Culture? *Georgia Review* 31, 830–50.

Hauerwas, Stanley, 1981, *A Community of Character*, Indiana: University of Notre Dame Press.

Hawkesworth, Mary, 1989, Knowers, Knowing, Known: Feminist Theory and Claims of Truth, *Signs: Journal of Women in Culture and Society* 14(3), 533–57.

Hayes, D. and A. Hudson, 2001, *Basildon: The Mood of the Nation,* London: Demos.

Hayles, N. Katherine, 1999, *How We Became Posthuman: Virtual Bodies in Cybernetics: Literature and Informatics*, Chicago: Chicago University Press.

Hayles, N. Katherine, 2003, The Human in the Posthuman, *Cultural Critique* 53, 134–7.

Hebblethwaite, Margaret, 1993, *Basic Christian Communities: An Introduction,* London: Geoffrey Chapman.

Hefner, Philip, 2003, *Technology and Human Becoming,* Minneapolis: Fortress Press.

Heidegger, Martin, 1976 [1966], 'Only a God Can Save Us Now': An Interview with Martin Heidegger, *Philosophy Today* 20(4), 267–84.

Heidegger, Martin, 1993a [1954], The Question of Technology, in D. F. Krell, ed., *Basic Writings of Martin Heidegger*, London: Routledge, pp. 307–42.

Heidegger, M, 1993b [1971], Building Dwelling Thinking, in D. F. Krell, ed., *Basic Writings of Martin Heidegger*, London: Routledge, pp. 343–64.

Heim, Michael, 1993, *The Metaphysics of Virtual Reality*, Oxford: Oxford University Press.

Hekman, S. J., 1986, *Hermeneutics and the Sociology of Knowledge*, Cambridge: Polity Press.

Hendershot, H., 2004, *Shaking the World for Jesus: Media and Conservative Evangelical Culture*, Chicago: University of Chicago Press.

Hertz, N., 2001, Why we stayed away, *Observer*, 10 June, 15.

Herzfeld, Noreen, 2002, *In Our Image: Artificial Intelligence and the Human Spirit*, Minneapolis: Fortress Press.

Heskins, Jeffrey, 2001, *Unheard Voices*, London: Darton, Longman & Todd.

Hicks, D. A., 2000, *Inequality and Christian Ethics*, Cambridge: Cambridge University Press.

Hiltner, S., 1958, *Preface to Pastoral Theology*, Nashville: Abingdon.

HMSO (Her Majesty's Stationery Office), 1995, *Manchester: 50 Years of Change: Post-War Planning in Manchester*, London: HMSO.

Hodgson, Peter, 1994, *Winds of the Spirit: A Constructive Christian Theology*, London: SCM Press.

Hogan, Linda, 1995, *From Women's Experience to Feminist Theology*, Sheffield: Sheffield Academic Press.

Holifield, E. B., 1983, *A History of Pastoral Care in America: From Salvation to Self-Realization*, Nashville: Abingdon.

hooks, bell, 1982, *Ain't I a Woman: Black Women and Feminism*, London: Pluto Press.

Hoover, Stewart, 2006, *Religion in the Media Age*, London: Routledge.

Hopewell, James, 1987, *Congregation: Stories and Structures*, London: SCM Press.

Howard, K., ed., 1995, *True Stories of the Korean Comfort Women*, London: Cassell.

Hubbard, R., 1990, The Political Nature of 'Human Nature', in D. L. Rhode, ed., *Theoretical Perspectives on Sexual Difference*, New Haven: Yale University Press, pp. 63–73.

Hubbard, Ruth and Elijah Wald, 1997, *Exploding the Gene Myth*, Boston: Beacon Press.

Humm, Maggie, ed., 1992, *Feminisms: A Reader*, Brighton: Harvester Wheatsheaf.

Hunt, I., 2003, Our Responsibility for Future Lives [online], *The Drawing Board: An Australian Review of Public Affairs*, 21 July. Available at http://www.econ.usyd.edu.au/drawingboard/digest/0307/hunt.html [Accessed 16 November 2003].

Hurston, Zora Neale, 1937, *Their Eyes were Watching God*, Philadelphia: Lippincott.

Interrogate the Internet, 1996, Contradictions in Cyberspace: Collective Response, in R. Shields, ed., *Cultures of Internet: Virtual Spaces, Real Histories, Living Bodies*, London: Sage, pp. 126–32.

Irigaray, Luce, 1974, *Speculum of the Other Woman*, translated by G. Gill, Ithaca, NY: Cornell University Press.

Irigaray, Luce, 1985 [1977], *This Sex Which is Not One*, translated by C. Porter, Ithaca, NY: Cornell University Press.

Irigaray, Luce, 1986, The Fecundity of the Caress, in R. A. Cohen, ed., *Face to Face with Levinas*, translated by C. Burke, Albany: SUNY Press, pp. 231–56.

Irigaray, Luce, 1993a, A Personal Note: Equal or Different?, in *Je, Tu, Nous: Toward a Culture of Difference*, translated by A. Martin, London: Routledge, pp. 9–14.

Irigaray, Luce, 1993b [1987], Divine Women, in *Sexes and Genealogies*, translated by G. C. Gill, New York: Columbia University Press, pp. 55–72.

Irigaray, Luce, 1993c, *An Ethics of Sexual Difference*, translated by C. Burke and G. Gill, Ithaca, NY: Cornell University Press.

Irigaray, Luce, 1998, Equal to Whom?, in G. Ward, ed., *The Postmodern God*, Oxford: Blackwell, pp. 198–224.

Jackelén, A., 2002, The Image of God as Techno Sapiens, *Zygon* 37(2), 289–302.

Jaggar, A., 1983, *Feminist Politics and Human Nature,* Totowa, NJ: Rowman & Allenfeld.

James, Eric, 1991, Seven devils and the Church Urban Fund, *Crucible,* March–April, 68–71.

James, P., H. Pennington and D. Burke, 1999, GM Foods served at Doom Temperature, *Times Higher Education Supplement,* 19 February, 26–7.

Jameson, F., 1991, *Postmodernism: Or the Cultural Logic of Late Capitalism,* London: Verso.

Jantzen, Grace M., 1998a, *Becoming Divine,* Manchester: Manchester University Press.

Jantzen, Grace M., 1998b, Necrophilia and Natality, *Scottish Journal of Religious Studies* 19(1): 101–21.

Jantzen, Grace M., 2001, Flourishing: Towards an ethic of natality, *Feminist Theory* 2(2), 219–32.

Jenkins, Rachel, 1989, *Women and Poverty in Salford,* Manchester: William Temple Foundation.

Johnston, R., 2000, *Reel Spirituality: Theology and Film in Dialogue,* Grand Rapids, MN: Baker Academic.

Jones, A.R., 1986, Writing the Body: Toward an Understanding of Ecriture feminine, in E. Showalter, ed., *The New Feminist Criticism,* London: Virago, pp. 361–77.

Joseph, A., ed., 1990, *Through the Devil's Gateway: Women, Religion and Taboo,* London: SPCK.

Justes, Emma J., 1978, Theological Reflections on the Role of Women in Church and Society, *Journal of Pastoral Care* 32, 42–54.

Justes, Emma J., 1985, Women, in R. J. Wicks, R. D. Parsons and D. Capps, eds, *Handbook of Pastoral Counseling,* Mahwah, NJ: Integration/Paulist Press, pp. 279–99.

Justes, Emma J., 1996, Pastoral Care and Older Women's Secrets, in J. S. Moessner, ed., *Through the Eyes of Women,* pp. 240–53.

The Kairos Document: A Theological Comment on the Political Crisis in South Africa, 1985, London: Catholic Institute for International Relations.

Kaku, Michio, 1998, *Visions: How Science Will Revolutionize the Twenty-first Century and Beyond,* Oxford: Oxford University Press.

Kanyoro, M. R. A., ed., 1991, *Our Advent: African Women's Experiences in the Lutheran Tradition,* Geneva: Lutheran World Federation.

Kapor, Mitchell, 1993, Where is the Digital Highway Really Heading? [online] *Wired Magazine* 1.03. Available at http://www.wired.com/wired/archive/1.03/kapor.on.nii_pr.html [Accessed 28 June 2002].

Kaufman-Osborn, T. V., 1997, *Creatures of Prometheus: Gender and the Politics of Technology,* Lanham, MD: Rowman & Littlefield.

Kearney, Richard, 1994, *Modern Movements in European Philosophy: Phenomenology, Critical Theory, Structuralism,* 2nd edn, Manchester: Manchester University Press.

Kelly, L., 1988, *Surviving Sexual Violence,* Cambridge: Polity Press.

Kelsey, D. H., 1998, Human Being, in P. Hodgson and R. King, eds, *Christian Theology: An Introduction to its Traditions and Tasks,* London: SPCK.

Kennedy, Karen, 1993, The Unwritten Journal, in E. L. Graham and M. Halsey, eds, *Life-Cycles: Women and Pastoral Care,* London: SPCK, pp. 10–18.

Kepnes, Steven, 1988, Telling and Retelling: the use of narrative in psychoanalysis and religion, *Concilium* 156, 27–33.

Kinast, Robert L., 1990, Pastoral Theology, Roman Catholic, in R. J. Hunter, ed., *Dictionary of Pastoral Care and Counseling*, Nashville: Abingdon, pp. 873–4.

Kirby, Liz, 1993, Anchor Hold, in E. L. Graham and M. Halsey, eds, *Life-Cycles: Women and Pastoral Care*, London: SPCK, pp. 135–43.

Kirby, Vicky, 1991, Corpus delicti: The body at the scene of writing, in R. Diprose and R. Ferrell, eds, *Cartographies: Poststructuralism and the Mapping of Bodies and Spaces,* Sydney: Allen & Unwin, pp. 88–100.

Kristenson, O., 2005, Doing Theology by Learning from the Poor, in K. Hallencreutz, ed., *Gender, Poverty and Church Involvement: Missio 20,* Uppsala: Swedish Institute of Mission Research, pp. 121–31.

Kristeva, Julia, 1981, Women's Time, *Signs: Journal of Women in Culture and Society* 7(1), 13–35.

Kristeva, Julia, 1984, *Revolution in Poetic Language,* New York: Columbia University Press.

Kroker, Arthur, 1996, Virtual Capitalism, in S. Aronowitz, B. Martinsons and M. Menser, eds, *Technoscience and Cyberculture,* London: Routledge, pp. 167–79.

Krull, Anne, 2002, Speaking Cyborg: Technoculture and Technonature, *Zygon* 37(2), 79–87.

Kurzweil, Ray, 1999, *The Age of Spiritual Machines,* London. Orion.

Lacan, Jacques, 1977, *Ecrits: A Selection,* translated by A. Sheridan, New York: Norton.

Lacey, H. and Y. Kim, 1997, The Emperor's forgotten army, *Independent on Sunday,* 25 May, 40–1.

Lakeland, P., 1997, *Postmodernity: Christian Identity in a Fragmented Age*, Minneapolis: Fortress Press.

Lambourne, R. A., 1983, Counselling for Narcissus or Counselling for Christ?, in M, Wilson, ed., *Explorations in Health and Salvation*, University of Birmingham: Institute for the Study of Worship and Religious Architecture, pp. 135–61.

Latour, Bruno, 1993, *We have Never been Modern,* translated by C. Porter, Cambridge, MA: Harvard University Press.

Latour, Bruno and Steve Woolgar, 1986, *Laboratory Life: the Construction of Scientific Facts,* 2nd edn, Princeton: Princeton University Press.

Leder, Drew, 1990, *The Absent Body,* Chicago: University of Chicago Press.

Leech, Kenneth, 2006, *The Soul and the City: Urban Ministry and Theology 1956–2006,* The Samuel Ferguson Lecture, University of Manchester, 19 October.

Leonard, Graham, 1989, *Let God be God,* London: Darton, Longman & Todd.

Lerner, Gerda, 1986, *The Creation of Patriarchy*, Oxford: Oxford University Press.

Lewin, Ann, 1993, Mothercare, in E. L. Graham and M. Halsey, eds, *Life-Cycles: Women and Pastoral Care*, London: SPCK, pp. 43–58.

Lewis, Philip, 1994, *Islamic Britain: Religion, Politics and Identity among British Muslims*, London: I. B. Tauris.

Lewontin, R. C., S. Rose and L. J. Kamin, eds, 1984, *Not in Our Genes: Biology, Ideology and Human Nature,* New York: Pantheon.

Liturgical Commission, General Synod of the Church of England, 1989, *Making Women Visible,* London: Church House Publishing.

Lloyd, G., 1984, *The Man of Reason: 'Male' and 'Female' in Western Philosophy,* London: Methuen.

Loades, Ann, 1987, *Searching for Lost Coins: Explorations in Christianity and Feminism*, London: SPCK.

Loades, Ann, ed., 1990, *Feminist Theology: A Reader*, London: SPCK.

Long, D. Stephen, 2000, *Divine Economy: Theology and the Market,* London: Routledge.

Lorde, Audre, 1984, *Sister Outsider,* Freedom, California: Crossing Press.

Loughlin, Gerard, 1996, *Telling God's Story: Bible, Church and Narrative Theology,* Cambridge: Cambridge University Press.

Loughlin, Gerard, 2005, Cinéma Divinité: A Theological Introduction, in E. C. Christiansen, P. Francis and W. R. Telford, eds, *Cinéma Divinité: Religion, Theology and the Bible in Film,* London: SCM Press, pp. 1–12.

Löw, R., 1996, Anthropology as the Basis of Bioethics, in G. K, Becker, ed., *Changing Nature's Course: The Ethical Challenge of Biotechnology,* Hong Kong: Hong Kong University Press, pp. 147–58.

Lowe, Stephen, 2000, Should Empowerment be Important to the Urban Church? Manchester: Diocese of Manchester, unpublished paper.

Lyall, David, 1995, *Counselling in the Pastoral and Spiritual Context,* Buckingham: Open University Press.

Lyden, John, 2003, *Film as Religion: Myths, Morals, and Rituals,* New York University Press.

Lynch, Gordon, 2005, *Understanding Theology and Popular Culture,* London: Routledge.

Lyotard, Jean-François, 1984, *The Postmodern Condition: A Report on Knowedge,* translated by G. Bennington and B. Massumi, Manchester: Mancheser University Press.

Lyotard, Jean-François, 1991, *The Inhuman: Reflections on Time,* translated by G. Bennington and R. Bowlby, Oxford: Blackwell.

MacIntyre, A., 1987, *After Virtue: A Study in Moral Theology,* 2nd edn, London: Duckworth.

Mackay, M., 2006, Churches, Charities call on Government to End Poverty in UK by 2020 [online], *Christian Today,* 7 December. Available at http://www.christiantoday.com/articledir/print.htm?id=8643 [Accessed 16 December 2006].

MacKinnon, C., 1989, *Toward a Feminist Theory of the State,* Boston: Harvard University Press.

Maddox, R. L., 1990, The recovery of theology as a proactical discipline, *Theological Studies* 51(4), 650–72.

Maitland, Sara, 1993, *A Map of the New Country: Women and Christianity,* London: Routledge & Kegan Paul.

Manchester Health for All Working Party, 1993, *Health Inequalities and Manchester in the 1990s,* Manchester: Manchester City Council.

Manc-host2, 2006, Manchester Passion, message 1 [online], 27 January. Available at http://www.bbc.co.uk/dna/england/F2770282?thread=2090395&phrase=Manchester [Accessed 12 December 2006].

Markham, Ian, 1994, *Plurality and Christian Ethics,* Cambridge: Cambridge University Press.

Marsh, Clive, 1997, Film and Theologies of Culture, in C. Marsh and G. Ortiz, eds, *Explorations in Theology and Film,* Oxford: Blackwell, 21–34.

Marsh, Clive, 2004, *Cinema and Sentiment: Film's Challenge to Theology,* Milton Keynes: Paternoster.

Martin, Emily, 1987, *The Woman in the Body*, Milton Keynes: Open University.

May, M. A., 1995, *A Body Knows: A Theopoetics of Death and Resurrection*, New York: Continuum.

Maynard, M., 1987, Violence towards women, in D. Richardson and V. Robinson, eds, *Introducing Women's Studies*, Basingstoke: Palgrave Macmillan.

Mazlish, Bruce, 1993, *The Fourth Discontinuity: The Co-Evolution of Humans and Machines*, New Haven: Yale University Press.

McCarthy, B., 2006, A snapshot of poverty [online]. *New Start*, 29 November. Available at http://www.newstartmag.co.uk/povertyhearing.html [Accessed 16 December 2006].

McCarthy, K., 1996, Women's experience as a hermeneutical key to a Christian theology of religions, *Studies in Inter-religious Dialogue* 6(2), 163–73.

McCarthy, Marie, 1990, Vatican II and Pastoral Care, in R. J. Hunter, ed., *Dictionary of Pastoral Care and Counseling*, Nashville: Abingdon, pp. 1298–300.

McCarthy, Marie, 2000, Spirituality in a Postmodern Era, in S. Pattison and J. W. Woodward, eds, *The Blackwell Reader in Pastoral and Practical Theology*, Oxford: Blackwell, pp. 192–206.

McConnell, M. T., 1981, Women's Experiences: Implications for Theology and Pastoral Care, D. Min, Dallas, Texas: Perkins School of Theology.

McEver, M., 1998, The Messianic Figure in Film: Christology beyond the Biblical Epic [online], *Journal of Religion and Film* 2(2). Available at http://www.unomaha.edu/jrf/McEverMessiah.htm [Accessed 5 July 2006].

McEwan, Dorothea, ed., 1991, *Women Experiencing Church: A Documentation of Alienation*, Leominster: Gracewing.

McFadyen, Alastair I., 1990, *The Call to Personhood*, Cambridge: Cambridge University Press.

McFague, Sallie, 1983, *Metaphorical Theology: Models of God in Religious Language*, London, SCM Press.

McFague, Sallie, 1987, *Models of God: Theology for an Ecological Nuclear Age*, London: SCM Press.

McGovern, Arthur, 1989, *Liberation Theology and its Critics*, Maryknoll, NY: Orbis.

McRoberts, O., 2002, 'Worldly' or 'Other-Worldly'? Activism in an Urban Religious District, in M. Dillon, ed., *Handbook of the Sociology of Religion*, Cambridge: Cambridge University Press, pp. 412–22.

Metz, Johannes Baptist, 1969, *Theology of the World*, New York: Seabury.

Metz, Johannes Baptist, 1984, Productive Noncontemporaneity, in J. Habermas, ed., *Observations on 'The Spiritual Situation of the Age'*, Cambridge, MA: MIT Press, pp. 169–77.

Milhaven, Annie L., ed., 1991, *Sermons Seldom Heard: Women Proclaim Their Lives*, New York: Crossroad.

Miller, V., 2004, *Consuming Religion: Christian Faith and Practice in a Consumer Culture*, London: Continuum.

Miller-McLemore, Bonnie, 1991, Women Who Work and Love: Caught between Cultures, in M. Glaz and J. S. Moessner, eds, *Women in Travail and Transition*, Minneapolis: Fortress Press, pp. 63–85.

Miller-McLemore, Bonnie, 1994, *Also a Mother: Work and Family as Theological Dilemma*, Abingdon: Nashville.

Miller-McLemore, Bonnie, 1996, The Living Human Web: Pastoral Theology at the Turn of the Century. In Moessner, Jeanne Stevenson, ed., *Through the Eyes of Women: Insights for Pastoral Care*, Philadelphia: Augsburg Fortress, pp. 9–26.

Miller-McLemore, Bonnie, 1998, The Subject and Practice of Pastoral Theology, in D. Ackermann and R. Bons-Storm, eds, *Liberating Faith Practices: Feminist Practical Theologies in Context*, Leuven: Peeters, pp. 175–98.

Miller-McLemore, Bonnie and Herbert Anderson, 1995, Gender and Pastoral Care, in P. D. Couture and R. J. Hunter, eds, *Pastoral Care and Social Conflict*, Nashville: Abingdon, pp. 99–113.

Mitchell, Jolyon and Sophia Marriage, eds, 2003, *Mediating Religion: Conversations in Media, Religion and Culture*, Edinburgh: T&T Clark.

Moessner, Jeanne Stevenson, ed., 1996, *Through the Eyes of Women: Insights for Pastoral Care*, Philadelphia: Augsburg Fortress Press.

Moltmann, Jürgen, 1984, Theology in Germany Today, in J. Habermas, ed., *Observations on 'The Spiritual Situation of the Age'*, Cambridge, MA: MIT Press, pp. 181–205.

Monsanto Corporation, 1999, *Frankenstein Food? Take Another Look*.

Monsma, S. V., 1986, *Responsible Technology: A Christian Perspective*, Grand Rapids, Michigan: W. B. Eerdmans.

More, Max, 1999, The Extropian Principles: A Transhumanist Declaration, Version 3.0, Extropian Institute.

More, Max, 2003, Principles of Extropy, Version 3.11 [online]. Available at http:// extropy.org/principles.htm [Accessed 9 April 2005].

MORI, 2001, How Britain Voted in 2001 [online]. Available at http://www.mori. com/polls/2001/election.shtml [Accessed 31 July 2001].

Morley, Janet, 1984, 'The Faltering Words of Men' Exclusive Language in the Liturgy, in M. Furlong, ed., *Feminine in the Church*, London: SPCK, pp. 56–70.

Morley, Janet, 1988, *All Desires Known*, London: Movement for the Ordination of Women.

Morton, Nelle, 1985, *The Journey is Home*, Boston: Beacon Press.

Moyser, George, 1985, The Church of England and politics: patterns and trends, in G. Moyser, ed., *Church and Politics Today: Essays on the Role of the Church of England in Contemporary Politics*, Edinburgh, T&T Clark, pp. 1–24.

Mud Flower Collective, The, 1985, *God's Fierce Whimsy: Christian Feminism and Theological Education*, New York: Pilgrim Press.

Muesse, Mark W., 1999, Religious Studies and 'Heaven's Gate': Making the Strange Familiar and the Familiar Strange, in R. T. McCutcheon, ed., *The Insider/Outsider Problem in the Study of Religion*, London: Cassell.

Murphy, N. and J. W. McClendon, 1989, Distinguishing modern and postmodern theologies, *Modern Theology* 5(3), 191–214.

Murray, S. B., 2003, Reimagining Humanity: The Transforming Influence of Augmenting Technologies Upon Doctrines of Humanity, in M. Breen, E. Conway and B. McMillan, eds, *Technology and Transcendence*, Dublin: The Columba Press, 195–216.

Myerson, G., 2001, *Heidegger, Habermas and the Mobile Phone*, London: Icon Books.

Nelson, James B., 1983, *Embodiment: An Approach to Sexuality and Christian Theology*, London: SPCK.

Nelson, James B., 1992a, *The Intimate Connection: Male Sexuality, Masculine Spirituality*, London: SPCK.

Nelson, James B., 1992b, *Body Theology*, Louisville, Kentucky: Westminster John Knox Press.

Neuger, Christie, 1993, A Feminist Perspective on Pastoral Counseling with Women, in R. J. Wicks and R. Parsons, eds, *Clinical Handbook of Pastoral Counseling*, Vol. 2, New York: Paulist Press, pp. 195–209.

Neuger, Christie and James Newton Poling, eds, 1997, *The Care of Men,* Nashville: Abingdon.

Newton, K. and P. Norris, 1999, Confidence in Public Institutions: Faith, Culture or Performance? [online]. Available at http://kshome.harvard.edu/.pnorris.shorenstein. ksg/articles.htm [Accessed 10 August 2001].

Newton, P., D. Brown and C. Clover, 1999, Alarm Over 'Frankenstein Foods', *Daily Telegraph*, 12 February, 1–2.

Nguyen, D. T. and J. Alexander, 1996, The Coming of Cyberspacetime and the End of the Polity, in R. Shields, ed., *Cultures of Internet: Virtual Spaces, Real Histories, Living Bodies,* London: Sage, pp. 99–124.

Nichols, Barbara, 1998, Genetic Testing: The tree of the knowledge of good and evil, in D. Ackermann and R. Bons-Storm, eds, *Liberating Faith Practices: Feminist Practical Theologies in Context*, Leuven: Peeters, pp. 153–74.

Nickell, Jeremy, with Tom Beaudoin and Gordon Lynch, 2006, Meaning, Spirit and Popular Culture: An Interview with Tom Beaudoin, *Crucible*, July–Sept, 17–23.

Niebuhr, H. Richard, 1951, *Christ and Culture,* San Francisco: Harper & Row.

Noble, David F., 1999, *The Religion of Technology: The Divinity of Man and the Spirit of Invention*, 2nd edn, New York: Penguin.

Norris, Pippa, 2001a, Apathetic Landslide: The 2001 British General Election [online]. Available at http://ksghome.harvard.edu/~.pnorris.shorenstein.ksg/acrobat/ BritVote 2001%20Norris.pdf [Accessed 10 August 2001].

Norris, Pippa, 2001b, *Digital Divide: Civic Engagement, Information Poverty, and the Internet Worldwide*, Cambridge: Cambridge University Press.

Nouwen, Henri J. M., 1968, Anton T. Boisen and Theology through Living Human Documents, *Pastoral Psychology*, September, 49–63.

O'Brien, Richard, 1986, Introducing the Report, in *Faith in the Scottish City,* Edinburgh: Centre for Theology and Public Issues.

O'Leary, S., 1996, Cyberspace as sacred space: communicating religion on computer networks, *Journal of the American Academy of Religion* 59(4), 781–808.

Oakley, Ann, 1985 [1972], *Sex, Gender and Society*, London: Gower.

Oddie, William, 1984, *What Will Happen to God?* London: SPCK.

Oden, Thomas C., 1980, Recovering Lost Identity, *Journal of Pastoral Care* 34(1).

Oliver, Gordon, 1991, Counselling, Anarchy and the Kingdom of God, *Lingdale Papers* 16, Oxford: Clinical Theology Association.

Oliver, Simon, 1999, The Eucharist before Nature and Culture, *Modern Theology* 15(3), 331–53.

Ortega, O., ed., 1995, *Women's Visions: Theological Reflection, Celebration, Action,* Geneva: WCC Publications.

Ortner, Susan B., 1974, Is Female to Male as Nature is to Culture?, in M. Z. Rosaldo and L. Lamphere, eds, *Woman, Culture and Society,* Stanford, CA: Stanford University Press, pp. 67–87.

Ostwalt, C., 1998, Religion and Popular Movies [online], *Journal of Religion and Film* 2(3). Available at http://www.unomaha.edu/jrf/popular.htm [Accessed 5 July 2006].

Paden, William B., 1994, *Religious Worlds,* 2nd edn, Boston: Beacon Press.

Palley, M. L., 1994, Feminism in a Confucian society: the women's movement in Korea, in J. Gelb and M. L. Palley, eds, *Women of Japan and Korea: Continuity and Change,* Philadelphia: Temple University Press, pp. 274–96.

Parekh, B., 1981, *Hannah Arendt and the Search for a New Political Philosophy,* London: Macmillan.

Parsons, Susan Frank, 1996, *Feminism and Christian Ethics,* Cambridge: Cambridge University Press.

Pattison, Stephen, 1997, *Pastoral Care and Liberation Theology,* 2nd edn, London: SPCK.

Patton, John, 1993, *Pastoral Care in Context,* Louisville, Kentucky: Westminster John Knox.

Peacock, Alison, 1993, Take My Intellect, and Use, in E. L. Graham and M. Halsey, eds, *Life-Cycles: Women and Pastoral Care,* London: SPCK.

Peck, Jamie and Kevin Ward, eds, 2002, *City of Revolution: Restructuring Manchester,* Manchester: Manchester University Press.

Peperell, R., 1995, *The Posthuman Condition,* Oxford: Intellect.

Percy, Martyn, 2002, *Salt of the Earth: Religious Resilience in a Secular Age,* Sheffield: Sheffield Academic Press.

Peters, Ted, 1997, *Playing God? Genetic Determinism and Human Freedom,* London: Routledge.

Pinch, T. J. and W. E. Bijker, 2003 [1987], The Social Construction of Facts and Artifacts, in R. C. Scharff and V. Dusek, eds, *Philosophy of Technology: The Technological Condition,* Oxford: Blackwell, pp. 221–32.

Pitts, Eve, 1990, Black Womanist Ethic, in P. Grant and R. Patel, eds, *A Time to Speak: Perspectives of Black Christians in Britain,* Birmingham: Community and Race Relations Unit, pp. 29–35.

Plant, Raymond, 1989, Conservative capitalism: theological and moral challenges, in A. Harvey, ed., *Theology in the City,* London: SPCK, pp. 68–97.

Plant, Raymond, 1999, Crosland, Equality and New Labour, in D. Leonard, ed., *Crosland and New Labour,* Basingstoke: Macmillan, pp. 19–34.

Plumwood, Val, 1993, *Feminism and the Mastery of Nature,* London: Routledge.

Plunkett, J., 2005, Springer show not blasphemous, Thompson says, *Guardian,* 7 January.

Poling, James Newton, 1991, *The Abuse of Power: A Theological Problem,* Nashville: Abingdon.

Pope, S. J., 2001, Natural Law and Christian Ethics, in R. Gill, ed., *Cambridge Companion to Christian Ethics,* Cambridge: Cambridge University Press, pp. 77–95.

Poster, M., 1996, Postmodern Virtualities, in G. Robertson *et al.*, eds, *FutureNatural: Nature/Science/Cultural,* London: Routledge, pp. 183–202.

Poster, Mark, 2001, *What's the Matter with the Internet,* Minneapolis, MN: University of Minnesota Press.

Postman, Neil, 1987, *Amusing Ourselves to Death: Public Discourse in an Age of Showbusiness,* London: Methuen.

Postman, Neil, 1993, *The Surrender of Culture to Technology,* London: Vintage.

Prelinger, C. M., 1986, The Female Diaconate in the Anglican Church: What Kind of Ministry of Women?, in G. Malmgreen, ed., *Religion in the Lives of English Women, 1760–1930,* Croom Helm.

Preston, Ronald H., 1991, *Religion and the Ambiguities of Capitalism,* London: SCM Press.

Pringle, D., ed., 1997, *The Ultimate Encyclopedia of Science Fiction,* London: Carlton.

Pryce, Mark, 1996, *Finding a Voice: Men, Women and the Community of the Church,* London: SCM Press.

Pui-lan, Kwok, 2005, *Postcolonial Imagination and Feminist Theology,* London: SCM Press.

Putnam, Robert, 2000, *Bowling Alone: The Collapse and Revival of American Community,* New York: Simon & Schuster.

Qibla Cola, 2003. Available at: http://www.qibla-cola.com/index2.asp [Accessed 15 September 2008].

Rahner, Karl, 1968, *Theology of Pastoral Action,* New York: Herder & Herder.

Reader, John, 1997, *Beyond all Reason: The Limits of Post-Modern Theology,* Cardiff: Aureus.

Reddie, Anthony, 2003, *Nobodies to Somebodies: A Practical Theology for Education and Liberation,* London: Epworth.

Reiss, M. J. and Straughan, R., 1996, *Improving Nature? The Science and Ethics of Genetic Engineering,* Cambridge: Cambridge University Press.

Rheingold, Howard, 1991, *Virtual Reality,* London: Seeker and Warburg.

Rich, Adrienne, 1980a, *On Lies, Secrets and Silence: Selected Prose 1966–1978,* London: Virago.

Rich, Adrienne, 1980b, Compulsory heterosexuality and lesbian existence, *Signs: Journal of Women in Culture and Society* 5(4), 631–90.

Richardson, Diane, 1993, Sexuality and Male Dominance, in D. Richardson and V. Robinson, eds, *Introducing Women's Studies,* London: Macmillan.

The Road to Damascus: Kairos and Conversion, 1989, London: Catholic Institute for International Relations.

Robins, K., 1995, Cyberspace and the World We Live In, *Body and Society* 1(3–4), 135–55.

Rogers, Carl, 1942, *Counseling and Psychotherapy,* Boston: Houghton Miffin.

Rogers, Carl, 1951, *Client-Centred Therapy,* Boston: Houghton Miffin.

Rogers, Carl, 1961, *On Becoming a Person,* London: Constable.

Rose, G., 1993, *Feminism and Geography: The Limits of Geographical Knowledge,* Cambridge: Polity Press.

Rose, Hilary, 1994, *Love, Power and Knowledge: Towards a Feminist Transformation of the Sciences,* Cambridge: Polity Press.

Ross, Andrew, 1991, *Strange Weather,* Cambridge: Verso.

Rowbotham, Sheila, 1973, *Hidden from History,* London: Pluto Press, 1973.

Rowbotham, Sheila, Lynne Segal and Hilary Wainwright, eds, 1979, *Beyond the Fragments,* London: Merlin Press.

Ruether, Rosemary Radford, 1983, *Sexism and God-Talk,* Boston: Beacon Press.

Ruether, Rosemary Radford, 1985, *Women-Church: Theology and Practice,* San Francisco: Harper & Row.

Ruether, Rosemary Radford, 1993, *Sexism and God-Talk,* 2nd edn, Boston: Beacon Press.

Russell, Letty M., 1995, Reflections on White Feminist Theology in the United States, in O. Ortega, ed., *Women's Visions: Theological Reflection, Celebration, Action,* Geneva: World Council of Churches, pp. 102–11.

Russell, Letty M., Katie G. Cannon, Adela M. Isasi-Díaz and Kwok Pui-lan, eds, 1985, *Inheriting our Mothers' Gardens,* Philadelphia: Westminster.

Russell, R. J. and Wegter-McNally, K., 2002, Natural Law and Divine Action, in

E. Peters and G. Bennett, eds, *Bridging Science and Religion,* London: SCM Press, pp. 49–68.

Ryan, M. A., 1998, Feminist Theologies and the New Genetics, *Concilium* 2, 93–101.

Sacks, Jonathan, 1994, *Will We Have Jewish Grandchildren?,* London: Vallentine Mitchell.

Sacks, Oliver, 1984, *A Leg to Stand On,* London: Duckworth.

Saiving, Valerie, 1979, The Human Situation: A Feminine View, in Carol P. Christ and Judith Plastow, eds, *Womanspirit Rising: A Feminist Reader in Religion,* New York: Harper & Row, pp. 25–42.

Sanctus1, 2002, Who we are [online]. Available at http:www.sanctus1.co.uk/whoweare.php [Accessed 28 November 2005].

Sanday, Peggy R., 1981, *Female Power and Male Dominance: On the Origins of Sexual Inequality,* Cambridge: Cambridge University Press.

Sandercock, Leonie, 2003, *Cosmopolis II: Mongrel Cities in the Twenty-first Century,* London: Continuum.

Scarman Report on the Brixton Disorders, 1981, London: HMSO, cmnd paper 8427.

Scarry, Elaine, 1985, *The Body in Pain: The Making and Unmaking of the World,* New York: Oxford University Press.

Scharff, R. C. and V. Dusek, eds, 2003, *Philosophy of Technology: An Anthology,* Oxford: Blackwell.

Schenck, D., 1986, The Texture of Embodiment: Foundation for Medical Ethics, *Human Studies* 9, 43–54.

Schleiermacher, Freidrich, 1966 [1811], *Brief Outline on the Study of Theology,* translated by T. N. Tice, Richmond, VA: John Knox Press.

Schuster, H., 1967, Pastoral Theology, in K. Rahner *et al.*, eds, *Sacramentum Mundi,* New York: Herder & Herder, pp. 365–8.

Scott, J., 1992, Experience, in J. W. Scott and J. Butler, eds, *Feminists Theorize the Political,* London: Routledge, pp. 22–40.

Scott, Peter M., 1998, Imaging God: Creatureliness and Technology, *New Blackfriars* 75(928), 260–74.

Scott, Peter M., 2003, *A Political Theology of Nature,* Cambridge: Cambridge University Press.

Scott, S. and D. H. J. Morgan, eds, 1993, *Body Matters: Essays on the Sociology of the Body,* London: Falmer Press.

Sedgwick, Peter, 1997, Theology and Society, in D. F. Ford, ed., *The Modern Theologians,* 2nd edn, Oxford: Blackwell, pp. 286–305.

Segal, Lynne, 1987, *Is the Future Female? Troubled Thoughts on Contemporary Feminism,* London: Virago.

Segundo, J. L., 1982, *The Liberation of Theology,* Maryknoll, NY: Orbis.

Selby, Peter, 1983, *Liberating God,* London: SPCK.

Shakespeare, Tom, 1998, Choices and Rights: Eugenics, Genetics and Disability Equality, *Disability and Society* 13(5), 665–81.

Shildrick, M., 1997, *Leaky Bodies and Boundaries: Feminism, Postmodernism and (Bio)Ethics,* London: Routledge.

Shildrick, M. and J. Price, 1996, Breaking the Boundaries of the Broken Body, *Body and Society* 2(4), 93–113.

Shilling, Chris, 1993, *The Body and Social Theory,* London: Sage.

Silver, Lee, 1998, *Remaking Eden: How Genetic Engineering and Cloning will Transform the American Family*, New York: Avon Books.

Simms, A., 1999, *Selling Suicide: Farming, False Promises and Genetic Engineering in Developing Countries*, London: Christian Aid.

Simon, B., 2003, Toward a Critique of Posthuman Futures, *Cultural Critique* 53, 1–9.

Simons, M. A. and J. Benjamin, 1987, Simone de Beauvoir: An Interview, *Feminist Studies* 5, 330–45.

Smith, Greg, 2004, Faith in Community and Communities of Faith? Government Rhetoric and Religious Identity in Urban Britain, *Journal of Contemporary Religion* 19(2), 185–204.

Snyder, R., 1968, The Boisen Heritage in Theological Education, *Pastoral Psychology*, September, 9–14.

Sölle, Dorothee, 1984, Thou Shalt have no Other Jeans before Me, in J. Habermas, ed., *Observations on 'The Spiritual Situation of the Age'*, Cambridge, MA: MIT Press, pp. 157–68.

Sourbut, E., 1996, Gynogenesis: A Lesbian Appropriation of Reproductive Technologies, in N. Lykke and R. Braidotti, eds, *Between Monsters, Goddesses and Cyborgs*, London: Zed Books, pp. 227–41.

St Hilda Community, 1991, *Women Included: A Book of Services and Prayers*, London: SPCK.

Stanko, E., 1985, *Intimate Intrusions*, London: Routledge & Kegan Paul.

Stanworth, Michelle, 1987, *Reproductive Technologies*, Cambridge: Polity Press.

Stock, Gregory, 2002, *Redesigning Humans: Choosing Our Children's Genes*, London: Profile.

Stockton, K. B., 1994, *God Between Their Lips: Desire Between Women in Irigaray, Bronte and Eliot*, Stanford, California: Stanford University Press.

Stokes, Allison, 1985, *Ministry after Freud*, New York: Pilgrim Press.

Stout, Jeffrey, 1988, *Ethics after Babel: the Language of Morals and Their Discontents*, Boston: Beacon Press.

Strachan, E. and G. Strachan, 1985, *Freeing the Feminine*, Dunbar: Labarum.

Strathern, Marilyn, 1980, No Nature, No Culture: The Hagen Case, in C. P. MacCormack and M. Strathern, eds, *Nature, Culture & Gender*, New York: Cambridge University Press.

Strathern, Marilyn, 1987, An Awkward Relationship: the case of feminism and anthropology, *Signs: Journal of Women in Culture and Society* 12(2), 276–92.

Stroup, George, 1984, *The Promise of Narrative Theology*, London: SCM Press.

Stuart, Elizabeth, ed., 1992, *Daring to Speak Love's Name: A Gay and Lesbian Prayer Book*, London: Hamish Hamilton.

Swinton, John and Harriet Mowat, 2006, *Practical Theology and Qualitative Research*, London: SCM Press.

Sykes, Stephen, 2006, *Power and Christian Theology*, London: Continuum.

Tamez, Elsa, 1989, The Power of the Naked, in E. Tamez, ed., *Through her Eyes: Women's Theology from Latin America*, Maryknoll, NY: Orbis.

Telford, William R., 2005, Through a Lens Darkly: Critical Approaches to Theology and Film, in E. C. Christiansen, P. Francis and W. R. Telford, eds, *Cinéma Divinité: Religion, Theology and the Bible in Film*, London: SCM Press, pp. 15–43.

Thistlethwaite, Susan Brooks, 1994, Beyond Theological Tourism, in S. B. Thistlethwaite and G. F. Cairns, eds, *Beyond Theological Tourism: Mentoring as a Grassroots Approach to Theological Education*, Maryknoll, NY: Orbis, pp. 3–15.

Thorne, Brian, 2007, Spiritual intelligence and the person-centred therapist, in J. Baxter, ed., *Wounds that Heal: Theology, Imagination and Health*, London: SPCK, 215–28.

Tong, Rosemarie, 1989, *Feminist Thought: A Comprehensive Introduction*, Sydney: George Allen & Unwin.

Townsend, Peter, 1979, *Poverty in the United Kingdom*, Harmondsworth: Penguin.

Tracy, D., 1981, *The Analogical Imagination: Christian Theology and the Culure of Pluralism*, London: SCM Press.

Treasure, Catherine, 1991, *Walking on Glass: Women Deacons Speak Out*, London, SPCK.

Trible, Phyllis, 1978, *God and the Rhetoric of Sexuality*, New York: Fortress Press.

Turner, Bryan S., 1984, *The Body and Society*, Oxford: Blackwell.

Turney, Jon, 1998, *Frankenstein's Footsteps: Science, Genetics and Popular Culture*, New Haven: Yale University Press.

Vulliamy, E., 2006, Welcome to the new holy land [online], *The Observer*, 17 December. Available at http://observer.guardian.co.uk/print/0,,329664634–102280,00.html [Accessed 17 December 2006].

Wagner, R., 2003, Bewitching the Box Office: Harry Potter and Religious Controversy [online], *Journal of Religion and Film* 7(2). Available at: http://www.unomaha.edu/jrf/Vol7No2/bewitching.htm [Accessed 12 December 2006].

Wajcman, J., 1991, *Feminism Confronts Technology*, Cambridge: Polity Press.

Waldby, C., 2000, *The Visible Human Project: Informatic Bodies and Posthuman Medicine*, London: Routledge.

Walker, Alice, 1984, Looking for Zora, in L. M. Russell, K. G. Cannon, A. M. Isasi-Díaz and Kwok Pui-lan, eds, *In Search of our Mothers' Gardens*, Boston: Beacon Press, pp. 93–116.

Walton, Heather, 1993, Breaking Open the Bible, in E. L. Graham and M. Halsey, eds, *Life-Cycles: Women and Pastoral Care*, London: SPCK, pp. 192–9.

Walton, Heather, 1994, True Vine, in H. Walton and S. Durber, eds, *Silence in Heaven*, London: SCM Press, pp. 169–72.

Walton, Heather and Susan Durber, eds, 1994, *Silence in Heaven: A Book of Women's Preaching*, London: SCM Press.

Ward, Hannah and Jennifer Wild, eds, 1995, *Human Rites: Worship Resources for an Age of Change*, London: Mowbray.

Ward, Hannah, Jennifer Wild and Janet Morley, eds, 1995, *Celebrating Women*, 2nd edn, London: SPCK.

Ward, Graham, ed., 1997, *The Postmodern God*, Oxford: Blackwell.

Ward, Pete, 2002, *Liquid Church*, Milton Keynes: Paternoster.

Warwick, Kevin, 2000, I want to be a Cyborg, *Guardian*, 26 January.

Warwick, Kevin, 2002, *I, Cyborg*, London: Century.

Waters, Brent, 2004, From Imago Dei to Technosapien? The Theological Challenge of Transhumanism, unpublished paper.

Webster, Alison, ed., 1995, *Found Wanting: Women, Christianity and Sexuality*, London: Cassell.

Webstercat71, 2006, Manchester Passion, message 10 [online], 14 April. Available at http://www.bbc.co.uk/dna/england/F2770282?thread=2090395andphrase=Manchester [Accessed 12 December].

Welch, Sharon D., 1985, *Communities of Resistance and Solidarity: A Feminist Theology of Liberation*, Maryknoll, NY: Orbis.

Wheeler, B. G. and E. Farley, eds, 1991, *Shifting Boundaries: Contextual Approaches to the Structure of Theological Education*, Louisville, KY: Westminster John Knox Press.

Whitford, Margaret, 1991, *The Irigaray Reader*, Oxford: Blackwell.

Wilkinson, John, 1993, *Church in Black and White*, Edinburgh: St. Andrew Press.

Williams, Raymond, 1958, *Culture and Society 1780–1950*, London: Chatto & Windus.

Williams, Rowan, 2000, The Nature of a Sacrament, in R. Williams, *On Christian Theology*, Oxford: Blackwell, pp. 197–208.

Wilson, J. Q. and J. Sacks, 2002, *The Moral Sense*, London: The Smith Institute.

Wise, Sue and Elizabeth Stanley, 1987, *Georgie Porgie: Sexual Harassment in Everyday Life*, London: Pandora.

Witz, A., 1993, Women at Work, in D. Richardson and V. Robinson, eds, *Introducing Women's Studies*, London: Macmillan.

Wolffe, John, 1993, The Religion of the Silent Majority, in G. Parsons, ed., *The Growth of Religious Diversity: Britain from 1945*, London: Routledge, pp. 305–46.

Wood, R., 2003, Religion, Faith-based Community Organizing, and the Struggle for Justice, in M. Dillon, ed., *Handbook of the Sociology of Religion*, Cambridge: Cambridge University Press.

Wood, V., 1999, It's not nice to fool Mother Nature, *Austin Chronicle* (online), available at: http://www.weeklywire.com/ww/08-09-99/austin_food_featuref.html [Accessed 23/11/99].

Wren, Brian, 1989, *Bring Many Names*, Oxford: Oxford University Press.

Yanagisako, S. J. and J. Collier, 1990, The Mode of Reproduction in Anthropology, in D. L. Rhode, ed., *Theoretical Perspectives on Sexual Difference*, New Haven: Yale University Press, pp. 131–41.

Young, Hugo, 1990, *One of Us*, London: Macmillan.

Young, Iris Marion, 1990, *'Throwing Like a Girl' and Other Essays in Feminist Philosophy and Social Theory*, Bloomington, IN: Indiana University Press.

Young, Pamela Dickey, 1990, *Feminist Theology/Christian Theology*, Minneapolis: Fortress Press.

LIST OF PUBLICATIONS BY

ELAINE L. GRAHAM

Monographs

1995 *Making the Difference: Gender, Personhood and Theology*, London: Mowbray; Minneapolis: Fortress Press, 260pp.

1996 *Transforming Practice: Pastoral Theology in an Age of Uncertainty*, London: Mowbray. Reprinted 2002, Eugene, OR: Wipf & Stock, 234pp.

2002 *Representations of the Post/Human: Monsters, Aliens and Others in Popular Culture*, Studies in Religion, Culture and Gender, Manchester University Press and Rutgers University Press, xi+259pp.

Jointly-Authored Works

2005 *Theological Reflection: Volume I: Methods*, with Heather Walton and Frances Ward, London: SCM Press, iv+250pp.

Edited Works

1993 *Life-Cycles: Women and Pastoral Care*, with Margaret Halsey, London: SPCK, 239pp.

2007 *Theological Reflection: Volume II: Sources*, with Heather Walton and Frances Ward, London: SCM Press, viii+455pp.

Academic Journal Articles

1988 The Pastoral Significance of Community Work, *Modern Churchman* new series 30(2), 15–23.

1989 The Pastoral Needs of Women, *Contact: The Interdisciplinary Journal of Pastoral Studies* 100, 23–5.

1990 Pastoral Theology, Feminism and the Future, *Contact: The Interdisciplinary Journal of Pastoral Studies* 103, 2–9.

1994 Toward a Theology of Desire, *Theology and Sexuality* 1, 13–30.

1995 Truth or Dare: Sexuality, Liturgy and Pastoral Theology, *Contact: The Interdisciplinary Journal of Pastoral Studies* 115, 3–9. Reprinted 2000 in D. Willows and J. Swinton, eds, *The Spiritual Dimension of Pastoral Care: Practical Theology in a Multidisciplinary Context*, London: Jessica Kingsley, 2000, pp. 264–75.

1995 Gender, Personhood and Theology, *Scottish Journal of Theology* 48(3), 341–58.

1995 From 'Space' to 'Woman-Space', *Feminist Theology* 9, 11–34.

1996 Fundamentalism, Postmodernism and Spirituality, *The Way: Review of Contemporary Christian Spirituality* 16(3), 203–14.

1996 Theology in the City: Ten Years after *Faith in the City*, *Bulletin of the John Rylands Research Institute* 78(1), 179–97.

1998 Pastoral Care and Communitarianism, *Contact: The Interdisciplinary Journal of Pastoral Studies* 125, 2–9.

1999 'Only Bodies Suffer': Embodiment, Representation and the Practice of Ethics, *Bulletin of the John Rylands Research Institute* 80(3), 255–73.

1999 Theology and History in the Work of A. O. Dyson, *Modern Believing* 40(2), 20–28.

1999 From 'Terrible Silence' to 'Transforming Hope': The Impact of Feminist Theory on Practical Theology, *International Journal of Practical Theology* 2, 185–212.

1999 Cyborgs or Goddesses? Becoming Divine in a Cyberfeminist Age, *Information, Communication and Society* 2(4), 419–38. Reprinted 2001 in E. Green and A. Adam, eds, *Virtual Gender: Technology, Consumption and Identity*, London and New York: Routledge, pp. 302–22.

1999 Pastoral Theology: 'Therapy', 'Mission' or 'Liberation'? *Scottish Journal of Theology* 52(4), 430–54.

2000 Good News for the Socially Excluded? Political Theology and the Politics of New Labour, *Political Theology* 2, 77–100.

2000 Some Expressive forms of a Liberation Practical Theology: art forms as resistance to evil, with James N. Poling, *International Journal of Practical Theology* 4, 163–83.

2001 High Fidelity: Reading Sexuality and Scripture Faithfully, *Modern Believing*, 42(3), 41–50.

2002 'Nietzsche Gets a Modem': Transhumanism and the technological sublime, *Literature and Theology* 16(1), 65–80.

2003 Frankensteins and Cyborgs: Visions of the Global Future in an Age of Technology, *Studies in Christian Ethics*, 16(1), 29–43.

2004 Clergy Sexual Abuse: Theological and Gender Perspectives, with D. Cozzens, W. Schipper, M. Longwood and M. M. Fortune, *Journal of Religion and Abuse* 6(2), 3–29.

2004 Bioethics after Posthumanism: Natural Law, Communicative Ethics and the Problem of Self-Design, *Ecotheology* 9(2), 66–86.

2004 Post/Human Conditions, *Theology and Sexuality* special issue, *Representations of the Post/Human* 10(2), 9–30.

2005 Theological Reflection: Method or Mystique? with Heather Walton and Frances Ward, *Contact: Practical Theology and Pastoral Care* 146, 29–36.

2006 In Whose Image? Representations of technology and the 'ends' of humanity, *Ecotheology* 11(2), 159–82. Also published in an abridged form: 2006. In

Whose Image? Representations of Technology and the 'Ends' of Humanity, in C. Deane-Drummond and P. M. Scott, eds, *Future Perfect? God, Medicine and Human Identity*, London: T&T Clark International, 56–69.

2006 The Professional Doctorate in Practical Theology: an idea whose time has come?, *International Journal of Practical Theology* 10(1), 293–311.

2006 Words of Encouragement from One Pilgrim to Another: For Stephen, 12 November 2007, *Contact: Practical Theology and Pastoral Care* 152, 6–7.

2007 If the Church says 'No', does God say 'Yes!'? Theological reflection on sexuality in a consumer culture, *Modern Believing* 48(1), 14–25.

2007 Power, Knowledge and Authority in Public Theology, *International Journal of Public Theology* 1(1), 42–62.

2008 The Professional Doctorate: Developing the Researching Professional in Practical Theology in Higher Education, with Zoe Bennett, *Journal of Adult Theological Education* 5(1), 34–52.

2008 What makes a good city? Reflections on the Commission on Urban Life and Faith, *International Journal of Public Theology* 2(1), 7–26.

2008 Why Practical Theology Must Go Public, *Practical Theology* 1(1), 11–14.

Chapters in Edited Books

1993 The Sexual Politics of Pastoral Care, in E. L. Graham and M. Halsey, eds, *Life-Cycles: Women and Pastoral Care*, London: SPCK, pp. 210–24.

1997 Feminist Theology: 'Myth', 'Mystery' or 'Monster'?, in L. Stanley, ed., *Thinking Feminisms*, London and California: Sage, pp. 109–19.

1998 Woorden tot vlees gemaakt: belichaming en praktische theologie, in M. de Haardt, E. Maeckelberghe and M. van Dijk, eds, *Geroepen om te Spreken: Over verbeelding en creativiteit in theologie en pastoraat*, Kampen: Kok Pharos, pp. 100–14.

1998 A View from a Room, in D. Ackermann and R. Bons-Storm, eds, *Liberating Faith Practices: Feminist Practical Theologies in Context*, Leuven: Peeters, pp. 129–52.

2000 Pastoral theology as Transforming Practice, in S. Pattison and J. W. Woodward, eds, *The Blackwell Reader in Pastoral Theology*, Oxford: Blackwell, 100–14.

2000 'The Story' or 'our stories'? Narrative Theology, Vernacular Religion and the Birth of Jesus, in G. Brooke, ed., *The Birth of Jesus: Biblical and Theological Reflections*, Edinburgh: T&T Clark, pp. 89–98.

2002 Liberal Theology and Transformative Pedagogy, in M. Chapman, ed., *The Future of Liberal Theology*, Aldershot: Ashgate, pp. 129–38.

2003 Different Forms of Feminist Ethics, in Carl-Henric Grenholm and Normunds Kamergrauzis, eds, *Feminist Ethics: Perspectives, Problems and Possibilities*, Uppsala Studies in Social Ethics 29. Uppsala: Acta Universitatis Uppsaliensis, pp. 15–30.

2003 Feminist Theology, in William Cavanaugh and Peter Scott, eds, *Blackwell Companion to Political Theology*, Oxford and New York: Blackwell, pp. 210–26.

2004 'Big Brother' or 'New Jerusalem'? Anti-Utopia and Utopia in an Age of New Technologies, in Johnston Mackay, ed., *Netting Citizens*, Edinburgh: St. Andrew Press, pp. 144–71.

2004 Public Theology in an age of 'Voter Apathy', in W. Storrar and A. Morton, eds, *Public Theology in the Twenty-First Century*, Edinburgh and New York: T&T Clark International, pp. 385–403.

2005 'Our Real Witness': Windsor, Public Opinion and Sexuality, in A. Linzey and R. Kirker, eds, *Gays and the Future of Anglicanism*, London: John Hunt Publishing, pp. 199–212.

2005 A Genius of Place, with Chris Baker and John Atherton, in E. L. Graham and A. Rowlands, eds, *Pathways to the Public*, Münster: Lit Verlag, pp. 63–83.

2007 Embodying technology, becoming our tools: discussing the post/human, in J. Baxter, ed., *Wounds that Heal: Theology, Imagination and Health*, London: SPCK, pp. 125–48.

2007 What we make of the world: the turn to culture in theology and the study of religion, in Gordon Lynch, ed., *Between Sacred and Profane: Researching Religion and Popular Culture*, London: I. B. Tauris, pp. 63–81.

2009 Doing God? Public Theology under Blair, in P. M. Scott, E. L. Graham and C. R. Baker, eds, *Remoralising Britain? Ten years of New Labour: Faith, Morals and Governance*, London: Continuum.

Review Articles

1991 Public Theology after Thatcher. [Review of J. A. Beckford, *Religion and Advanced Industrial Society*, Unwin Hyman, 1989, D. B. Forrester, *Beliefs, Values and Policies*, Clarendon, 1989 and J. Sacks, *The Persistence of Faith*, BBC, 1990], *Modern Churchman* New Series 32(5), 1–7.

2001 The Right Question is Theological. [Review of Alastair McFadyen, *Bound to Sin: Abuse, Holocaust and the Christian Doctrine of Sin*, Cambridge University Press, 2000] *Reviews in Religion and Theology*, June, 256–62.

Conference Proceedings

2004 Editor, with Chris Baker, *Religious Capital in Regenerating Communities*, Proceedings of launch conference of Manchester Centre for Public Theology, Manchester: William Temple Foundation/Northwest Development Agency, 37pp.

2004 Editor, with Esther D. Reed, *The Future of Christian Social Ethics: Essays on the work of Ronald H, Preston, 1913–2001*. *Studies in Christian Ethics* special issue 17(2), viii+215pp.

2005 Editor, with Anna Rowlands, *Pathways to the Public Square*. Proceedings of 2003 International Academy of Practical Theology, Manchester, Münster: Lit Verlag, International Practical Theology, Vol, 1, iii+318pp.

Contributions to Reference Works

1995 Théologie Féministe. In Pierre Gisel, ed., *L'Encyclopédie du Protestantism* ed., Geneva: Labor et Fides, pp. 1555–7. Reprinted 2005.

1995 Gender, in P. B. Clarke and A. Linzey, eds, *Dictionary of Ethics, Theology and Society*, London: Routledge, pp. 396–400.

1996   Gender. In L. Isherwood and D. McEwan, eds, *An A–Z of Feminist Theology*, Sheffield: Sheffield Academic Press, pp. 78–80.

1996   Pastoral Theology. In L. Isherwood and D. McEwan, eds, *An A–Z of Feminist Theology*, Sheffield: Sheffield Academic Press, pp. 171–3.

1996   Psychology of Women. In Letty Russell and Shannon Clark, eds, *Dictionary of Feminist Theologies*, Louisville, KY: Westminster John Knox Press, pp. 231–2.

2000   Pastoral Theology. In A. Hastings, ed., *Oxford Companion to Christian Thought*, Oxford: Oxford University Press, pp. 519–20.

SOURCES AND ACKNOWLEDGEMENTS

'A View From a Room: Feminist Practical Theology from Academy, Kitchen and Sanctuary', *Liberating Faith Practices: Feminist Practical Theologies in Context*, pp. 129–52 © Peeters Publishers 1988.

'Big Brother or New Jerusalem? Anti-Utopia and Utopia in a Virtual Age', in *Netting Citizens*, pp. 144–71 © Saint Andrew Press, 2004.

'Bioethics after Posthumanism: Natural Law, Communicative Ethics and the Problem of Self-Design' *Ecotheology* 9:2, pp. 66–86 © Equinox Publishing, 2004.

'From "Space" to "Woman-Space"', *Feminist Theology* 9, pp. 11–34 © Sheffield Academic Press, 1995.

'From "Terrible Silence" to "Transforming Hope": Feminist Theory and Practical Theology', *International Journal of Practical Theology* 2, pp. 185–212 © Walter de Gruyter GmbH & Co. KG, 1999.

'Gender, Personhood and Theology', *Scottish Journal of Theology* 48:3, pp. 341–58 © Cambridge University Press, 1995.

'In whose image? Representations of technology and the "ends" of humanity', *Ecotheology* 11:2, pp. 159–82 © Equinox Publishing, 2006.

'The Pastoral Needs of Women', *Contact* 100, pp. 23–5 © Contact Pastoral Ltd., 1989.

'Pastoral Theology as Transforming Practice', *The Blackwell Reader in Pastoral Theology*, pp. 100–14 © Blackwell Publishing, 2000.

'Pastoral Theology, Feminism and the Future', *Contact* 103, pp. 2–9 © Contact Pastoral Ltd., 1990.

'Pastoral Theology: "Therapy", "Mission" or "Liberation"?', *Scottish Journal of Theology* 52:4, pp. 430–54 © Cambridge University Press, 1999.

'Post/Human Conditions', *Theology and Sexuality* 10:2, pp. 9–30 © Sage Publications Ltd, 2004.

'Public Theology in an Age of Voter Apathy', *Public Theology for the 21st Century*, pp. 385–403 © T&T Clark/Continuum, 2004.

'The Sexual Politics of Pastoral Care', in *Life-Cycles: Women and Pastoral Care*, pp. 210–24 © SPCK, 1993.

'"The Story" and "Our Stories": Narrative Theology, Vernacular Religion and the Birth of Jesus', in *The Birth of Jesus*, pp. 89–98 © T&T Clark/Continuum, 2000.

'Words Made Flesh: Women, Embodiment and Practical Theology', *Feminist Theology* 21, pp. 109–21 © Sheffield Academic Press, 1999.

'Words of Encouragements from One Pilgrim to Another', *Contact* 152, pp. 6–7 © Contact Pastoral Ltd. Ltd, 2006.